LEARNING TO THINK SPATIALLY

Committee on Support for Thinking Spatially: The Incorporation of Geographic Information Science Across the K–12 Curriculum

Geographical Sciences Committee

Board on Earth Sciences and Resources

Division on Earth and Life Studies

NATIONAL RESEARCH COUNCIL
OF THE NATIONAL ACADEMIES

THE NATIONAL ACADEMIES PRESS
Washington, D.C.
www.nap.edu

THE NATIONAL ACADEMIES PRESS • **500 Fifth Street, N.W., • Washington, DC 20001**

NOTICE: The project that is the subject of this report was approved by the Governing Board of the National Research Council, whose members are drawn from the councils of the National Academy of Sciences, the National Academy of Engineering, and the Institute of Medicine. The members of the committee responsible for the report were chosen for their special competences and with regard for appropriate balance.

This study was supported by Environmental Systems Research Institute, Department of Interior/U.S. Geological Survey Grant No. 00HQAG0011, National Aeronautics and Space Administration Grant No. NAG5-9857, National Geographic Society Education Foundation Grant No. 200-0123, and National Science Foundation Grant No. BCS-0076284. Any opinions, findings, conclusions, or recommendations expressed in this publication are those of the author(s) and do not necessarily reflect the views of the organizations or agencies that provided support for the project.

Library of Congress Cataloging-in-Publication Data

Learning to think spatially : GIS as a support system in the K-12 curriculum.
   p. cm.
   Includes bibliographical references and index.
   ISBN 0-309-09208-6 (pbk.) — ISBN 0-309-53191-8 (PDF)
   1. Space perception—Study and teaching. 2. Geographic information systems.   I. National Academies Press (U.S.)
   BF723.S63L43 2006
   370.15'2—dc22
                                    2005032115

Additional copies of this report are available from the National Academies Press, 500 Fifth Street, N.W., Lockbox 285, Washington, DC 20055; (800) 624-6242 or (202) 334-3313 (in the Washington metropolitan area); Internet, http://www.nap.edu.

Cover designed by Van Nguyen. Photo © Blauel/Gnamm—ARTOTHEK. Courtesy of the Städelsches Kunstinstitut, Frankfurt.

THE NATIONAL ACADEMIES
Advisers to the Nation on Science, Engineering, and Medicine

The **National Academy of Sciences** is a private, nonprofit, self-perpetuating society of distinguished scholars engaged in scientific and engineering research, dedicated to the furtherance of science and technology and to their use for the general welfare. Upon the authority of the charter granted to it by the Congress in 1863, the Academy has a mandate that requires it to advise the federal government on scientific and technical matters. Dr. Ralph J. Cicerone is president of the National Academy of Sciences.

The **National Academy of Engineering** was established in 1964, under the charter of the National Academy of Sciences, as a parallel organization of outstanding engineers. It is autonomous in its administration and in the selection of its members, sharing with the National Academy of Sciences the responsibility for advising the federal government. The National Academy of Engineering also sponsors engineering programs aimed at meeting national needs, encourages education and research, and recognizes the superior achievements of engineers. Dr. Wm. A. Wulf is president of the National Academy of Engineering.

The **Institute of Medicine** was established in 1970 by the National Academy of Sciences to secure the services of eminent members of appropriate professions in the examination of policy matters pertaining to the health of the public. The Institute acts under the responsibility given to the National Academy of Sciences by its congressional charter to be an adviser to the federal government and, upon its own initiative, to identify issues of medical care, research, and education. Dr. Harvey V. Fineberg is president of the Institute of Medicine.

The **National Research Council** was organized by the National Academy of Sciences in 1916 to associate the broad community of science and technology with the Academy's purposes of furthering knowledge and advising the federal government. Functioning in accordance with general policies determined by the Academy, the Council has become the principal operating agency of both the National Academy of Sciences and the National Academy of Engineering in providing services to the government, the public, and the scientific and engineering communities. The Council is administered jointly by both Academies and the Institute of Medicine. Dr. Ralph J. Cicerone and Dr. Wm. A. Wulf are chair and vice chair, respectively, of the National Research Council.

www.national-academies.org

SUPPORT FOR THINKING SPATIALLY: THE INCORPORATION OF GEOGRAPHIC INFORMATION SCIENCE ACROSS THE K–12 CURRICULUM

ROGER M. DOWNS, *Chair*, The Pennsylvania State University, University Park
SARAH WITHAM BEDNARZ, Texas A & M University, College Station
ROBERT A. BJORK, University of California, Los Angeles
PETER B. DOW, First Hand Learning, Inc., Buffalo, New York
KENNETH E. FOOTE, University of Colorado, Boulder
J. FREEMAN GILBERT, University of California, San Diego, La Jolla
REGINALD G. GOLLEDGE, University of California, Santa Barbara
KIM A. KASTENS, Lamont-Doherty Earth Observatory of Columbia University, Palisades, New York
GAEA LEINHARDT (member until February 28, 2002), University of Pittsburgh, Pennsylvania
LYNN S. LIBEN, The Pennsylvania State University, University Park
MARCIA C. LINN, University of California, Berkeley
JOHN J. RIESER, Vanderbilt University, Nashville, Tennessee
GERALD M. STOKES, University of Maryland and Pacific Northwest National Laboratory, College Park
BARBARA TVERSKY, Stanford University, Palo Alto, California

National Research Council Staff

ANTHONY R. DE SOUZA, Director, Board on Earth Sciences and Resources
KRISTEN L. KRAPF, Program Officer (until November 2004)
YVONNE P. FORSBERGH, Research Assistant (until November 2002)
MONICA R. LIPSCOMB, Research Assistant (until June 2004)
VERNA J. BOWEN, Financial and Administrative Associate
RADHIKA S. CHARI, Senior Project Assistant (from November 2002 to November 2003)
AMANDA M. ROBERTS, Program Assistant (from April 2004)
TERESIA K. WILMORE, Project Assistant (from November 2003 to April 2004)

GEOGRAPHICAL SCIENCES COMMITTEE

ROGER M. DOWNS, *Chair*, The Pennsylvania State University, University Park
BRIAN J. L. BERRY, The University of Texas at Dallas, Richardson
SUSAN L. CUTTER, University of South Carolina, Columbia
RUTH S. DeFRIES, University of Maryland, College Park
WILLIAM E. EASTERLING III, The Pennsylvania State University, University Park
PATRICIA GOBER, Arizona State University, Tempe
MICHAEL F. GOODCHILD, University of California, Santa Barbara
SUSAN HANSON, Clark University, Worcester, Massachusetts
JONATHAN D. MAYER, University of Washington, Seattle
EMILIO F. MORAN, Indiana University, Bloomington
DAVID L. SKOLE, Michigan State University, East Lansing

National Research Council Staff

HEDY J. ROSSMEISSL, Senior Scholar
VERNA J. BOWEN, Financial and Administrative Associate

Acknowledgments

This report has been reviewed in draft form by individuals chosen for their diverse perspectives and technical expertise, in accordance with procedures approved by the National Research Council's Report Review Committee. The purpose of this independent review is to provide candid and critical comments that will assist the institution in making its published report as sound as possible and to ensure that the report meets institutional standards for objectivity, evidence, and responsiveness to the study charge. The review comments and draft manuscript remain confidential to protect the integrity of the deliberative process. We wish to thank the following individuals for their review of this report:

Tanya M. Atwater, University of California, Santa Barbara
Victor R. Baker, University of Arizona, Tucson
Angelo Collins, Knowles Science Teaching Foundation, Haddonfield, New Jersey
Mary D. Gunnels, National Highway Traffic Safety Administration, Washington, D.C.
Mary Hegarty, University of California, Santa Barbara
Roberta L. Klatzky, Carnegie Mellon University, Pittsburgh, Pennsylvania
Mark Monmonier, Syracuse University, New York
M. Duane Nellis, Kansas State University, Manhattan
Herbert L. Pick, Jr., University of Minnesota, Minneapolis
Nancy Rankin, Hillview Middle School, Menlo Park, California
Cary I. Sneider, Museum of Science, Boston, Massachusetts

Although the reviewers listed above have provided many constructive comments and suggestions, they were not asked to endorse the conclusions or recommendations nor did they see the final draft of the report before its release. The review of this report was overseen by David J. Cowen, University of South Carolina, Columbia, and Lyle V. Jones, The University of North Carolina, Chapel Hill. Appointed by the National Research Council, they were responsible for making certain that an independent examination of this report was carried out in accordance with institutional procedures and that all review comments were carefully considered. Responsibility for the final content of this report rests entirely with the authoring committee and the institution.

Frontispiece: Young students in a GIS learning laboratory.

Preface

The title of this report, *Learning to Think Spatially*, is a description of its contents and, at the same time, a description of the process that led to the report. Although the original charge to the committee appeared clear and definitive when the study proposal was approved by the National Academy of Sciences, the writing process has been a less linear path than we expected. To begin with, the committee comprised a wide range of disciplinary backgrounds: astronomy, education, geography, the geosciences, and psychology (for biographical sketches, see Appendix A). Learning about and from each other took considerable time and effort. It became clear that the original charge had to be reshaped; we could not address that charge until spatial thinking itself had been explored and explained. Only after that was done could we focus on the second part of the title: *GIS as a Support System in the K–12 Curriculum.*

Spatial thinking—one form of thinking—is based on a constructive amalgam of three elements: concepts of space, tools of representation, and processes of reasoning. It is the concept of space that makes spatial thinking a distinctive form of thinking. By understanding the meaning of space, we can use its properties (e.g., dimensionality, continuity, proximity, and separation) as a vehicle for structuring problems, for finding answers, and for expressing solutions. By expressing relationships within spatial structures (e.g., maps, multidimensional scaling models, computer-assisted design [CAD] renderings), we can perceive, remember, and analyze the static and, via transformations, the dynamic properties of objects and the relationships between objects. (Abbreviations are spelled out in full at their first use in the body of the report and are defined in Appendix I.) We can use representations in a variety of modes and media (graphic [text, image, and video], tactile, auditory, kinesthetic, and olfactory) to describe, explain, and communicate about the structure, operation, and function of objects and their relationships. Spatial thinking is not restricted to any domain of knowledge, although it may be more characteristic of architecture, medicine, physics, and biology, for example, than of philosophy, business administration, linguistics, and comparative literature.

Although spatial thinking is a universal mode of thinking, it has distinctly different manifestations in different disciplines. Part of the nonlinear committee process involved understanding and taking advantage of those differences. Committee members presented interpretations of the process of spatial thinking from their disciplinary perspective. Spatial thinking uses space to integrate and structure ideas. Many of the committee meetings were, therefore, seminar exercises in the representation and integration of ideas from different disciplines. In this respect, we were fortunate to receive the support of numerous individuals (see Appendix B for a list of people who contributed to the committee's work). Without their support, the committee could not have constructed an amalgam of ideas about space, representation, and reasoning, especially as they relate to geographic information systems. We have lost count of the times that contributors responded to yet another e-mail containing another (small) request.

That people were so willing to respond is one measure of the importance of the topic. Another is the willingness of committee members to provide draft materials and comments on the drafts of other committee members. Two of us——Roger Downs and Anthony de Souza—took the responsibility for creating the overall report structure, for weaving together the disparate pieces, and for writing the final report. However, *Learning to Think Spatially* represents the collective belief of an interdisciplinary group of scholars that spatial thinking merits—if not demands—the focused and systematic attention of scientists and educators alike. We must understand the process of spatial thinking, we must develop systems for supporting the process, and we must ensure that all students have the opportunity to learn about spatial thinking. We need to invest in a systematic educational program to enhance levels of spatial thinking in K–12 students. Our goal must be to foster a generation of students (1) who have the habit of mind of thinking spatially, (2) who can practice spatial thinking in an informed way, and (3) who adopt a critical stance to spatial thinking. These conclusions and recommendations were driven by the breadth and depth of the educational experiences of members of the committee. Three of us had been K–12 school teachers and most of us had worked extensively at the intersection of research and educational policy, helping to develop national standards, curricula, assessments, and specific educational programs for federal, state, and local education agencies.

As with any committee process, *Learning to Think Spatially* would not have been possible without the generous support, patience, and active encouragement and participation of our five sponsors. The committee gratefully acknowledges the support of the Environmental Systems Research Institute (ESRI), the National Aeronautics and Space Administration (NASA), the National Geographic Society (NGS), the National Science Foundation (NSF), and the U.S. Geological Survey (USGS).

Anthony de Souza and I would also like to thank the numerous staff members at the National Academies who helped during the committee, writing, and publication processes: Kristen L. Krapf, program officer; Yvonne P. Forsbergh, research assistant; Monica R. Lipscomb, research assistant; Verna J. Bowen, financial and administrative associate; Jennifer T. Estep, financial associate; Radhika S. Chari, senior program assistant; Amanda M. Roberts, program assistant; and Teresia K. Wilmore, program assistant.

Through the committee process, we all came to realize the extent to which spatial thinking pervades our lives as scientists, our roles in the workforce, and our everyday lives. To a person, we enjoyed the challenges of learning about thinking spatially. That it took us more than three years to produce this report is a testament to the size, importance, and difficulty of the topic. The road has been long and winding, but if we reach the goal of spatial literacy for American students then our time has been well spent.

Roger M. Downs
Department of Geography
The Pennsylvania State University

Contents

EXECUTIVE SUMMARY   1

1   INTRODUCTION   11
   1.1   The Challenge to Learn, 11
   1.2   Spatial Thinking, 12
   1.3   Charge to the Committee, 13
   1.4   An Outcome of the Report: Fostering Spatial Literacy, 15
   1.5   Audiences for *Learning to Think Spatially*, 20
   1.6   Structure of This Report, 21

PART I: THE NATURE AND FUNCTIONS OF SPATIAL THINKING

2   THE NATURE OF SPATIAL THINKING   25
   2.1   Introduction, 25
   2.2   Approaches to Spatial Thinking, 25
   2.3   The Use of Space as a Framework for Understanding, 28
   2.4   The Three Functions of Spatial Thinking, 33
   2.5   Space as the Basis for Spatial Thinking, 36
   2.6   The Process of Spatial Thinking, 40
   2.7   Conclusion, 48

3   SPATIAL THINKING IN EVERYDAY LIFE, AT WORK, AND IN SCIENCE   49
   3.1   Introduction, 49
   3.2   Spatial Thinking in Everyday Life, 49
   3.3   Spatial Thinking at Work, 52
   3.4   Spatial Thinking in Science, 55
   3.5   Spatial Thinking in Astronomy, 56

3.6   Spatial Thinking in Geoscience, 68
3.7   Thinking Spatially in Geoscience: The Seafloor Maps of Marie Tharp, 83
3.8   Thinking Spatially in Geography: Walter Christaller's Discovery of Central Place Theory, 88
3.9   Conclusion, 93

4   TEACHING AND LEARNING ABOUT SPATIAL THINKING   94
4.1   Introduction, 94
4.2   Expertise Differences in Spatial Thinking: The Effects of Experience, 95
4.3   The Challenge of Developing Expertise in Spatial Thinking, 103
4.4   The Transfer of Spatial Thinking Across Subjects in the Curriculum, 105
4.5   The Fostering of Expertise in Spatial Thinking, 107
4.6   Conclusion, 109

5   RESPONDING TO THE NEED FOR SPATIAL THINKERS   110
5.1   Introduction, 110
5.2   The Increasing Need for Spatial Thinking Skills, 110
5.3   Providing Skilled Spatial Thinkers, 111
5.4   The 1999 Trends in International Mathematics and Science Study (TIMSS), 113
5.5   Spatial Thinking in the National Education Standards, 114
5.6   Spatial Thinking and Education for the Next Generation, 131

6   TOOLS FOR THOUGHT: THE CONCEPT OF A SUPPORT SYSTEM   135
6.1   Introduction, 135
6.2   The Nature of a Support System, 135
6.3   The Functions of a Support System, 140
6.4   Tools for Thought: The Limits to Power, 141
6.5   General Criteria for the Design of a Support System in the K–12 Educational Context, 145
6.6   The Need for Support Systems for Spatial Thinking (SSST), 147
6.7   The Requirements of a Support System for Spatial Thinking, 148
6.8   Support Systems for Spatial Thinking in the K–12 Context, 150
6.9   The Implementation of a Support System for Spatial Thinking in the K–12 Educational Context, 151

PART II: SUPPORT FOR SPATIAL THINKING

7   HIGH-TECH SUPPORT SYSTEMS FOR SPATIAL THINKING   155
7.1   Introduction, 155
7.2   High-Tech Systems for Supporting Spatial Thinking, 156
7.3   The Nature and Functions of GIS, 158
7.4   The Current Status of GIS, 164

8   AN ASSESSMENT OF GIS AS A SYSTEM FOR SUPPORTING SPATIAL
THINKING IN THE K–12 CONTEXT   166
8.1   Introduction, 166
8.2   The Capacity of GIS as a Support System for Spatial Thinking, 167
8.3   The Design of GIS as a Support System for Spatial Thinking in the K–12 Educational Context, 176

8.4   The Implementation of GIS as a Support System for Spatial Thinking, 203
8.5   Mechanisms for the Redesign of GIS Educational Software, 214
8.6   Conclusion, 216

9   GIS AS A SUPPORT SYSTEM FOR SPATIAL THINKING   217
9.1   Introduction, 217
9.2   The Necessary Requirements of a Support System for Spatial Thinking, 217
9.3   The Design of GIS as a Support System for Spatial Thinking in the
      K–12 Educational Context, 218
9.4   The Implementation of GIS as a Support System for Spatial Thinking, 219
9.5   The Redesign of GIS Educational Software, 220
9.6   Conclusion, 220

PART III: SUPPORTING SPATIAL THINKING IN THE FUTURE

10   CONCLUSIONS AND RECOMMENDATIONS   229
10.1   Introduction, 229
10.2   Charge to the Committee, 229
10.3   The Nature and Functions of Spatial Thinking, 230
10.4   Support for Spatial Thinking, 233
10.5   Conclusion, 235

11   THE SPATIAL THINKER   237
11.1   GIS and the Challenge of Thinking Spatially, 237
11.2   An Example of Using GIS to Think Spatially, 237
11.3   Meeting the Challenge to Learn to Think Spatially, 241

REFERENCES   243

APPENDIXES

A   Biographical Sketches of Committee Members and Staff   259
B   Oral Presentations and Written Statements   264
C   Individual Differences in Spatial Thinking: The Effects of Age,
     Development, and Sex   266
D   The Role of Spatial Representations in Learning, Problem Solving, and Transfer   281
E   Software Descriptions and Resources   285
F   What Is GIScience?   287
G   The Introduction of GIS into K–12 Education   289
H   Seasonal Differences: A Customized Eighth-Grade GIS Module   293
I   List of Acronyms   298

INDEX   301

LIST OF BOXES

1.1   Mapping of Cholera in Nineteenth-Century England, 14
1.2   Mapping of Arsenic in Twenty-First-Century Bangladesh, 16
1.3   Role of GIS in Spatial Thinking, 18

2.1   Browsing in Library Space, 34
2.2   A Personal Guidance System, 38

4.1   Reconceptualizations of the Concept of Transfer, 106

5.1   Spatial Thinking and the *National Geography Standards*, 116

6.1   Ocean Navigation in Micronesia, 137
6.2   Vehicle Navigation Systems in the United States, 142
6.3   Thinking Inside the Box, 151

7.1   High-Tech Systems to Support Spatial Thinking, 156

8.1   Functions of a GIS, 175
8.2   Students Analyzing a Real-World Problem with GIS: Characteristics and
      Potential Problems of a School's Tree Population, 180
8.3   *ArcVoyager*, 185
8.4   Open Versus Closed Software System Architectures, 188
8.5   Illustrative Difficulties That Teachers and Students Confront When Working with GIS, 194
8.6   What Teachers Should Know to Be Successful with GIS in the Classroom, 206

9.1   Technological Evolution in GIS, 222

C.1   Use of the Terms Sex and Gender, 269
C.2   Shadow Projection Task, 274

LIST OF FIGURES

Frontispiece: Young students in a GIS learning laboratory

ES.1 Diagram of the DNA structure, 2
ES.2 James Watson and Francis Crick with their DNA model, 2

1.1   Snow's 1855 map showing the areas of south London served by two water
      companies, 15
1.2   Spatial distribution of arsenic levels in wells in Arailhazar Upazilla, Bangladesh, 17

2.1   Spatial visualization items, 26
2.2   Underneath a typical urban street corner, 29
2.3   Units of length arrayed in a scalar progression from the micro to the macro, 31
2.4   A concept map depicting how various information sources are used to synthesize a
      geophysical gravity model, 32

2.5 An information landscape depicting demographic similarities and differences between the 50 states, 33

2.6 Visual browsing query process, 34

2.7 Spatialized query user interface, 35

2.8 Three modules of the Personal Guidance System, 38

2.9 Representations can be brought into direct contact with the real world using wearable computers, 39

3.1 A set of instructions for installing a ceiling fan, 51

3.2 Eratosthenes' technique for determining the size of Earth, 58

3.3 Ptolemaic system, 60

3.4 Epicycles in the Ptolemaic system, 61

3.5 Retrograde motion, 61

3.6 Astronomical parallax, 62

3.7 The Hertzsprung-Russell (H-R) diagram, 63

3.8 Map of the solar neighborhood, 65

3.9 The period-luminosity diagram for the Cepheids, 66

3.10 The characteristic light curve of a Cepheid variable, 66

3.11 Cepheids in the Andromeda galaxy, 67

3.12 The redshift distance relationship, 68

3.13 Describing the shapes of natural objects, rigorously and unambiguously: stereograms of crystals, 69

3.14 Describing the shapes of natural objects, rigorously and unambiguously: classification of folds, 70

3.15 Diagrammatic representation of equal-area projection of various fabric elements, 71

3.16 Flow chart for identifying minerals, 72

3.17 Ascribing meaning to the shape of a natural object: jigsaw-like fit of the coastlines of Africa and South America, 73

3.18 Ascribing meaning to the shape of a natural object: Siccar Point, 73

3.19 Ascribing meaning to the shape of a natural object: distribution of modern species of planktonic foraminifera, 74

3.20 Ascribing meaning to the shape of a natural object: carbonate-shelled microfossils, 75

3.21 Ascribing meaning to the shape of a natural object: the shape and orientation of the mineral grain in this photomicrograph are interpreted as evidence that the rock has undergone shearing, 76

3.22 Ascribing meaning to the shape of a natural object: reasoning from first principles, 77

3.23 Recognizing a shape or pattern amid a cluttered, noisy background, 78

3.24 Visualizing a three-dimensional object, structure, or process by examining observations collected in one or two dimensions, 78

3.25 Describing the position and orientation of objects in the real world relative to a coordinate system anchored to Earth, 79

3.26 William Smith's geological map of England and Wales, 80

3.27 Mentally manipulating a volume by folding, faulting, and eroding: geometry of the lower duplex at Hénaux, 81

3.28 Marie Tharp in 1960, 83

3.29 Tharp's original hand contouring of a portion of the mid-Atlantic ridge, 85

3.30 World ocean floor panorama, 85

3.31 Diagram of central places in southern Germany, 89

3.32 Diagram of a classic central place system, 91

4.1   A sample mental rotation task, 99

5.1   Specify locations and describe spatial relationships using coordinate geometry and other representational systems, 121
5.2   Use visualization, spatial reasoning, and geometric modeling to solve problems, 121
5.3   Specify locations and describe spatial relationships using coordinate geometry and other representational systems, 122
5.4   Specify locations and describe spatial relationships using coordinate geometry and other representational systems, 122
5.5   Use visualization, spatial reasoning, and geometric modeling to solve problems: developing spatial thinking, 125
5.6   Use visualization, spatial reasoning, and geometric modeling to solve problems: building additional spatial thinking skills, 126
5.7   Guide to the content standard for physical science for grades K–4, 127
5.8   Guide to the content standard for physical science in grades 9–12, 128
5.9   Guide to the content standard for Earth science in grades 9–12, 129
5.10 Specify locations and describe spatial relationships using coordinate geometry and other representational systems, 130
5.11 Use visualization, spatial reasoning, and geometric modeling to solve problems, 131
5.12 Specify locations and describe spatial relationships using coordinate geometry and other representational systems, 132
5.13 Geometry Standard: Specify locations and describe spatial relationships using coordinate geometry and other representational systems, 132
5.14 Use visualization, spatial reasoning, and geometric modeling to solve problems, 133

6.1   Using a calculator to solve a mathematical problem, 136
6.2   A Puluwatan canoe, 137
6.3   A mattang stick chart, 138
6.4   Representation of the Etak method, a system for tracking position at sea, 139
6.5   The dangers of an inappropriate map projection, 146

7.1   Components of a GIS, 160
7.2   A raster-based map of Santa Barbara County, 161
7.3   Map of the United States recorded on a vector GIS of polygons, lines, and points, 161
7.4   A geographic information system, 162
7.5   Geographical data can be divided into geometric data and attribute data, 162
7.6   Attribute data consist of qualitative or quantitative data, 163
7.7   Phases in the scientific method, 164

8.1   Six graphic variables that can be used to symbolize geographic phenomena, 170
8.2   Two screenshots from *Earthviewer*, 172
8.3   The WIMP (windows, icons, menus, pointers) environment for computing, 174
8.4   Multistage analysis in a pictorially based GIS, 178
8.5   Trees conflicting with utility lines, 180
8.6   Hazardous trees: trees in poor or dying condition, 181
8.7   A screen display from a user-built map generated from Level 4 of *ArcVoyager*, 185
8.8   *ArcView* digitizing, 186

8.9   "On-screen" representation of a haptic choropleth map of southern California, 189

8.10 *ArcView* Quick Reference Graphical User Interface, 190

8.11 On or off themes: adding a theme in *ArcView 3*, 194

8.12 Active and inactive themes: one active theme, 195

8.13 Active and inactive themes: two active themes, 195

8.14 Logical queries: query window in *ArcView 3*, 196

8.15 Logical queries: query windows in *ArcView 8*, 197

8.16 Logical queries: select by theme, 197

8.17 Zooming in: *ArcView 3* zooming tool, 198

8.18 Zooming in: standard procedure for defining a box to create a rescaled map, 199

8.19 Zooming in: what happens when a user clicks in a site and accidentally wiggles before releasing the mouse?, 199

8.20 Teachers' feelings of preparedness to incorporate digital content into their classrooms, 208

8.21 Browsing the DLESE library for educational resources by subject, 210

8.22 A page from ESRI's Geography Network web site from which users can access a huge collection of geospatial datasets, 211

9.1   The U.S. map, showing average annual precipitation superimposed on county and state boundaries, is based on a built-in project in ESRI's *ArcExplorer Java Edition for Education*, 223

9.2   This map of elevation and earthquakes, superimposed on state borders, is part of a project generated by ESRI's *ArcView 9*, 224

9.3   An oblique perspective view of North America showing earthquakes (greater than 3.0 on the Richter scale), 225

9.4   A frame, showing Mount Everest, from a QuickTime video file exported from *ArcGlobe*, 226

10.1 Timetable for implementing Recommendations 2–6, 236

11.1 Map of infant mortality rates, 238

11.2 Maps of variables affecting infant mortality, 239

C.1   Shadow projection drawing tasks, 275

H.1   Map of South Asia with countries, rivers, and major cities named with graphs contrasting total and annual rainfall for Bombay and Mangalore, 294

H.2   Map of South Asia with countries, rivers, and annual precipitation, 295

H.3   Map of South Asia with countries, rivers, and types of agriculture, 296

H.4   Map of South Asia with countries, rivers, and population density, 297

LIST OF TABLES

5.1   The Geospatial Technology Competency Model, 113

5.2   Table of Standards and Expectations for School Mathematics, 117

7.1   Comparison of the Current Capabilities of High-Tech Systems That Can Support Spatial Thinking, 158

8.1 Major GIS Software Products Used in K–12 Education, 167

8.2 Potential GIS Database Volumes for Some Typical Applications, 168

8.3 Assessment of the Capacity of GIS to Spatialize, Visualize, and Perform Functions, 176

8.4 Assessment of the Design of GIS to Meet Educational Goals, 183

8.5 Assessment of GIS in Terms of Its Appropriateness to Meet Student Needs, 192

8.6 Computational Requirements for *Idrisi* and *ArcView* Software, 201

8.7 Assessment of GIS to Match the Educational Context, 203

8.8 Assessment of Programs for the Implementation of GIS as a Support System, 213

Executive Summary

THE DOUBLE HELIX: A CLASSIC EXAMPLE OF SPATIAL THINKING

We wish to suggest a structure for the salt of deoxyribose nucleic acid (D.N.A.). This structure has novel features which are of considerable biological interest. (Watson and Crick, 1953, p. 737)

Those two deceptively low-key sentences are the introduction to a short (two-page) paper that marks one of the greatest achievements of twentieth century science. James Watson and Francis Crick described the molecular structure of the gene, work that is seen as the cornerstone of molecular biology and is still, 52 years later, "of considerable . . . interest."

The committee's interest in this discovery is considerable but different. We see Watson and Crick's paper as exemplifying the power of a way of thinking, spatial thinking. We suggest that spatial thinking is at the heart of many great discoveries in science, that it underpins many of the activities of the modern workforce, and that it pervades the everyday activities of modern life.

The challenge faced by Watson and Crick and their many competitors in the race to understand the molecular structure of the gene was to provide a three-dimensional model that met certain criteria including compatibility with (1) "the usual chemical assumptions," (2) experimental data, and (3) two-dimensional X-ray images. Watson and Crick (1953, p. 737) rejected, for example, the structural model proposed by Pauling and Corey in part because ". . . some of the van der Waals distances appear too small." Fraser's model was not even commented upon because it was ". . . rather ill-defined" (Watson and Crick, 1953, p. 737).

Their solution is the now-famous double helix, comprising two intertwined, complementary, and displaced phosphate-sugar chains. Both right-handed helices are coiled around the same axis and are connected to each other by bonds of the bases on the inside of the chains. Sugar residues are perpendicular to the attached bases. Watson and Crick assumed an angle, 36 degrees, between residues on the chain and this led to a structure that repeats after 10 residues or 34 A. They also specified a distance, 10 A, of a phosphorus atom from the fiber axis. They noted that

1

(t)he previously published X-ray data on deoxyribose nucleic acid are insufficient for a rigorous test of our structure. So far as we can tell, it is roughly compatible with the experimental data, but it must be regarded as unproved until it has been checked against more exact results. Some of these are given in the following communications. We were not aware of the details of the results presented there when we devised our structure, which rests mainly though not entirely on published experimental data and stereochemical arguments. (Watson and Crick, 1953, p. 737)

As we know, the structure is indeed compatible with experimental data and it stands as proven. The power of their reasoning, based on experimental data and stereochemical arguments, is remarkable.

Here, the committee emphasizes the explicitly spatial nature of their solution. They developed a three-dimensional structure that is scaled in both distance and angular terms. They specified the "handedness" of the structure (right handed) and showed how it was repeated at a fixed spatial interval. However, it is more than simply a structural description. In passing, they coyly and correctly noted:

It has not escaped our notice that the specific pairing we have postulated immediately suggests a possible copying mechanism for the genetic material. (Watson and Crick, 1953, p. 737)

Although their original figure (Figure ES. 1) is described as "purely diagrammatic," physical models (see Figure ES. 2) demonstrated the power of their biological, chemical, and spatial intuitions.

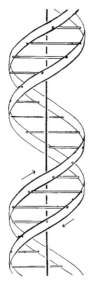

FIGURE ES.1 Diagram of the DNA structure. The two ribbons symbolize the two phosphate-sugar chains, and the horizontal rods the pairs of bases holding the chains together. The vertical line marks the fiber axis. Reprinted by permission from *Nature*, Watson and Crick, 1953, p. 737; Macmillan Publishers Ltd.

FIGURE ES.2 James Watson (*left*) and Francis Crick (*right*) with their DNA model. (From A. Barrington Brown/Science Photo Library.) Reprinted with permission from Photo Researchers, Inc.

> The novel feature of the structure is the manner in which the two chains are held together by the purine and pyrimidine bases. The planes of the bases are perpendicular to the fibre axis. They are joined together in pairs, a single base from one chain being hydrogen-bonded to a single base for the other chain, so that the two lie side by side with identical z-co-ordinates. One of the pair must be a purine and the other a pyrimidine for bonding to occur. (Watson and Crick, 1953, p. 737)

The three-dimensional structure is complex—two parallel but displaced spiraling chains; simple—the base bonds hold it together and fix angular distances; and beautiful—its elegance and explanatory power. It is the result of a brilliant exercise of imaginative visualization that is constrained by empirical data, expressed by two-dimensional images, and guided by deep scientific knowledge and incisive spatial intuition.

THE PROCESS OF SPATIAL THINKING

Watson and Crick's achievement is an intellectual tour de force, but the committee views the process of spatial thinking as a universal mode of thinking, one that is accessible to everyone to different degrees in different contexts. Spatial thinking is based on a constructive amalgam of three elements: concepts of space, tools of representation, and processes of reasoning. It depends on understanding the meaning of space and using the properties of space as a vehicle for structuring problems, for finding answers, and for expressing solutions. By visualizing relationships within spatial structures, we can perceive, remember, and analyze the static and, via transformations, the dynamic properties of objects and the relationships between objects. We can use representations in a variety of modes and media (graphic [text, image, and video], tactile, auditory, and kinesthetic) to describe, explain, and communicate about the structure, operation, and function of those objects and their relationships.

TEACHING AND LEARNING ABOUT SPATIAL THINKING

Spatial thinking can be learned, *and* it can and should be taught at all levels in the education system. With advances in computational systems (hardware and software), spatial thinking can now be supported in ways that enhance the speed, accuracy, and flexibility of its operation and open up the process to increasing numbers of people, working collaboratively and at higher levels of performance. Because of these newly available computational technologies, support for spatial thinking is more readily possible today and in the immediate future, but concomitantly, more challenging cognitive skills are necessary to take advantage of the rapidly changing support systems.

To think spatially entails knowing about (1) space—for example, different ways of calculating distance (e.g., in miles, in travel time, in travel cost), the basis of coordinate systems (e.g., Cartesian versus polar coordinates), and the nature of spaces (e.g., in terms of the number of dimensions [two versus three]); (2) representation—for example, the relationships among views (e.g., plans versus elevations of buildings, orthogonal versus perspective maps), the effect of projections (e.g., Mercator versus equal-area map projections), and the principles of graphic design (e.g., the roles of legibility, visual contrast, and figure-ground organization in the readability of graphs and maps); and (3) reasoning—for example, the different ways of thinking about shortest distances (e.g., as the crow flies versus route distance in a rectangular street grid), the ability to extrapolate and interpolate (e.g., projecting a functional relationship on a graph into the future, estimating the slope of a hillside from a map of contour lines), and making decisions (e.g., given traffic reports on a radio, selecting a detour).

Therefore we need to invest in a systematic educational program to foster spatial literacy by enhancing levels of spatial thinking in K–12 students. Our goal must be to foster a generation of students (1) who have the habit of mind of thinking spatially, (2) who can practice spatial thinking in an informed way, and (3) who adopt a critical stance to spatial thinking.

THE FOSTERING OF SPATIAL LITERACY

Literacy is a normative statement of what members of a culture should know and be able to do with that knowledge. The Workforce Investment Act of 1998 (Public Law 105-220) stated that ". . . (t)he term literacy means an individual's ability to read, write, and speak in English, compute, and solve problems, at levels of proficiency necessary to function on the job, in the family of the individual, and in society" (Title II, Section 203, Number 12).

Spatially literate students who have developed appropriate levels of spatial knowledge and skills in spatial ways of thinking and acting, together with sets of spatial capabilities, have the following characteristics:

1. They have the habit of mind of thinking spatially—they know where, when, how, and why to think spatially.
2. They practice spatial thinking in an informed way—they have a broad and deep knowledge of spatial concepts and spatial representations, a command over spatial reasoning using a variety of spatial ways of thinking and acting, and well-developed spatial capabilities for using supporting tools and technologies.
3. They adopt a critical stance to spatial thinking—they can evaluate the quality of spatial data based on its source and its likely accuracy and reliability; can use spatial data to construct, articulate, and defend a line of reasoning or point of view in solving problems and answering questions; and can evaluate the validity of arguments based on spatial information.

THE CHARGE TO THE COMMITTEE

The title of the proposal that led to the formation of the committee was *Support for Thinking Spatially: The Incorporation of Geographic Information Science Across the K–12 Curriculum*. The original charge contained two questions:

1. How might current versions of GIS (geographic information system) be incorporated into existing standards-based instruction in all knowledge domains across the school curriculum?
2. How can cognitive developmental and educational theory be used to develop new versions of GIS that are age appropriate in their design and to implement new GIS curricula that are age appropriate in their scope and sequence?

The first question was intended to generate recommendations for levels of technology (hardware and software), system support (e.g., software, hardware, teaching materials), curriculum scope and sequence (e.g., the role of necessary precursors), and pre-service and in-service training. The second question was intended to generate recommendations based on an assessment of theoretical and empirical approaches, in psychology and education, relevant to the development of knowledge and skills that underpin the use of GIS.

However, the committee recognized that these two questions could not be answered without first addressing the educational role of spatial thinking itself. New and better support tools for education—such as GIS—may well be necessary and appropriate but to what purpose and in what contexts? The answer might seem obvious from the proposal title: to support spatial thinking across the K–12 curriculum. However, such a response raises some more fundamental questions: Why—and where—do we need to support spatial thinking across the K–12 curriculum? Why should we invest in better GIS or other support tools? What is the role of spatial thinking in everyday life, the workplace, and science?

After coming to appreciate the fundamental importance of spatial thinking and realizing that it was not just undersupported but underappreciated, undervalued, and therefore underinstructed, the committee came to a new understanding of the charge. The two original questions about the current role and future development of GIS as a support system could be satisfactorily answered only after we addressed two additional questions, one about the societal and educational need for spatial thinking and the other about the ways in which we learn to think spatially. Therefore, the committee developed an understanding of two additional questions:

1. What are the nature and character of spatial thinking: what is it, why do we need to know about it, and what do we need to know about it?

2. How does the capacity for spatial thinking develop and how might it be fostered systematically by education and training?

This led to a more coherent and comprehensive set of recommendations. With this reorganization of the task, Part I of this report, "The Nature and Functions of Spatial Thinking" (Chapters 2 through 6) led to Recommendation 1. Part II of the report, "Support for Spatial Thinking" (Chapters 7 through 9) led to Recommendations 2–6.

PART I: THE NATURE AND FUNCTIONS OF SPATIAL THINKING

The committee arrived at a position on the educational necessity for teaching and learning about spatial thinking:

• Spatial thinking is a collection of cognitive skills. The skills consist of declarative and perceptual forms of knowledge and some cognitive operations that can be used to transform, combine, or otherwise operate on this knowledge. The key to spatial thinking is a constructive amalgam of three elements: concepts of space, tools of representation, and processes of reasoning (see Chapter 1.2).

• Spatial thinking is integral to everyday life. People, natural objects, human-made objects, and human-made structures exist somewhere *in* space, and the interactions of people and things must be understood in terms of locations, distances, directions, shapes, and patterns (see Chapter 2).

• Spatial thinking is powerful. It solves problems by managing, transforming, and analyzing data, especially complex and large data sets, and by communicating the results of those processes to one's self and to others (see Chapter 2).

• Spatial thinking is integral to the everyday work of scientists and engineers, and it has underpinned many scientific and technical breakthroughs (see Chapter 3).

• Spatial thinking is a skill that can—and should—be learned by everyone, but there are significant individual and group differences in levels of performance (see Chapters 2 and 4 and Appendix C).

• Spatial thinking develops uniquely in individuals, depending on their experience, education, and inclination (see Chapter 4 and Appendix C).

• Expertise in spatial thinking draws on both general spatial skills that cross many domains of knowledge and spatial skills that are a particular domain of knowledge (see Chapter 4).

• Expertise in spatial thinking develops in the context of specific disciplines and becomes transformed and refined through training and extensive practice (see Chapters 3 and 4).

• While transfer of spatial thinking skills from one domain of knowledge to another is neither automatic nor easy, appropriately designed curricula that encourage infusion across school subjects can facilitate transfer (see Chapter 4).

•   Spatial thinking is currently not systematically instructed in the K–12 curriculum despite its fundamental importance and despite its significant role in the sets of national standards for science, mathematics, geography, and so forth (see Chapter 5). There is a major blind spot in the American educational system.

•   Support systems leverage the power of the human capacity to think and to solve problems (see Chapter 6.1).

•   Spatial thinking is a complex, powerful, and challenging process and support systems provide an interactive environment within which spatial thinking can take place by helping students to spatialize data sets, visualize working and final results, and perform analytic functions (see Chapter 6.6).

•   Given the increasing need for lifelong learning skills in a technologically changing world, students need opportunities to learn a range of low- and high-tech support systems for spatial thinking (see Chapter 6).

•   Implementing any support system in the K–12 context requires coordinated programs for material, logistical, instructional, curriculum, and community support (see Chapter 6.4).

Therefore, the committee views spatial thinking as a basic and essential skill that can be learned, that can be taught formally to all students, and that can be supported by appropriately designed tools, technologies, and curricula. With appropriate instruction and commensurate levels of low- and high-tech support, spatial thinking can become an invaluable lifelong habit of mind.

However, the problem with respect to teaching and learning about spatial thinking is far deeper than simply a lack of adequate supporting tools. Tools are means to an end: tools are therefore necessary but not sufficient. Schools teach what society values. Society values that for which there is a clear and explicit need and therefore educational rationale. Thus, two of the most valued school subjects are mathematics and science. As Chapter 5 makes clear, however, underpinning success in mathematics and science is the capacity to think spatially. Also, as Chapter 3 makes clear, spatial thinking underpins many tasks in everyday life, the workplace, and science. Ironically, those underpinnings are not yet matched by either a deep scientific understanding of the process of spatial thinking or a broadly accepted educational rationale for learning how to think spatially.

Chapters 3 and 5 provide a powerful educational rationale for teaching spatial thinking. Chapter 2 offers a first attempt to describe and understand the process of spatial thinking, and Chapter 4 and Appendix C summarize what is known about the learning and teaching of spatial thinking, leading to a position statement on the fostering of expertise in spatial thinking (see Chapter 4.5).

Chapter 5 demonstrates that there is no systematic and comprehensive attempt to teach about spatial thinking as part of the national Science and Mathematics Standards. Nowadays, school curricula are designed to meet content standards for specific disciplines, originating at either the national or the state level, that express what students should know and be able to do at various points throughout their school careers. Schools, and increasingly society at large, measure their success against benchmarks using standards-based assessments. As the educational saying goes, "We assess what we value and we value what we assess."

There are neither content standards nor valid and reliable assessments dedicated solely to spatial thinking. Without such standards and assessments, spatial thinking will remain locked in a curious educational twilight zone: extensively relied on across the K–12 curriculum but not explicitly and systematically instructed in any part of the curriculum. No matter how well designed support tools for spatial thinking might be, they will not be effective without societal recognition of the importance of spatial thinking and without an educational commitment to teaching spatial thinking to all students in all grades.

However, spatial thinking itself is not a content-based discipline in the way that physics, biology, and economics are disciplines: it is not a stand-alone subject in its own right. Spatial thinking is a way of thinking that permeates those disciplines and, the committee would argue, virtually all other subject matter disciplines. Instruction in spatial thinking should play an equivalent role to that of the "writing across the curriculum" approach. Standards for spatial thinking, therefore, should be general guidelines for what students need to know about concepts of space, tools of representation, and processes of reasoning in order to be able to solve problems. These general guidelines must be integrated into the particular content knowledge expectations for various subject matter disciplines. The guidelines should, therefore, be infused across the curriculum in as many disciplines as possible. Spatial thinking is the lever to enable students to achieve a deeper and more insightful understanding of subjects across the curriculum.

Spatial thinking is *not* an add-on to an already crowded school curriculum, but rather a missing link across that curriculum. Integration and infusion of spatial thinking can help to achieve existing curricular objectives. Spatial thinking is another lever to enable students to achieve a deeper and more insightful understanding of subjects across the curriculum.

Instruction in spatial thinking would help to foster a new generation of spatially literate students who are proficient in terms of spatial knowledge, spatial ways of thinking and acting, and spatial capabilities (see Chapter 1.4.1). With this proficiency, students will have established the habit of mind of thinking spatially, seeing opportunities for approaching problems by using their knowledge of concepts of space. They will be able to practice spatial thinking in an informed way, drawing on their knowledge of tools of representation. They will adopt a critical stance to spatial thinking, using the appropriate processes of spatial reasoning (see Chapter 1.4.2). Chapter 11 shows eighth-grade students practicing spatial thinking in a remarkably sophisticated way with the support of a tool, GIS, and with the guidance of an enlightened teacher.

The first recommendation is designed to help to achieve the goal of spatial literacy for all American students.

Recommendation 1

Through the support of federal funding agencies (i.e., the National Science Foundation [NSF], the National Institutes of Health, and the Department of Education), there should be a systematic research program into the nature, characteristics, and operations of spatial thinking. The recent NSF competition for "Science of Learning Centers" provides one program model for developing knowledge about spatial thinking.

The findings of this research program would be expected to highlight the importance of spatial thinking across the K–12 curriculum as well as to encourage the development of spatial thinking standards and curriculum materials to train K–12 students in spatial thinking.

The ultimate goal should be to foster a new generation of spatially literate students who have the habit of mind of thinking spatially, can practice spatial thinking in an informed way, and can adopt a critical stance to spatial thinking. Meeting this long-term goal will require careful articulation of the links between spatial thinking standards and existing disciplinary-based content standards. It will necessitate the development of innovative teaching methods and programs to train teachers, together with new ways to assess levels of spatial thinking and the performance of educational support programs. There should be a national commitment to the systemic educational efforts necessary to meet the goal of spatial literacy.

PART II: SUPPORT FOR SPATIAL THINKING

The committee arrived at a position on the educational challenges of providing systems for supporting spatial thinking in K–12 education:

• Spatial thinking can be supported and facilitated by the development of a coherent suite of supporting tools, ranging from low to high technology in nature, that can (1) address a range of types of problems, (2) use a range of types and amounts of data, and (3) require different levels of skill and experience (see Chapter 6).

• Support systems for spatial thinking must meet three requirements to be successful: they must (1) allow for the spatialization of data, (2) facilitate the visualization of working and final results, and (3) perform a range of functions (transformations, operations, and analyses) (see Chapter 6).

• The success of a support system in the K–12 context is a function of its design (see the ten criteria in Chapter 6) and its implementation across the curriculum (see the five support needs in Chapter 6).

• Geographic information science has significant but as yet unrealized potential for supporting spatial thinking across a range of subjects in the K–12 curriculum (see Chapters 7, 8, and 9).

• However, there are significant design and implementation challenges to be met before GIS can play a significant role alongside other tools for teaching standards-based spatial thinking across the curriculum. GIS should be redesigned to accommodate the full range of learners and school contexts, to be more developmentally and educationally appropriate, to be easier to teach and to learn, and to accommodate the current levels of computing equipment (see Chapters 8 and 9).

• GIS must be supported by a systematic implementation program that incorporates teacher training, curriculum development, and material support (see Chapters 8 and 9).

The committee sees GIS as exemplifying both the theoretical power of a high-tech system for supporting spatial thinking and the practical design and implementation problems that must be faced in the K–12 context:

• The power of GIS lies in its ability to support the scientific research process and to provide policy-related answers to significant real-world problems arising in a range of disciplinary contexts.

• The appeal of GIS lies in its direct connection to significant workforce opportunities in the information technology (IT) sector.

• The potential of GIS lies in its ability to accommodate the full range of learners and to be adapted to a range of educational settings.

• The practical problems of adapting GIS to the K–12 environment are equally striking. As an expert-based, "industrial strength" technology, it is, in one sense, too powerful for most K–12 needs. It is challenging and inviting, yet intimidating and difficult to learn. While the design issues can be addressed, the implementation challenges are immense. All of the essential implementation supports—for materials, logistics, instruction, curriculum, and in the community—are either weak or nonexistent.

Therefore, while GIS can make a significant impact on teaching and learning about spatial thinking, it must be situated in a context wherein there is a systematic, standards-based approach to teaching spatial thinking, along with a suite of supporting tools available to do so. Taken alone, GIS is not *the* answer to the problem of teaching spatial thinking in American schools; however, it can play a significant role in *an* answer. For GIS to be able to play that significant role, the committee identified a set of recommendations:

Recommendation 2

There should be a coordinated effort among GIS designers, psychologists, and educators to redesign GIS to accommodate the needs of the K–12 education community. Among the many design issues that must be addressed are

- broadening the accessibility of GIS to the full range of learners (e.g., adding alternative sensory input and output modes);
- strengthening the capacity to spatialize nonspatial data;
- overcoming the visualization limitations (e.g., with respect to time and to full three-dimensional capacity);
- providing graded versions of GIS that are age and/or experience appropriate (e.g., that are easy to learn, cumulative, and flexible);
- redesigning interfaces to be more intuitive and to provide help and guidance (e.g., providing reflective wizards);
- making the software customizable (e.g., adopting an open system architecture; making it possible for teachers to hide or expose functionality as needed); and
- making the software "teacher friendly" in terms of ease of installation, maintenance, and use.

The committee recognizes that many of these design challenges are not specific to the K–12 context and that their solution may not occur with that context in mind. Should this be the case, then someone must take responsibility for adapting the solutions to the particular needs of K–12 teachers and students. Teachers and students should not be expected to adapt to a "one-size-fits-all" GIS that does not reflect their special needs.

The committee identified three mechanisms that led to the development of GIS software: the academic model, the commercial model, and the collaborative model. These three models offer distinct options for the redesign of GIS software for the K–12 context. All three mechanisms appear to have merit, as well as potential pitfalls. The choice among them, therefore, should be made by the appropriate funding agencies.

Based on the levels of investment being made by commercial vendors and on experience from many GIS development projects, it would be reasonable to assume that a suitable GIS could be developed over a period of three years. Therefore, the committee makes the following recommendations.

Recommendation 3

To coordinate the development of GIS software, a "Federation of GIS Education Partners" should be established. The federation should consist of GIS developer and user partners, drawn from academia, government, the private sector, and the K–12 user community.

To be successful, the following should be considered in the design of a GIS educational software federation:

- The federation should be a grass-roots, community-driven effort.
- The governance basis of the federation should be to ensure that the priorities of the broader community are honored. However, some centralized management would be necessary for making major decisions on behalf of the federation's constituents, for representing the federation's interests, and for conducting day-to-day operations. The instrument of centralized management should be used sparingly.

• The federation should be flexible. Thus, the initial rules and procedures should not be overspecified.

• The federation should manage the tensions that may arise from constituents with differing expectations (e.g., software companies, teachers).

Recommendation 4

Working in collaboration, GIS system designers, educational IT specialists, and teachers should develop guidelines for a model GIS-enabled school.

The guidelines should address software and hardware needs (including schedules for upgrades), local and global network design and access requirements, classroom layouts for different modes of instruction, and levels of technical support for hardware and software.

Recommendation 5

Working in collaboration, representatives of colleges of education and GIS educators should

• establish guidelines for pre- and in-service teacher training programs for teaching spatial thinking using GIS; and
• develop a model standards-based curriculum for teaching about GIS.

Recommendation 6

With funding from either a government agency (e.g., the National Science Foundation, the Department of Education) or a private philanthropy, a research program should be developed to determine whether or not an understanding of GIS improves academic achievement across the curriculum. Without credible assessment of results, the value of GIS and other support systems for spatial thinking cannot be evaluated.

This set of recommendations (2-6) contains overlaps and critical interdependencies. Thus, for example, the GIS redesign process must inform the development of guidelines for GIS-enabled schools. The model curriculum must be linked to assessment procedures and to the research program on the impact of GIS on academic achievement.

IN CONCLUSION

The premise for this report is the need for systemic educational change. Fundamental to that change is a national commitment to the goal of spatial literacy. Spatial thinking must be recognized as a fundamental and necessary part of the process of K–12 education. The committee does not view spatial thinking as one more piece to be added on to an already overburdened curricular structure. Instead, it sees spatial thinking as an integrator and a facilitator for problem solving across the curriculum. Spatial thinking does not and should not stand alone, but equally well, without explicit attention to it, we cannot meet our responsibility for equipping the next generation of students for life and work in the twenty-first century.

1

Introduction

1.1 THE CHALLENGE TO LEARN

Of the many contributions that Jerome Bruner made to the scientific study of education, perhaps none is more important than his insistence that we must challenge students to learn and to think *and* that we must support their doing so. In 1959, Bruner offered a classic example of how to foster thinking, using only the simplest of tools. The work grew out of his concern with the "passivity of knowledge-getting," an approach he saw as depriving students of the thinking that is the reward for learning.

Fifth-grade students learned about the geography of the north central states in the United States in one of two ways:

> One group learned geography as a set of rational acts of induction—that cities spring up where there is water, where there are natural resources, where there are things to be processed and shipped. The other group learned passively that there were arbitrary cities at arbitrary places by arbitrary bodies of water and arbitrary sources of supply. One learned geography as a form of activity. The other stored some names and positions as a passive form of registration. (Bruner, 1959, p. 188)

Bruner's description of the work of the first group captures the power and excitement of thinking:

> We hit upon the happy idea of presenting this chunk of geography not as a set of knowns, but as a set of unknowns. One class was presented blank maps, containing only tracings of the rivers and lakes of the area as well as the natural resources. They were asked as a first exercise to indicate where the principal cities would be located, where the railroads, and where the main highways. Books and maps were not permitted and "looking up the facts" was cast in a sinful light. Upon completing this exercise, a class discussion was begun in which children attempted to justify why the major city would be here, a large city there, a railroad on this line, etc.
>
> The discussion was a hot one. After an hour, and much pleading, permission was given to consult the rolled up wall map. I will never forget one young student, as he pointed his finger at the foot of Lake Michigan, shouting, "Yipee, *Chicago* is at the end of the pointing-down lake." And another replying, "Well, OK: but Chicago's no good for the rivers and it should be here where there

is a big city (St. Louis)." These children were thinking, and learning was an instrument for checking and improving the process. To at least a half dozen children in the class it is not a matter of indifference that no big city is to be found at the junction of Lake Huron, Lake Michigan, and Lake Superior. They were slightly shaken up transportation theorists when the facts were in. (Bruner, 1959, pp. 187–188)

The first group of children was practicing a vital form of thinking—spatial thinking—and their work was supported by a simple outline map. Hidden behind many of the daily operations of everyday life, the workplace, and science, spatial thinking is integral to successful problem solving. Section 1.2 defines spatial thinking and presents two examples of spatial thinking in epidemiology. Section 1.3 discusses the committee's charge. The first group of children in Bruner's study was successful in spatial thinking, and the purpose of this report (Section 1.4) is to foster a generation of students who are spatially literate, who can match the accepted norms for what should be known about space, representation, and reasoning. Fostering spatial literacy can be achieved only by systemic educational reform, and central to the reform process are members of the four audiences of this report (Section 1.5). Section 1.6 describes the structure of the report.

1.2 SPATIAL THINKING

There are many forms of thinking: verbal, logical, metaphorical, hypothetical, mathematical, statistical, and so forth. They can be distinguished in terms of their representational system (e.g., verbal, using linguistic symbols; mathematical, using mathematical symbols) or their reasoning system (e.g., logic, metaphor). In any domain of knowledge, multiple forms of thinking are used: science, for example, uses linguistic, hypothetical, mathematical, logical, and many other thinking processes.

Spatial thinking, one form of thinking, is a collection of cognitive skills. The skills consist of declarative and perceptual forms of knowledge and some cognitive operations that can be used to transform, combine, or otherwise operate on this knowledge. The key to spatial thinking is a constructive amalgam of three elements: concepts of space, tools of representation, and processes of reasoning. It is the concept of space that makes spatial thinking a distinctive form of thinking. By understanding the meanings of space, we can use its properties (e.g., dimensionality, continuity, proximity, separation) as a vehicle for structuring problems, finding answers, and expressing and communicating solutions. By expressing relationships within spatial structures (e.g., maps, multidimensional scaling models, computer-assisted design [CAD] renderings), we can perceive, remember, and analyze the static and, via transformations, the dynamic properties of objects and the relationships between objects. We can use representations in a variety of modes and media (graphic [text, image, and video], tactile, auditory, kinesthetic, and olfactory) to describe, explain, and communicate about the structure, operation, and function of objects and their relationships. Spatial thinking is not restricted to any domain of knowledge, although it may be more characteristic, for example, of architecture, medicine, physics, and biology than of philosophy, business administration, linguistics, and comparative literature.

To think spatially entails knowing about (1) *space*—for example, the relationships among units of measurement (e.g., kilometers versus miles), different ways of calculating distance (e.g., miles, travel time, travel cost), the basis of coordinate systems (e.g., Cartesian versus polar coordinates), the nature of spaces (e.g., number of dimensions [two- versus three-dimensional]); (2) *representation*—for example, the relationships among views (e.g., plans versus elevations of buildings, or orthogonal versus perspective maps), the effect of projections (e.g., Mercator versus equal-area map projections), the principles of graphic design (e.g., the roles of legibility, visual contrast, and figure-ground organization in the readability of graphs and maps); and (3) *reasoning*—for example, the different ways of thinking about shortest distances (e.g., as the crow flies versus route distance in a rectangular street grid), the ability to extrapolate and interpolate (e.g., projecting a functional relationship on a graph into the future or estimating the slope of a hillside from a map of contour lines), and making decisions (e.g., given traffic reports on a radio, selecting an alternative detour).

Boxes 1.1 and 1.2 illustrate the process and power of spatial thinking. While both deal with waterborne threats to public health, the key parallels lie in their imaginative treatments of epidemiological data. Mapped patterns of spatial variability in levels of cholera incidence and dissolved arsenic can be understood in terms of the source of drinking water—in the first case as a function of the differential surface location of the wells and, in the second case, the differential depth of the wells. Both cases depend on visualization in three dimensions, with the differential contamination levels within the spatial structure of subsurface aquifers providing the explanation for the patterns of spatial variability in health impacts. In the first case, the technology of data acquisition and graphic production is relatively simple; in the second case, it depends on sophisticated technologies that produce remarkable levels of locational accuracy. In both cases, the technology enables an exploratory and explanatory approach to problem solving that draws on the scientific knowledge, intuition, and experience of researchers.

1.3 CHARGE TO THE COMMITTEE

The title of the proposal for this report was *Support for Thinking Spatially: The Incorporation of Geographic Information Science Across the K–12 Curriculum.* Given the need for increased scientific and technological literacy in the workforce and in everyday life, we must equip K–12 graduates with skills that will enable them to think spatially and to take advantage of tools and technologies—such as GIS (geographic information systems) (see Box 1.3)—for supporting spatial thinking. Therefore, the charge contained two questions, the first of which was intended to generate recommendations for levels of technology (hardware and software), system supports (e.g., teaching materials), curriculum scope and sequence (e.g., the role of necessary precursors), and pre-service and in-service training, while the second was intended to generate recommendations based on an assessment of theoretical and empirical approaches, in psychology and education, relevant to the development of knowledge and skills that underpin the use of GIS.

However, the committee recognized that the charge could not be met without first addressing the educational role of spatial thinking itself. New and better support tools for education—such as GIS—may well be necessary and appropriate, but to what purpose and in what contexts? The answer might seem obvious from the proposal title: to support spatial thinking across the K–12 curriculum. However, such a response points to a fundamental question: Why—and where—do we need to support spatial thinking across the K–12 curriculum? Why should we invest in better GIS or other support tools? What is the role of spatial thinking in everyday life, the workplace, and science?

After learning to appreciate the fundamental importance of spatial thinking, the committee came to a new understanding of the charge. Questions about the current role and future development of GIS as a support system could be answered satisfactorily only after the societal and therefore educational need for spatial thinking, and the ways in which we learn to think spatially, were understood.

Therefore, the committee developed an understanding of two additional questions: (1) What are the nature and character of spatial thinking? (2) How does the capacity for spatial thinking develop and how might it be fostered systematically by education and training? This revision to the committee charge was approved by the National Research Council (NRC) and met with consent from the project sponsors.

BOX 1.1
Mapping of Cholera in Nineteenth-Century England

Dr. John Snow (1813–1858), an English medical health officer, is celebrated for his now-famous and often-reproduced map of the relationship between cholera deaths and water pumps in central London, depicting what he called "the topography of the outbreak" of cholera in the late summer of 1854. On the basis of this map, he recommended the removal of the handle of a water pump that proved to be a source of contaminated drinking water. For that feat alone, he merits the soubriquet of the "father of epidemiology."

However, in a less well-known section of his book *On the Mode of Communication of Cholera* (1855), Snow is responsible for an even more remarkable exercise in spatial thinking. (This analysis is based on Robinson, 1982, pp. 175–180.) After establishing to his satisfaction the link between contaminated water and the incidence of cholera, Snow undertook an exercise in data collection, representation, and interpretation that captures the essence of spatial thinking. He knew that there were differential death rates from cholera throughout London. He also knew that at least two major water companies, the Southwark & Vauxhall Company and the Lambeth Company, provided water to more than 300,000 Londoners. He did not know, however, the service area of each water supply company because the data either did not exist or were not available to him.

Knowing that Southwark & Vauxhall Company drew its water from the River Thames and the Lambeth Company from inland wells, Snow developed a simple test for water salinity to differentiate water derived from the two sources. Based on tests of the salinity of samples gathered by collaborators from locations throughout the city, he mapped the distribution of salinity values, and from this map, he inferred the service areas of the two companies. Interestingly, there was an area of spatial overlap in the pattern of water distribution (Figure 1.1).

Snow also had a map of the rates of cholera deaths per 1,000 houses. He correlated data from the water distribution and cholera death maps. Interestingly again, the two "sole-service" areas and the "both-providers" service area had different death rates. The South & Vauxhall Company sole-service area experienced a death rate of 71 per 1,000 and the Lambeth Company sole-service area experienced a death rate of 5 per 1,000. Crucial to his reasoning, the area with both providers experienced an intermediate cholera death rate. Death rates were, therefore, correlated with water source. The resultant explanation for the variation in death rates was simple: the Southwark & Vauxhall Company drew its water from a river that also served as a depository for untreated sewage, whereas the Lambeth Company had switched from the river source to less-polluted inland wells in 1852.

Snow's approach exemplifies spatial thinking. After collecting data, he used maps to integrate the data. From these maps, he identified spatial patterns (service areas and differential death rates). He correlated the two patterns and reasoned about the spatial variation in one (death rates) as a function

This report, therefore, answers four questions:

1. What are the nature and character of spatial thinking: what is it, why do we need to know about it, and what do we need to know about it?

2. How does the capacity for spatial thinking develop and how might it be fostered systematically by education and training?

3. How might current versions of GIS be incorporated into existing standards-based instruction in all knowledge domains across the school curriculum?

4. How can cognitive developmental and educational theory be used to develop new versions of GIS that are age appropriate in their design and to implement new GIS curricula that are age appropriate in their scope and sequence?

The committee came to believe that spatial thinking is pervasive: it is vital across a wide range of domains of practical and scientific knowledge; yet it is underrecognized, undervalued,

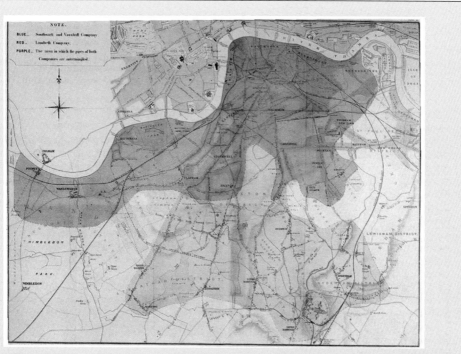

FIGURE 1.1 Snow's 1855 map showing the areas of south London served by two water companies. Original 535 × 410 mm. Lithograph 7560.e.67, printed color. SOURCE: Robinson, 1982, p. 179. Reproduced by permission of the British Library.

of spatial variations in the other (water sources). From this analysis, he drew a causal explanation and accounted for the differential death rates.

This brilliant exercise in thinking would now be accomplished more rapidly and accurately with the support of global positioning system (GPS) technology and a geographic information system. Nevertheless, the fundamental properties of the thinking process would remain the same. Data are represented in a spatial context, and through a reasoning process, a problem is solved.

underappreciated, and therefore, underinstructed. Despite the practical importance of spatial thinking—historical and contemporary—the committee recognized that scientists and educators have not yet clearly identified and described the operations of spatial thinking. Without a clear understanding of the nature and character of spatial thinking, it is impossible to design instructional systems and technologies to support it.

1.4 AN OUTCOME OF THE REPORT: FOSTERING SPATIAL LITERACY

The committee was charged with exploring ways of supporting the process of thinking spatially. If this charge is met successfully, then American students will become more spatially literate. Section 1.4.1 defines the components of spatial literacy, and Section 1.4.2 presents the characteristics of a student who is spatially literate.

BOX 1.2
Mapping of Arsenic in Twenty-First-Century Bangladesh

In many areas of the world, arsenicosis—arsenic poisoning that leads to cancers and other debilitating diseases—is an increasing problem. In Bangladesh, the cause of the problem is arsenic from groundwater that is pumped from wells, the source of drinking water for 97 percent of the population.

van Geen et al. (2003) analyzed the spatial variability of arsenic in tube wells in a 25 km^2 area in Araihazar Upazilla (an administrative unit). The parallels to the work of Snow are obvious: a public health crisis, a waterborne agent, the use of wells, the need for mapping, and the ideas of spatial patterns and variability. The differences are equally obvious: access to sophisticated technologies, knowledge of the causative agent, and the deployment of teams of well-equipped scientific researchers.

The challenge in the case of arsenic in the watertable in Bangladesh is one of understanding what the authors refer to as ". . . the bewildering degree of spatial variability of groundwater arsenic contaminations" (van Geen et al., 2003, p. 3-1). The variability in arsenic levels over very short distances is remarkable (where levels of ≤10 μ*g*/L meet the World Health Organization guidelines for safe drinking water and levels of ≤50 μ*g*/L meet the U.S. Environmental Protection Agency guidelines). The researchers sampled water from 5,971 wells, recording arsenic levels, the position of the well (via a global positioning system [GPS]), and well characteristics (e.g., date of installation, depth). Data were mapped onto an *IKONOS* satellite image.

Figure 1.2 shows the spatial pattern of variability. Each color-coded circle on the map (right) corresponds to a well whose location was determined by students using a hand-held GPS receiver. The wells are clustered in two villages. Water from each well was sampled and analyzed for arsenic. The safer wells are color-coded in green, and the more dangerous wells are color-coded as red or red-brown dots. (Interestingly, public health authorities in parts of Bangladesh paint the handles of the safer wells green and those of the high-arsenic-level wells red, matching the universal symbols for stop and go, safe and dangerous). The background is an *IKONOS* satellite image showing rectangular patches corresponding to rice fields that separate the villages.

The parallel section (left) shows the same information as a function of depth. Well owners know the depth of their wells, the majority of which were installed in the past 10 years, because they paid for each 15-foot PVC (polyvinyl chloride) pipe section that went into the well construction.

The map shows that most households in the northern village have access to low-arsenic water, whereas only some households in the southern village do. The explanation is that in the northern village, a shallow clay layer has forced villagers to install wells that tap into a deeper, but low-arsenic, sandy aquifer. A shallower aquifer with highly variable arsenic levels was available in the southern village, and therefore, many (but not all) villagers chose to install their wells as inexpensively as possible by minimizing well depth. Now that villagers and local well drillers are aware of the depth distribution of arsenic in this area, most new wells are being installed to tap into the deeper aquifer.

This analysis is an equally brilliant exercise in spatial thinking that follows the same steps as those of Snow: from data to maps to patterns to causal explanations. Apart from the technical sophistication, the major difference is the spatial complexity. van Geen and his colleagues are looking at arsenic levels in a three-dimensional context: two surface coordinates and a depth coordinate. The complexity of the surface patterns of safer versus less safe wells can be understood only in terms of subsurface structures that vary in all three dimensions.

1.4.1 Components of Spatial Literacy

Bruner refers to his students as being "slightly shaken up transportation theorists." He points out that ". . . [t]hese children were thinking, and learning was an instrument for checking and improving the process." Although the committee does not necessarily want fifth-grade students to become better transportation theorists, it does want all students to learn to be better spatial thinkers.

Learning to think is a key educational goal. Achieving this goal leads to literacy, where literacy is a normative statement of what members of a culture should know and be able to do with that

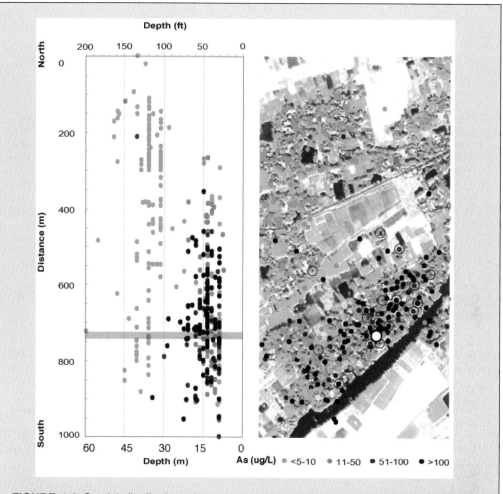

FIGURE 1.2 Spatial distribution of arsenic levels in wells in Arailhazar Upazilla, Bangladesh. SOURCE: van Geen et al., 2003, p. 3-11. Reproduced by permission of American Geophysical Union.

knowledge. The Workforce Investment Act of 1998 (Public Law 105-220) stated that ". . . [t]he term 'literacy' means an individual's ability to read, write, and speak in English, compute, and solve problems, at levels of proficiency necessary to function on the job, in the family of the individual, and in society" (Title II, Section 203, Number 12). The committee would add spatial thinking to this list of necessary abilities. A person proficient in spatial thinking is spatially literate and can match the norms for what should be known about space, representation, and reasoning.

These norms are set within a framework derived from *Technically Speaking: Why All Americans Need to Know More About Technology* (NRC, 2002c). That NRC report saw a technologically

BOX 1.3
Role of GIS in Spatial Thinking

A geographic information system mirrors many of the functions and operations of spatial thinking. A GIS can serve as one means of support for spatial thinking and as a model for exemplifying the challenges and ways of incorporating spatial thinking into K–12 education.

A GIS is an integrated system of hardware, software, and procedures designed to support the collection, management, manipulation, analysis, modeling, and display of spatially referenced data about Earth's surface in order to solve complex planning and management problems. The power of a GIS is that it allows us to ask questions of data and to perform spatial operations on spatial databases. A GIS can answer five generic questions:

Question	Type of Task
1. What is at . . . ?	Inventory and/or monitoring
2. Where is . . . ?	Inventory and/or monitoring
3. What has changed since . . . ?	Inventory and/or monitoring
4. What spatial pattern exists . . . ?	Spatial analysis
5. What if . . . ?	Modeling

SOURCE: Geography Education Standards Project, 1994, p. 256.

literate person as displaying three characteristics: knowledge of concepts, command over ways of thinking and acting, and development of capabilities. "Like literacy in reading, mathematics, science, or history, the goal of technological literacy is to provide people with the tools to participate intelligently and thoughtfully in the world around them" (NRCc, 2002, p. 3).

Given the resonances between this view of technological literacy and the committee's view of spatial literacy, and given the shared emphasis on the importance of tools for thought, the committee offers a parallel characterization of spatial literacy as constituting proficiency in terms of spatial knowledge, spatial ways of thinking and acting, and spatial capabilities.

Spatial Knowledge

Students need to know the concepts that are the building blocks for spatial thinking. There are general spatial concepts that are found in many disciplines, such as symmetry, isomorphism, reflection, orientation, rotation, and function, and spatial concepts that are tailored to a particular discipline, such as relative versus absolute distance, small versus large scale, and distance decay in geography.

Students learn the meanings and uses of concepts relevant to spatial thinking in the context of specific disciplines or school subjects. Thus, in mathematics, students learn about general concepts, such as minima and maxima, and their specific forms, such as hyperbolas and parabolas. In geometry, they learn about conic sections: hyperbola, parabola, ellipse, and circle. They learn to distinguish among a torus, Mobius strip, and Klein bottle. In physics, they learn that the equilibrium position of a fixed chain is a catenary curve (or hyperbolic cosine).

Even this cursory listing of concepts by discipline illustrates two fundamental educational challenges. First, there is a rich, complex, conceptual structure to the description and explanation of space to be learned within each discipline. Second, rather than coming up with an omnibus list of concepts for spatial thinking, students—and especially teachers—should identify concepts relevant to specific disciplines but should also look for common themes. They should reflect on how concepts of one discipline might inform or interfere with learning about concepts in another disci-pline. For example, in algebra, geometry, and science, the concept of function has different mean-ings. Similarly, in geometry, a point is a dimensionless location, whereas in geography, a point in space is a specific place with a small but definite area.

Spatial Ways of Thinking and Acting

People draw upon strategies that emphasize the use of spatial thinking to carry out projects. They set ideas into spatial contexts, seeing similar things as being close together and dissimilar things as far apart. They draw diagrams and graphs. They look for patterns and note outliers (anomalies) from the patterns. They look for clusters. They use statistical analyses to test for spatial relationships. They look for relationships among different spatial patterns. They disentangle change over space from change over time. Some representations are sketches used only during the thinking process, whereas others are created for an audience. In each case, there is an interplay between thinking and acting, between ideas and their representation, between expression for one's self and communication and dissemination to others.

The educational challenge is to teach students strategies for spatial thinking; to teach how, where, and when to use them; and to convey a critical awareness of the strengths and limitations of each strategy.

Spatial Capabilities

Skills in spatial thinking are learned within a specific context. Skills can be supported by tools and technologies (see Chapter 6 for the concept of support systems and Chapter 7 for a range of high-tech spatial support systems). Disciplines adapt particular supporting tools and technologies: in mathematics, students learn to use graphing calculators; in design, students learn to use CAD programs; and in geography, students learn to use GIS. As a result of the human genome project, students must learn new representational schemes and develop sophistication in spatial thinking.

Tools and technologies support different tasks: concept maps are used for structuring ideas, CAD for design, GIS for geospatial data analysis, and so forth. For each task category, there are often competing versions of tools: for GIS, there are low-tech approaches, such as traditional techniques for overlaying paper or mylar maps at the same scale on a light table; for high-tech approaches, there are software programs by Environmental Systems Research Institute (ESRI), Intergraph, Idrisi, etc. (see Chapters 7 and 8). Moreover, new categories of tools and technologies emerge as fields advance. For example, developing a robust spatial representation of the brain has become feasible as magnetic resonance imaging (MRI), functional magnetic resonance imaging (fMRI), and other techniques become available.

The educational challenge is threefold: (1) to provide students with experience using low-tech tools (paper, pencils, protractors, compasses, etc.); (2) to provide students with opportunities to learn several, general-purpose, high-tech applications that support spatial thinking (e.g., *Excel*, *Powerpoint*, *Photoshop*); and (3) to develop the skills that will allow them to learn new low- but especially new high-tech applications. When students specialize in a discipline, they often need to learn a complex application relatively quickly. However, expert use of many high-tech support systems requires a lengthy investment of time. Often students have difficulty determining how support systems work. Moreover, teachers question the value of investing in the instruction time necessary for students to attain a level of proficiency that allows them to solve interesting problems with the tools.

Taken together, the educational challenges for teachers and students are complex. On the one hand, students need to learn how to use a relatively small number of discipline-specific tools as quickly as possible. On the other hand, in the longer run, students also need to learn how to learn new supporting tools as they emerge. Each tool is costly to learn in terms of time. New tools become available and old tools are revised or discarded (e.g., the slide rule). Focused tools—such as CAD—are very powerful, but they do not necessarily offer opportunities across disciplines and therefore across the curriculum.

If these educational challenges are met, we can also meet the goal of fostering a new generation of spatially literate students. To do so, we need to invest in a systematic educational program to enhance levels of spatial thinking in all K–12 students.

1.4.2 Three Characteristics of a Spatially Literate Student

Spatially literate students who have developed appropriate levels of spatial knowledge and skills in spatial ways of thinking and acting, together with sets of spatial capabilities,

- have the habit of mind of thinking spatially—they know where, when, how, and why to think spatially;
- practice spatial thinking in an informed way—they have a broad and deep knowledge of spatial concepts and spatial representations, a command over spatial reasoning using a variety of spatial ways of thinking and acting, have well-developed spatial capabilities for using supporting tools and technologies; and
- adopt a critical stance to spatial thinking—they can evaluate the quality of spatial data based on their source, likely accuracy, and reliability; they can use spatial data to construct, articulate, and defend a line of reasoning or point of view in solving problems and answering questions; and they can evaluate the validity of arguments based on spatial information.

The committee believes that students can derive pleasure from thinking spatially. The children in Jerome Bruner's first group of active, engaged, and excited spatial thinkers should represent the rule, not the exception.

1.5 AUDIENCES FOR *LEARNING TO THINK SPATIALLY*

Fostering a new generation of spatial thinkers requires systemic educational reform. Such reform cannot be achieved without the long-term participation, cooperation, and commitment of many individuals. Therefore, this report is aimed at four groups of people, often overlapping in composition, who are central to educational reform.

Its first audience is the educational establishment—those federal, state, and local officials who are charged with establishing educational policy and practice. These officials establish content and performance standards for what students should know and be able to do; they adopt assessment programs to measure levels of student performance; they establish criteria for teacher preparation and certification; they provide the supplies and equipment necessary for instruction; and they provide instructional programs for pre- and in-service teachers. The educational establishment can mandate or encourage systemic change. However, the successful implementation of change is possible only with the active participation and cooperation of the second audience—members of the educational infrastructure. This audience ranges from the leadership of teachers' unions to pre-service trainers to curriculum developers, textbook writers, educational publishers, courseware developers, and test and assessment developers. The precise direction of change and reform will depend on members of the third audience—researchers in education and psychology. As argued earlier, without a clear understanding of the nature and character of spatial thinking it is impossible to design instructional systems and technologies to support spatial thinking. The design of one such instructional system, GIS, falls under the aegis of the fourth audience—the developers of GIS software.

Some of the recommendations in Chapter 10 are aimed specifically at particular audiences (e.g., members of the educational establishment or GIS software developers). Other recommendations require the collaboration of members of all four audiences. The committee believes that the set of recommendations provides the basis for actions to ensure that the next generation of American students is spatially literate.

Spatial thinking can be learned; it should be taught at all levels in the education system. With advances in the tools and technologies of computation (hardware and software), spatial thinking can be supported in ways that enhance the speed, accuracy, capacity (to manage large amounts of data), and flexibility of its operation and open up the process to increasing numbers of people, working collaboratively and at higher levels of performance. Because of newly available computational technologies, support for spatial thinking is more readily possible today, but concomitantly, more challenging cognitive skills are necessary to take advantage of rapidly changing support systems. Given the rapid change in supporting tools and technologies, therefore, spatially literate students must be lifelong learners.

1.6 STRUCTURE OF THIS REPORT

In Part I, "The Nature and Function of Spatial Thinking" (Chapters 2 through 6), the committee focuses on the first pair of questions of the charge about spatial thinking and its support: its definition, character, and operations (Chapter 2); its roles in everyday life, work, and science (Chapter 3); its incorporation into instruction in the K–12 curriculum (Chapter 4); and its central role in workforce needs, and its implicit, unacknowledged role in standards-based K–12 education (Chapter 5). The nature and characteristics of a support system for spatial thinking are defined in the K–12 context (Chapter 6).

The committee sees spatial thinking as a basic and essential skill that can be learned, that can be taught formally to all students, and that can be supported by appropriately designed tools and technologies. With appropriate instruction and support, spatial thinking can become a lifelong habit of mind. The committee presents a set of educational guidelines for developing instructional systems and curricula that can foster spatial literacy in American students. Therefore, Part I generates one recommendation.

On the basis of this understanding, Part II, "Support for Spatial Thinking" (Chapters 7 through 9), focuses on questions three and four of the charge. The committee reviews a range of high-tech systems for supporting spatial thinking (Chapter 7), evaluates the design and implementation of GIS as a system for supporting spatial thinking in the K–12 context (Chapter 8), and assesses the current status and potential of GIS as a support system in the K–12 context (Chapter 9).

The committee believes that although GIS can make a significant impact on teaching and learning about spatial thinking, it must be situated in a context wherein there is a systematic, standards-based approach to teaching spatial thinking, along with a suite of supporting tools available to do so. Taken alone, GIS is not *the* answer to the problem of teaching spatial thinking in American schools; however, it can play a significant role in *an* answer. Therefore, Part II generates five recommendations.

In Part III, "Supporting Spatial Thinking in the Future" (Chapters 10 and 11), the committee addresses the role of spatial thinking in general, and in K–12 education in particular, and illustrates the role of GIS in supporting spatial thinking. Chapter 10 presents the committee's conclusions and a set of six recommendations, and Chapter 11 describes students who are spatially literate and who are using GIS to solve interesting and important problems.

Part I

The Nature and Functions of Spatial Thinking

2

The Nature of Spatial Thinking

2.1 INTRODUCTION

In Chapter 1, the committee defines spatial thinking as a constructive amalgam of three elements: concepts of space, tools of representation, and processes of reasoning. Space provides the conceptual and analytical framework within which data can be integrated, related, and structured into a whole. Representations—either internal and cognitive or external and graphic, linguistic, physical, and so forth—provide the forms within which structured information can be stored, analyzed, comprehended, and communicated to others. Reasoning processes provide the means of manipulating, interpreting, and explaining the structured information.

In this chapter, the committee describes and explains spatial thinking in more detail. It begins in Section 2.2 by looking at the current understanding of spatial thinking, distinguishing it from narrower concepts such as spatial ability, and viewing it as a means of problem solving. Section 2.3 explores the use of space as a framework for understanding, identifying the three contexts in which spatial thinking operates and pointing to the key role of spatialization. Section 2.4 turns to the three functions of spatial thinking: description, analysis, and inference. The basis for spatial thinking is the structure of space and the operations that can be performed on and in that structure. Section 2.5 builds a four-part structure of space based on primitives, languages of space, spatial concepts, and operations. The chapter ends in Section 2.6 with a psychological analysis of the cognitive processes underlying spatial thinking.

2.2 APPROACHES TO SPATIAL THINKING

2.2.1 Forms of Thinking About Space

In terms of its power and pervasiveness, spatial thinking is on a par with, although perhaps not yet as well recognized and certainly not as well formalized as, mathematical or verbal thinking. It can be contrasted with verbal thinking. Language allows us to express the output of direct sensory perceptions of the world; it allows us to develop metaphors; and it can support abstractions such as meanings that are counterfactual or hypothetical, or do not rely on direct sense perceptions. Another quality of verbal thinking is that it can be and most often is public and external. After millennia of talking and writing, there are well-established, formal conventions of meaning and pragmatics that ensure considerable consensus across people within a language community. We have a good understanding of what it means to be articulate and literate in the verbal domain. We can assess performance in spoken and written forms, and we focus on the teaching and learning of verbal thinking.

By contrast, there is as yet no clear consensus about spatial thinking and, therefore, spatial literacy. Thus, there are many related concepts in use: we speak about spatial ability, spatial reasoning, spatial cognition, spatial concepts, spatial intelligence, environmental cognition, cognitive mapping, and mental maps (see for example, Eliot, 1987; Gardner, 1983; Golledge and Stimson, 1997; Gould and White, 1974; Kitchin, 1994; Kitchin and Freundschuh, 2000; Newcombe and Huttenlocher, 2000; Portugali, 1996; Tversky, 2000a,b).

Perhaps the most familiar of these terms is spatial ability. Spatial ability is conceptualized as a trait that a person has and as a way of characterizing a person's ability to perform mentally such operations as rotation, perspective change, and so forth. The concept derives in part from the psychometric tradition of intelligence measurement and testing with, for example, the French (French et al., 1963) reference test kit identifying types of spatial ability such as spatial orientation and visualization. By classifying the cognitive processes used to solve tasks thought to measure spatial ability, Linn and Petersen (1986) identified three categories of spatial ability: spatial perception, mental rotation, and spatial visualization. For example, spatial visualization is measured by tests such as the paper folding test (in which respondents are presented with drawings of folded pieces of paper that have hole(s) punched in them and are asked to select which drawing indicates how the paper would look when unfolded), and the embedded figures test (in which respondents are asked to find a simple shape within a complex one) (see Figure 2.1). Spatial ability has been studied in terms of group and individual performance differences (see Eliot, 1987; Golledge et al., 1983; Linn and Petersen, 1985).

Spatial ability is clearly related to but much more restricted in its scope than spatial thinking, as are all of the competing concepts. It is the links among space, representation, and reasoning that give the process of spatial thinking its power, versatility, and applicability. Spatial thinking is multifaceted in its operation: just as there is no single recipe for how to think verbally or mathematically, there is no single way to think spatially. Instead, the process of spatial thinking comprises broad sets of interconnected competencies that can be taught and learned.

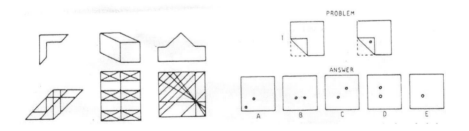

FIGURE 2.1 Spatial visualization items. Left, embedded figures: respondents are asked to find the simple shape shown on the top in the complex shape shown on the bottom. Right, paper folding: respondents are asked to indicate how the paper would look when folded. SOURCE: Linn and Petersen, 1985. Reprinted with permission of the Society for Research in Child Development.

At one level, we can learn to read the pressure and temperature axes of a phase diagram in physics, to understand the relations between elements in the atomic chart in chemistry, to recognize the particular shapes and locations that are indicative of tumors in an MRI, to understand the spatial properties that are preserved by a modified Mercator projection in cartography, and to visualize the three-dimensional spatial relations between different air masses and the associated types of fronts in meteorology. In each case, we can identify a particular set of spatial concepts that must be known and understood and the interpretive skills, parts of spatial ways of thinking and acting, that must be mastered. Taken together, the set of concepts and skills forms a cognitive spatial tool kit that is tuned to the practice of a particular discipline (for example, see Chapter 3.6.1). The tool kit mixes domain-specific spatial knowledge (concepts, models, and theories) with the use of generic representational forms and spatial structures (e.g., Cartesian coordinate systems, linear and nonlinear relations, scale transformations, rotations and perspective change). To the extent that there are tools and technologies to be learned (e.g., how to take an MRI reading or to create a map projection using a computer algorithm), we learn the spatial capabilities that make us proficient in a domain of knowledge.

At another level, as we become spatially literate, we develop a general spatial attitude. This entails a willingness and ability to frame problems in spatial terms, to use the language of space to express the elements of a problem, to think about relations between objects in terms of distances or directions or patterns, to imagine alternative graphical representations, to change viewing perspective or viewing angle, to zoom in or out, to hypothesize and visualize the effects of different rates of change, to predict what might happen to spatial patterns or structures or relations if . . . By linking spatial knowledge, spatial ways of thinking and acting, and spatial capabilities with this general spatial attitude, we have a flexible and powerful way of thinking that is transferable to and applicable in a wide range of contexts in everyday life, the workplace, and science.

2.2.2 Spatial Thinking as Problem Solving

Our concept of spatial thinking is broader than spatial ability and related concepts in that it approaches the process of problem solving via the coordinated use of space, representation, and reasoning. Scientists in general and educators in particular have not paid sufficient attention to identifying and articulating the nature, characteristics, and operation of what is arguably a defining characteristic of the scientific approach.

Spatial thinking uses representations to help us remember, understand, reason, and communicate about the properties of and relations between objects represented *in* space, whether or not those objects themselves are inherently spatial. Objects can be concrete things (as in a cognitive map of roads and neighborhoods in a city) or abstract concepts (as in a two-dimensional graphic plot from a multidimensional scaling model of the love-hate relationships between characters in a Shakespeare play). In the first case, there is an objective geographic space within which the objects exist and from which, on the basis of experience, we can calculate distances and directions. The subjective cognitive map is a mental representation that may transform and systematically distort objective distances and directions between places. In the second case, the number and types of words exchanged between characters are converted into similarity measures and then distances between characters. The graphic plot locates characters in a space in which one dimension is hate and the other love. Location in space can be used to understand the relationships between characters.

Representations can be internal, a mental image of the workings of a pulley system, or external, a printed cross section of a geological structure or an immersive virtual reality display of the interior of a new building. The forms of representation can range from a schematic diagram of a pulley system to a photograph or movie of actual pulleys, lines, and weights. The cross-sectional diagram can be two dimensional, showing depth and extent, or a pseudo-perspective diagram showing depth and two horizontal dimensions. It could be a geological cross section in which time replaces depth as the vertical axis. Instead of an immersive space, the representation of the building could be a plan and elevation, an architect's three-dimensional physical model, or an ordered series of architectural renderings, viewing the interior from different places in the building with a near-photographic appearance. Representations can capture what is (e.g., a map of a city), what might be (e.g., a sketch of an addition to a house on a lunchroom napkin), and what should be (e.g., a score for a piece of music or dance).

Reasoning processes can ask: What happens if we add weight to one part of the pulley system, if we remove weight from another part, or if the string breaks in a particular place? We can ask which parts move, how far, and what the equilibrium position is. In the other cases, we can ask how the thickness of the rock layers varies with depth, or what the "sense" of space is that we "feel" as we move through the lobby of the building. The questions can capture either the results of change or the process of change. They can deal with possible or hypothetical ("what would it look like if") situations (e.g., a fly's-eye view of the atrium of the building or David Macaulay's images of parts of the urban infrastructure "floating" in three-dimensional space without the surrounding and supporting physical ground) (Figure 2.2).

Spatial thinking occurs in private and in public. On the one hand, spatial thinking encompasses a range of cognitive processes that support exploration and discovery: we can visualize relations, imagine transformations from one scale to another, rotate an object to look at its other sides, create novel viewing angles or perspectives, evoke images of places and spaces, and so forth (see Hanson and Hanson, 1993). On the other hand, spatial thinking allows us to externalize these operations by creating spatial representations in a range of media, forms, and sensory modalities: tactile maps or graphs, auditory maps, vibrotactile surfaces, traditional cartographic maps, two-dimensional graphs, link or flow diagrams, tree diagrams of hierarchical relations, three-dimensional (3-D) scale models, exploded views of a structure, and so on. The representations can be created as part of a personal working dialogue. They can be shared with others, thus exposing the representational and reasoning processes of spatial thinking to public scrutiny. The representations are simultaneously ways of expressing personal understanding and rhetorical acts of communication and persuasion that can establish a public consensus.

2.3 THE USE OF SPACE AS A FRAMEWORK FOR UNDERSTANDING

2.3.1 Spaces for Interpreting Data

Crucial to the power of spatial thinking is our ability to use space as a framework for understanding. The process of interpretation begins with data:

> Data consists of numbers, text, or symbols which are in some sense neutral and almost context-free. Raw geographic facts, such as the temperature at a specific time and location, are examples of data. When data are transmitted, they are treated as a stream of bits; and the internal meaning of the data is irrelevant to the transfer process.
>
> Information is differentiated from data by implying some degree of selection, organization, and preparation for a particular purpose—information is data serving some purpose, or data that have been given some interpretation. (Longley et al., 2001, p. 6)

There are three spatial contexts within which we can make the data-to-information transition: those of life spaces, physical spaces, and intellectual spaces. In each case, space provides the essential interpretive context that gives meaning to the data.

FIGURE 2.2 Underneath a typical urban street corner. SOURCE: Illustration from Underground by David Macaulay. Copyright 1976 by David Macaulay. Used by permission of Houghton Mifflin Company. All rights reserved.

2.3.2 The Three Contexts for Spatial Thinking

The first context is that of the everyday or physical geographic world of four-dimensional space-time. Variously called spatial perception, environmental cognition, cognitive mapping, and so forth, in this context spatial thinking is a means of coming to grips with the static and dynamic spatial relations between and among self and other objects in the physical environment. The domain of concern is locations defined on the surface and near-surface of Earth, at resolutions between millimeters and hundreds of kilometers.

This is cognition *in* space and involves thinking about the world in which we live. It is exemplified by wayfinding and navigation, actions that we perform in space. It extends to other everyday activities: assembling a child's toy from a set of parts using printed instructions; packing the trunk of a car to maximize carrying capacity; and building a dog kennel using tools, a pile of lumber, and a general model of what dog kennels typically look like. We might call this context *the geography of our life spaces* (see Chapter 3.2).

The second context is built on the four-dimensional world of space-time, but in this case the focus is on a scientific understanding of the nature, structure, and function of phenomena that range from the microscopic to the astronomical scales. It is the world of the structure of the atom, the structure of Earth, and the structure of the universe (as expressed, for example, in Figure 2.3, see also http://www.falstad.com/scale and Chapter 3.5). This is cognition *about* space and involves thinking about the ways in which the "world" works. We might call this the *geography of our physical spaces*.

The third context is in relationship to concepts and objects—the focus of our thoughts—that are not in and of themselves necessarily spatial but can be assigned locations via space-time coordinates and therefore can be *spatialized*. The key premise is the conversion of some data relationship between objects—for example, similarity or dissimilarity, order or sequence, time of appearance—into locations and therefore arrangements of the objects in a space. The domain of concern and therefore the nature of the space is defined by the particular problem. It could be the space of compact versus midsized cars that might be purchased, the familial relations between European languages, or the newspaper article space representing the thematic content of two issues of the *New York Times* (Skupin and Buttenfeld, 1996, 1997).

This is cognition *with* space and involves thinking with or through the medium of space in the abstract. It is exemplified by the conversion of linguistic statements into spatially ordered sequences to answer questions, and therefore the process depends on representations that we develop of concepts in space. Thus, we can take two linguistic propositions, Mary is nicer than Jane and Jane is nicer than Sally; interrelate them by converting them into an ordered left-to-right or top-to-bottom sequence image or diagram of Mary, Jane, and Sally; and then, by using visual inspection, answer the transitive question: Who is nicer, Mary or Sally? We might call this context the *geography of our intellectual spaces*.

A classic example of the geography of an intellectual space is a concept map. A concept map treats concepts within a domain of discourse as features to be mapped, and it defines their position and ordering in space using similarity measures. The similarity can be in terms of function, genesis, structure, or appearance. The underlying data are not inherently spatial in the geographic sense, lacking positional coordinates, but geographic space and representations provide a useful canvas—a familiar two-dimensional (2-D) space on which ideas can be represented—and a metaphor for similarity—in that near things are more alike than distant things. This approach has taken on new significance in the form of tools for visually exploring complex data sets, where software converts data into spatial forms, calculates distance metrics, displays the outcomes graphically, and supports the exploration of data sets using visualization methods. Figure 2.4 shows a concept map of the utility of data sources for constructing a map of gravitational anomalies that can be used to understand the deep geological structure of Earth.

Figure 2.5 uses another geographic metaphor, the idea of a landscape, where surface morphology, as well as planar distance, contribute to the perception of similarity between places. Familiarity with interpreting landscape structures such as mountains and valleys is leveraged to provide insight into a more complex, but hidden, high-dimensional structure. Figure 2.5 shows an information landscape produced from year 2000 Census demographics. States with a similar demographic profile appear clustered together. Height is used to show the absolute difference between two states, so that the presence of "hills" between states indicates that they are in fact quite different.

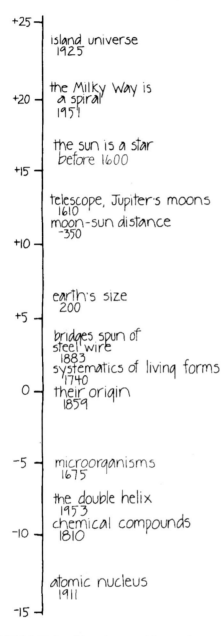

This list is a selection of the dates and authors of discoveries, inventions, early developments, and first persuasive formulations of concepts that have built the present understanding of the world. The list is not ordered by date, but roughly by the physical scale to which each finding is related. It shows when we came to understand each order of magnitude.

We know that a simple listing is somewhat misleading; the history of these ideas and experiences is too complicated to describe fully in so summary a form. Even the dates are a little uncertain; sometimes they refer to discovery, sometimes to publication. Most of these discoveries have had their forerunners and their rivals. We have tried to point out the influential beginnings. Some famous names are included, partly to place the great works in time. The list favors events with strong effect on the visual model and on the underlying evidence.

FIGURE 2.3 Units of length arrayed in a scalar progression from the micro to the macro. SOURCE: Morrison et al., 1982, p. 122.

2.3.3 Spatialization

These contexts for thinking spatially—life spaces, physical spaces, and intellectual spaces—are *not* independent of one another. The ability to spatialize is built on the understanding of space that comes initially from our interactions with the everyday world of four-dimensional space-time. The processes of spatial thinking (e.g., perspective change, scale change, transformation, rotation,

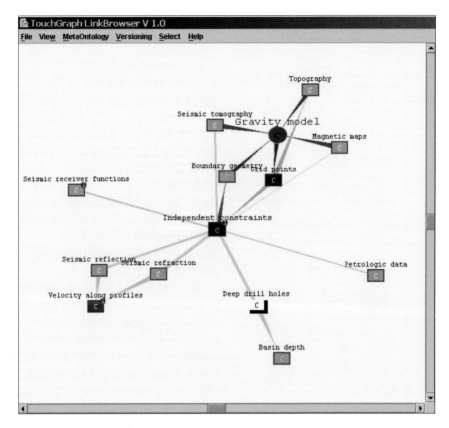

FIGURE 2.4 A concept map depicting how various information sources are used to synthesize a geophysical gravity model (represented by the red, circular node). The concepts are spatialized around this node according to their importance, so closer concepts represent the more useful data sources. SOURCE: Concept graph courtesy of Dr. Randy Keller, University of Texas, software developed by the GeoVISTA Center, Penn State. Reproduced by permission from Dr. Randy Keller.

pattern searching) are identical in the life and physical space contexts. Many forms of representation are derived from our interactions with the everyday world (e.g., images, graphs, maps). These representations support visualization whereby we convert information into a spatial form that can be perused by sight.

While the initial and intuitive roots of spatial thinking are grounded, literally, in the geographies of our life and physical spaces, a major part of its scientific and therefore educational importance lies in the process of spatialization that creates intellectual spaces. With the advent of computers and scientific instrumentation, we have gone from a problem-rich, data-poor world to one that is both data-rich and problem-rich, but is currently lacking the capacity to bring data to bear on solving problems. The solution to problems will depend on the capacity to process, analyze, and represent the vast quantities of data that we can gather and store. Some of these data are already geospatial in nature, as in the case of pixel or raster data derived from remote-sensing platforms. Much of the remainder of the data, although nonspatial in its original manifestation, can be spatialized. By embedding and representing these data in spaces, we can bring powerful spatial reasoning procedures to bear and therefore solve problems (see Box 2.1).

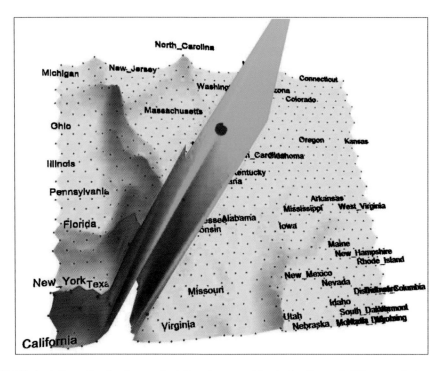

FIGURE 2.5 An information landscape depicting demographic similarities and differences between the 50 states. The high peak at the front represents California, which is very different from all other states. Image produced using a self-organizing map (neural network) and data from the 2000 Census.

2.4 THE THREE FUNCTIONS OF SPATIAL THINKING

Spatial thinking serves three purposes. It has (1) a descriptive function, capturing, preserving, and conveying the appearances of and relations among objects; (2) an analytic function, enabling an understanding of the structure of objects; and (3) an inferential function, generating answers to questions about the evolution and function of objects.

The power of spatial thinking resides in its capacity to provide an understanding of structure and of function. By an understanding of *structure* is meant a description of how something is organized—what part is where in relation to other parts. We can capture the arrangement of objects in space and speak about order, relation, and pattern. By *function* is meant an understanding of how and why something works. It can express how something changes with time (kinematics) and allow us to explain the reasons for the changing arrangements of time-varying spatial patterns (dynamics). Therefore, spatial thinking is not static. It is a dynamic process that allows us to describe, explain, and predict the structure and functions of objects and their relationships in real and imagined spatial worlds. It allows us to generate hypotheses, to make predictions, and to test their consequences.

The archetypal case of a spatial representation is a cartographic map, and we can see the three functions of spatial thinking at work in map reading and interpretation. The most commonly available map form, a road map, provides a two-dimensional picture of part of the world, depicting places and the roads that connect them. Spatial thinking is the analytical and inferential process that allows us to select a route connecting two places subject to criteria such that the route is easy to follow (e.g., contains a minimum number of decision points [intersections, turns, etc.]) and that it

BOX 2.1
Browsing in Library Space

At present, the capacity to store digital information far exceeds the capacity to retrieve desired information. There is a premium on methods for knowledge discovery in databases, using exploratory techniques and data mining. Spatialization and visualization are central to information retrieval processes. Spatialization provides structures for organizing information, and visualization displays the results of searches.

Fabrikant (2000, p. 69) provides a classic statement of the power of spatial thinking: "Spatialization, which combines powerful visualization techniques with spatial metaphors, has a great potential to overcome current impediments in information access and retrieval. Spatialization is utilised to create lower-dimensional digital representations of higher-dimensional data sets, whose characteristics are often quite complex. These digital data sets may not be spatial in nature. Common spatial concepts such as distance, direction, scale, and arrangement which are part of the human's experience in everyday life are applied to construct abstract information spaces."

She applies these ideas to the information about places stored in the Alexandria Digital Library (ADL) collection (http://www.alexandria.ucsb.edu). Fabrikant (2000, p. 69) begins with a model of the visual information-gathering process, based on what she describes as ". . . the visual-information-seeking mantra. The mantra includes three parts: 'Overview first, zoom and filter, then details-on-demand.'"

Figure 2.6 is an abstract model of the information-gathering process that is implemented into an experimental query interface allowing a user to visually browse through the ADL data-type catalog.

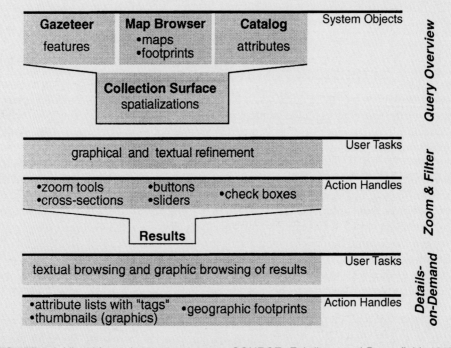

FIGURE 2.6 Visual browsing query process. SOURCE: Fabrikant and Buttenfield, 1997, p. 688. Reproduced by permission from Blackwell Publishing.

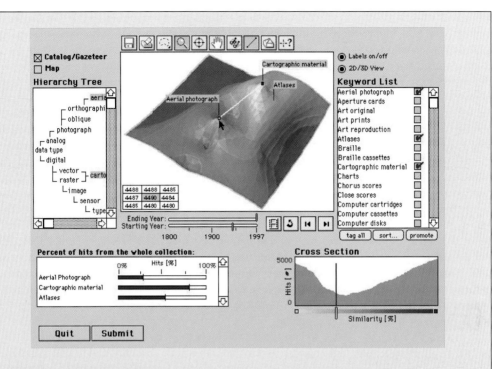

FIGURE 2.7 Spatialized query user interface. SOURCE: Modified from Fabrikant and Buttenfield, 1997, p. 689. Reproduced by permission from Blackwell Publishing.

"The design of this direct manipulation interface is based on three spatial concepts, including distance (similarity), scale (level of detail), and arrangement (dispersion and concentration)" (Fabrikant, 2000, p. 72). The interface applies the visual-information-seeking mantra to a landscape of keywords from the catalog entries (Figure 2.7).

The landscape is based on the similarities between lists of key words, with proximity reflecting high degrees of similarity. As Fabrikant (2000, p. 74) notes:

This landscape affords a user to:

- look at the surface and get a sense of the structure of the library space (overview first),
- navigate in this landscape to discover items of interest,
- selectively perceive the landscape by changing the level of detail of the document space (zoom and filter),
- select individual documents or groups of documents, and
- discover relations between documents (details-on-demand).

The interface contains other spatial thinking approaches: level of detail is available through a zoom function; there is a "looking glass" tool that allows detailed inspection of the surface of the landscape; and the cross-section window shows the magnitude of related documents to be found under the white line of the landscape.

The physical act of browsing on library shelves has been replaced by spatial search through a document keyword landscape, a model that exemplifies both spatialization as a way of structuring information and spatial thinking as a way of developing an understanding of a nonspatial domain, library items.

minimizes travel time (e.g., trades off travel time for distance by maximizing the distance traveled on limited-access, higher-speed highways). Spatial thinking allows us to follow the selected route, to anticipate junctions and turns, and to make a detour, working from memory or from the map itself, if traffic and road conditions necessitate it. The travel time calculation can account for levels of congestion according to time of day, day of week, and even weather conditions. Spatial thinking is also powerfully evocative. By interpreting the shaded relief symbols on the map, we can visualize the texture of the topography over which we are passing. By interpreting symbols for urban areas and forests, we can conjure up images of typical built-up or natural landscapes through which we might pass. The place names may remind us of other places that we have known and visited.

However, it is crucial to recognize that spatial thinking is *not* limited to graphic representations of the visual world. We access the world through multiple senses, and each sensory modality can provide a basis for spatial thinking. We can locate a crying child or an approaching car by estimating its position from the ways that sound arrives differentially at each ear. Smells can characterize places. A dressmaker can use touch to match the nap of fabric pieces by running a hand up and down the fabric. Neither spaces nor representations are necessarily sense specific. In scientific visualization, for example, spatial information can be presented visually and auditorally at the same time. Virtual reality systems can mix visual, auditory, and kinesthetic modalities in the presentation of information. For visually impaired people, tactile, kinesthetic, and auditory systems support and enable spatial thinking (see Box 2.2). Although vision dominates the process and language of spatial thinking for most people, spatial thinking is not restricted to the visual modality: it is multimodal. Whatever the sense modality of the representation, its contents can be scanned (to gain an overview), disaggregated into parts, reassembled into wholes, transformed in scale, analyzed in terms of patterns, and interpreted in terms of processes. Some operations may be easier, faster, and more precise in one particular modality as a function of channel capacity and "bandwidth." Nevertheless, part of the power of spatial thinking lies in the access to multiple sensory modalities, with the opportunities for backup, redundancy, and parallel processing.

2.5 SPACE AS THE BASIS FOR SPATIAL THINKING

The basis for spatial thinking is the structure of space and the operations that we can perform on and in that structure. We can think about spatial structure and spatial operations from a number of perspectives, each of which is built from a root metaphor. For example, geography and cartography give us the map as a way of describing, representing, and understanding spatial relations. Mathematics gives us the analytic power of geometry and topology. Each root metaphor can be expressed in a form that is inherently spatial. For example, the concepts of maps and mappings exist in cartography and mathematics, and they can lead to a remarkable range of representational forms: cartographic maps, tree diagrams, graphs of phase spaces, cross tabulations, flow charts, networks, nonplanar graphs, etc.

To illustrate the basis for spatial thinking, we use a combination of the map, geometry, topology, and graphics metaphors. The idea of spatial structure can be understood in terms of sets of primitives and the concepts that can be derived from them. The idea of spatial operations can be understood in terms of the transformations that are possible within the space and the interpretations that can be generated from the spatial structures.

Spatial thinking can be decomposed into competencies that allow us to understand four ideas: (1) we can start with a set of primitives, (2) to which we can add some languages of space, (3) from which we can derive spatial concepts, and (4) on the basis of which we can perform operations.

1. The set of *primitives* is a way of capturing our encounters with a world full of objects (occurrences of phenomena): objects are the things that we are trying to understand (Golledge,

1995, 2002). For each domain of scientific knowledge, there are different sets of objects: in biology they might include genes, cells, proteins, biota, and so forth, and in sociology they might include neighborhoods, stereotypes, organizations, etc. In any domain, we can specify at least four fundamental properties of objects that allow us to reason and think about features of objects such as their (a) identity or name, (b) location in space, (c) magnitude, and (d) temporal specificity and duration. These properties allow for the identification of an object.

In the case of geographic location, for example, identification requires a coordinate system that can be globally applied and understood, as in the latitude-longitude system, or can be locally contingent, as in terms of street names and numbers. Georeferencing ensures that each object has an unambiguous location specification, and thus the entire set of objects can be located in a space (e.g., the set of georeferenced place names in an atlas gazetteer, the set of nine-digit zip codes for addresses in the United States).

2. The *languages of space* allow us to capture the fundamental properties of objects. One language is based on dimensionality and uses a geometric (and graphic) dimensional series: by limiting ourselves to objects in three-space for the moment, we can think about objects as instances of a point, a line, an area, or a volume. As is clear from looking at a large- and a small-scale map of an area of Earth's surface, a point on a large-scale map can become an area on a small-scale map. (To geographers, a large-scale map encompasses a small area of Earth's surface and vice versa. This is an instance of the tuning of spatial thinking by means of a disciplinary convention that is perhaps counter-intuitive.) The language is a flexible way of capturing the spatial properties of objects. However, we must be careful in using this language across knowledge domains: a point in geometry is a dimensionless location, whereas a point on a map is an area, perhaps very small, on the surface of Earth.

A second language is based on scale and uses scalar relations between objects to arrive at a sense of context (Montello, 1993). Context can be established by means of the terminal values that encompass the scale sequence, the lower bound of which often acts as a datum. The choice of terminal values can reflect extremes in our understanding of the phenomena studied. Thus, the stunning realization of the span of contemporary knowledge in *Powers of Ten* (Morrison et al., 1982) offers a visual model of the world that ranges from 10^{25} to 10^{-16}, encompassing 42 powers of ten arranged around the datum of 1 meter, roughly the world at arm's length (see Figure 2.3). Thus:

> The pages offer a reference frame, a marker for exploration of experience in the domain of astronomy, or of geography, or of biology, or of chemistry. Any physical object can be sought out in its proper place along the journey, and so given an appropriate context. (Morrison et al., 1982, p. 190)

The choice of bounds reflects a convention about the phenomenal range of the particular domain of knowledge (see also Packard, 1994). We can consider other properties related to scale: the limit of resolution, the units of measurement and the calibration of a scale, the conversion between different scales, and the standard benchmarks against which objects are compared. Other languages of space deal with frames of reference and directions.

3. The third step allows us to derive a series of *spatial concepts* from the (spatial or temporal) location properties of sets of objects. In two-space representations, we can specify distance, angle, and direction (relative to a given frame of reference), sequence and order, connection and linkage. We can understand the structural properties of sets of objects in terms of boundaries, density, dispersion, shape, pattern, and region. In three-space, we can also consider the properties of slope or gradient, peaks, and valleys.

4. The fourth—and crucial—step captures the *operations* that allow us to manipulate and transform the space that we have created and to interpret the relations among objects in the set. We could, for example, translate or rotate sets of objects within the space or change the spatial scale at

BOX 2.2
A Personal Guidance System

The University of California Santa Barbara Personal Guidance System (PGS) is a support system for travelers developed from an innovative 1985 conceptualization by Loomis (Loomis, 1985). A group under Loomis, Klatzky, and Golledge, graduate students, and technicians have cooperated in undertaking basic research, technical development, and laboratory and field experimentation to build a series of testbed PGSs.

The goal of this research is to determine how to develop a means of spatial information processing about real-world environments *without* the use of vision, the spatial sense par excellence. To achieve this goal requires convincing evidence that human wayfinding in a complex real-world context can be undertaken systematically and successfully without the use of sight. This has required

1.   demonstrating that people without vision (i.e., blindfolded but otherwise sighted people and those who are vision impaired or blind) can think spatially, learn routes and environmental layouts, and spatially update positions with respect to landmarks or a home base;

2.   developing wayfinding strategies that allow independent wayfinding and travel activities; and

3.   learning to build and adapt state-of-the-art technology that assists in environmental learning and wayfinding.

To achieve these goals, Loomis conceptualized three interconnected modules (Figure 2.8). The first module—the localization and tracking component—focused on using the U.S. Navstar global positioning system (GPS) of 24 geosynchronous satellites to fix the current spatial position in real time. The GPS used satellite triangulation to determine a traveler's starting position and to track movement by recording a location fix about every second. The GPS unit consisted of a receiver with liquid crystal display (LCD) to display latitude-longitude coordinates (and height above sea level if needed); the locating signals were received via an antenna, and the system was battery operated and portable. Because latitude and longitude coordinates are not well understood by most people, the coordinate information is converted to a local coordinate system.

The second module consists of a laptop computer with GIS software that includes a digitized spatial database, a routine for locating the GPS coordinate on the local base map, and a set of

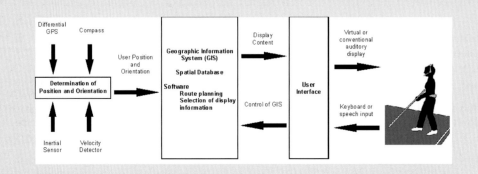

FIGURE 2.8 Three modules of the Personal Guidance System. SOURCE: Loomis, 1985.

FIGURE 2.9 Representations can be brought into direct contact with the real world using wearable computers.

functionalities that perform spatial manipulations on digitized data sets. In particular, the GIS (1) calculated shortest paths through the local network between the traveler's current location and a given destination, (2) identified local environmental features that fell within a given radius of the traveler (called buffering), (3) defined a corridor of specific width along the chosen path to allow for local veering without departing too far from the line of travel, and (4) defined waypoints, places en route where a spatial choice must be made (e.g., turn left, turn right, go straight ahead).

The third module is a unique creation by Loomis—an interface consisting of a virtual auditory display. As the traveler moves from choice point to choice point along a route, the GPS and GIS combine to provide simultaneous tracking of the traveler's position along the path in the spatial database (digitized maps). A buffer centered on the traveler moves simultaneously. Any database feature (e.g., buildings, bus stops, roads) that falls within the range of the buffer identifies itself (by speech) to the traveler. Although the identification is heard through stereophonic headphones, the Loomis virtual system makes it seem *as if* the spoken label emanates from the real-world location of the object (i.e., sound appears to be projected from outside the traveler's head, emanating from a specific location so that the traveler can accurately point to the direction and estimate the distance to a real-world feature). This allows blind travelers to develop a "mental map" of the area through which they are traveling, thus providing them with a system that gives information about their local setting similar to what would be obtained by visual processing. With repeated experience of a route and with changes in the buffer size, the traveler can build up an increasingly detailed mental map of the environment (Figure 2.9).

Ongoing research is exploring the basis for wayfinding instruction. Choices range from spatial language instructions (e.g., go left, go right, go straight ahead), orienting and directional styles (e.g., using clock face directions such as "2 o'clock, 150 yards"), angular advice (e.g., "veer 50 degrees"), or geographic advice (e.g., "turn northeast"). The question is which type of instruction is clearest and most easily interpreted by the traveler.

which we are operating (by zooming in or out) or change the distance metric (e.g., using a Manhattan or city-block metric versus a Euclidean or as-the-crow-flies metric) or change the dimensionality of the space (collapsing from three to two dimensions).

Through processes of simplification, generalization, and classification, we can identify patterns in distributions of objects (see Chapter 3.8). We could describe patterns as random versus systematic, recognizing that these descriptions suggest something about the processes that may have given rise to the patterns, thus linking space and time. Systematic patterns can be clustered or uniform; uniform patterns in two-space can be built on either a rectangular or a triangular lattice. Shapes and patterns can display symmetry or be asymmetrical. We can look for outliers to patterns, breaks or discontinuities, and distortions in portions of the pattern.

We could identify higher-order structures in the spatial structure such as systems, networks, or hierarchies based on concepts of sequence, linkage, dominance, and subordination. We can overlay sets of objects in the same space, looking for associations and correlations, or disaggregate complex spatial patterns into separate layers. We look for correlations (positive or negative) between layers. We can identify—and try to interpret—outliers or exceptions that do not conform to a pattern. We can interpolate between or extrapolate from objects. We can bring to bear interpretive axioms: for example, nearby objects are likely to be similar, but closer objects are likely to be more similar. From this we can consider nearest neighbors, distance decay effects, spatial autocorrelation, and so forth. (All of these operations can be performed on a GIS working with geospatial data; see Chapters 7 and 8.)

At this point, the basis for the power of spatial thinking is clear: it lies in the range of operations that we can bring to bear on the description and explanation of spatial structures and the range of representations that we can use to capture those spatial structures. We can appreciate that power in another way, as well. This discussion of three sets of ideas—the language of space, spatial concepts, and operations—is based on only one member of the set of four primitives—spatial location. Each of the other three primitives—identity, magnitude, and temporal specificity and duration—can be approached spatially. Thus, identity gives rise to taxonomies and a range of spatial representations can be used to express the structure of classifications (trees, Venn diagrams, etc.). We can capture branching relations and ordination (super- and subordinates) and think about families, hierarchies, etc. The property of time gives rise to ideas such as growth, change, and development, all of which can be spatialized and represented. Magnitude can be considered an ordered series and therefore easily spatialized.

2.6 THE PROCESS OF SPATIAL THINKING

Spatial thinking is not unitary in character and operation (as demonstrated in Section 2.2.2). It can appear in many flavors and varieties—some appropriate for one task, some for another. For example, mental rotation is involved in describing the world as it appears from another's point of view, while distinguishing figure from ground is involved in finding a face in a crowd. Individuals may excel at some aspects of spatial thinking and not at others. Facility in using the components increases with experience, most obviously expressed in expertise in a knowledge domain, such as finding tumors in X-rays, inferring the presence of oil-bearing strata in a geological cross section, or imagining three-dimensional shapes from two-dimensional architectural drawings (see Chapter 3).

What follows is a framework for organizing the components of spatial thinking (Tversky, 2005). Any complex spatial reasoning task, such as comprehending a weather map or planning a route, will use several components in concert. To characterize the nature and varieties of spatial thinking, we have to make a distinction about thinking in general.

In analyzing any kind of thought, it is useful to distinguish representations from transformations—that is, data from manipulations performed on data or information from operations applied to the information. The distinction is not hard and fast; it is easy to argue that representations and transformations can be decomposed into finer levels of representations and transformations (Rumelhart, 1980). Spatial thinking rests on the interplay between mental representations that capture spatial features of the world and the transformations that can be applied to those representations. The transformations are similar to the perceptual transformations that are applied to the visuospatial world (Podgorny and Shepard, 1978). However, this statement, too, must be qualified because people can use spatialization to think about abstract concepts that are metaphorically spatial, a powerful feature of spatial thinking. Such uses are reflected in language; we say that someone is on top of the world or has fallen into a depression or become closer.

The committee proposes an organized catalog of elements of spatial thinking, beginning simply with the properties of representations, first static and then dynamic. It continues by describing the properties of transformations that can be performed on either external stimuli or mental representations. Then the committee turns to issues such as the process of complex spatial reasoning, the role of distortions in spatial thinking, using spatial thinking in abstract domains, and spatial thinking using external diagrammatic representations as opposed to internal mental representations. Finally, links between levels of expertise and the process of spatial thinking are discussed.

Representations: The Properties of Entities Representations, whether in the mind or external, map elements and their relations in the world to elements and their relations in the represented world. Thus, representations consist of elements and the spatial or conceptual relations among the elements with respect to a reference frame. An important component of spatial thinking, then, is encoding of the attributes of the spatial world. What follows is a partial list of the kinds of attributes that can be encoded and the processes that encode them. Saying that these attributes can be encoded does not say that they are encoded faithfully; indeed, there are systematic distortions in at least some of the encoding operations, distortions that appear to function to ease information-processing demands. For example, the location of an entity is encoded with respect to the locations of other entities or to a reference frame, and normalized to the reference frame so that entities are remembered as more aligned with the reference frame. Which attributes of entities are encoded will depend on the task and on the experience of the perceiver. Recognizing patterns, for example, may entail evaluating the shapes and sizes of the parts of the pattern.

Spatial thinking can be said to begin with distinguishing and encoding spatial features of the world (Hochberg, 1978). First, figures must be distinguished; then their features and their relations to each other and to their context can be encoded into mental representations. A partial list of encoding operations that establish mental representations follows; it is suggestive of the sorts of perceptual features that people encode, and it is ordered in terms of the importance of the process in terms of spatial thinking. Encoding processes are not atomistic in themselves; they result from prior information processing and, in turn, serve as components for more complex spatial judgments and inferences. Encoding processes include

- distinguishing figures from ground;
- recognizing patterns, both outline shapes and internal configurations;
- evaluating size;
- discerning texture;
- recognizing color; and
- determining other attributes.

For example, the process of *distinguishing figures from ground* occurs early in information processing, so early that we are rarely aware of it. However, on dark, foggy nights, it is sometimes difficult to discern what is a figure—an object, vehicle, or building—and what is shadow or fog. Novices have that experience when looking at X-rays: what is bone, what is tissue, what is tumor?

Pattern recognition is of special significance in everyday life and in specialized knowledge domains. In everyday life, it underlies recognition of faces and places. For recognizing that something is a face, the outside contour is important; for recognizing that a face is that of a particular individual, the inside configuration is critical (Farah et al., 1998). In specialized knowledge domains, pattern recognition underlies recognition of a multitude of spatial categories from flight paths on radar screens and interactions in graphs to fault lines in aerial photographs. For shapes, it underlies object and letter recognition in everyday life, as well as recognition of rare subspecies in biology, protein molecules in chemistry, rock types in geology, and symbols in mathematics. Learning to correctly distinguish one pattern from another can take considerable experience and often depends on first discerning figure from ground. Expertise in many domains requires recognition of specific patterns, but the principles are the same as those for recognizing the objects and patterns in the world around us. For everyday and expert situations, recognizing patterns entails discerning relevant features and their appropriate spatial relations.

In everyday life, *evaluating size* is essential for navigation, packing, and rearranging furniture. In scientific thinking, size evaluation is used in thinking about structures in geology, biology, and many aspects of engineering. Size evaluations are subject to many perceptual illusions, so learning to overcome them is important.

Texture is one important clue to depth and distance, so *evaluating texture* is important in navigating the world (Gibson, 1979). It is also a clue to object recognition: the furriness of a cat, the sleekness of an automobile, and the coarseness of freshly sawed wood. Texture is also a clue to how something should be handled and interpreted. In science, texture can distinguish one kind of rock from another (see Chapter 3.6), one kind of tissue from another, or one kind of vegetation from another in a remotely sensed image.

Color evaluation is a clue to object recognition. Small round things that are orange are more likely to be apricots than plums. Similarly, in science, color distinguishes one chemical, rock, or tissue from another.

Representations: The Relations Between Static Entities Often spatial judgments, such as size, shape, distance, or direction comparisons, are not evaluations of properties of entities but rather evaluations that depend on relating an entity to a reference frame (e.g., determining whether something is upright), or relating one entity to another (e.g., deciding whether one glass is closer than another or filled higher than another). Important spatial evaluations and comparisons that depend on relating an entity to a reference frame or comparing two entities are

- determining orientation,
- determining location,
- assessing distance,
- comparing size,
- comparing color,
- comparing shape,
- comparing texture,
- comparing location,
- comparing direction, and
- comparing other attributes.

Thus, in the case of *determining orientation*, we can ask: Is the picture on the wall upright or tilted? Evaluating orientation requires comparing the intrinsic frame of reference of an object—in this case, the picture—to the extrinsic frame of reference—in this case, the room. Determining orientation is often critical to identifying what something is, for example, distinguishing a letter *M* from a *W,* a *b* from a *d,* or a diamond from a square. Similarly in science and engineering, ascertaining orientation is an essential spatial judgment: in chemistry, for identifying molecules and predicting their behavior; in geology, for identifying rock strata and inferring the conditions that produced them; in building design, for identifying sources of light and predicting their seasonal and daily changes.

Representations: The Relations Between Dynamic Entities The world is not static, and the mind finds ways to encode, interpret, and represent moving objects. Evaluating characteristics of a dynamic entity is also done with respect to other entities or to a frame of reference. Dynamic features that can be evaluated include the following:

- direction of movement,
- manner of motion,
- speed or acceleration, and
- intersection or collision.

Evaluating *direction of movement* can be critical for survival: Is an object headed toward me? Is that beast turning around? Note that encoding change in size can underlie perception of direction of movement; thus, if something is growing larger, it is likely to be coming closer. The direction in which something animate is going is a clue to the organism's intent: Is the motion toward a restaurant or a movie theater? Evaluating direction of movement underlies scientific reasoning as well, for example, the directions of tectonic plates or weather fronts.

Evaluating *manner of motion* is important for understanding the world; manner of motion distinguishes one animal from another—indeed, one individual human being from another. Running, swaggering, stumbling are all clues to the state of another person. Differences in manner of motion distinguish different physical entities, the weight and shape of rocks for example. Manner of motion can diagnose an unhealthy heart or, on a more abstract level, an irregular electroencephalogram (EEG).

Each of these judgments about relations among dynamic entities plays a role in everyday interactions in the world, in walking along crowded streets and in driving on the highway; in avoiding flying objects or trying to catch them in baseball (McBeath et al., 1995) or return them in tennis. These judgments underlie scientific inferences as well, in understanding the operations of a machine, anticipating weather conditions, or predicting traffic flows and bottlenecks.

Transformations of Representations of Entities These encoding operations establish mental representations of the spatial world. A powerful feature of spatial thinking is transforming, manipulating, and operating on representations. By mentally extrapolating a path of movement, we can predict time and place of arrival. By mentally rotating an object, we can determine whether it will fit into a room, a dishwasher, or a suitcase. By mentally extending a line in a graph, we can detect a trend.

According to the dominant theory of mental imagery, the mental operations that we perform on actual and mental representations are internalizations of the physical changes that we perceive as we interact in the world (Finke and Shepard, 1986). In the world, things move in different manners and directions; they change shape, color, and texture in regular and predictable ways. For this reason, many mental transformations parallel the changes encoded in forming mental representations of changing entities. Anticipating these changes is critical to interacting with the world. Anticipating changes entails mentally enacting those changes. The extraordinary flexibility of the human mind then allows these mental spatial operations to be applied to imagined stimuli as well as to perceived ones, providing the means not only to anticipate states and processes in the world, but also to create new states and processes in the imagination. That said, not all the changes we observe in the world are faithfully reflected in mental transformations.

Manipulations of spatial representations are the bases of inference, prediction, and creativity. We have already mentioned the cases of catching fly balls and predicting trends from graphs. Transforming spatial representations is elementary to scientific reasoning, from comprehending new situations to creating and testing new ideas. Surgeons use spatial transformations to envisage a new surgical procedure; geologists use spatial transformations to understand how earthquakes could have produced the rock formations they observe; microbiologists use spatial transformations to test whether vaccines may fit large molecules (Shepard, 1984). Some of the spatial transformations that people can apply include

- changing perspective (reference frame),
- changing orientation (mental rotation),
- transforming shapes,
- changing size,
- moving wholes,
- reconfiguring parts,
- zooming in or out,
- enacting, and
- panning.

Changing perspective entails imagining a new point of view in an environment or taking a new point of view on an object. Whenever we shake hands, we have to mentally change reference frame, though this piece of spatial behavior has become automatized for most adults. However, we become aware of the difficulties of mentally changing reference frame when we give directions to strangers who have lost their way. In scientific spatial thinking, surgeons need to mentally change perspective to plan and perform an operation, and geologists need to mentally change perspective to go from frontal views to cross sections.

Changing perspective is closely related to changing orientation (mental rotation). People can imagine an object changing its position in an environment. For example, people can imagine rotating a picture on a wall to determine if it would look better in another orientation. Mental rotation is useful for geometricians in determining properties of triangles and squares and for chemists in determining whether molecules will fit or bind.

Several transformations are of special significance because skill in performing them correlates with performance on complex spatial reasoning tasks. Notably, mental rotation or changing orientation (Shepard and Cooper, 1982), changing perspective or reference frames (Franklin and Tversky, 1990), and reconfiguring parts or detecting embedded figures (Suwa and Tversky, 2001) seem to be involved in a large number of spatial tasks: mental rotation in catching or manipulating objects, changing perspective in navigating the world, reconfiguring parts in rearranging the spatial world, and detecting embedded figures in recognizing people in crowds. (These skills are also addressed in the discussion of individual differences in Appendix C.)

Enacting is a special case of spatial transformation that combines spatial thinking with motoric thinking (Schwartz, 1999). Just as spatial thinking is based on perceptual processing, motor thinking has action as its foundation. Action is accomplished by the interaction of the space of the body in the space of the world. Enacting underlies the mental practice techniques used by athletes, musicians, orators, and others to rehearse performances. Enactions can be coopted to understand forces as well as the mechanics and sequences of actions. For example, enaction is involved in imagining steering a boat or car or bicycle, and in understanding the forces of wind on all three, and the effects of ocean currents on the boat and gravity on the car or bicycle. There is a famous story about Einstein, well-known for his prodigious powers of spatial thinking, that in developing the theory of relativity, he imagined himself hurtling in space at the speed of light. Enactions can underlie the ordering of spatial transformations when several transformations are applied in sequence to the same representation. Thus, when people have to apply several transformations to the same figure in order to solve geometric analogies, they first move the figure, then change its orientation, then determine its size, and finally add parts to the figure. This order corresponds exactly to the order in which people draw figures; they first decide where to begin drawing, then what direction to draw in, and then how far to draw (Novick and Tversky, 1987). Thus, the order of performing the mental transformations in this complex reasoning task corresponds to the order of executing the analogous external task, suggesting that the enactment of drawing is internalized and applied to other mental tasks.

The Process of Complex Spatial Reasoning Representations and transformations are the components that enter into complex spatial reasoning. Combining components enables complex spatial reasoning, such as solving geometric analogies or developing relativity theory. In actual practice, spatial reasoning often uses several representations, several comparisons, and multiple transformations. For example, planning a route requires determining a location, then a direction of movement to the next location, then reorientation at each successive location. Deciding which route is the most efficient entails constructing, then comparing several possible routes on several spatial attributes: distance, complexity (number of turns), and type of path, city street or highway. Determining whether two independent variables interact requires making successive magnitude estimations, first on each variable, then between variables. Imagining chemical bondings requires moving elements into an array, then rearranging them as a consequence of the bonding. For some spatial inferences, the spatial-temporal information may be suggestive but not sufficient, for example, for determining force and mass.

Role of Distortions in Spatial Thinking The processes that establish representations and execute transformations are schematic. That is, they delete some information and add or emphasize other information. The schematization is systematic and not random, driven by perceptual organizing principles and leading to predictable distortions in memory and judgment. For example, one way in which perception is organized is with respect to the frame of reference the world provides, one vertical and two horizontal axes. We localize objects in the world with respect to those axes, in an approximate fashion. Organization with respect to a reference frame carries over to the north-south-east-west canonical axes of geographic space and to the axes provided by a diagram in graphic space. One result is that when an entity's location is coded relative to the surrounding frame of reference, it is remembered as more aligned with the reference frame than it actually is. Thus, people remember "tilted" entities, such as South America, as more "upright," or aligned north-south, than they actually are (Tversky, 1981). Motion paths are similarly schematized and hence distorted; slightly oblique motion is coded as vertical or horizontal (Pani et al., 1996; Shiffrar and Shepard, 1991).

Role of Abstract Spatial Thinking People use spatial thinking metaphorically in everyday life as well as in science. We say that we feel "close" to one person, that another has "fallen out" of favor, that a third is "on top of the world," and that yet another has "lost his center" (Lakoff and Johnson, 1980). The periodic table, flow diagrams in heat transfer and computer programs, and the "solar system" model of atoms are but some of the spatial representations used to summarize and organize abstract information. They have multiple effects on ways that scientists think about these concepts and teach them to their students. They enable spatial reasoning to be applied to complex causal phenomena. Because people have had a lifetime of experience in reasoning spatially (indeed, survival depends on it), they come to science with a spatial toolbox that can be applied to abstract concepts. Applying these spatial thinking tools is by no means automatic; in fact, one of the great challenges of education is facilitating transfer of tools acquired in one domain to another (see

Chapter 4.4). The key to effective transfer of skills, such as spatial ones, from one domain to another is going from concrete content to the abstractions that cut across domains. (Ways to facilitate transfer are discussed in Chapter 4.5.)

Role of External Spatial Representations in Spatial Thinking Note that many of the previous examples (e.g., the periodic table, flow diagrams, molecular models) are external spatial representations. That is, they are visible on paper or some other physical medium, though they do exist in some form in the mind as well. People have been creating external representations since before recorded history, from maps in the sand to bent trees as trail markers to notches on wood to record heads of cattle. The advantages of externalizing spatial representations are multiple (Tversky, 2001). They provide a semipermanent record that can be examined by a community, unlike mental representations that may be forgotten and are accessible only to an individual. For science and engineering, external representations have the advantage of being visible to other members of a community. They can be referred to by gesture as well as language in explaining, inferring, and discovery. They relieve the burden of limited working memory to maintain a representation, freeing it to perform transformations and operations on an external representation. Thus, one important function of external spatial representations is to augment working memory. Another is to focus attention on critical aspects of the conceptions. Like internal spatial representations, external spatial representations schematize; they omit irrelevant information and highlight the relevant. External representations may also be supplemented with diagrammatic devices that focus attention, such as arrows, guidelines, boxes, brackets, and boldface large type. Many external representations are pictorial. All other things equal, pictures are easier to remember than comparable words, so spatial representations also facilitate long-term memory for the concepts they convey.

Effective External Representations We have already mentioned the key to creating effective external representations: they must convey the essential conceptual information and eliminate the irrelevant information that can clutter and distract. This is harder than it sounds. For example, what information should be included in a tourist map? Which facilities of use to tourists—historic buildings, museums, restaurants, hotels, and so on—should be included, without cluttering the map with so much information that none of it is legible? Similar problems arise in scientific visualizations. Another issue in designing effective visualizations is deciding how to depict elements and mapping spatial relations. Ideally elements should be easy to recognize and decipher, associated in some way with what they represent. Spatial relations among elements, especially distance, should reflect conceptual relations in the abstract domain (Tversky, 2001). Animated diagrams have their appeal, yet they turn out to be no more effective than comparable still diagrams across a broad range of content areas in conveying conceptual information. This is partly because animations are typically complex and fleeting, so learners have trouble knowing what to attend to. Perhaps more important is that animations are continuous but people think about continuous processes as discrete steps. A well-designed sequence of still diagrams can convey the information essential to each step (Tversky et al., 2002).

Role of Expertise in Spatial Thinking As with all cognitive competencies, there are significant differences among people as to how, how quickly, and how well they do something. Spatial thinking is no exception. Within domains of knowledge, there are experts and novices. Differences between experts and novices can be accounted for by training and experience. Across domains of knowledge, there are disciplines within which spatial thinking is emphasized and taught and those within which it plays a hidden and relatively minor role. Across groups, there are also significant variations in how people approach spatial thinking. Across age, for example, children and adults do not think spatially in the same way. Those differences can be accounted for by maturation, education, and experience. All of these issues are addressed in Chapter 4 and Appendix C.

If, for the moment, the effects of domain are ignored, the expert-novice distinction can be used to understand some of the major differences in the ways in which people think spatially. A key goal, especially in science, is to learn to extract functional information from spatial structures and to understand how and why something works. In learning to do this, we can order component tasks of spatial thinking in terms of relative difficulty.

The first and easiest step is *extracting spatial structures*. This process of pattern description involves identifying relations between the components of a spatial representation and understanding them in terms of the parts and wholes that give rise to patterns and coherent wholes. The second step, *performing spatial transformations*, is harder. Translations in space or scale transformations (changes in viewing distance) are easier than rotations or changes of perspective (changes in viewing angle or azimuth). Imagining the motions of different parts in relation to each other—running the object—can be very difficult. The third step, *drawing functional inferences*, is the most difficult and yet the most central to the process of scientific thinking. It requires establishing temporal sequences and cause-and-effect relations.

The difficulty of each of these three steps increases with increasing *dimensionality*: spatial structures in two-space are easier to understand than those in three-space. In scientific applications, difficulty also increases as a *function of data quality and quantity*. Missing data require extrapolation and interpolation. Data error leads to uncertainty and increasing difficulty. Partial and incomplete data require an even more skilled use of extrapolation and interpolation and more complex inference processes.

People use representations, whether in the mind or external, to comprehend and remember a set of concepts as well as to make inferences and discoveries about those concepts. Understanding the spatial relations and structure of a diagrammed system is relatively straightforward for most learners, because a diagram shows the parts in their spatial relations, using diagrammatic space to map real space. Most people can grasp the essential parts and their spatial relations from a diagram, such as a bicycle pump or a heart. What is much harder to understand is the meaning, interpretation, function, and causal chain that the diagram is meant to convey. While a novice can understand the spatial structure of a bicycle pump or heart from a diagram, only those with some expertise can grasp the functional and causal relations among the parts, that is, understand how the pump or the heart works (Heiser and Tversky, 2002).

For most scientific and engineering contexts, diagrams are meant to convey not just the structure of a system but also its behavior or the causal chain of its parts or the function of its operations. These are exactly the aspects of diagrams that students of all ages find difficult. Diagrams show structure, but they do not show function or behavior or causal relations. Language can compensate by stating this information directly. However, diagrams can also be enriched with extrapictorial devices, notably lines, arrows, boxes, and brackets, to convey abstract information. For example, when asked to describe a diagram of a bicycle pump, students describe the structural relations among the parts. When arrows are added to the diagram that denote the sequence of actions of the pump, students describe the causal, functional actions of the pump (Heiser and Tversky, 2002). Even the addition of arrows may not be sufficient to convey the functional information. For understanding bicycle pumps and car brakes, diagrams were sufficient for undergraduates of high mechanical ability but not for those of low ability; for those of low mechanical ability, language compensated (Heiser and Tversky, 2002).

In many educational settings, diagrams are taken for granted. These studies suggest that teaching how to reason from diagrams could reap great benefits. Such teaching would be needed in a number of domains: geography, arithmetic and mathematics, biology, geology, chemistry, physics, and engineering. Diagrams are common in history and the humanities as well. Across the curriculum, what is needed is exercises in interpreting the spatial entities and spatial relations of diagrams, making inferences as well as making discoveries. Constructing diagrams is an integral part of this instruction, especially in groups. Junior high school dyads working together produced diagrams of, for example, plant ecology that were more abstract and contained less irrelevant, pictorial information than those produced by individuals.

2.7 CONCLUSION

Spatial thinking *is* a powerful tool. It is fundamental to problem solving in a variety of contexts: in life spaces, physical spaces, and intellectual spaces. In each case, it can offer increasingly powerful understandings, moving from description through analysis to inference. In each case, it depends upon a level of spatial knowledge, skills in spatial ways of thinking and acting, and the development of spatial capabilities. All of the component skills can, to some significant degree, be learned and this points to the crucial need for education in spatial thinking.

In Chapter 3, the committee shows how spatial thinking plays a fundamental role in everyday life, the workplace, and science. In everyday life, the necessary skills are rarely learned in formal contexts: we learn by informal means and by doing. In the workplace and scientific contexts, there are increasing demands in terms of levels of spatial knowledge, spatial ways of thinking and acting, and spatial capabilities: those demands are often met by formal instruction. Chapter 3 shows how demands have changed over time (in, for example, astronomy), how they are met by learning within a domain of knowledge (in, for example, the geosciences), and how some people become particularly skilled at spatial thinking (in the cases of Marie Tharp and Walter Christaller). People use spatial thinking daily, to find the things they need at home and their ways in the world. Spatial tools that everyone possesses can be articulated and refined to turn learners into powerful scientific thinkers.

3

Spatial Thinking in Everyday Life, at Work, and in Science

3.1 INTRODUCTION

Literacy in the classically linguistic sense means that someone can read, write, and speak in a language. Those abilities can be seen in all aspects of our existence: in spoken and written communications in everyday life, in the workplace, and in science. Spatial literacy follows a similar pattern: people draw upon their spatial knowledge, their repertoire of spatial ways of thinking and acting, and their spatial capabilities to solve problems in all aspects of their lives.

Section 3.2 explores the ways in which spatial thinking underpins activities that range across the fabric of our everyday lives. For the vast majority of these activities, there is no formal instruction in how to use spatial thinking to solve problems. This lack of formal instruction is in direct contrast to the formal learning that enables the use of spatial thinking in the workplace and science. Section 3.3 illustrates how novices and experts in various crafts and professions use spatial thinking skills in their work. Section 3.4 introduces the fundamental link between doing science and thinking spatially, explaining the parallels among the three disciplines—astronomy, geoscience, and geography—that are the basis for four case studies. The case studies illustrate a set of themes: the role of spatial thinking in historical changes in our most fundamental understandings of the physical world (Section 3.5 on spatial thinking in astronomy), the challenges of learning the component operations of spatial thinking during the novice-to-expert transition in a discipline (Section 3.6 on learning to think spatially in the geosciences), and the role of particularly gifted spatial thinkers in shaping understanding in a discipline (Section 3.7 on Marie Tharp in geoscience and Section 3.8 on Walter Christaller in geography).

3.2 SPATIAL THINKING IN EVERYDAY LIFE

In March 2003, Mark Wegner and Deborah Girasek published a study in *Pediatrics* on the readability of printed instructions for car safety seat (CSS) installation. They were motivated by a report that 79 to 94 percent of child safety seats were improperly installed, while 46 percent of accident-related deaths among children aged 1 to 14 resulted from motor vehicle collisions.

Our data indicate that CSS instructions in the United States are currently written at a reading level that is too high. Experts in the arena of health literacy recommend that materials be targeted to the fifth- or sixth-grade reading level. . . . The average readability level of the instruction sets that we tested was 10th grade. Researchers . . . found that approximately two thirds of parents tested in an outpatient clinic could not read at more than a ninth-grade level. . . . Because parents would be expected to be the main target for CSS instruction sets, this lends additional evidence that the instruction sets may not be reaching the people most likely to benefit from the message. (Wegner and Girasek, 2003, p. 590)

On the face of it, the study confirms general beliefs about the failure of American education to produce verbally literate people who can read polysyllabic words; the authors used the SMOG (Simple Measure of Gobbledygook) statistic based on the number of three or more syllable words in text samples. They recommended that "manufacturers of CSS rewrite their instruction sets to a fifth-grade reading level. This could be accomplished by using shorter sentences and simpler words" (Wegner and Girasek, 2003, p. 591).

In the committee's judgment, a second message can be drawn. Wegner and Girasek (2003, p. 590) noted that "[t]his study did not take into account some factors that tend to increase comprehensibility, such as the use of illustrations and empty space . . ." because ". . . [p]ictures and diagrams were not considered, neither were captions that stood apart from the rest of the instruction set and applied only to pictures" (Wegner and Girasek, 2003, p. 589).

That many car safety seats are improperly installed should come as no surprise to any adult American. The problem is not simply one of comprehension as a function of word complexity, sentence length, and therefore, verbal literacy. Comprehension is a function of another form of literacy, one that is equally essential but largely overlooked. Spatial literacy lies at the heart of spatial thinking. It was unfortunate that Wegner and Girasek chose not to include the pictures and diagrams because installation instructions are a complex combination of text and graphics.

For anyone who has attempted to assemble a child's bicycle, a piece of furniture, a stereo system, or a ceiling fan (Figure 3.1), the challenge of language is only part of the problem. Instructions control actions. Words have referents, physical objects, and those referents must be correctly identified, aligned, and brought together. Directions such as up and down, front and back, on top of and behind, and left and right become crucial in establishing relations between parts. Parts must be linked into a working whole. Motions involving clockwise versus counterclockwise turns, through versus over versus under, and push versus pull must be distinguished. The coordination among text, schematic diagram, and required actions is critical to success in the assembly process.

Spatial thinking is so deeply embedded in the activities of daily life and thought that it is difficult to disentangle and appreciate its role. We may not even realize its role, but it is fundamental to many taken-for-granted activities, underpinning their successful performance and sometimes accounting for their spectacular failure. Imagine, therefore, a classic middle-class family with two parents and children of various ages. Imagine a typical day in the life of that family. Imagine solving the problems of everyday life.

A phone call in late August to a daughter on a study-abroad program in Europe requires, among other things, working out the right time to call. This requires an understanding of time zones and the use of daylight saving time. A trip to take a son to college involves packing things into boxes and packing boxes into a car trunk and back seat in the most efficient way such that space use is maximized, nothing gets crushed or broken, and things are easy to remove. Getting to the college town and apartment building involves using a web-based search engine to print a route map, and then following written and map directions. The exercise machine that was disassembled and packed has to be reassembled without, unfortunately, the instructions, which have been lost. The now-assembled bunk bed, desk, and shelves have to be fitted into the room without blocking heating vents, electrical outlets, telephone outlets, and the passage to the window, closet, and door in the

Preliminary Assembly

continued from page 2.

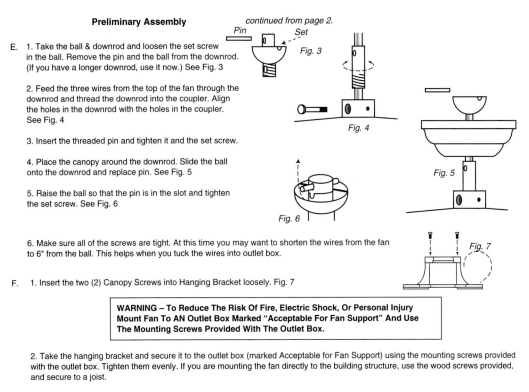

E. 1. Take the ball & downrod and loosen the set screw in the ball. Remove the pin and the ball from the downrod. (If you have a longer downrod, use it now.) See Fig. 3

2. Feed the three wires from the top of the fan through the downrod and thread the downrod into the coupler. Align the holes in the downrod with the holes in the coupler. See Fig. 4

3. Insert the threaded pin and tighten it and the set screw.

4. Place the canopy around the downrod. Slide the ball onto the downrod and replace pin. See Fig. 5

5. Raise the ball so that the pin is in the slot and tighten the set screw. See Fig. 6

6. Make sure all of the screws are tight. At this time you may want to shorten the wires from the fan to 6" from the ball. This helps when you tuck the wires into outlet box.

F. 1. Insert the two (2) Canopy Screws into Hanging Bracket loosely. Fig. 7

> **WARNING – To Reduce The Risk Of Fire, Electric Shock, Or Personal Injury Mount Fan To AN Outlet Box Marked "Acceptable For Fan Support" And Use The Mounting Screws Provided With The Outlet Box.**

2. Take the hanging bracket and secure it to the outlet box (marked Acceptable for Fan Support) using the mounting screws provided with the outlet box. Tighten them evenly. If you are mounting the fan directly to the building structure, use the wood screws provided, and secure to a joist.

3. Make sure all of the wires are accessible and are not being pinched. Also, make sure the bracket doesn't wobble.

To begin with, the site of installation must be clear of any obstructions. Walls, cabinet or cupboard doors, and AC/heating vents (strong air currents will cause fan to wobble) are common obstructions. Also, you will need a securely mounted outlet box that is listed for fan support.

The only tools you will need are: A medium Phillips screwdriver, common sense, and a little caution.

FIGURE 3.1 A set of instructions for installing a ceiling fan. Note the appeal to common sense and caution.

apartment. A trip to a supermarket to stock up on food for the refrigerator requires getting verbal driving directions from a neighbor, remembering and following them, and finding where things are located in a store that is organized in ways subtly different from the one that the family is used to. A written grocery list has to be mapped onto the floor plan of the supermarket in an efficient way. To amuse a younger child on the journey home, someone has to help her to put together pieces of a complex jigsaw puzzle. The journey home is complicated by the need to make a detour around construction that was not marked on the downloaded route map. It is also complicated by a flat tire: replacing it with the spare requires understanding the instructions on the side of the jack, removing the bolts and the wheel, and then tightening the bolts in the correct direction and sequence. Returning home, another son is asked to take over lawn mowing duties and has to find an efficient way to maneuver around flower beds and trees in the garden. The youngest child's shoelace has come undone and there is yet another lesson in how to tie a shoelace properly, a double knot this time. The costume for the middle daughter's school play has to be cut from fabric, fitted, and sewn by tomorrow's dress rehearsal.

Everyday life is impregnated with tasks that, on the surface, are routine and trivial. Viewed as problems requiring solutions, these tasks are far from trivial in nature. All of the tasks involve the concept of space in general and various spaces in particular: global time-space, car trunk space, neighborhood space, supermarket space, room space, machine space, puzzle space, garden space, the space of shoelaces, and the space of dress patterns. Many of the tasks involve graphic representations: the time zone diagram in the telephone directory, the web search engine map, the floor plan of the supermarket, the grocery list, the picture of the completed jigsaw puzzle, and the dress pattern. All tasks involve complex sequences of operations: finding the clock times of the two places and subtracting the right one to work out the time difference; choosing boxes of the right size for the space available, orienting and rotating them, and stacking them; rotating parts, twisting parts, and tightening fastenings; breaking an operation into discrete parts and demonstrating and explaining the operations; making a loop with one lace, putting the other part of the shoe lace over the top of the loop, and so forth. Some of the tasks can be taught formally, such as map reading, whereas others, such as dress making, are no longer taught formally in schools, and still others, such as tying shoelaces, are learned informally as part of everyday life. There is transfer of learning from one task to another; jigsaw puzzles and exercise machine assembly have things in common.

Tasks can be performed in different ways. The web search engine offers three different representations: lists of text instructions, maps with straight-line segments, and conventional road maps. Strategies for solving jigsaw puzzles differ: some people sort straight edge pieces first, then match by shape. Others use color and patterns to make decisions. Some performance differences are significant and lead to faster and more efficient solutions: others, especially shoelace tying styles, are matters of preference (single versus double knots). There are differences based on age and sex in solving problems. Some people approach the trunk-packing task analytically, gauging the dimensions of boxes and thinking about alternative arrangements; others plunge ahead, using trial and error. For many activities, we are not consciously aware of spatial thinking; in other instances, the challenge is explicit and we monitor our own process.

3.3 SPATIAL THINKING AT WORK

Spatial thinking at work begins before work, during the daily challenge of commuting. Many drivers simplify the complex two-dimensional plane between home and work to a line that contains a sequence of turns at landmarks. The rest of the environmental context is not relevant to the task of commuting and therefore is largely ignored during the commute. The path, specifying where to turn and which direction to take, is crucial. As a consequence, people pay more attention to landmarks that mark changes in direction, and they remember those landmarks better than other places along the route (Tom and Denis, 2004).

The cognitive importance of landmarks and turns is reflected in neurophysiology. Using brain imaging technology, researchers have shown connections between cognitive processes and brain functioning (Aguirre et al., 1998; Maguire et al., 1997). There is a greater neurophysiological response to landmarks signaling turns than to landmarks that are simply en route in those areas of the brain underpinning the construction of mental maps (Janzen and van Turennout, 2003). These areas of the brain are larger in people who are expert at navigation, such as London taxi drivers who undergo considerable training before they are allowed to pursue their profession. Neurophysiological findings suggest that extensive spatial experience may lead to physical changes in the brain that may, in turn, further enhance spatial thinking.

Experienced taxi drivers have more extensive and detailed mental maps of the areas they service than do ordinary residents. Nevertheless, taxi drivers' mental maps are simplified in the same ways as those of regular commuters. For example, taxi drivers think about the main arteries of a city as being straighter and more aligned with cardinal directions than they actually are. This illustrates an important characteristic of expertise. Expertise draws on the same mechanisms as normal, everyday cognitive processing; the novice-expert difference is a consequence of the degree and type of practice and experience in a domain.

Getting to work is not the only spatial task shared by different occupations. In order to operate, workers need a mental model of the structure and functioning of the institution: they need to know who to turn to for help on what task. Sometimes information is mentally represented as a spatial network, much like a rudimentary mental map of an environment. In this institutional mental space, links are tasks and nodes are people who perform tasks. Often information is explicitly represented in an organizational chart and depicted as a spatial network that must be "navigated." Managers must decide how to allocate resources or what new projects to undertake. To do so, they consult charts and graphs of performance. Charts and graphs provide spatial representations of data, but do not in themselves provide solutions to problems. Solutions depend on making inferences from charts and graphs, projections of future sales, changes in personnel and equipment, and more.

Beyond generic problem-solving similarities, many jobs require the use of specific spatial skills. Recognition of complex patterns is required in many professions. Think of the time you saw an X-ray image in a doctor's office. You could probably pick out bones but little else. In the clouds that X-rays resemble, highly trained radiologists can discern tumors, blood clots, and faulty valves. Recognizing these patterns takes years of training and is by no means perfect (see Ericsson, 1996, for an overview of the literature on expertise; see the November 2003 issue of the *Educational Researcher* on expertise in the context of education).

Recognition skill does *not* transfer to other domains. Skilled radiologists are no better than novices at recognizing skin diseases that dermatologists are expert in diagnosing or plant diseases that botanists excel at discerning. Expertise in pattern recognition is domain specific. It requires discerning features characteristic of specific sensory categories. Typically, domain expertise in pattern recognition also requires learning the proper configurations of distinctive features. The practice that polishes this skill requires categorizing many examples of related and different phenomena and getting feedback on the categorization process. Simply seeing examples is not sufficient; to become expert, people must learn to differentiate and discriminate one category from another (Nickerson and Adams, 1979). A classroom demonstration illustrates that seeing, however frequent, is insufficient to ensure learning critical features. Students are asked to name what is shown on both sides of a penny or whether their (analog) watch dial has lines or numbers to mark minutes. Few succeed at the penny task, and many are surprisingly poor at the watch task. Although we "look" at pennies and watches frequently, often many times a day, we do not have to distinguish one penny or watch face from another (Nickerson and Adams, 1979). We do, however, need to distinguish a penny from a nickel or dime, and we do so based on color or shape or size without paying attention to the face of the coin. In watches, we only consult the lengths of hands and their angles. When we need to make fine distinctions, such as those required to differentiating types of tumors or diagnosing skin diseases, we must learn the fine details distinguishing among tumors or skin diseases.

Pattern recognition, then, is a spatial skill demanded by many disciplines. People learn to distinguish critical features in their proper, two-dimensional spatial configurations. Other professions, however, require skill in thinking about three-dimensional configurations, a process especially difficult for the human mind. Although the physical world is (at least) three dimensional, the image captured on the retina and represented topographically in visual areas of the cortex is two dimensional. Thus, the three-dimensional world is a mental construct built from numerous cues to depth as well as experience navigating the world. Experience teaches us how to integrate two-dimensional views into three-dimensional representations. Integration of two-dimensional views can be accomplished by means of features, objects, and landmarks common to different views. Integration of two-dimensional views is also accomplished by means of a frame of reference that is shared by the views (Tversky, 2003). Expertise in dealing with three-dimensional representations is, like pattern recognition, also domain specific.

Buildings and devices are three-dimensional structures; so architects and product designers face the challenge of three-dimensional thinking. They cope with the challenge by externalizing thought to the sketch-pad or computer screen, working with a series of two-dimensional slices. This is, of course, what radiologists do; they examine two-dimensional images of the human body. For architecture, there is a canonical set of two-dimensional slices: plan, elevation, and cross section. The slices facilitate design by simplifying a three-dimensional problem to a standard set of two-dimensional ones. Each slice serves different functions in the design process (Arnheim, 1977; O'Gorman, 1998). Plans or overviews capture spatial relations among the rooms of a building or among the buildings, open spaces, and paths of a complex. They are important for understanding the functions of the structure because they show the proximity of rooms or buildings to each other and ways to navigate among them. Elevations show how a building or complex will appear; the outside skin establishes the aesthetic value of the building. Finally, cross sections show how the infrastructure—for example, plumbing, heating and air-conditioning systems—interconnects parts of the structure.

Design in architecture is facilitated by partitioning three-dimensional space into two-dimensional representations. Architects typically begin with sketches of plans or overviews of the site. Early in the process, architects like to keep designs sketchy, literally and figuratively. They do not want to commit too soon to specific shapes or exact spatial relations. Sketches are a test bed for architects (Goldschmidt, 1994; Schon, 1983). Architects begin with an idea and turn it into a sketch. When they inspect the sketch, they often see spatial features and relations that they did not explicitly design, but that were a consequence of other design decisions (Suwa et al., 2001). Unintended spatial features and relations have implications that may or may not be desirable. As a consequence of such discoveries, architects revise ideas. They re-sketch the building and critically reexamine the new sketches. Architects interact with the sketches in a kind of conversation that refines their ideas (Goldschmidt, 1994; Schon, 1983). Experienced architects are more expert at this conversation. They get more new ideas from examining sketches than do novice architects. They see more functional implications than do novices (Suwa and Tversky, 1997). For example, experts see functional information such as changes in traffic flow and lighting throughout the day and year. Novice architects are less likely to make functional inferences from sketches. As is true for pattern recognition, considerable experience is needed to "see" behavior or function in sketches. For pattern recognition, the necessary information is in the depiction; experts learn to pay attention to the right features in the right organization. In the case of architecture, information about traffic flow or lighting is not in the depiction; it must be inferred from the depiction. The inference process is analogous to the expertise required to read written text or music. The sounds and meanings of words and notes must be derived from the depictions, and this process requires training and practice.

As architects' ideas become more refined, sketches become more specific. The three-dimensional task of the architect is, therefore, simplified by the set of two-dimensional layers. It turns out, however, that simplification—division into planes—serves design in another important way because the different planes also correspond to differing sets of design considerations. Plans determine how people will navigate a building; elevations determine how a building will look; cross sections determine how the infrastructure is organized.

Air traffic control is another profession that requires spatial thinking in three dimensions. The process is even more difficult because of the added dimension of time; controllers must operate in three-dimensional space-time. Aircraft are in motion, so controllers must keep track of the changing positions of numerous aircraft at different and changing altitudes, speeds, and directions. As in the case of commuting routes on the ground, the key to success in the air is simplifying the information in functional ways. Architects slice space into two-dimensional planes. Air traffic controllers slice space into two-dimensional layers and time into slices.

Researchers have investigated how air traffic controllers think about space and time in order to create display systems that conform to the process of spatial thinking (Wickens, 1992, 1998; Wickens and Mayor, 1997). Air traffic controllers think about space as an ordered stack of two-dimensional layers varying in altitude and can deal with each layer separately, turning a three-dimensional task into a series of two-dimensional tasks. This way of thinking has affected the design of visual support systems for air traffic controllers and the way in which flows of incoming and departing aircraft are organized. Aircraft are confined to altitude layers as a function of flight distance and destination. There are complex interactions between the ways in which the mind structures a multifaceted problem and the way in which we design cognitive tools and support systems to facilitate performance.

Earlier, we observed that one hallmark of an experienced architect is the ability to make behavioral or functional inferences from structural spatial information. This ability characterizes expertise in other domains as well. Experts at mechanical thinking, for example, can "see" how a device will behave from its structure (Heiser and Tversky, submitted). They can look at the structure of a bicycle pump or car brake or pulley system and anticipate its operation, understanding how parts move and affect each other to produce desired outcomes. Novices or people low in spatial ability can also understand the structural relations among the parts of a device, but they have difficulty anticipating its behavior or function. Teaching this spatial thinking skill is part of the process of turning novices into experts in everyday life, in the workplace, and in science.

3.4 SPATIAL THINKING IN SCIENCE

> The effectiveness of nonverbal processes of mental imagery and spatial visualization . . . can be explained, at least in part, by reference to the following interrelated aspects of such processes: their private and therefore not socially, conventionally, or institutionally controlled nature; their richly concrete and isomorphic structure; their engagement of highly developed, innate mechanisms of spatial intuition; and their direct emotional impact. (Shepard, 1988, p. 174)

Spatial thinking is deeply implicated in the conduct of science. This is not to argue that science can only be done by means of spatial thinking. It is to argue that many classic discoveries and everyday procedures of science draw extensively on the processes of spatial thinking.

The Executive Summary describes the role of spatial thinking in one of the great discoveries in modern science, Crick and Watson's double-helix model of the structure of DNA in biochemistry. Chapter 1 illustrates the role of spatial thinking in epidemiology. Here, the committee focuses on spatial thinking in astronomy, geoscience, and geography. These sciences have many things in common. They are Earth-centric. They are empirical sciences that are predominantly nonexperimental in character, relying on interpretation of hard-won observations of existing situations. In recent decades, each has experienced floods of data from newly developed observational technologies: sensors (such as seismographs and high-resolution hydrophones), sampling devices (such as deep sea and ice core drilling technologies), satellites (including multispectral imagery and global positioning systems [GPS]), and platforms (such as the Hubble telescope and the *Alvin* submersible).

Astronomy, geoscience, and geography have gone from being data impoverished to data enriched, if not data overwhelmed, placing a premium on the ability to manage and interpret data. At the same time, each has developed procedures to deal with data problems: generalization to cope with overspecificity and detail; extrapolation and interpolation to deal with missing data; correction procedures to deal with error and uncertainty. Because of the inherently spatial nature of their concerns, they have been at the forefront of developing and practicing spatial thinking through the use of root metaphors (e.g., maps), analytic techniques (e.g., trend surface analysis), and representational systems (e.g., spectral diagrams). They show similar sensitivities to the effects of spatial scale and the need for multiscalar analyses, to interrelationships between space and time, to the importance of spatial context, and to the needs for visualization and spatialization (see Chapters 2 and 8).

Four case studies are presented here. The first, from astronomy, is a long-term, historical account of the development of one approach to spatial thinking, astrophysical spatialization, within a discipline. The second, from geoscience, contrasts spatial thinking from two perspectives, that of an expert practicing the craft and that of a novice learning the craft. The third and fourth case studies focus on two scientists whose work exemplifies the power of spatial thinking. The third describes the work of Marie Tharp, a marine geologist, who created a pioneering series of seafloor maps. The last case study analyzes the work of Walter Christaller, a geographer who developed central place theory. The focus in each case study is the way in which spatial thinking is integral to the work of scientists and therefore to scientific discovery and progress.

3.5 SPATIAL THINKING IN ASTRONOMY

3.5.1 From the Celestial Sphere to the Structure of the Universe

The process of moving from the human wonder at the glory of the night sky to a scientific understanding of the structure and evolution of the universe is a remarkable story, made possible to a significant degree by insights and inferences generated by spatial thinkers.

The fundamental problem in astronomy is that it has a limited set of basic measurements from which to work. The measurements are simple. At any position in the sky, and at a particular time and location, we can measure the amount of energy flowing toward the observer as a function of wavelength. As the ancients looked at the sky through the limited window of the visible spectrum, they saw the refracted and reflected light of the Sun, Moon, stars, and planets.

The challenge was to make sense of the colors, patterns, movements, and changes. The basic intellectual structure was spatial, built on primitives and concepts that could be derived from those primitives (this analysis of astronomical primitives is based on Golledge's 1995 and 2002 articles on geographic primitives). In the sky, they saw objects at particular locations. Those objects were of varying brightness, now referred to as differing relative magnitudes. They gave the brighter of these objects names, labeling, and noticed how the appearance of the sky changed systematically with time. In passing, it is interesting to note that several of our basic time measurements—days, months, and years—are tied to observations of the sky, and that one of the basic functions of astronomers from ancient times until the late twentieth century was time keeping. The ancients used other spatial concepts to describe the objects they saw on the celestial sphere. Very early on they recognized that several objects moved against the background of the stars, the planets, the Moon, and the Sun. Therefore, they employed concepts such as relative direction and orientation. They used another fundamental spatial concept, frame of reference, viewing the "fixed" stars as a background against which other objects moved in terms of relative motion. They also saw patterns of stars or constellations in the sky.

3.5.2 The Structure and Evolution of the Universe

While it is interesting to discuss the relative sophistication of the ancient observations, particularly those associated with time keeping, there are many ways to illustrate the fundamental role of spatial thinking in astronomy. Here the focus is on the astronomical process of the spatialization of the universe. This is the process by which generations of astronomers have attempted to infer the structure and evolution of the universe from the basic observations, the spatial primitives of astronomy. They did so by converting data about energy into representations, often graphic, that allowed them to draw inferences about the physics of the stars and the cosmos. Spatial thinking is so pervasive in astronomy that in our illustrative story, we will further restrict the discussion to some of the key steps that built up a cosmic distance scale and enabled us to place objects in space, and eventually in time, with increasing precision.

3.5.3 The First Step: The Shape and Size of Earth

The first step in the process involved inferences about the shape and size of Earth. Central to this process were the attempts to measure the size of Earth and, outstanding among those attempts, was the work of Eratosthenes.

Of the remarkable series of polymaths who were librarians of the Great Library in Alexandria, Egypt, none was more remarkable than Eratosthenes of Cyrene (275–194 BC) (see Casson, 2001). Eratosthenes was, among other things, a mathematician, a philosopher, and a geographer. In the last of these avocations, he was a pioneer. He produced a remarkably accurate world map, centered on the "known" world of the Mediterranean Sea. The map was the first to include parallel lines of latitude. He suggested that Africa might be circumnavigated and that the major seas were connected. He calculated the length of the year and proposed adding a leap year to accommodate for the progressive discrepancy between Earth's orbit and the calendar.

Of his geographic achievements, Eratosthenes is best remembered for his work in geodesy, establishing the scientific grounding for that discipline through a brilliant exercise in spatial thinking. He calculated the circumference of Earth:

> He did this by employing a method that was perfectly sound in principle: first ascertaining by astronomical observations the difference between the latitudes of two stations situated on the same meridian, also by terrestrially measuring the distance between the same two stations, and finally, on the assumption that the earth was spherical in shape, by computing its circumference. (Vrettos, 2002, p. 52)

The details of the actual procedure are even more remarkable. It combined knowledge, observation, calculation, inference, and intuition in a way that captures the essence of spatial thinking.

Eratosthenes was aware of the idea, which had been proposed by earlier Greek natural philosophers, that Earth is spherical in shape. When he learned from travelers that at noon on the summer solstice in Syene (modern Aswan) the Sun shone directly into a deep well and its reflection was visible on the surface of the water in the well, he realized that the Sun must be directly overhead at that date and time, so that a gnomon (vertical stick) would cast no shadow. If Earth is indeed spherical, on the same date and time, a gnomon where he lived, in Alexandria, would cast a shadow. A smaller Earth, with a greater curvature, would produce a longer shadow than a larger Earth.

He realized that this general argument could be turned into a quantitative measurement by envisioning a frame of reference with an origin at the center of Earth, and by assuming that the Sun is so far away that its rays would be nearly parallel at Syene and Alexandria (Figure 3.2). In that case, the angle formed by a gnomon and the tip of its shadow in Alexandria, would be the same angular distance between Syene and Alexandria that would be observed from the center of Earth. He measured this angle and found it to be 7 degrees and 12 minutes, or approximately 1/50th of a circle. Since the overland distance between Alexandria and Syene had been measured by travelers (5,000 stade), he multiplied that number by 50 to arrive at a distance for the circumference of Earth.

Starting from the generally accepted belief that Alexandria and Syene (modern Aswan) were on the same meridian and his belief that Earth was spherical, Eratosthenes used a frame of reference

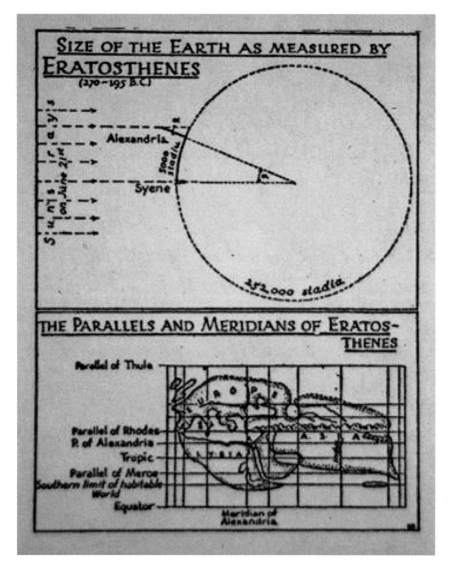

FIGURE 3.2 Eratosthenes' technique for determining the size of Earth. SOURCE: The Eratosthenes Project, http://www.phys-astro.sonoma.edu/observatory/eratosthenes/#original.

with an origin at the center of Earth and measured the relative orientation of sunlight as it struck Earth. The key to his spatial analysis was the measurement of angles relative to a plane perpendicular to a radius to the center of Earth, an absolute measure of direction (Figure 3.2).

The debates over his data (e.g., the interpretation of the distance of a stade and the accuracy of the distance measurement) and the fact that Alexandria and Syene do not lie on the same meridian are incidental to the magnitude of his achievement. It is the integration of geography and geometry, the use of observation and empirical data, the use of a superb sense of spatial intuition, and the marriage of deduction and calculation that make Eratosthenes' feat quite remarkable. From a few pieces of data and some beliefs, he used the power of spatial thinking to capture the size of Earth.

3.5.4 The Next Steps: The Spatial Structure of the Solar System

From this work on the shape and size of Earth, the next 2,000 years were marked by a struggle to come to grips with the spatial structure of the solar system. The search was an interesting one from the perspective of spatial thinking. Frequently, this search for an understanding of the structure of the solar system is described as a process of replacing the geocentric view of the universe with a heliocentric view. In a more fundamental spatial view, the search illustrates the power and implications of selecting an appropriate frame of reference.

From the time that individuals began to make systematic observations of the objects in the sky, and until the time of Copernicus, the crucial task of astronomers was predicting the position of the moving celestial bodies as a function of time. These predictions were essential for their primary functions of time keeping, eclipse prediction, and generating horoscopes. The Ptolemaic universe, the dominant geocentric cosmology for many centuries, is a spatialization of a method used to predict the position of various celestial objects, such as the Moon and the planets that appeared to move against the backdrop of the fixed stars. In general, the "fixed stars" tended to retain their positions with respect to one another on an imaginary "celestial sphere," which appeared to turn slowly around Earth, making one circuit every 24 hours. In contrast, the planets (then taken to be the Sun, Moon, Mercury, Venus, Mars, Jupiter, and Saturn) appeared to move irregularly with respect to the stars. The Sun and Moon always moved in one direction with respect to the stars, while the other planets moved at different speeds and sometimes even moved backwards (retrograde motion). Furthermore, the planets Mercury and Venus were never seen far from the Sun. These features were well known even to the earliest observers, and any explanation of the structure of the solar system had to explain these motions.

The Ptolemaic system, set forth by Claudius Ptolemy in the *Almagest* around AD 150, was a refinement of earlier ideas. The major feature of the Ptolemaic system was the use of epicycles (Figure 3.3), or circles on circles, as a mathematical device to predict where a planet would be at any given time. The appropriate choice of epicycles could explain why Mercury and Venus were never seen too far from the Sun and could even explain the retrograde motion of the planets. The result was a remarkably good description of the relative motion of the objects in the solar system from the frame of reference of Earth.

The major feature of the Ptolemaic view was the use of epicycles (Figure 3.4) to explain the retrograde motion of the outer planets (Figure 3.5). In essence, however, the result is simply a description of the relative motion of the objects in the solar system from the frame of reference of Earth.

The Copernican cosmology can be viewed as a simple transformation of the motion of the same objects to the frame of reference of a fixed Sun. To the extent that the models of these respective universes are calibrated by observations, they have the same predictive power for a terrestrial observer interested in prediction. However, several steps, theology aside, led to the acceptance of the Copernican model. First, its elegant spatial simplicity was appealing. Next, the laws of planetary motion, derived from the model by Kepler, gave it some deeper appeal. Kepler's laws were significant spatial generalizations about the relationships between the planets and the Sun. He not only inferred the elliptical nature of the orbits of the planets, but also provided a generalization that explained the orbits of all objects in terms of the period of rotation around the Sun and their distance from the Sun. By adopting elliptical orbits in a heliocentric system, Kepler was the first to be able to explain the retrograde orbit of the outer planets in modern terms (Figure 3.5). Finally, through the application of the theory of gravitation, Newton gave the Copernican system grounding in first principles, assigning primacy to the mass of the Sun as a referent for the entire solar system.

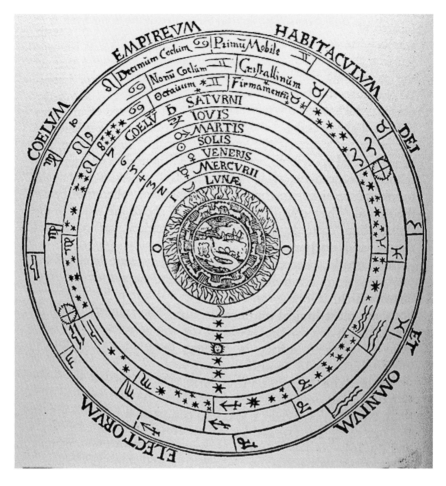

FIGURE 3.3 Ptolemaic system. The basic ordering of the planets around Earth is a feature of the Ptolemaic system. SOURCE: http://abyss.uoregon.edu/~js/glossary/ptolemy.html. Reproduced by permission of the Whipple Library, University of Cambridge.

3.5.5 Next Steps: Distances Beyond the Solar System

The next step in building a picture of the universe depended on creating a distance scale that could accommodate distances beyond the solar system. The key method for doing so involved the concept of astronomical parallax (Figure 3.6). From the perspective of spatial thinking, the measurement of astronomical parallax plays an interesting role in resolving the debate between the geocentric and heliocentric models of the solar system.

The essential challenge of astronomical observation in the middle of the second millennium was the accurate measurement of the position of the planets and the stars. The master of this challenge was Tycho Brahe. At his observatory, Uraniborg, he assembled the most accurate instruments of the day for his observations, observations that made Kepler's work possible. Tycho, who arguably had the best understanding of the relative positions of the astronomical objects of the time, opposed the Copernican view because he was unable to observe stellar parallax. His observations of stellar positions were by far the most accurate of the time and, therefore, he would have been the

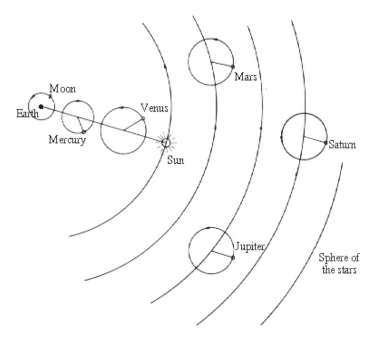

FIGURE 3.4 Epicycles in the Ptolemaic system. SOURCE: http://abyss.uoregon.edu/~js/glossary/ptolemy.html. Reproduced by permission from Dr. Jose Wudka.

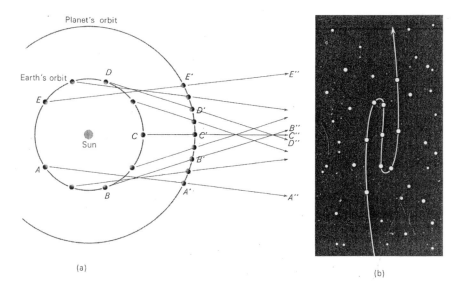

FIGURE 3.5 Retrograde motion. In modern heliocentric theory, the relative motions of the planets around the Sun causes the outer planets, those further away from the Sun than Earth, to appear to move backwards relative to the fixed stars on a regular basis. Note also that the inner planets are never seen at a large angular separation from the Sun. These two features were well known even to prehistoric observers, and any explanation of the structure of the solar system had to explain these motions. SOURCE: Abell, 1969.

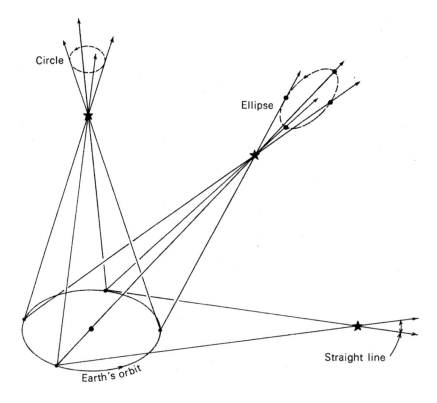

FIGURE 3.6 Astronomical parallax. The measurement of astronomical parallax is a triangulation of the distance to a star, using the orbit of Earth around the Sun as a baseline. A star is said be 1 parsec away if the angle p is 1 second of arc. Tycho's difficulty with measuring this angle was that it was well below the limit of his ability to detect. The nearest star is Proxima Centauri, 1.3 parsecs away, making the parallax angle less than 1 second. In practice this technique works only for relatively nearby stars, and the parallactic motion is measured against stars much further away that have no detectable parallax. SOURCE: Abell, 1969.

most likely to detect stellar parallaxes. However, the largest observed stellar parallax is less than 1 second of arc and 60 times smaller than the limit of Tycho's instrumentation of approximately 1 arc minute. The detection of stellar parallax led to the eventual proof that not only was Earth *not* the center of the universe, but the Sun was just an ordinary star of modest luminosity.

The breakthrough came in 1838 when three astronomers—Bessel, Henderson, and Struve—reported measuring the parallax of three nearby stars, 61 Cygni, Alpha Centuri, and Vega. This measurement served two critical purposes. First, it established the parsec as the basic unit of astronomy. Using the Sun-Earth distance as the baseline, a parsec is defined as the distance at which an object would have a parallax of 1 arc second, a distance equal to 206,265 times the distance of Earth from the Sun. Second, it established the scale of the universe, as then perceived, to be very large. The nearest stars were found to be more than 1 parsec away.

Following the first detection of stellar parallax, astronomers slowly began to build up a picture of the solar neighborhood, the region around the Sun where the parallax of objects could be measured. Edward Hertzsprung in 1911 and, independently, Henry Norris Russell in 1913 gave astronomy its first astrophysical spatialization—the Hertzsprung-Russell (H-R) diagram (Figure 3.7). This diagram plotted absolute magnitude against the newly identified spectral type of nearby stars. Two key concepts were merged in the diagram. The first was that of absolute magnitude,

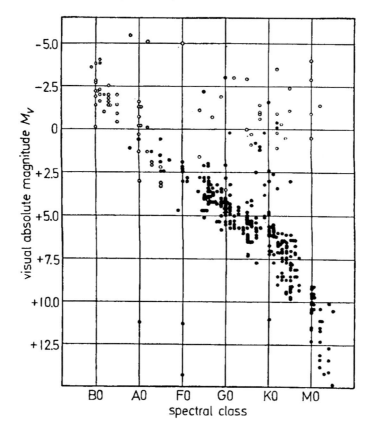

FIGURE 3.7 The Hertzsprung-Russell (H-R) diagram. Developed independently by the two astronomers for whom it is named, the H-R diagram shows absolute magnitude versus spectral type. Since the spectral type is a surrogate for temperature, hot blue stars are found on the left of the diagram and cool red stars on the right. The Sun is a star of intermediate temperature (G spectral type) with an absolute magnitude of approximately 5. The group of stars running from upper left to lower right is called the main sequence and is where most stars are found on the diagram. A simple consideration of the Stefan Boltzman law suggests that a star above the main sequence at the same spectral type (temperature) must be large and one lower is smaller. This led to the designation of the stars in the upper right as red giants and those in the lower left as white dwarfs. Later work showed that the position in the H-R diagram was a product of stellar mass and age. The magnitude scale is a logarithmic scale of luminosity. Stars whose absolute magnitude differs by 5 differ in intrinsic luminosity by a factor of 100. SOURCE: Unsöld, 1969.

which is simply the brightness of a star if it were placed at a standard distance of 10 parsecs. Examining the visible spectrum of a star and classifying it according to the observed distribution of features seen in its spectrum determines the spectral type of the star. Second, as ideas of modern quantum mechanics explained the reason for the existence of different spectral features in stellar spectra, it was realized that the star's spectral type was a surrogate for temperature, so that the horizontal axis of the H-R diagram ran from hot blue stars on the left to cool red stars on the right. When spectral type and absolute magnitude were plotted, most stars were found to fall on a single broad band, called the main sequence, with some hot dim stars found below the main sequence and some cool bright stars found above. In one diagram, therefore, the concept of red giant and white dwarf stars was given meaning.

Over the next several years, there were two approaches to building a picture of the structure of the universe, as revealed by the distribution of the stars. Both approaches involved the concept of a "standard candle," thus establishing the absolute brightness (magnitude) of a star by nonparallax means. Using the absolute and the apparent brightness, it was possible to infer the distance of the star. Both methods were tied to stars whose parallax had been measured, but they allowed the extension of the distance scale beyond the solar neighborhood and the reach of the measurement of parallax.

One approach built on the H-R diagram and developed what became known as "spectroscopic parallaxes." In this approach, the spectrum of a star was examined and then classified. By the time of the development of this method, it had been shown that spectra gave evidence not only of the temperature but also of the luminosity of a star. For example, it was possible from an examination of a star's spectrum to distinguish between a main sequence star of spectral K0 (Figure 3.7) and a brighter (giant) star of the same temperature. So, by observing a star's spectrum, we know about how bright it is if seen from a given distance. By comparing its known absolute brightness with its apparent brightness in the sky, we can infer how far away it is. In fact, the classification approach was sufficiently precise that the magnitude of a star's absolute brightness could be established within approximately 10–25 percent (a few tenths of a magnitude) and the distance inferred to comparable accuracy.

In 1953, Morgan, Whitford, and Code used this technique of spectroscopic parallax to map the spatial distribution of young clusters of stars around the Sun (Figure 3.8). This analysis shows the distribution of these objects forming three distinct arms, and it was a key step in creating a sense of the spatial structure of our galaxy.

The second set of standard candles emerged through yet another astrophysical spatialization, called the period-luminosity diagram (Figure 3.9). This approach was made possible by Leavitt's observation in 1911 that the period of a particular class of pulsating stars is an excellent predictor of its average absolute magnitude. This class of stars, called Cepheids after the prototype delta Delta Cephei, is also easy to identify from its distinctive light curve (the change in brightness over the period of pulsation) (Figure 3.10). Leavitt made her discovery by observing Cepheid variables in a nearby galaxy, the Small Magellanic Cloud. Because the distance of these variable stars relative to each other was small in comparison to their absolute distance from Earth, the scatter in their distance did not hide the relationship.

In 1924, Edwin Hubble used this new standard candle and the 100-inch telescope on Mount Wilson to identify Cepheids in the Andromeda Nebula (Figure 3.11), establishing once and for all that it was a galaxy like our own.

Hubble went on to extend his system of standard candles and measures to establish the distances to increasingly distant galaxies. In 1929, Hubble made a discovery that opened up the universe even further and thus began the age of modern cosmology. He found that the further a galaxy was from Earth, the faster it was moving away (Figure 3.12).

This led to the idea of an expanding universe, which in turn led to the "Big Bang" theory—that the universe was once all together, in a single place. With the discovery from this picture of an expanding universe, astronomy moved on to concepts such as the Big Bang, the discovery of quasars and other objects moving at very high velocities relative to Earth. The Hubble relationship became not only a map of space, but also a map of time. More distant objects, because of the finite velocity of light, are being observed at an earlier time in the history of the universe, opening up a window into the evolution of galaxies and clusters of galaxies and the "three degree" background radiation.

However, it is interesting to note that the "Hubble Constant," the quantity that describes the expansion velocity of the universe, has the units of kilometers per second per megaparsec (a million

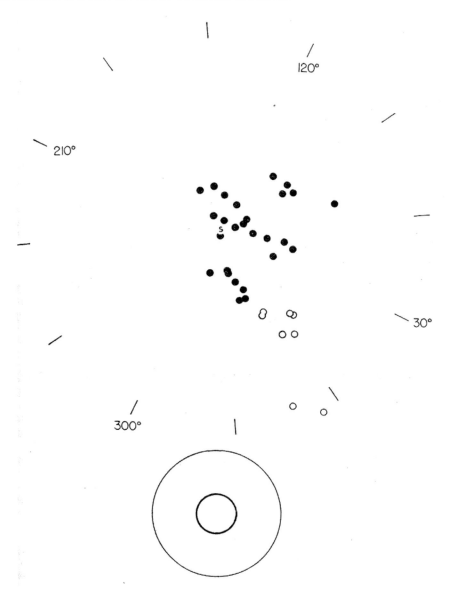

FIGURE 3.8 Map of the solar neighborhood. This diagram projects the position of younger clusters of stars onto the galactic plane. The Sun is denoted by S in the diagram. From observations of external galaxies we know that the spiral arms are apparent largely because of the presence of bright stars in relatively young clusters of stars. In showing the position of these stars near the Sun we can see a similar pattern. Parts of three arms of our galaxy are visible from the diagram. SOURCE: Morgan et al., 1953, p. 318. Reproduced by permission from the American Astronomical Society.

parsecs). So even in our description of the far reaches of the universe, the distance scale is tied to the distance from Earth to the Sun. This distance scale is an appropriate homage to the process of spatial thinking that led from measuring the diameter of Earth to an understanding of some of the most fundamental properties of the universe.

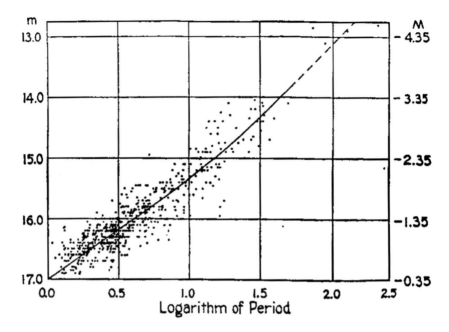

FIGURE 3.9 The period-luminosity diagram for the Cepheids. This diagram shows Henrietta Leavitt's graph of data for the Small Magellanic Cloud. It illustrates the relationship between the period of a Cepheid variable and its average luminosity. *Left*: m refers to the average apparent magnitude of the variable as observed; *right*: M refers to absolute magnitude of the variable stars. SOURCE: http://www.astro.livjm.ac.uk/courses/one/ NOTES/Garry%20Pilkington/cepinp1.htm.

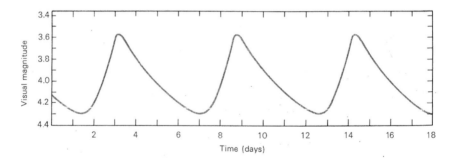

FIGURE 3.10 The characteristic light curve of a Cepheid variable. This star has a period of approximately 5.5 days (log 0.74), which implies that it has an absolute magnitude of approximately −1.5. Recalling from Figure 3.9 that the magnitude scale is a logarithmic scale of luminosity and that stars whose absolute magnitude differs by 5 differ in intrinsic luminosity by a factor of 100, we can calculate the distance to the star. The average apparent magnitude (visual magnitude in the figure) is 3.75, making the difference between absolute and apparent magnitude slightly more than 5. Therefore, the star appears approximately 100 times less luminous than it would if it were at the standard distance of 10 parsecs. Applying the inverse square law (luminosity decreases in proportion to $1/r^2$), one can infer that this star would be slightly more than 100 parsecs away. SOURCE: Abell, 1969, p. 480.

FIGURE 3.11 Cepheids in the Andromeda galaxy. Using the 100-inch Hooker telescope at Mt. Wilson, Hubble managed to measure the light curves of variable stars in the Andromeda galaxy, which he identified as Cepheids, and used to infer the distance to the galaxy. SOURCE: Hubble, 1936.

3.5.6 Thinking Spatially in Astronomy: The Role of Astrophysical Spatialization

Astronomy has at its core a long and powerful practice of spatial thinking. Two factors enabled its advancement: (1) a careful and systematic observation of the heavens and (2) a series of intellectual breakthroughs achieved by some of the finest spatial thinkers in the history of science. Breakthroughs enabled astronomy to build a picture of the universe in space and time, starting from the seemingly simple observation of the apparent position and brightness of celestial objects in the night sky. The boundary of our knowledge of the four-dimensional structure of the universe spread out from Earth like a ripple from a rock thrown in the pond. Eratosthenes' work provided a baseline, the shape and size of Earth. Kepler used the observations of Brahe to build a rational view of the spatial structure of the solar system and the motion of planets and other objects within it. With time,

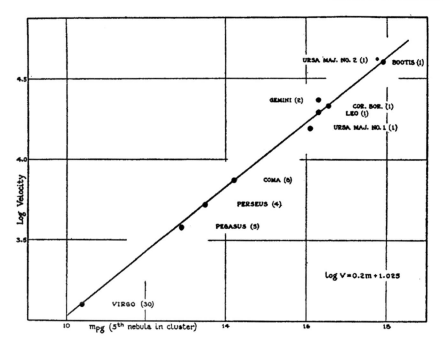

FIGURE 3.12 The redshift distance relationship. This diagram shows that galaxies further away are receding from our galaxy at faster rate. The slope of the relationship is given by the Hubble constant (*H*) measured in kilometers per second per megaparsec. The inverse of the Hubble constant is a simple estimate of the age of the universe. SOURCE: Hubble, 1936.

these efforts created distance scales to accommodate distances beyond the solar system: moving from the solar neighborhood to another spatial context, that of our galaxy, and finally, to a vision of an expanding universe enabled by Edwin Hubble's work. At this scale, distance becomes time. Thus, spatial thinking brought us not only a picture of the spatial structure of the Universe, but an understanding of its history as well.

3.6 SPATIAL THINKING IN GEOSCIENCE

3.6.1 Thinking Spatially in Geoscience: The Operations

As with any complex scientific practice, it is difficult to identify the component operations and impossible to specify a single sequence in which they are performed. Based on the experience of geoscientists, the committee presents a descriptive catalog of the spatial thinking operations typically performed in the process of doing geoscience. It is based on two categories of thinkers: expert geoscientists, especially those undertaking a spatial challenge that is novel to anyone, and beginning students, undertaking a spatial challenge that is novel to them. Thinking spatially by geoscientists and geoscience students involves, among other things,

- describing the shape of an object, rigorously and unambiguously;
- identifying or classifying an object by its shape;
- ascribing meaning to the shape of a natural object;
- recognizing a shape or pattern amid a cluttered or noisy background;

- visualizing a three-dimensional object or structure or process by examining observations collected in one or two dimensions;
- describing the position and orientation of objects you encounter in the real world relative to a conceptual coordinate system anchored to Earth;
- remembering the location and appearance of previously seen items;
- envisioning the motion of objects or materials through space in three dimensions;
- envisioning the processes by which objects change shape;
- using spatial thinking to think about time; and
- considering two-, three-, and four-dimensional systems where the axes are not distance.

Describing the Shape of an Object, Rigorously and Unambiguously

Untold person-lifetimes have been invested in the task of describing natural objects in a way that is rigorous and unambiguous, and attends to all of the important observable parameters. Faced with the huge range of objects found in nature, mineralogists, petrologists, geomorphologists, structural geologists, sedimentologists, zoologists, and botantists had to begin by agreeing upon words, measurements, and concepts with which to describe these natural objects.

Given a collection of objects that intuitively seem related in some way, what should you observe, and what should you measure, in order to capture the shape of each object? After much spatial thinking, crystallographers decided that you should observe how many planes of symmetry the crystal has and whether or not the angles between those planes of symmetry are right angles. Size and color of the crystal are not so important (Figure 3.13). After much spatial thinking, structural geologists decided that you should describe a fold in a sedimentary layer by imagining a plane cutting through the axis of symmetry of the fold, and then measuring the dip and strike of this plane, and the plunge of the intersection between this axial plane and the fold itself (Figure 3.14).

Although this descriptive style of geoscience and biology tends to be disparaged nowadays, the worldwide effort, in the eighteenth through twentieth centuries, to develop methodologies describing the objects of nature was crucial to the success of the discipline.

The processes on the part of expert observers as they develop a new description methodology include (1) careful observation of the shape of a large number of objects; (2) integrating these observations into a mental model of what constitutes the common characteristics among this group of objects; (3) identifying ways in which individual objects can differ while still remaining within the group; and (4) developing a methodical, reproducible set of observation parameters that can describe the range of natural variability within the group, thus defining a class. Step (4) may include developing a lexicon or taxonomy of terms, developing measuring instruments, developing units of

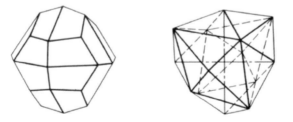

FIGURE 3.13 Describing the shapes of natural objects, rigorously and unambiguously: stereograms of crystals. SOURCE: Hurlbut, 1971. Copyright © 1971 by C. S. Hurlbut. Reproduced by permission of John Wiley & Sons, Inc.

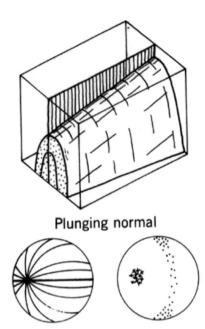

The fold at left is classified based on the orientation of the hinge line and axial surface. Diagrammatic projections below the block diagram show orientation data.

Plunging normal

FIGURE 3.14 Describing the shapes of natural objects, rigorously and unambiguously: classification of folds. SOURCE: Hobbs et al., 1976.

measurement, and/or developing two-dimensional graphical representations of some aspect of the three-dimensional objects.

For the novice, developing this descriptive skill involves becoming facile with the terms and techniques used by specialists who have previously studied this class of objects. In some cases, these descriptive techniques call upon projective and Euclidean spatial skills that many learners find extremely difficult. For example, when structural geologists collect data on which to apply their fold classification system, they record the vector that is perpendicular to the surface of the fold at many points on the fold, mentally extend those vectors until they intersect an imaginary hemisphere beneath the fold, and convey this information as points on a lower-hemisphere equal-area projection diagram. Command of projective spatial skills is required either to record or to interpret such data (Figure 3.15).

Similarly, many students have difficulties in spotting the subtle planes of symmetry that are required to make use of the crystallographers' descriptive methodology. Then, when it comes time to describe the angular relationships between crystal faces (using a system called Miller indices in which the three faces of a cube, for example, are labeled 001, 010, and 100) most students find that their Euclidean spatial ability initially fails them (Figure 3.13).

Identifying or Classifying an Object by Its Shape

Paleontologists or micropaleontologists identify fossils or microfossils according to shape or morphology. A variant of this task is identifying an object according to its shape, texture, and color. Mineralogists or petrologists identify minerals in a hand sample or photomicrograph by their shape, their color (including how their color changes under different lighting conditions), and their texture

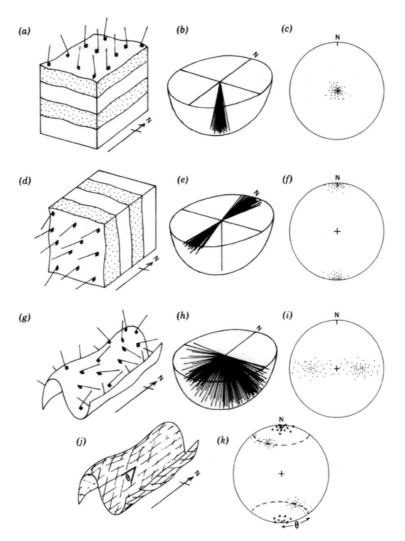

FIGURE 3.15 Diagrammatic representation of equal-area projection of various fabric elements. SOURCE: Hobbs et al., 1976.

(e.g., Does it have stripes? Does it have a shiny surface?). However, individual grains of the same mineralogy and individual fossils of the same species are not identical, but tend to share certain diagnostic properties (e.g., plagioclase grains tend to be much longer than they are wide, whereas olivine grains tend to be roughly as long as they are wide) (Figure 3.16).

Novices learn this identification skill by comparing unknown fossils or minerals against a physical catalog, using the descriptive terms and measurements mentioned above. To become experts, students must construct a mental catalog of the properties of dozens to hundreds of fossils or minerals, and then develop facility at comparing each unknown new mineral or fossil against this mental catalog.

Classifying or categorizing an object by its shape.

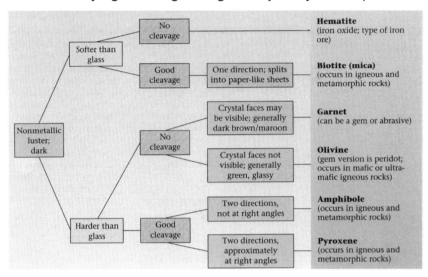

FIGURE 3.16 Flow chart for identifying minerals. SOURCE: Marshak, 2002. Earth Portrait of a Planet, New York, W.W. Norton & Co. Inc., Appendix B-2 Flow Charts for Identifying Minerals.

Ascribing Meaning to the Shape of a Natural Object

The shape of a natural object found in situ (including its size and orientation) carries clues about its history and formative processes.

One of the most famous instances of ascribing meaning to the shape of a natural object is the work of Alfred Wegener (1880–1930). He noted the apparent jigsaw-like fit of the coastlines of Africa and South America, and inferred that the continents were previously connected (Wegener, 1929) (Figure 3.17). James Hutton (1726–1797) noted the contrast in shape and texture of underlying and overlying rocks at his famous Scottish outcrop, and inferred the existence of unconformities and thus the immensity of geologic time (Hutton, 1788) (Figure 3.18). Both instances reflect brilliant spatial thinking.

In everyday practice, micropaleontologists use morphologic clues to make inferences about the geologic age and the paleoenvironment within which planktonic microfossils lived and died (Figure 3.19). One group of diatom (a form of phytoplankton) fossils might have thick silicate shells, whereas another group of diatoms has delicate thin shells. This difference could be attributed to the latter group's growing in water impoverished in dissolved silicon or it could be an evolutionary difference. The carbonate-shelled microfossils (foraminifera) in a sediment sample might be pitted and lack delicate protruberances (Figure 3.20). This could be attributed to the sediment sample being deposited near the calcite compensation depth, the depth in the ocean below which calcium carbonate dissolves and above which calcium carbonate is preserved in sediment. The observation that a group of microfossils are much smaller than typical for their species could be attributed to their living in a stressed environment, for example a marine species living in brackish water.

Structural geologists look at distortions in the shapes of crystals and fossils to infer the strain (and thereby stress) that a body of rock has undergone (Figure 3.21). Sedimentologists use the presence of ripples and other sedimentary structures to infer that a sedimentary stratum was depos-

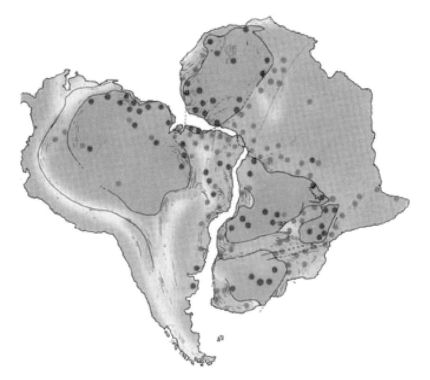

FIGURE 3.17 Ascribing meaning to the shape of a natural object: jigsaw-like fit of the coastlines of Africa and South America. SOURCE: Hamblin, 1994. Reprinted by permission of Pearson Education, Inc., Upper Saddle River, N.J.

FIGURE 3.18 Ascribing meaning to the shape of a natural object: Siccar Point. SOURCE: Dr. Clifford E. Ford, 2004, http://www.geos.ed.ac.uk/undergraduate/field/siccarpoint/images.htm.

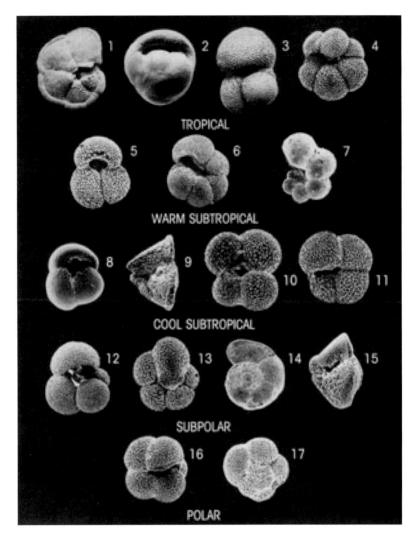

FIGURE 3.19 Ascribing meaning to the shape of a natural object: distribution of modern species of plank-tonic foraminifera. SOURCE: Kennett, 1982. Reprinted by permission of Pearson Education, Inc., Upper Saddle River, N.J.

ited under flowing water, and they use the orientation and asymmetry of the ripples to determine which way the current was flowing in the ancient body of water. Whether a river is meandering, straight, or braided tells geomorphologists about the energy regime (velocity) of a river. Similarly, the grain-size distribution of sedimentary particles tells sedimentologists about the velocity of an ancient river; it takes a higher energy flow to carry gravel rather than sand.

To summarize from these examples, the shape of a natural object can be influenced by (1) its strain history, (2) the energy regime under which it was formed, (3) the chemical environment under which it formed, and (4) changes in the physical or chemical environments experienced after its initial formation. Geoscientists seek to reason backwards from observing the morphology to

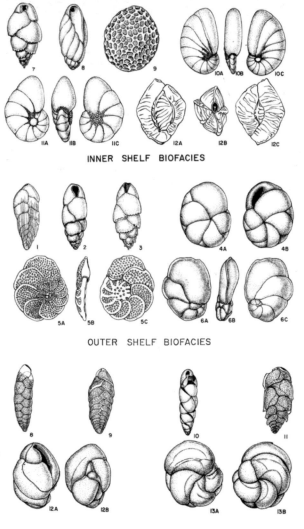

INNER SHELF BIOFACIES

OUTER SHELF BIOFACIES

UPPER BATHYAL BIOFACIES

Representative benthonic foraminifera typical of inner and outer shelf biofacies and upper bathyal biofacies in the Gulf of California.

FIGURE 3.20 Ascribing meaning to the shape of a natural object: carbonate-shelled microfossils. SOURCE: Kennett, 1982. Reprinted by permission of Pearson Education, Inc., Upper Saddle River, N.J.

inferring the influencing processes. The key questions are: What processes or forces could have acted upon this mineral, landform, fossil, or organism (the fossil before it died) to cause it to have this shape? What function could this form have served in the life of the organism?

The novice generally begins by applying learned rules of thumb. At the expert level, this thought process involves reasoning from first principles about the connection among form, function, and history and doing so in the context of an expert knowledge base about the normal characteristics of the class of objects under study. Students, as novices however, may misunderstand fundamental processes (Figure 3.22). The ability to reason from first principles well is one of the abilities people have in mind when they say that someone has good "geologic intuition."

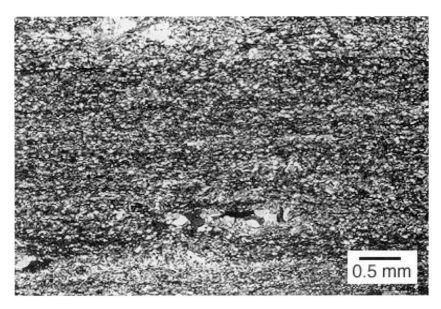

FIGURE 3.21 Ascribing meaning to the shape of a natural object: the shape and orientation of the mineral grain in this photomicrograph are interpreted as evidence that the rock has undergone shearing. SOURCE: The University of North Carolina, Chapel Hill, Department of Geological Sciences.

Recognizing a Shape or Pattern amid a Cluttered or Noisy Background

An experienced interpreter of seismic reflection data can confidently and reproducibly trace seismic reflectors across a graphic profile that looks like uniform gray noise to the untrained eye (Figure 3.23). A gifted paleontologist can stand at an outcrop with a bus full of geologists and spot fossils where others see nothing.

Visualizing a Three-Dimensional Object, Structure, or Process by Examining Observations Collected in One or Two Dimensions

Physical oceanographers measure the temperature and salinity of seawater by lowering an instrument package on a wire vertically down from a ship and recording the temperature, conductivity, and pressure at the instrument. Thousands of vertical conductivity-temperature-depth profiles have been combined to create our current understanding of the three-dimensional interfingering of the water masses of the world's oceans.

A field geologist examines rock layers and structures where they are exposed at Earth's surface in outcrop, taking advantage of differently oriented road cuts, stream cuts, wave cuts, or quarries to glimpse the third dimension. From these fragmented surficial views, he or she constructs a mental view of the interior of the rock body or, more commonly, multiple possible views.

The expert's visualization of the parts of a structure that cannot be seen is guided by more than simple mechanical interpolation between observable sections or profiles. The physical oceanographer's visualization is, for example, shaped by physics that decrees that lower-density water masses overlie higher-density water masses (Figure 3.24). The field geologist's visualization is shaped by the understanding that marine sedimentation processes tend to produce layers roughly horizontal and roughly uniform in thickness before deformation. Marie Tharp's case (see Section

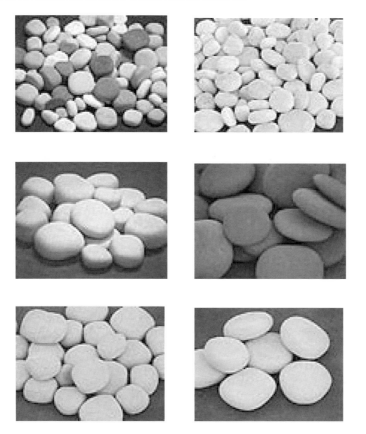

FIGURE 3.22 Ascribing meaning to the shape of a natural object: reasoning from first principles. SOURCE: Kusnick, 2002.

3.7) is interesting because neither she nor anyone else knew any details about the tectonic and volcanic processes that form the seafloor geomorphology; yet her maps in areas of sparse data (the Southern Oceans, for example) are far better than would have been possible by interpolating from data alone. In these examples, the physical oceanographer and the field geologist are guided by knowledge of the processes that shaped the unseen parts of the puzzle, but in Tharp's case she seems to have developed a spatial intuition or feel for the nature of the seafloor before the formative processes were understood.

Describing the Position and Orientation of Objects Encountered in the Real World Relative to a Conceptual Coordinate System Anchored to Earth

Learning to measure the dip and strike of a sedimentary strata or other planar surface is a rite of passage for introductory geoscience students (Figure 3.25). This technique requires Euclidean spatial skills (see Appendix C). Many students seem incapable of grasping this technique at any kind of deep or intuitive level; at best, they can learn to memorize a sequence of steps and apply them mechanically.

Until the advent of GPS navigation for research vessels, navigation was a huge issue for seagoing oceanographers. The challenge is to make the most precise seafloor maps, ground-truthed

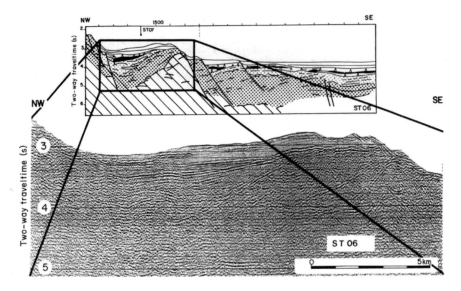

FIGURE 3.23 Recognizing a shape or pattern amid a cluttered, noisy background. Multichannel seismic line ST06 across a small tilted block at the base of the Monte Baronie structure. SOURCE: Rehault et al., 1987.

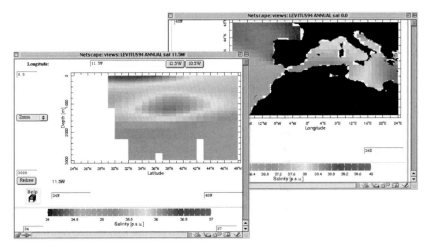

FIGURE 3.24 Visualizing a three-dimensional object, structure, or process by examining observations collected in one or two dimensions.

with the most precisely located samples, measurements, and photographs. This requires navigational understanding of ships, samples, and towed vehicles. Every navigation technique—dead reckoning, sextant, Loran, doppler satellite navigation, seafloor-based acoustic transponders, or GPS—requires thinking about how angles and/or distances change as a function of the relative motions between objects.

This suite of tasks is difficult because it involves angular estimations. Dealing with angles is a skill that can be improved with practice and lost through disuse. As a result of practice, a marine geologist can learn to estimate a compass course on a map by eye to within better than 5 degrees,

FIGURE 3.25 Describing the position and orientation of objects in the real world relative to a coordinate system anchored to Earth.

changes of heading to within 1 degree, and then mentally integrate the angular effect of wind, current, and wire pull on the ship's heading.

Learning how to figure out where you are on a topographic map is another rite of passage for geology students. This skill has a real life counterpart in figuring out where you are on a road map. The mental process involves making connections between the three-dimensional, horizontally viewed, infinitely detailed, ever-changing landscape that surrounds you and through which you are moving, and the two-dimensional, vertically viewed, schematic, unchanging representation of that landscape on a little piece of paper. Although navigating through an unfamiliar terrain by referring to a map is probably the most common map-using task for nonprofessional map users, this skill is rarely taught in school.

Remembering the Location and Appearance of Previously Seen Items

The great Appalachian field geologist John Rodgers (Rodgers, 2001) knew the location of every outcrop and every ice cream stand from Maine to Georgia. Students recall that he remembered the salient sedimentary and structural characteristics of every outcrop he had ever seen in any mountain range in the world, and where it was located. His ability to remember the relationships among rock bodies at those outcrops allowed him to construct, over a long lifetime in the field, a mental catalog of occurrences of geologic structures, which he drew on to create a masterful synthesis of how fold-and-faulted mountain ranges form (Rodgers, 1990).

William Smith (1769–1839) made the world's first geological map (Figure 3.26), a map of England and Wales showing rocks of different ages in different colors (Winchester, 2001). When Smith began his field work, it was not understood that rocks occurred on Earth's surface in organized spatial patterns; he figured out that the organizing principle was the age of the rocks as recorded in their fossils. As with Marie Tharp, Smith made his map before the causal processes that underlay the observations on his map were understood, and he worked from incomplete data, primarily outcrops revealed in canal cuts. As with Marie Tharp's map, Smith's map stands up very well to comparison with modern maps. Many spatial skills must have contributed to Smith's effort,

FIGURE 3.26 William Smith's geological map of England and Wales. SOURCE: Winchester, 2001.

but among them was his ability to remember and organize, aided only by the simplest of paper and pencil records, a huge body of spatially referenced observations. His nephew, John Phillips, wrote of William Smith: "A fine specimen of this ammonite was here laid by a particular tree on the road's side, as it was large and inconvenient for the pocket, according to the custom often observed by Mr. Smith, *whose memory for localities was so exact* that he has often, after many years, gone direct to some hoard of nature to recover his fossils." [emphasis added] (from *Memoirs of William Smith* by John Phillips cited in Winchester, 2001, p. 270).

Envisioning the Motion of Objects or Materials Through Space in Three Dimensions

Physical oceanographers and marine geochemists envision water moving along the "great ocean conveyor belt" of density-driven ocean currents (Broecker, 1991). Atmospheric physicists envision a spiraling pattern of air currents in latitudinally bounded bands. Geophysicists envision mantle rising beneath ridge crests and sinking at subduction zones. Today's students have brightly colored textbook drawings and animated web sites to help them visualize these complex three-dimensional flows. The first thinkers to envision these flows, which cannot be seen literally even in part by human eyes, must have made gigantic leaps of spatial thinking.

For these pioneer thinkers, to what extent did the visualization grow from data and to what extent from understanding of causative processes? The simplistic notion is that one collects a mass of data about the distribution of some property or process, combines the data into a mental picture or computer-aided visualization, and then interprets it. This may understate and underestimate the skill of a spatial thinker.

Consider the example of global atmospheric circulation. Certainly, the existence and orientation of trade winds, a fundamental observation, was known from long ago. Yet the northward counterflow at high altitude cannot have been documented observationally by those pioneers; they must have inferred it and included it in their mental picture because the picture did not make physical sense without it. Some of the great leaps of visualization of three-dimensional Earth processes have progressed by a hybrid process, in which the visualization is partly shaped by data and observations and partly by intuitive understanding of driving forces. Modern models of oceanic and atmospheric circulation try to formalize this hybrid cognitive process. The models are built around equations that purport to represent physical forces, and then data are used to "train" the models through a process of "data assimilation."

Envisioning the Processes by Which Objects Change Shape

Whereas the fluid parts of the Earth system generally respond to imposed forces by moving through space, the solid parts may respond by changing their shape, by deforming, by folding, and by faulting. After struggling to visualize the internal three-dimensional structure of a rock body, the geologist's next step is often to try to figure out the sequence of folding and faulting events that has created the observed structures. This task may be attacked either forwards or backwards: backwards, by "unfolding" the folds and "unfaulting" the faults; or forwards, by applying various combinations of folds and faults to an initially undeformed sequence of rock layers until you find a combination that resembles the observed structure (Figure 3.27). The forward approach resembles the paper-folding task used by psychologists who study spatial thinking (see Chapter 2).

Elements of solid Earth also change their shape through erosion, through the uneven removal of parts of a whole. Thinking about eroded terrains requires the ability to envision negative spaces, the shape and internal structure of the material that is no longer present.

Using Spatial Thinking to Think About Time

It is common in thinking about Earth to find that variation or progression through space is closely connected with variation or progression through time. For example, within a basin of undeformed sedimentary rocks, the downward direction corresponds to increasing time since deposition. On the seafloor, distance away from the mid-ocean ridge spreading center corresponds to increasing time since the formation of that sliver of seafloor.

As a consequence, geologists often think about distance in space when they really want to think

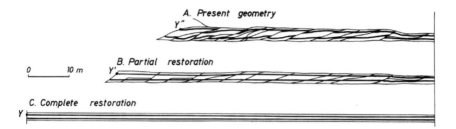

FIGURE 3.27 Mentally manipulating a volume by folding, faulting, and eroding: geometry of the lower duplex at Hénaux. SOURCE: Ramsay and Huber, 1987. Copyright 1987, reprinted with permission from Elsevier.

about duration of geological time. Distance in space is easy to measure, in vertical meters of stratal thickness or horizontal kilometers of distance from ridge crest. Duration in geological time is hard to measure, and subject to ongoing revision, involving complicated forays into seafloor magnetic anomalies, radiometric dating, stable isotope ratios, or biostratigraphy.

In another kind of interaction between space and time, geologists use spatial relationships in rock bodies to figure out the sequence of events. If a volcanic dike cuts across certain layers of sedimentary rocks, then the intrusion of the dike must have happened after the deposition of the sediments. Sediments in a fault-bounded basin that form a wedge, in which the deeper layers dip more steeply than the shallow layers, are interpreted as "syn-rift" sediments, sediments deposited during the interval of time when the basin's bounding normal faults were slipping.

Considering Two-, Three-, and Four-Dimensional Systems Where the Axes Are Not Distance

Specialists within different branches of geosciences have a tendency to use "space" as a metaphor for variation in observable but nonspatial parameters of natural systems. For example, petrologists visualize a tetrahedron, in which each corner is occupied by a chemical element or by a mineral of pure composition (e.g., one end member of a solid solution). Any given rock can be placed at a point within the tetrahedron according to the concentration of each of the components in the rock. To communicate this tetrahedron to colleagues, they project the data down onto one of the sides of the tetrahedron, where it appears on the page as a triangle, with each rock sample appearing as a dot.

Igneous petrologists deal in "pressure-temperature space." The pressure dimension of this space is something like distance beneath Earth's surface, but it is denominated in units of downwardly increasing pressure rather than in units of distance. The temperature dimension is also related to distance beneath Earth's surface, with temperature increasing downwards. The chemical composition of an igneous rock depends in part on where in pressure-temperature space the initial melt separated out of the mantle.

Physical oceanographers deal in "T-S" diagrams, where T is the temperature and S the salinity of water mass. Temperature and salinity together control the density of the water mass, and density in turn controls whether the water mass will sink relative to other water masses in the same ocean. Water samples that share a common history will likely cluster together in T-S space, and water masses with different histories of formation will usually occupy different areas of T-S space.

The processes for thinking about these non-distance-denominated "geospaces" feel similar to the processes for thinking about the distribution of objects and their movement through "regular" distance space. A clue is that the vocabulary is the same. Two water masses are "close together" or "far apart" in T-S space. A body of rock in the mantle "moves" through pressure-temperature space on a "trajectory."

This habit of mind of using spatial representations for nonspatial observables seems particularly common among geoscientists. People trained in other disciplines tend to use statistics, equations, or verbal descriptions to describe variability in the objects or systems they study, rather than the visually displayed, spatially based approaches so common in the geosciences.

3.6.2 Thinking Spatially in Geoscience: The Processes

Given this depiction of some of the operations of spatial thinking in geoscience, we can characterize spatial thinking as consisting of five major processes. These linked operations begin with observing, describing, recording, classifying, recognizing, remembering, and communicating the two- or three-dimensional shape, internal structure, orientation, and/or position of objects, properties, or processes. The next step involves mentally manipulating those shapes, structures, orientations or positions—for example, by rotation, translation, deformation, or partial removal. The third step involves making interpretations about what caused the objects, properties, or processes to have those particular shapes, structures, orientations, and/or positions. With this understanding in mind, it is possible to make predictions about the consequences or implications of the observed shapes, internal structures, orientations, and/or positions. Finally, geoscientists can use spatial thinking processes as a short-cut, metaphor, or mental crutch to think about processes or properties that are distributed across some dimension other than physical space.

3.7 THINKING SPATIALLY IN GEOSCIENCE: THE SEAFLOOR MAPS OF MARIE THARP

3.7.1 Introduction: Seafloor Mapping

Marie Tharp (1920–) is a marine cartographer who made some of the first maps of the seafloor between the 1950s and the 1970s (Figure 3.28). With kilometers of water obscuring her direct vision, she was able to visualize and depict the shapes of terrain that no human eye had ever seen.

FIGURE 3.28 Marie Tharp in 1960. SOURCE: Columbia University, Earth Institute. World Ocean Floor, Bruce C. Heezen and Marie Tharp. Copyright by Marie Tharp 1977/2003. Reproduced by permission of the Marie Tharp Oceanographic Cartography, One Washington Ave., South Nyack, New York 10960.

Her maps have stood the test of time amazingly well when compared against modern maps made with sophisticated swath-mapping and satellite-based mapping systems.

She created the maps using sparse and flawed echograms based on echo sounder data and her remarkable capacity for spatial thinking. Tharp's decades-long effort involved synthesizing vast amounts of spatial data, visualizing what was previously unseen, and interpreting spatial observations in terms of causal processes.

Marie Tharp worked at the Lamont-Doherty Earth Observatory of Columbia University in the research group of Professor Bruce Heezen. Earlier accounts (e.g., Menard, 1986) tended to give all or most of the intellectual credit to Heezen, recognizing Tharp only as the person who plotted the echograms. More recently, however, Tharp has been given credit for discovering the mid-Atlantic rift valley, correlating the rift valley and earthquake locations, and insisting on the validity of this as evidence for seafloor spreading at a time and place when this was considered to be heresy (Lamont-Doherty Earth Observatory, 2001).

3.7.2 The Nature of What Tharp and Heezen Did

Measure Water Depths from Precision Data Recorders (PDRs). Echo sounders measure the depth of the water beneath a ship by measuring the travel time of an electronic ping of sound as it travels from the ship to the seafloor and back. In Tharp's era, the state of the art was the precision depth recorder, as refined by the U.S. Navy during World War II. The echoes from the seafloor were recorded as burn marks on a roll of paper by a stylus that swept across the paper once per second. Tharp and her assistants manually converted the location of these burn marks into water depths, measuring a water depth for each 5 minutes of time along the track of a ship's travel.

Reconcile and Plot Navigation. Ship's tracks were plotted by hand on table-sized plotting sheets at a scale of 4 inches to a degree of longitude, based on celestial navigation and dead reckoning by the ship's officers. (On a modern research vessel, a navigation fix would be taken from the GPS every minute, the navigation would be logged by computer, and the ship's track would be plotted automatically in real time.)

Plot Soundings on Navigation Plots. Water depths were written by hand onto plotting sheets, alongside the ship's track.

Make Profiles and Contour Maps. Contours were drawn by hand on overlays of the plotting sheets. Profiles were made along azimuths that seemed interesting, sometimes combining segments of several different ship tracks to make a composite track (Figure 3.29). At this point we can begin to appreciate Tharp's skill as a spatial thinker. Profiles and contour maps require judgments as to what is or is not interesting—which tracks to include or to discount.

Plot Complementary Data at the Same Scale. Earthquake epicenter location and sediment data were plotted, by hand, at the same scale as the bathymetric data. This strategy revealed that earthquakes and thin sediment cover occurred along the axis of the mid-Atlantic ridge.

Convert Profiles and Contours into Physiographic Diagrams. Heezen and Tharp's most famous products are physiographic diagrams, scaled drawings or paintings of the seafloor as though all of the water had been drained away. Given the large gaps between track lines (tens to hundreds of kilometers even in the best covered areas; see Figure 3.30), creating a continuous physiographic diagram required substantial interpolation. Tharp gained a feel for the fabric or texture of the seafloor in areas of more abundant data and then used that "feel" to guide her mapping in the areas of less abundant data. We should note that this feeling was spatial or visual and intuitive, rather than being grounded in an understanding of the processes that formed the seafloor features because no-one understood those processes during the early years of Tharp's mapping career.

The decision to use physiographic diagrams was initially motivated by the U.S. Navy's classification and hence restriction of use of quantitative bathymetric data such as contours (Lawrence,

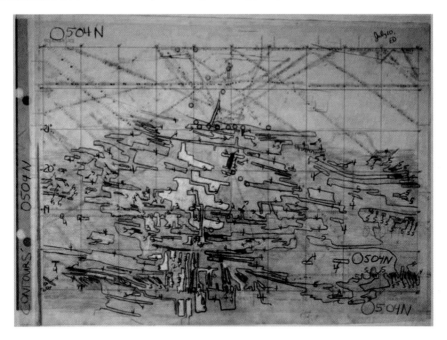

FIGURE 3.29 Tharp's original hand contouring of a portion of the mid-Atlantic ridge. In the background, you can discern the tracklines with hand-written bathymetric sounding data points along them. Despite the sparseness of the tracklines, Tharp detected and depicted the rift valley along the axis of the mid-Atlantic ridge, which was one of the early lines of evidence for seafloor spreading. Tharp's map also shows clearly the fabric of transform faults and fracture zones (the roughly east-west trends), although it was many years before an explanation of transform faults emerged. SOURCE: Library of Congress, http://www.loc.gov/exhibits/treasures/trr078.html.

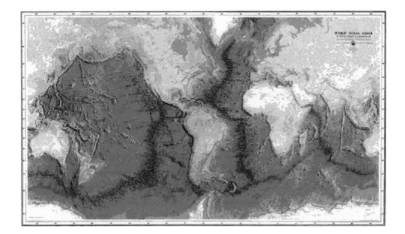

FIGURE 3.30 World ocean floor panorama. SOURCE: Heezen and Tharp, 1977. Copyright by Marie Tharp 1977/2003. Reproduced by permission of the Marie Tharp Oceanographic Cartography, One Washington Ave., South Nyack, New York 10960.

1999, 2002; Menard, 1986). In fact, however, the physiographic diagram approach proved to be a powerful visualization tool that probably facilitated the interpretation of morphology in terms of the formative processes. The physiographic diagrams foreshadowed the modern shaded-relief displays of digital elevation models.

Find Trends, Patterns, Consistencies, and Symmetries in the Data. The most famous example of this process was Tharp's realization that the mid-Atlantic ridge has a deep, symmetrical, steep-sided valley running down its center. Heezen was at first unwilling to accept the existence of this valley, dismissing it as "girl talk" (Wertenbaker, 1974, p. 144), but after additional patient work, they were able to construct a compelling case for the widespread existence of this valley (Heezen and Tharp, 1956).

Interpret Physiographic Diagrams and Profiles in Terms of Formative Processes. The symmetrical, steep-sided valley in the mid-Atlantic ridge was reminiscent of the rift valleys of Africa that were formed by extensional tectonics. Extensional tectonics in the center of the ocean would be compatible with the then-new and controversial hypothesis of seafloor spreading. After some apparent mental struggles, Heezen and Lamont Director Maurice Ewing presented the mid-Atlantic rift valley as evidence of seafloor spreading (Ewing and Heezen, 1956; Menard, 1986; Lawrence, 2002).

The seafloor mapping task was a signal achievement in spatial thinking. As with any process of science, it combined remarkable patience and dedication over long periods of time, scrupulous care and meticulous accuracy, trial and error, the willingness to make interpretative leaps, and relentless determination. It also exemplified some of the component skills of spatial thinking. The supports were, by modern standards, primitive. Data were managed in paper records, graphics were produced by hand, the demands on eyes and hands and minds were intense. Nowadays, such tasks would be supported by a tool such as GIS.

3.7.3 The Importance of Marie Tharp's Work

Prior to the work of Heezen, Tharp, and a handful of contemporaries at other major oceanographic institutions, most geoscientists did not think at all about the seafloor. If they did do so, considered it to be a muddy plain, the dumping ground for sediments eroded from the continents.

After the seafloor mapping activities of the 1950s and 1960s, much of educated humanity appreciated that the seafloor was as complicated—and interesting—as the continents. Geoscientists knew that the seafloor was shaped by an almost totally different set of processes than those which shape continental geomorphology. The concept of seafloor spreading—centered about the rift valley on the axis of the mid-Atlantic ridge—became a cornerstone of the hypothesis of plate tectonics, which in turn revolutionized almost all of our thinking about the physical workings of planet Earth.

3.7.4 The Nature of the Challenge

Tharp, Heezen, and their colleagues faced a set of challenges that were physical, technical, and intellectual. The entire process, whose outcomes could not have even been guessed in advance, took many person-years of detailed, patient work. Significant spatial patterns emerged slowly, and it must have been difficult to see the forest amid so many trees.

The raw data posed a set of interrelated challenges. They were discontinuous, subject to recording error, potentially confounded in terms of angle, based on unsystematic sampling grids, and locationally inaccurate. Many of the echo sounders of Tharp's era did not present a straightforward profile of the bathymetry beneath the ship. Every time the water depth changed by 400 fathoms (1 second of two-way travel time, ship to bottom and back, or approximately 750 m), there was a tear in the continuity of the profile. For an area of rugged terrain therefore, Tharp could not see the shape of the seafloor by looking directly at the shipboard data.

The actual display on the graphic recorded in the ship showed the fractional part of the acoustic travel time in seconds. The integer part of the travel time was not displayed directly, but had to be "book-kept" by keeping track of the upward and downward changes of sweep. In other words, every 0.5 second of travel time (200 fathoms) looks in the shipboard data exactly like 1.5 seconds of travel time (600 fathoms) and 2.5 seconds (1,000 fathoms). If the shipboard watchstanders did not bookkeep accurately, the water depth could easily be off by 400, 800, or more fathoms.

To ensure that some of the outgoing acoustic energy traveled downwards toward the seafloor despite the rolling and pitching of the ship, echo sounders of Tharp's era emitted a 60 degree wide cone of sound, rather than a narrowly focused beam. In steep terrain such as a mid-ocean ridge crest, the first returning echo might be from a point off to the side of the ship rather than directly beneath the ship. In that case a mass of overlapping "side echoes" could partially or totally obscure the vertical seafloor echo on the data record.

The ship tracks that Tharp worked with were irregularly spaced opportunistic crossings of the central Atlantic rather than the results of a systematic survey. The gaps between ship tracks were often large (hundreds of kilometers) relative to the size of the features being mapped, requiring rather bold interpolation between tracklines. The ships' navigation was by celestial navigation and dead reckoning. The charted positions of the ships could be off by miles in any direction. Consequently, the bathymetric data on crossing tracks often did not agree.

The intellectual challenge was in one sense the problem to be solved. There was no conceptual framework with which to guide the eye toward detecting spatial patterns in the data. There were few expectations as to what might or even could exist. The processes by which seafloor morphology is formed were almost completely unknown. There was no way of knowing, at the beginning of the work, where or when the process would end, and there were few guides as to where to begin looking for pattern and meaning. One obvious source, continental geomorphology, was in fact misleading. As it turned out, seafloor morphology is shaped by quite different processes than those that dominate in continental settings, and as a result, there are no familiar land surface analogues for many seafloor bathymetric features.

3.7.5 Marie Tharp: A Skillful Spatial Thinker at Work

In creating maps of the seafloor, Marie Tharp epitomizes the skillful spatial thinker at work. We can see many of the dimensions of skilled performance. In doing so, it is important to re-emphasize the extent to which she worked with limited technological support. Many of the tasks that she undertook with paper and pencil would today be supported by technology.

A skilled spatial thinker is capable of detecting spatial patterns and regularities from a sparse, discontinuous, and error-laden data set. Even today, it would be a challenge for a geoscientist, knowledgeable about the processes that shape seafloor morphology, to generate sensible seafloor contours from the scattered ship tracks that Tharp had available. A skilled spatial thinker can depict and interpret spatial information despite noisy, ugly data. Tharp literally saw through the masses of side echoes and navigation errors in her data set.

Part of her success is a reflection of another component of spatial thinking. She could shift easily back and forth among different vantage points and representations of spatial data. Tharp's raw data were profiles; her intermediate products were lines of tiny handwritten numbers; and her final products were maps and paintings.

A skilled spatial thinker is also creative in terms of using or, more significantly, creating new representational modes to convey spatial data. When the U.S. Navy prohibited Heezen and Tharp from publishing their data in the form of contour maps, they developed the physiographic diagram technique (Menard, 1986).

A skilled spatial thinker can combine multiple kinds of spatial and nonspatial information. By having one of her helpers plot earthquake epicenter locations at the same spatial scale as her bathymetric maps, Tharp was able to extrapolate the location of the mid-ocean ridge axis to regions for which there was no bathymetric coverage available.

A skilled spatial thinker must be capable of holding large amounts of spatial information in mind at one time and browsing through these data. The rolls of PDR data from which Tharp worked eventually filled every room of a very large house, but it seemed that she could remember what bathymetric features she had seen and, of equal importance, where she had seen them (M. Tharp, March 2001 interview, Oral History Project of the John Heinz III Center for Science, Economics and the Environment).

The ultimate power of spatial thinking enables one to see connections between observable or inferred spatial patterns and distributions, on the one hand, and those processes that may have caused those patterns to come into existence, on the other. Tharp recognized that a continuous, symmetrical, steep-sided valley, co-located with abundant earthquakes, could be formed by rifting (extensional tectonics) as predicted by the then-new and controversial theory of seafloor spreading.

In Marie Tharp, all of these skills were intertwined with a passion and determination to solve a problem that many of her colleagues did not even recognize. Spatial thinking is not the only characteristic that accounts for Marie Tharp's success, but it is fundamental to the successful mapping of the seafloor.

3.8 THINKING SPATIALLY IN GEOGRAPHY: WALTER CHRISTALLER'S DISCOVERY OF CENTRAL PLACE THEORY

3.8.1 The German Tradition of Location Theory

Throughout the nineteenth century and during the first half of the twentieth century, Germany was a—if not the—center of geographical scholarship. As a respected discipline, geography was strongly entrenched in the German university system. A long tradition of German scholars had defined many of the key ideas in the discipline: Alexander von Humboldt and the science of exploration; Carl Ritter and the concept of the region; Friedrich Ratzel and the study of anthropogeography; and Alfred Hettner and the idea of chorology (or regional differentiation).

One branch focused on the idea of location theory. At its simplest, location theory asked: Why are things located where they are? It sought to answer the question by finding general laws that would explain spatial patterns of such things as agricultural production, based on Johann Heinrich von Thunen's (1826) model of agriculture, and manufacturing, based on Alfred Weber's (1909) theory of industrial location.

In 1933, Walter Christaller (1893–1969) published a doctoral dissertation that added another strand to location theory, accounting for settlement patterns with his central place theory (Figure 3.31). The echoes of that remarkable discovery still play a role in geography, sociology, and planning today. For some, central place theory is emblematic of the spatial analysis approach to geography, an approach that seeks to understand and model the processes that give rise to patterns on Earth's surface.

For all scholars, however, the discovery of central place theory is an illustration of the power of spatial thinking in geography. This analysis draws heavily on an autobiographical essay written in 1955 (translated and reprinted in Christaller, 1972): "How I Discovered the Theory of Central Places: A Report About the Origin of Central Places."

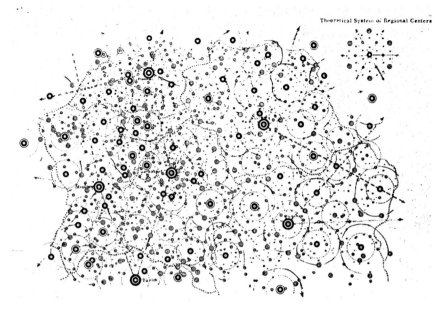

FIGURE 3.31 Diagram of central places in southern Germany. SOURCE: Baskin, 1957.

3.8.2 The Roots of Walter Christaller's Work

Three sets of formative influences shaped Christaller's work: those derived from his childhood, from his career, and from the intellectual context in which he worked.

One of the formative influences in his childhood was the gift of an atlas from an aunt, a gift suggested by Christaller's mother: "My aunt was quite disappointed that she 'just' sent a 'useful' gift, and not something to play with, which would really make one happy" (Christaller, 1972, p. 601).

Reflecting a view that would be echoed by many geographers, Christaller saw the atlas in a different light: "The atlas then became a plaything, not only something to look at and study. I drew in new railroad lines, put a new city somewhere or other, or changed the borders of nations, straightening them out or delineating them along mountain ranges" (Christaller, 1972, p. 601).

The world is not a given to be captured and frozen, as is, on the map: a world is but one possible world to be depicted, as we choose to imagine it, on a map. To a geographer, human patterns are contingent possibilities, not necessities entailed and determined by environmental constraints. Christaller was visualizing and drawing hypothetical worlds, albeit worlds that had to conform to some geographical rationale. There is a logic to placing borders along the mountain ranges that separate groups of people or to dividing human systems on the basis of physical systems, in this case watersheds. The playfulness of this activity is crucial: the map was the inspiration for possible worlds.

Another childhood formative influence is what Christaller (1972, pp. 601–602) called "statistics":

> I designed new administrative divisions and calculated their populations—because I also had a passion for statistics. When I found a statistical handbook advertised for about two marks, I pleaded with my father to buy it for me. He, who was only interested in literature, tried to dissuade me. From disappointment, I broke into tears, and then, nevertheless, was given the statistical handbook.

We would refer to statistics as data, although the calculation of the population of administrative divisions is close to a modern approach to statistical analysis. We can also see this as a passion for collecting and using geospatial data.

The third childhood formative influence that Christaller (1972, p. 602) reports is the deliberate fostering of an inquiring mind as a result of active field work:

> In school in Darmstadt I had an excellent geography teacher. Often we went with him through the woods and fields; suddenly he stood still and asked: What do you see here? We discovered, more or less, that the beech tree branches on one side were green with lichens, and not on the other side. And we found the explanation: on the moist windward side the lichens can grow, but on the dry lee side they cannot. Our geography teacher Völsing taught us to observe and look for causes.

The young Christaller exemplifies the development of a spatial thinker: he was fascinated by maps and data and patterns, emboldened to imagine and depict alternative worlds, grounded in the description and explanation of actual worlds, and prompted to ask questions about existing patterns and relationships.

His career shows both the power of these childhood formative influences and the effects of persistence, constraint, and opportunity. He began to study the idea of national economy at university, but those studies were interrupted by World War I. Even here, the passions of his childhood came through strongly:

> When I was wounded in the First World War at Stralsand and put in a military hospital, and my mother asked me what I would like sent to me, I wrote: a Perth Pocket Atlas. In my bed I completely painted this atlas, and I always took it with me, when I was cured and returned to the front. (Christaller, 1972, p. 602)

World War I was followed by marriage, a family, and the need to earn money. This led to a career in city planning, particularly in Berlin, work whose connection with spatial thinking is clear. The third set of formative influences come from the intellectual context in which Christaller worked. In 1930, he returned to university at Erlangen, working on a doctorate in economics: "Due to personal interest, I . . . went to lectures of Robert Gradmann. My old love for geography awoke in all its force and drew me, as . . . almost a forty-year-old man, completely under its power" (Christaller, 1972, p. 602).

Christaller includes an extended passage from a seminar paper that he wrote for Gradmann, commenting on two articles. In this passage, we can see some of the intellectual roots of his thinking, views that shaped his dissertation research. Christaller wrote about the nature of spaces (abstract and concrete); about the search for "laws, causalities, and functional relations"; about location theory; and about the evolution of spatial patterns—all of which underpinned his discovery of central place theory.

3.8.3 The Discovery of Central Place Theory

Christaller was determined to solve an age-old problem in human geography: how to explain the fundamental properties (size, number, and location) of settlements. Prior accounts had approached explanations in terms of geographic necessity: a city "had" to be here, not there, because of something particular about the site. It could be on a promontory near a river or at the intersection of several transportation routes. Such explanations failed because there were often comparable sites at which cities had not developed, and the transportation route explanation failed on grounds of cause and effect. Which came first? Which accounted for which? Historical studies of the formation, growth, and demise of particular cities were rich, fascinating accounts that described what happened in a particular place, but even if such accounts were obtained for all cities, it was not clear that any general rules would emerge. Statistical accounts could describe patterns and develop classifications, but not necessarily generate the rules or laws that Christaller sought.

Christaller brought these three streams of scholarship—necessity, history, and statistics—to bear on the problem of settlements. On the one hand, he was a theoretician, interested in explanations drawn from the intersections of geography, history, economics, and statistics and from the generalities of space. In so doing, he described himself as an "outsider" to all of these disciplines. On the other hand, he was an empiricist, drawn to the details of maps and regional landscapes, to the particularities of places (in this case, southern Germany in the 1930s).

What distinguished his particular approach was the interplay between theory and observation, driven by a remarkable capacity for spatial thinking. In his work, we can see a variety of complementary approaches: space as in graphics, space as in the description and analysis of patterns, space as in a structure for a model, and space as in algebraic relations in the form of hierarchies.

The observational component drew on the formative influences of his childhood. As he reports:

> I continued my games with maps: I connected cities of equal size by straight lines, first of all, in order to determine if certain rules were recognizable in the railroad and road network, whether regular traffic networks existed, and, second of all, in order to measure the distances between cities of equal size. (Christaller, 1972, p. 607)

Maps again become tools for experimentation, the basis of a search for regularity, pattern, and rules. In this stage, Christaller was successful, identifying latticework patterns of spatial relationships that have become iconic and, to some geographers, beautiful: "Thereby, the map became filled with triangles, often equilateral triangles (the distances of cities of equal size from each other were thus approximately equal), which then crystallized as six-sided figures (hexagons)" (Christaller, 1972, p. 607).

He also identified a previously known spatial relationship whereby small towns were ". . . very frequently and very precisely 21 kilometers apart from each other." The accepted explanation was based on a day's travel by cart, the small towns serving as stopover points for travel between major cities. Understanding the reasons for the geometric pattern and this spacing regularity was the result of his theorizing, a step that took only nine months (see Figure 3.32).

The key to this step was an imaginative leap out of the real space of southern Germany into an abstract economic model of space: "a symmetrical plain, without obstructions such as rivers or mountain ranges, with a uniformly distributed population, in order to then determine where, under such conditions, the site of a central city or market would form" (Christaller, 1972, p. 608).

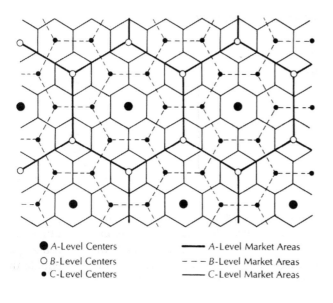

● A-Level Centers   —— A-Level Market Areas
O B-Level Centers   – – – B-Level Market Areas
• C-Level Centers   —— C-Level Market Areas

FIGURE 3.32 Diagram of a classic central place system (market areas: a $K = 3$ hierarchy). SOURCE: de Souza, 1990, p. 258.

Christaller understood the power of this model of an economic landscape (now referred to as an isotropic plane):

> This model is "correct" in itself, even if it is never to be found in the reality of settlement landscape in pure form: mountain ranges, variable ground; but also variable density of population, variable income ratios and sociological structure of the population, historical developments and political realities bring about deviations from the pure model. (Christaller, 1972, p. 608)

In effect, the model allows Christaller to separate the signal (pattern) from the noise (deviations) and, at the same time, to offer explanations for both signal and noise. He also recognized the link between space and time, pattern and change:

> I thus did not satisfy myself with setting up a model for an invariable and constant economic landscape (thus, for a static condition)—but instead I also tried to show how the number, size and distribution of the central places change, when the economic factors change. . . . (Christaller, 1972, p. 608)

The explanations were built on the concept of a central place. Christaller saw settlements of all sizes as serving functions (commercial, governmental, educational, recreational, medical, etc.) for themselves and for a surrounding population. To use this conceptual building block, Christaller had to find a way of measuring the quality of centrality, and to do so, he used the number of telephone connections as an indicator, scaled to the population size of the place. Here we can see echoes of his childhood preoccupation with "statistics."

According to Christaller (1972, p. 609), given this connection indicator: "I was able to assign all central places in South Germany value indication numbers from 1 to 2825 (Munich)." After arraying the values into size classes: "I was able to mark in the central places in South Germany, according to their significance as central places, on a map, to measure the distances among them, and to determine their rank in the hierarchy of their 'complementary areas' which belonged to them (i.e., of their surrounding territory)."

At this point, the mapped patterns and the theoretical patterns intersect in a brilliant exercise in spatial thinking. Settlements are scaled by size—and therefore distance—classes, and these classes are organized into a hierarchy that captures size, number, spacing, and spatial arrangements. Different types of hierarchy arranged settlements on the basis of different logics of grouping and dependency: K-3 for efficiency or markets, K-4 for optimal traffic flows, and K-7 for efficiency of administration:

> . . . the lowest ranked central places have a surrounding territory with a radius of 4–5 kilometers, and an average population of 3,000 (in the central place and surrounding territory) and their distances from the nearest central places, which according to the model lie within hexagonal (six-sided) connections, amount to seven kilometers. Within the completely regular hexagonal system of central places, the distances of all higher ranked central places can be derived, inasmuch as one multiplies the distance of the next lowest ranking central place by $\sqrt{3}$; the sequence of distances is thus: 7–12–21–36–62–108–185 . . . km. (Christaller, 1972, p. 609)

Christaller had explained the size, number, and distribution of settlements in one theoretical structure that has both an economic and a geographic rationale to it. It has both an algebraic and a geometrical interpretation. It is both static and dynamic. It is both abstract and concrete: "Thus, I was able to find surprising concurrences between geographical reality and the abstract schema of the central places (the theoretical model) especially in the predominantly agrarian areas of North and South Bavaria" (Christaller, 1972, p. 609).

The process of development of this intellectual structure also showed echoes of Christaller's youth:

> On Sundays, or also Saturday and Sunday, I used to hike around in the beautiful landscapes of

the Frankish Alps. While hiking, I mentally developed the progress of my work. . . . Thus, many an idea which helped me progress . . . gave me the happiness of a discoverer; it was connected in my memory to some forest path or other, just where I was, where the sun cast its light patches through the foliage onto the earth. . . . (Christaller, 1972, p. 609)

Christaller's thinking was grounded in space, it was about space, and it was captured in spatial diagrams.

3.8.4 Walter Christaller as a Spatial Thinker

To many geographers in the decades between the 1950s and 1970s, Christaller's work was an inspiration, a model to be applied literally and to be followed metaphorically. It was one of the cornerstones of the spatial analysis approach to geography. It was tested in many places, adapted, and rejected by some. It served as a planning tool in many parts of the world. For later generations of geographers, it became an emblem.

Whatever one's judgment of the theory, the discovery itself was an extended exercise that shows the power and process of spatial thinking:

> If I may very briefly once again describe my methodology: first of all play, paint on the maps, draw in lines and points, but in a very playful fashion—then problems suddenly emerge. Then I tried, while hiking, to elucidate them, to solve them, while hiking the thoughts are shaken back into their proper places. And, last of all, comes the completion and formulation. Thereby, the language should be of a sort that chimes, that is audible, and not just something for reading. In general, the opinion predominates that creative scholarly work is born at the desk. It must not be so. Mine was created while hiking, in nature. I, moreover, am glad to consider myself a geographer. (Christaller, 1972, p. 610)

As William Bunge (1966, p. 133) wrote: "With the possible exception of cartography, this author is of the opinion that the initial and growing beauty of central place theory is geography's finest intellectual product and puts Christaller in a place of great honor."

3.9 CONCLUSION

As the examples in this chapter illustrate, there are different levels of performance in spatial thinking as a function of age and experience, and there are different modes of performance in spatial thinking in different contexts. Marie Tharp and Walter Christaller exemplify the power of spatial thinking in the process of scientific discovery. Some geoscience students never seem to master the relations between dip and strike in rock formations. An air traffic controller may not be any more effective at assembling a child's toy than an artist. A child who has learned to tie a shoelace may not yet be able to tie a necktie. For some of these activities, years of formal training are required. For others, learning is informal and unstructured.

There are three messages about the role of spatial thinking in everyday life, at work, and in science. The first is the pervasiveness, power, and flexibility of the process of spatial thinking: successful problem solving in many contexts depends to a significant degree upon spatial thinking. The second is the extent to which there are significant variations in how and how well the process is executed: there is no single "best" way of thinking spatially. The third is the importance of meeting the challenge of formal training in spatial thinking: workplace-relevant skills require considerable investment of individual and societal resources. Although some learning occurs informally, much depends upon the formal education system. Chapter 4 considers the teaching and learning of spatial thinking skills: How do people acquire the spatial knowledge, spatial ways of thinking and acting, and spatial capabilities that are increasingly important in an information technology-driven society and economy?

4

Teaching and Learning About Spatial Thinking

4.1 INTRODUCTION

Spatial thinking is powerful and pervasive, underpinning everyday life, work, and science (Chapter 3). It plays a role in activities ranging from understanding metaphors, becoming good at wayfinding, and interpreting works of art, to engaging in molecular modeling, generating geometry proofs, and interpreting astronomical data. Spatial thinking comes in many guises (Chapter 2). It can rely on any of the senses; it can take place entirely in the mind or it can be supported by tools that are simple—a pencil and paper—or complex—a GIS program (Chapters 7 and 8). Spatial thinking can be a basis for sophisticated expertise—as in the calculations of a world-class orienteer—or for everyday judgments—as in the rough-and-ready estimates of the amount of paint needed to cover the walls of a room.

Although everyone can and does think spatially, people do so in different ways and with varying degrees of confidence and success in different situations. Some people are good at spatial reasoning, and others struggle; the results of giving travel directions exemplify the difference in levels of success. In giving directions, strategies vary: directions can be given as turns, as landmarks, or as a sketch map. Some people are good at spatial thinking only in a limited domain of knowledge and literally cannot find their way out of the proverbial paper bag, whereas others seem able to tackle a wide range of spatial problems (see, for example, discussions of spatial agnosia and spatial amnesia; Amorim, 1999).

In this chapter, the committee explores the nature of and explanations for differences in the process of spatial thinking and discusses ways to incorporate spatial thinking into the K–12 curriculum. How can we account for differences in the ability to think spatially? What does it mean to be good at spatial thinking? How can one learn to become a better spatial thinker? Answers to these questions are crucial to the challenge of teaching and supporting spatial thinking in American schools. If, for example, the capacity to think spatially is innate and immutable, then presumably educational programs would be of no value. If, on the other hand, one can learn to think spatially, then what types of learning experiences are helpful? Are they helpful to everybody in the same way in the same context, or should different people be helped in different ways in different contexts?

Section 4.2 asks: What do we mean by being good at spatial thinking? Experts think more deeply and remember in more detail within their domain of expertise, but not necessarily outside of that domain. Given the domain specificity of expertise, what does it mean to achieve expertise in spatial thinking? Section 4.2 describes the processes involved in generating spatial representations and explains ways in which those processes can facilitate and limit thinking. Our conclusions are that similar processes underpin some aspects of spatial thinking in all domains, whether thinking about tectonic plates, troop movements in the Civil War, or weather. Of equal importance, we believe that practicing spatial thinking pays off. Some features of practice and expertise at spatial thinking in one domain do transfer to other domains (for example, knowing what it takes to construct a spatial representation). Yet many features do not transfer and, therefore, spatial thinking needs to be practiced in specific contexts where it is appropriate.

Section 4.3 turns to the development of expertise in spatial thinking, showing how expertise is a function of time and how it involves the use of spatial representations. Given an objective of infusing and integrating diverse spatial thinking activities throughout the K–12 curriculum, Section 4.4 addresses the question: To what extent is learning to think spatially transferable from one context or from one domain to another? Section 4.5 presents a position statement on fostering expertise in spatial thinking. Section 4.6 presents the committee's conclusions regarding the teaching and learning of spatial thinking and derives two educational principles that should inform the development of curricula to foster spatial literacy.

4.2 EXPERTISE DIFFERENCES IN SPATIAL THINKING: THE EFFECTS OF EXPERIENCE

4.2.1 The Nature of Expertise

In everyday life and in cognitive science, we equate superior performance in a domain of activity—sport or classical music or nuclear physics—with expertise. Experts in an intellectual knowledge domain think fluently and deeply within their domain of expertise (as in the case of Marie Tharp with respect to marine geosciences and Walter Christaller with respect to human geography [Chapter 3]), but experts do not necessarily think with comparable fluency or depth outside of those domains. Expertise is not an automatic result of high intelligence. Instead experts have acquired extensive understanding of the spatial knowledge, spatial ways of thinking and acting, and spatial capabilities within their domains. The knowledge and skills shape what they attend to and notice, how they organize new information, and how they solve problems.

Fluent and deep expert thinking occurs in every knowledge domain, and reasoning with spatial representations often serves as a central feature of expertise in a range of areas: electronic circuit design (Biswas et al., 1995; Cheng, 2002), reading X-rays (Manning and Leach, 2002), air traffic control (Ackerman and Cianciolo, 2002), architecture (Salthouse et al., 1990), video gaming (Greenfield et al., 1994; Sims and Mayer, 2002), and driving a taxi (Maguire et al., 1997).

Experts often acknowledge the role of spatial representations and imagery. Shepard (1988) compiled autobiographical accounts from notable figures in the sciences, arts, and literature in which these experts attributed the emergence of their original ideas at least in part to the use of spatial imagery. For example, Einstein described developing the concept of special relativity in part through thought experiments in which he imagined the properties of space and time while he was traveling at different speeds. Kekulé described developing the molecular model of the structure of benzene in part as a consequence of dreaming about a snake coiled in a circle, biting its own tail.

We do not know the extent to which experts are correct in believing that their scientific discoveries emerged from using spatial representations of actual or hypothetical events: the images may have simply allowed them to describe and explain their discoveries, which may have emerged without using spatial representations. Expert and nonexpert learners, however, often use spatial models strategically to help remember and understand when reading new information (Cariglia-Bull and Pressley, 1990) and when using diagrams to understand technical texts (Hegarty and Just, 1993; Simon, 2001).

4.2.2 Domain-Specific Expertise: The Case of Chess

Chess has been a major task in cognitive analyses of expertise. de Groot (1978) conducted pioneering studies comparing the chess playing of grand masters with that of lesser ranked but highly competitive players. He wanted to identify the cognitive skills and strategies that enabled grand masters to outscore their opponents. His hypothesis was that masters would show greater breadth of search (by thinking through a greater number of possible moves) and greater depth of search (by thinking through more "if I do this, and my opponent does that ..." possibilities). To test this hypothesis, he asked masters and non-masters to think aloud while they selected moves. Neither masters nor skilled opponents thought exhaustively through all possibilities, though both groups did show impressive breadth and depth of searches. Yet somehow, masters selected "better" moves than did their opponents.

Chase and Simon (1973) hypothesized that the difference between masters and non-masters involved spatial pattern learning; masters "see" the arrangements of chess pieces in larger and more meaningful chunks and are faster at recognizing different board patterns. As a test of this hypothesis, they created configurations of pieces on schematic chessboards, and asked masters and non-masters to study the configurations in order to identify them in a later recognition test. Some patterns were realistic and fitted the rules of chess, whereas others were determined by randomly assigning identical sets of pieces to positions on the board. Masters and non-masters showed similar levels of memory for randomly determined boards, whereas masters significantly outperformed non-masters in remembering meaningful patterns. Expertise in chess helps players recognize meaningful spatial patterns and remember them easily and well. Highly skilled players excel at thinking through moves, reflecting their deep and easily accessed knowledge of the spatial patterns of games. Differences between players reflect depth of knowledge of spatial patterns in the domain of chess.

Expertise in chess (like expertise in the sciences, mathematics, humanities, and arts) is, therefore, specific to a domain. Experts generally are not more intelligent, nor do they think more deeply (Ericsson and Charness, 1994). The fluent reasoning and problem solving that characterize expertise result from the build-up of a store of domain-specific knowledge (Bransford et al., 1999).

Given this position about expertise in general, what does it mean to have expertise in spatial thinking? In what ways might expertise in spatial thinking be domain specific and in what ways might it cut across all domains where spatial thinking is useful? Because spatial imagery, a form of human memory, is the realm of spatial thinking best understood by cognitive psychologists, we begin by discussing spatial imagery and memory.

4.2.3 The Role of Memory in Expertise

People remember and think about spatial information in many forms. Perceptual images, for example, preserve many of the features of the original input modality, such that imagining visual experiences results in activation of the visual cortex, or auditory experiences of the auditory cortex, and so forth (Barsalou et al., 2003). Experts and novices use perceptually rich images to help them think about the kinematics and dynamics of physical systems such as springs (Clement, 2003) and interlocking gears (Schwartz and Black, 1996). Spatial thinking that taps perceptual images is embodied in the sense that images of a thinker's physical actions, such as physically pulling a spring or turning a gear wheel, make it easier to imagine the resulting spring forces and gear movements.

People are versatile in their ability to generate and use images. They can call to mind the physical appearance of static objects or dynamic events they have directly experienced through vision, audition, and touch (Kosslyn and Koenig, 1992). They can generate spatial images from nonspatial forms of input such as reading text (Franklin and Tversky, 1990), listening to conversation, or ideas they have imagined on their own (Finke, 1989). Although imagery often results from visual input and is often described in visual terms, spatial images are *not* necessarily visual; they are accessible to persons who lack life experience seeing (de-Beni and Cornoldi, 1988; Cornoldi and Vecchi, 2003; Farah, 1989). Children younger than about 7 years of age do not tend to use imagery strategically to help them learn new information, but even pre-school age children can generate and process images based on perceptual input. Kosslyn et al. (1990) showed that children in kindergarten can look at a visual stimulus and then generate an image of it later in order to make decisions about what they saw. Ray and Rieser (2003) showed that children 3–4 years of age can listen to short stories and generate spatial representations of the story in order to judge the relative locations of objects described in the story.

Psychologists distinguish memory in terms of its structures and the types of knowledge that are represented. A classic model of memory (Baddeley, 1986) includes three major structural types: sensory storage, short-term or working memory, and long-term memory (although a unitary view of memory is a viable alternative; see Cowan, 1997). Memory is highly selective, and much of what is perceived is forgotten or reconstructed as a result of organizing schema (for a classic treatment of this issue, see Bartlett, 1932).

Three features of the memory system can help us to understand how and why spatial thinking does and does not work: the automaticity of overlearning, the use of strategies to reduce memory demands, and the capacity of multiple working memory subsystems to operate in parallel.

The first feature is that calling to mind overlearned materials is more automatic than recalling less familiar materials, thus placing a smaller demand on working memory. The idea of automaticity might explain why attempts to use spatial aids such as maps or graphics to understand historical events sometimes interferes with learning instead of facilitating it. If the content *and* form of the map or graph are relatively unfamiliar, then too much working memory capacity is required to process both the unfamiliar form and the intended content of the representation.

A second feature is the skillful use of strategies to reduce demands on long-term memory. For example, chunking numbers by combining them into larger units, each of which is meaningful, is an effective memory strategy. It is easier to remember a list of numbers in this form [526 924 018 682] rather than this form [526924018682]. Even more effective is a way to chunk information so that it relates to things (or meaningful chunks) one already knows well. It is more difficult, therefore, to remember this list of arbitrarily defined chunks [219 171 918 194 119 45] than this list of meaningful chunks [the start and end years of the United States participation in the two World Wars are 1917–1918 and 1941–1945].

Most of the research on the use of memory strategies is aimed at understanding memory for verbal materials. We need to find out about analogous memory strategies for spatial information— what are efficient ways to "chunk" the information in graphics to make it easier to remember? What are efficient ways of chunking new graphics so they can be related to graphics that have already been learned?

Perceptual learning processes can lead to the rapid and accurate identification of the patterns that are central to expertise (Fahle and Poggio, 2000; Gibson, 1969; Gibson and Pick, 2000). Examples include pilots learning to judge air and ground speed (Haber, 1987); machinists and architects learning to "see" the three-dimensional shape of a solid object or house from top, side, and front views (Garling and Evans, 1991); radiologists learning to spot tumors on X-rays (Lesgold,

1988); and meteorologists learning to see patterns on satellite images (Lowe, 2001). Just as Chase and Simon indicated that chess masters rapidly distinguished meaningful chess configurations from random patterns, work on perceptual learning shows analogous results for a wide variety of materials. These range from increasing sensitivity to smaller and smaller gaps between simple lines with practice (Fahle et al., 1995), to comprehending variations in elevation when reading topographic maps (Pick et al., 1995), to discriminating relevant from irrelevant information in mathematics problems (Littlefield and Rieser, 1993; Schwartz and Bransford, 1998). These findings apply directly to the tools (e.g., models, graphics, maps) for learning about spatial patterns that are used in schools (Rieser, 2002).

The third feature of working memory is its structural differentiation. Working memory consists of multiple subsystems, some of which operate in parallel and do not interfere with others. So, for example, Brooks (1968) showed that effectiveness at solving a spatial problem is reduced more by a simultaneous spatial task than by a verbal task. Baddeley (1986) argued that there are three storage systems in working memory. One serves central executive functions such as reasoning and decision making. The other two store different types of information—the articulatory loop for verbal information and the visuospatial sketch-pad for spatial information. A broad range of research has built on these observations. Thus, for example, in the case of readers elaborating on their understanding of verbal information, spatial representations can be more helpful than additional verbal information because they result in less mutual interference.

4.2.4 The Processing of Spatial Information

Kosslyn (1978) distinguished four stages in the cognitive processing of spatial information:

1. generating a representation, either by recalling an object or event from long-term memory or by creating an image from words or ideas;
2. maintaining a representation in working memory in order to use it for reasoning or problem solving;
3. scanning a representation that is maintained in working memory, in order to focus attention on some of its parts; and
4. transforming a representation, for example, by rotating it to a new viewing perspective, shrinking it, or imagining its shape if it were transformed by being folded or compressed.

Each of these stages requires cognitive effort and uses some of the resources and capacity of working memory (Kosslyn et al., 1990). Shepard and his colleagues (Shepard and Metzler, 1971; Shepard and Cooper, 1986) pioneered studies of the relationship between spatial imagery and the cognitive effort involved in mental rotation. Shepard and Metzler (1971) showed adults representations of pairs of novel three-dimensional objects in various orientations (Figure 4.1). On a given trial, the two objects were either the same (sometimes they were oriented in the same direction and sometimes their orientations differed relative to each other) or they were different, representing mirror images of each other. Subjects were asked to say whether the two were the same or different and decision times were recorded. The results showed consistent patterns—response times for correctly judging two shapes as the same increased linearly with increasing angular differences in orientation. The response time increase applied to stimuli differing in orientation in the two-dimensional picture plane and stimuli differing in orientation in three-dimensional depth (that is, rotated through the picture plane).

Practice does make it easier to create and to transform spatial representations. Familiarity and practice imagining specific types of objects and events sharply improves the ease of cognitive processing of spatial representations. For example, Lohman and Nichols (1990) asked adults to

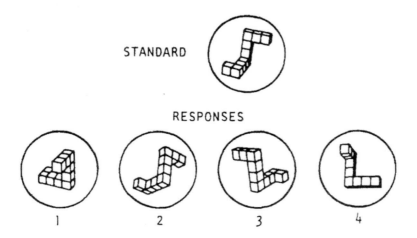

STANDARD

RESPONSES

1   2   3   4

FIGURE 4.1 A sample mental rotation task. SOURCE: Shepard and Metzler, 1971. Reprinted with permission from Mental Rotation of Three-Dimensional Objects, *Science* 171:701–703. Copyright 1971 American Association for the Advancement of Science.

perform about 1,000 mental rotation trials of the Shepard and Metzler type. Although some people completed the trials rapidly and accurately from the beginning, others were slow and labored in responding. Practice clearly helped, however; after more than 1,000 trials, every subject's speed increased, and the average speed of the whole group improved by two standard deviations. However, people find it more difficult to generate spatial representations and to mentally rotate representations of novel and complex objects than of familiar and simple objects.

The question of what is learned during practice is crucial in terms of transfer of learning from one context to another and in terms of designing educational programs. During intense practice in judging pairs of shapes as same or different, for example, one has the opportunity to learn what particular shapes look like in different orientations; thus, part of the learning is pattern learning. However, there are two other possibilities: practice might result in improvements in the speed of mentally rotating those particular shapes involved in the practice, or practice might result in an improvement in the skill of mentally rotating shapes in general. Insofar as practice results in improvement in a general mental rotation skill, then benefits of practice gained with one set of shapes should transfer and show up as benefits when people are asked to judge novel shapes. On the other hand, if practice results in building specific pattern knowledge of particular shapes from different orientations, then practice with one set of shapes should transfer only to highly similar shapes with little or no transfer to different shapes.

Laboratory research has resolved this issue for short periods of practice at mental rotation ranging up to several hours in duration. The benefit of extended practice results in pattern learning that contributes to gains in mental rotation speed (Bethell-Fox and Shepard, 1988; Lohman and Nichols, 1990; Tarr and Pinker, 1989). Some evidence indicates that practice increases the speed of mentally rotating those specific shapes involved in practice (Sims and Mayer, 2002). There is little or no evidence that mental rotation practice leads to a domain general skill because improvements do not transfer to novel shapes.

Studies are limited, however, in terms of the amount of practice and the variety of shapes practiced. As a consequence, we do not know the degree to which extended periods of practice and the degree to which practice with a larger set of shapes might result in improvement in either generalized mental rotation or other stages of image processing. Thus, for example, we do not know whether the expertise of an architect at visualizing buildings from different perspectives and in various configurations would transfer to skill at visualizing molecular structures or geological structures.

The research most relevant to this question focused on video game experts (Greenfield et al., 1994; Sims and Mayer, 2002). Sims and Mayer compared college students highly skilled at *Tetris* with those who were not so skilled. *Tetris* is a computer game in which success depends on rotating shapes so that later-appearing shapes interlock cleanly with earlier-appearing shapes. The game begins with a blank screen; one of seven shapes appears at the top of the screen and descends toward the bottom. During its descent the goal is to rotate and translate the shape, so that when it reaches the bottom of the screen it is in position to fit nicely with the shapes that follow in a continuous series. Speed is a critical factor; players have to anticipate how much to rotate shapes to fit them together.

Experts are rapid and accurate in deciding how much to rotate shapes to optimize fit. Sims and Mayer (2002) wanted to find out whether high levels of skill at mentally rotating *Tetris* shapes would transfer to rotating other shapes in the *Tetris* context. Results show a limited amount of *near transfer*: experts were better able than novices to play a *Tetris*-like game in rotating shapes that—although not identical to the shapes used in *Tetris*—were very similar to them. However, there was no evidence for *far transfer*. That is, experts did not show the same advantage in rotating shapes that were unlike those used in *Tetris* (even when those shapes were familiar from another context such as capital letters).

Based on laboratory studies, pattern learning and spatial transformations such as mental rotation are relatively domain specific. Learning to recognize and classify types of spatial patterns that characterize one field of expertise does not transfer when trying to learn other types of spatial patterns from another field. The benefits of practicing transformations of spatial patterns that characterize one field of study do not seem to transfer to other fields.

4.2.5 A Model of the Acquisition of Expertise in Spatial Thinking

A model of the acquisition of expertise in spatial thinking involves at least four components:

1. Domain-specific long-term memory of patterns: in order to learn to identify patterns in a knowledge domain more rapidly and accurately, one needs to study those particular shapes. There is little or no benefit from studying one set of shapes in perceiving another set of shapes.

2. However, perceptual learning of patterns goes hand in hand with the meta-cognitive knowledge that (a) patterns can be multiply classified and (b) studying patterns and practicing pattern identification makes those patterns come faster and more readily to mind when they are relevant to a task.

3. Domain-specific mental transformations of patterns in working memory: in order to learn to imagine how molecular structures will appear when rotated or expanded, one needs to practice mentally transforming those structures and highly similar ones. In order to learn to imagine the cross sections resulting from folds and structural events theorized within plate tectonics, one needs to practice those mental transformations for those types of patterns.

4. However, practice in mental transformation goes hand in hand with the meta-cognitive knowledge that such practice (a) pays off and (b) makes it easier to think and reason within that domain.

This position on the acquisition of expertise in spatial thinking has two possible sets of implications for the design of K–12 programs to foster spatial thinking. One approach builds on the first and third components of the expertise acquisition model. Expertise consists of domain-specific knowledge; therefore, this is also true for areas of expertise specifically involving spatial thinking to greater and lesser degrees. If you want to think fluently and well about particular types of patterns, you have to put in time studying those patterns. Practice at constructing spatial representations reduces the drain on working memory when constructing spatial representations of objects and situations like others in the domain of study, but practice at spatial representations in one domain transfers minimally to representations in other domains. Practice at mental spatial operations shows a similar degree of domain specificity. However, there is limited "near transfer," and practice discriminating or mentally rotating one set of shapes does benefit discriminating and mentally rotating highly similar shapes. Unfortunately, we do not know the metric that defines degrees of similarity.

The other approach builds on the second and fourth components of the expertise acquisition model and is based on the concept of "learning to learn." With expertise comes the ability to "know what it takes to learn." Students can learn that practice at spatial thinking really helps—it helps them to call spatial patterns to mind more rapidly and accurately, and it helps them to imagine transformations in those patterns more rapidly and accurately. They can also understand that the benefits of pattern learning are specific to the types of pattern learned and that the benefits of practicing mental transformation are specific to the types of patterns involved in the practice.

Expertise in spatial thinking is strongly linked to a particular knowledge domain. Through practice and experience, experts build the domain knowledge base and skills that allow them to think fluently and deeply. Central to expertise is pattern learning; skill in creating representations, especially spatial representations; and the ability to transform information. Although much of expertise is internal or cognitive, it also draws on external supports in the form of tools and representations (especially spatial representations).

Learners who have had more versus less experience in a domain, in using certain kinds of representations, or in reasoning about domain-specific problems approach new spatial learning tasks differently. Differences in domain-specific expertise are, however, not the only way of characterizing distinctions among learners. Appendix C addresses other ways in which differences among learners are relevant for spatial thinking. It discusses the notion of learner differences in general and then considers the links between three learner characteristics—chronological age, developmental level, and biological sex and cultural gender—and the process of spatial thinking.

4.2.6 The Role of Expertise in Spatial Thinking

As with all cognitive competencies, there are significant differences among people as to how, how quickly, and how well they can do something. Spatial thinking is no exception. Within domains of knowledge, there are experts and novices (see Section 3.6). Differences between experts and novices can be accounted for by training and experience (see Section 5.6). Across domains of knowledge, there are disciplines, such as geoscience, within which spatial thinking is emphasized and taught, and those, such as philosophy, within which it plays a hidden and relatively minor role. Across groups, there are also significant variations in how people approach spatial thinking. Across age, for example, children and adults do not think spatially in the same way. These differences can be accounted for by maturation, education, and experience (see Appendix C).

If, for the moment, we ignore the effects of domain, we can use the expert-novice distinction to understand some of the major differences in the ways in which people think spatially. A key goal, especially in science, is to learn to extract functional information from spatial structures and to understand how and why something works. In learning to do this, we must master three component tasks of spatial thinking.

The first step is *extracting spatial structures*. This process of pattern description involves identifying relations between the components of a spatial representation and understanding them in terms of the parts and wholes that give rise to patterns and coherent wholes. The second step is *performing spatial transformations*. Translations in space or scale transformations (changes in viewing distance) are easier than rotations or changes of perspective (changes in viewing angle or azimuth). Imagining the motions of different parts in relation to each other—running the object—can be very difficult. The third step, *drawing functional inferences*, is central to the process of scientific thinking. It requires establishing temporal sequences and cause-and-effect relations.

The difficulty of each of these steps increases with increasing *dimensionality*: spatial structures in two-space are easier to understand than those in three-space. In scientific applications, difficulty also increases as a *function of data quality and quantity*. Missing data require extrapolation and interpolation. Data error leads to uncertainty and increasing difficulty. Partial and incomplete data require an even more skilled use of extrapolation and interpolation, as well as more complex inference processes.

People use representations, whether in the mind or external, to comprehend and remember a set of concepts as well as to make inferences and discoveries about those concepts. Understanding the spatial relations and structure of a diagrammed system is relatively straightforward for most learners, because a diagram shows the parts in their spatial relations, using diagrammatic space to map real space. Most people can grasp the essential parts and their spatial relations from a diagram, such as a bicycle pump or a heart. What is much harder to understand is the meaning, interpretation, function, and causal chain that the diagram is meant to convey. While a novice can understand the spatial structure of a bicycle pump or heart from a diagram, only those with some expertise can grasp the functional and causal relations among the parts—that is, understand how the pump or the heart works (Heiser and Tversky, 2002).

For most scientific and engineering contexts, diagrams are meant to convey not just the structure of a system but also its behavior or the causal chain of its parts or the function of its operations. Yet, these are exactly the aspects of diagrams that students of all ages find difficult. Diagrams show structure, but they do not "show" function or behavior or causal relations. Language can compensate by stating this information directly. However, diagrams can also be enriched with extrapictorial devices, notably lines, arrows, boxes, and brackets, to convey abstract information. For example, when asked to describe a diagram of a bicycle pump, students describe the structural relations among the parts. When arrows are added to the diagram that denote the sequence of actions of the pump, students describe the causal, functional actions of the pump (Heiser and Tversky, 2002). Still, even the addition of arrows may not be sufficient to convey the functional information. For understanding bicycle pumps and car brakes, diagrams were sufficient for undergraduates with high mechanical ability but not for those of low ability; for those of low mechanical ability, language compensated (Heiser and Tversky, 2002).

In many educational settings, diagrams are taken for granted. These studies suggest that teaching how to reason from diagrams could reap significant benefits. Such teaching would be needed in a number of domains: geography, arithmetic and mathematics, biology, geology, chemistry, physics, engineering, and so forth. Diagrams are common in history and in the humanities as well. Across the curriculum, students need exercises in interpreting the spatial entities and spatial relations of diagrams, making inferences as well as making discoveries. Constructing diagrams is an integral part of this instruction, especially in groups. Junior high school dyads working together produced diagrams of, for example, plant ecology, that were more abstract and contained less irrelevant pictorial information than those produced by individuals.

4.3 THE CHALLENGE OF DEVELOPING EXPERTISE IN SPATIAL THINKING

Scientific phenomena that have physical representations in space, such as DNA replication, weather patterns, ocean floor spreading, and trajectories of airplanes, lend themselves immediately to spatial thinking. However, the physical manifestation of explanatory scientific concepts such as entropy, heat flow, and fusion is often hidden from direct inspection. Relevant phenomena can be microscopic or obscured by other information as in the case of molecules, folds of Earth, plate movement, and chemical reactions.

Expertise in science takes time and practice to develop. The challenge for educators is to provide the instructional time, the appropriately designed materials and activities (especially representations), and the supportive environment that will allow students to build expertise in particular school subjects and, at the same time, develop expertise in spatial thinking. Therefore, to learn about complex systems in science, students need three things: (1) knowledge of a wide range of scientific concepts, (2) skills in generating and interpreting spatial representations of information, and (3) opportunities to practice spatial thinking skills in challenging but well-supported projects.

Concepts and representations make sense to experts because they have had numerous opportunities to use them over extended periods. Considerable instructional time is required for those concepts and representations to become useful to students. Given the scarcity of such time, however, students frequently end up as perennial novices, always facing a new set of topics and a new assortment of representations that they are expected to connect and employ in dealing with another set of challenging questions.

4.3.1 Developing Expertise Through the Acquisition of Knowledge

Chapter 3 presents examples of experts in geoscience, geography, and astronomy using spatial thinking in the process of scientific discovery and explanation. To achieve insights, experts link varied data sources, use their knowledge of processes such as volcanism or evolution, and incorporate their understanding of principles such as thermal equilibrium or biodiversity. Successful researchers reorganize, combine, prioritize, compare, question, and discuss their ideas over extended periods. Experts develop proficiency in their fields over years and often find the methods they use to assess complex displays of data difficult to explain and, therefore, teach to others. Skilled programmers, for example, can inspect a 300-line program and rapidly identify bugs, whereas novices can look at the same 300 lines essentially forever without finding the problem (Soloway and Spohrer, 1989).

Experts specialize in particular aspects of their field. They need time and experience not only to understand the representations used in new aspects of the field, but also to learn the domain-specific principles and ideas to interpret and critique this information. Experts reformulate representations of complex information such as plate movements or crystal configurations and engage in discipline-specific disputes about appropriate ways to reduce data to formats that are maximally open to inspection (cf. work on the human genome, molecular pathways, and electron microscope materials). Each year *Science* magazine recognizes researchers who create visualizations that are acclaimed by their peers (Bradford et al., 2003). To those outside a particular scientific domain, however, the representations can perplex and confuse as much as inform. Some representations, such as patterns of earthquakes superimposed on the outlines of continents, communicate information that would be difficult to capture in words, whereas others, such as the methods for representing the structure of crystals, can confuse even experts (Chapter 3) as well as nonexperts. Even ingenious representations, such as modern algebraic systems, have sometimes thwarted as well as hastened scientific discovery (e.g., diSessa, 2000).

Experts in one application of spatial thinking, such as architecture, may not find those skills useful in another application of spatial thinking, such as interpreting weather maps, because the representations and their underlying scientific principles are different. Clement (1998), for example, asked expert mathematicians to interpret visual displays of the behavior of springs varying in diameter and flexibility. The mathematicians behaved similarly to students encountering the material about springs for the first time (Clement, 1998). Lewis and Linn (1994) reported similar results when they asked expert chemists and physicists to explain everyday phenomena that exemplify principles that they understand well. One expert, for example, preferred aluminum foil over wool as an insulator because it is a common practice to wrap cold drinks in aluminum. Expertise is, therefore, domain specific. Expertise takes significant time to develop in depth.

4.3.2 Developing Expertise Through the Understanding of Representations

Educators often devise new representations to help novices. Tests of these representations in contexts as diverse as weather maps (Edelson et al., 1999), molecular models (Linn and Hsi, 2000; Wiser and Carey, 1983), and the rock cycle (Kali et al., 2003) have proven humbling. Students cannot readily interpret diagrams and representations (Hegarty et al., 1999), and when they attempt to use them, they often become more, rather than less confused. Students have interpreted representations of heat that use color intensity as implying that heat has mass, for example. Most commonly colored weather maps show only the predicted weather on land rather than showing the weather patterns as extending over the oceans. The maps also show weather only over the United States rather than extending into both Canada and Mexico. Such representations can deter students from thinking about the weather as large-scale, complex systems influenced by differential surface temperatures over land and water (Edelson et al., 1999).

4.3.3 Developing Expertise Through Challenging Projects

Interpretations of the superficial features of spatial information can persuade students that scientific phenomena follow different principles from those endorsed by experts. For example, novice observers of geological features such as rock outcrops, streams, or basins may impute formation processes that consider only surface features (Liben et al., 2002). Novice observers of patterns—the flight of flocks of birds or the flow of traffic—impute more causality to individuals and their actions than is justified (Resnick, 1994). Observers typically believe, for example, that a lead bird has special status, or that all traffic jams are caused by accidents, rather than recognizing the systemic nature of emergent phenomena (Resnick, 1994). Understanding can be improved by instructional programs that enable students to build models of these phenomena by embedding "instructions" in individual birds or cars and then observing the emergence of patterns.

Students pay attention to perceptual information that is salient but not necessarily relevant (Hegarty, 1992; Lowe, 2003; Morrison et al., 2002). To overcome distracting perceptual cues—when they are inevitable—students need supports including ways to structure information and opportunities to reflect in order to make connections among ideas (Reiser et al., 2001; Davis, 2003a,b; Linn and Hsi, 2000). Curriculum designers have identified ways to direct attention to important information using everything from overlays to simplified versions of the materials to translating the information into less complex representations.

To enable students to develop expertise in spatial thinking, it makes sense to engage them in extended projects that are challenging. In science, however, most students flounder when asked to undertake complex, multistage projects where they must manage and sequence multiple tasks: design methods for collecting data; devise representations for information; and combine principles, experimental results, and representations of results (Edelson, 1999; Feldman et al., 2000; Reiser et al., 2001). In addition to basic knowledge about and practice in spatial thinking, students need guidance and support in working through first projects, and appropriate guidance can have significant impacts on student learning. In helping students to research Galapagos finches, Reiser and Tabak (http://www.letus.org/bguile/finches/finch_overview.html) created data tables to represent results, and the tables helped students to reach more compelling conclusions. In studying how students interpret weather maps, Edelson (1999) found that the map colors did not convey information effectively without substantial support. This support included simplification of the displays, presenting outlines of continents, and designing activities to communicate interactions between land and sea and the impact of such interactions on wind, temperature, and the day-night cycle. Hoadley (2004), in collaboration with Cuthbert et al. (2002), asked students to design a desert house that was cool during the day and warm at night. Many students failed to connect the day-night cycle to their designs and/or combined design elements without considering how they interacted.

Students are slow to learn how to monitor their own progress, frequently misjudging their abilities and progress. They cannot easily make links between representations and observed phenomena. For example, in the *GenScope* project, students used software to explore topics in genetics illustrated by a fictitious dragon species. Students were expected to transfer understanding from the dragon software to the case of worms studied using paper and pencil materials. The first study, however, failed to demonstrate any significant impact from the software use (Lobato, 2003). In a replication, the researchers added a "Dragon Investigations" module based on paper-and-pencil activities. It encouraged students to reflect on parallels between dragons and worms, and to monitor their performance. This approach was more successful.

Students need support—scaffolding and guidance—to allow them to bring their fragmented knowledge to bear on a compelling problem. Central to the support process is the use of static or animated representations, although studies have revealed a series of barriers to understanding such representations.

4.4 THE TRANSFER OF SPATIAL THINKING ACROSS SUBJECTS IN THE CURRICULUM

Central to all of these instructional design efforts to meet the many challenges of fostering spatial literacy is a basic question: To what extent is student learning of spatial knowledge, spatial ways of thinking and acting, and spatial capabilities *specific* to a particular domain of knowledge? If, for example, the learning of spatial thinking is inherently domain specific, then the instructional challenge is different than it would be if learning in one domain readily transfers to and supports learning in another—and very different—domain. We turn next to this fundamental question of transfer. Can well-learned spatial thinking skills transfer to reasoning about and solving new problems in a different area?

De Corte (2003, p. 142) has noted that "the concept [of transfer] has been very controversial, conceptually as well as empirically." That learning frequently does not transfer to situations in which it is relevant is a puzzle to researchers and a concern for educators. Knowledge and skills that have been well learned, as indexed by performance at the end of instruction, often fail to transfer to new times and contexts in which they would be helpful. Box 4.1, based on De Corte's work, contrasts a traditional view of transfer with a modern reconceptualization.

Before we discuss the roles that spatial imagery and spatial representations may play in fostering transfer of spatial thinking, we must distinguish between the ideas of "near" and "far" transfer. The former refers to the transfer of what has been learned to tasks and settings that resemble the original learning situations perceptually and in terms of their obvious themes. Far transfer refers to situations in which what has been learned is successfully applied to situations where there is less perceptual similarity (see the discussion of *Tetris*, in Section 4.2.4).

BOX 4.1
Reconceptualizations of the Concept of Transfer

Proposals to reconceptualize the transfer construct are making an important contribution toward advancing theory and research. An analysis of the literature shows that traditionally transfer was very narrowly conceived as the independent and immediate application of knowledge and skills acquired in one situation to another. Accordingly, narrow criteria of successful transfer were adopted. Bransford and Schwartz (1999) called this narrow definition the *direct-application theory of transfer*. In this framework, the key question is, Can people apply something they learned directly and independently to a new setting? A typical characteristic of this approach to transfer is that the final transfer task (i.e., the experimental task that is used to test whether transfer has taken place) takes the form of sequestered problem solving. That is, while solving the transfer task, subjects do not get opportunities to invoke support from other resources, such as texts or colleagues, or to try things out, receive feedback, or revise their work.

As an alternative to this view, Bransford and Schwartz proposed a broader perspective emphasizing *preparation for future learning* (PFL) as the major aspect of transfer. Under this framework, the focus in assessing transfer is on subjects' abilities to learn in novel, resource-rich contexts. This view is much more in line with the now-prevailing notion of learning as an active and constructive process, but emphasizes, in addition, the active nature of transfer itself. Indeed, in this approach a novel context is not conceived as just "given"; using one's prior knowledge and the available resources, one can modify the situation and its perception. For instance, confronted with a fellow learner's perspective about a problem situation, one can revise one's own perception of the problem. In this respect, Bransford and Schwartz also emphasized the important role of metacognitive (or self-regulatory) skills. Such active control of the transfer situation is lacking in the direct-application model. Another benefit of the PFL model of transfer is that it suggests affective and motivational qualities, in addition to cognitive skills, are candidates for transfer.

The PFL approach is convergent with a redefinition of transfer by Hatano and Greeno (1999), who criticized traditional models of transfer for both treating knowledge as a static property of an individual and adopting inappropriately narrow criteria of successful transfer. They considered the conceptualization of transfer as the direct application of acquired elements from one situation to another as incompatible with current perspectives on the contextualized or situated nature of knowledge. That is, the direct-application theory is static, in the sense that it neglects how aspects of thinking that arise from interactions among people, and between people and other material and informational systems, might affect performance in the transfer situation. Hatano and Greeno proposed replacing the term *transfer* with the term *productivity*, to refer to the generality of learning (i.e., the degree to which learning in some situation has effects on task-related activities in a variety of other situations). The latter situations can, in accordance with the PFL perspective, involve hints or other kinds of support that facilitate the recall of relevant prior knowledge. Hatano and Greeno rightly claimed that in everyday learning environments, people rarely need to use previously acquired knowledge and skills without also having access to external support (De Corte, 2003).

The committee makes two generalizations about links between instruction and transfer: the role of learning general principles and the value of learning multiple examples. First, instruction that explains general principles supports far transfer better than does instruction that is more specific and focused. Judd (1908), for example, asked fifth- and sixth-grade students to throw darts at a target under water, initially with the target submerged 12 inches under the surface. He found that practice with feedback was effective at helping students hit the target when it was submerged at the 12-inch learning level, but did not help them to hit the target when its depth was varied. Instruction explaining the underlying principles of light refraction led to much better transfer to throwing darts at new depths.

Wertheimer (1959) compared two methods of instructing students to find the area of a parallelogram, one that emphasized structural relationships in parallelograms and one that involved a fixed solution routine (dropping a perpendicular line and applying a formula). On problems that involved finding the area of standard parallelograms that varied in base, height, and the degree to which the corner angles differed from 90 degrees, both groups performed well. On novel problems, where the shapes were atypical but amenable to the same solution logic, the method that emphasized understanding structural relationships produced far better transfer. Similar findings have been obtained with a wide range of tasks, such as solving binomial probability problems (Mayer and Greeno, 1972), debugging computer programs (Klahr and Carver, 1988), and even determining the sex of chicks (Biederman and Shiffrar, 1987).

The second generalization is that using multiple examples during initial learning and/or varying the conditions of practice also facilitates far transfer. This applies to the benefits of varying the conditions of practice when learning motor skills (e.g., Catalano and Kleiner, 1984; Shea and Morgan, 1979), the benefits of using multiple examples when teaching students how to solve complex problems (e.g., Gick and Holyoak, 1983; Homa and Cultice, 1984), and the benefits of varying the outlines of an advanced-organizer text (that is, material read before some to-be-learned text) as opposed to rereading the to-be-learned article itself (Mannes and Kintsch, 1987).

Given these two generalizations, spatial representations might be expected to foster far transfer in problem solving by leading learners to induce general principles and relationships among the problems being studied. For example, a geology instructor could take students on a field trip to several local outcrops in the Appalachian Mountains and then use spatial representations to provide comparable information about parts of the Appalachians further north or south where the style of rock deformation differs. By comparing and contrasting these multiple examples (some from direct experience, other learned only through spatial representations), students could construct an understanding of the general properties of folded or faulted mountains and the underlying deformation processes. To the extent that generating schematic-spatial representations of information requires learners to generate their own ideas about general principles and about relationships that cut across different specific problems, instruction emphasizing the role of spatial representations should foster transfer to new problems.

There is nothing to suggest that the transfer of information by means of or even about spatial thinking is any easier or more difficult than transfer in any other medium or domain. However, spatial representations can aid in transfer and spatial representations can play major roles in learning, remembering, and problem solving (see Appendix D).

4.5 THE FOSTERING OF EXPERTISE IN SPATIAL THINKING

Expertise in any area of knowledge is hard won, and expertise in spatial thinking is no exception to this generalization. Developing expertise takes time, commitment, and opportunity to learn the spatial knowledge, spatial ways of thinking and acting, and spatial capabilities that are characteristics of any domain of knowledge.

There are components of cognitive processing that enter into learning to think spatially just as they enter other kinds of cognitive mastery (e.g., quantitative thinking, verbal reasoning). Even though they are not themselves "spatial" in nature, they must also be taken into account because they are relevant to how successful one is in solving spatial problems. Working memory, for example, allows a person to keep pieces of problems in mind simultaneously and, thereby, makes it possible to see relations. When we visualize rotating an object to fit into some opening, we depend on working memory to hold both pieces in mind at once. Thus, skill in spatial thinking cannot be seen as isolated from other cognitive skills.

Expertise in spatial thinking draws on both general spatial skills and spatial skills that are particular to parts of a domain of knowledge. It is unlikely that there will be instant transfer of some skill to a problem in another domain of knowledge, yet some components of existing spatial skills can be drawn upon to tackle the new problem. Thus, it might be necessary to develop expertise in particular contexts before one can see the connections to some more general spatial skill (e.g., one might become expert at seeing things in three dimensions in biology, but still need considerable practice to learn to apply the skill to seeing new kinds of forms, shapes, and positions in chemistry or geology).

The benefits of practicing spatial thinking initially tend to be domain specific, and as is the case for other forms of expertise, learning to think spatially is best conducted in the context of the types of materials one is seeking to learn and understand. Thus, practicing spatial skills is most effective if it is contextualized within a domain of knowledge.

Structured, systematic practice greatly improves the speed and accuracy with which people can generate spatial representations and transform spatial information. Thus, it is important to identify the types and forms of spatial representations and transformations that are critical for different learning goals and encourage students to practice them (see Appendix D).

Spatial representations can help students in learning and problem solving. The evidence suggests that we should (1) have students generate their own spatial representations; (2) use spatial representations to provide multiple and, where possible, interlocking and complementary representations of situations, especially where the phenomena are not readily available to direct sensory perception; (3) use a wide variety of spatial representations; (4) use spatial representations to convey a variety of kinds of thinking (e.g., data about how something is structured now, how it could or should appear in the future or did appear in the past); and (5) learn where—and which types of—spatial representations can be useful. The evidence also suggests that we should not (1) force students to use a spatial approach to a problem when another approach is equally or better suited; (2) overload students' cognitive capabilities by exposing then to a novel spatial representation while simultaneously asking them to reason about a complex situation; or (3) assume that animations are necessarily better than sequences of static representations (see Appendix D).

Expertise in spatial thinking varies among different groups. There are different average levels of skills or expertise associated with different groups (e.g., younger and older children). There is also, however, significant variation within any given group on any given spatial skill. This means that one cannot automatically infer what any given learner brings to the task. Thus, from an instructional standpoint, it will be necessary to have tasks with multiple levels of achievement and multiple strategies for achieving them.

The distributions of performance on spatial tasks shows a great deal of overlap for boys and girls and some average differences too. Boys and girls show differences on average performance of some spatial skills, where boys outperform girls on some skills and girls outperform boys on others. Thus, it is important not to "discount" the spatial learning capabilities of either boys or girls— practice and learning significantly boost the performance of both boys and girls (see Appendix C).

People vary in how rapidly they can create and transform spatial representations, and their levels of spatial thinking skill can help or hinder their learning across the broad range of sciences. Students with higher levels of initial skill will find learning that involves spatial thinking easier than those with lower levels of initial skill. For students with critically low levels of skill in spatial thinking, the use of tools for spatial thinking, such as graphics and figures, may actually interfere with, not facilitate, learning.

Effective learning depends on having sufficient levels of general and particular spatial thinking skills. Thus, it is important to assess the strengths and limitations that individual learners bring to their learning goals.

4.6 CONCLUSION

The three key conclusions from this chapter are that spatial thinking can be taught; that learning to think spatially must take place within domain contexts; and that while transfer from one specific domain of knowledge to another is neither automatic nor easy, it is possible with appropriately structured programs and curricula. On the basis of these conclusions, the committee derives two educational principles: first, instruction should be infused across and throughout the curriculum; second, instruction should create skills that promote a lifelong interest in spatial thinking. These two principles lead in turn to ideals for the design of a K–12 curriculum that would promote and support spatial thinking. Chapter 5 explores the extent to which such curricula ideals are met by current standards-based curricula in sciences and mathematics.

5

Responding to the Need for Spatial Thinkers

5.1 INTRODUCTION

On March 15, 2003, the *Economist* published an article with the provocative title of "The Revenge of Geography." The thesis is that "… it was naive to imagine that the global reach of the internet would make geography irrelevant. Wireline and wireless technologies have bound the virtual and physical worlds closer than ever" (Economist, 2003, p. 19). The virtual world overlays and intersects with the real world in which we live. For example, Internet protocol (IP) addresses have a physical expression in the geographic location of the computer and its user. The geographic location of mobile devices can be determined through GPS. The committee would argue that the global reach of the Internet will make the understanding of space even more important. Access to and intelligent use of the virtual world will place a premium on spatial thinking in everyday life, in the workplace, and in science. To what extent is the American K–12 educational system responding to such needs by producing students who are at least familiar with, if not expert at, spatial thinking?

This chapter reviews the extent to which the educational system is meeting societal needs for spatial thinkers. Sections 5.2 and 5.3 show how the increasing importance of the information technology sector is generating demands for skilled workers with spatial skills and for citizens who can use spatial tools and technologies in their everyday lives. Sections 5.4 and 5.5 look at educational responses, first in terms of international comparisons of spatial skills of students and second in terms of the role of spatial thinking in standards-based education. Given the arguments in the four chapters in Part 1 of this report, in Section 5.6 the committee develops a position statement advocating the need to teach spatial thinking to every K–12 student.

5.2 THE INCREASING NEED FOR SPATIAL THINKING SKILLS

At the simplest level, the root metaphors for describing access to the virtual world of the Internet are spatial: portals, desktops, connectivity, traffic, speed, addresses, geocodes and geotags, cyberspace, navigation, and search. As the *Economist* argues, "Finding information relevant to a particular place, or the location associated with a specific piece of information, is not always easy.

This has caused a surge of innovation, as new technologies have developed to link places on the internet with places in the real world—stitching together the supposedly separate virtual and physical worlds" (Economist, 2003, p. 19). Geolocation systems match Internet addresses and physical locations. Thus, we are moving into a world of personal computing functionality (such as geo-enabled Personal Digital Assistants [PDAs] in car navigation systems [see Box 6.2] and cell phones with GPS functions), which provide us with and enable us to use spatial information. For example, Location Based Services (LBS), which link mobile devices (cell phones, PDAs, etc.) with GPS technology, allow for the tracking of people in geographical space and for the provision of real-time information to people as they move in space (Did you know that store X, only 50 yards away, has a sale on item Y?). That information would come from access to your recent purchasing patterns, your current location, and the proximity to a store offering similar goods. As Dobson and Fisher (2003, p. 52) pointed out, "LBS offers major benefits on the one hand and horrendous risks on the other." In either case, the spatial thinking skills of the user are an essential prerequisite.

At a more fundamental level, there is an intersection between information technology (IT) and the idea of space. The intersection takes a variety of forms. It is estimated, for example, that 80 percent of all data can be given spatial coordinates and therefore spatialized. It is similarly estimated that 80 percent of all text documents contain geographical references (M. F. Goodchild, personal communication, 2003). Fabrikant and Buttenfield (2001) show that it is possible to spatialize various forms of knowledge and that the spatialization of mapping domains has become a topic of great interest in information science. The management of increasingly massive databases depends on data mining, a technique that draws extensively on spatial concepts, and visualization, an approach that is equally spatial in its foundations. The classic example of this convergence of spatialization and visualization is the analytic technique of multidimensional scaling (MDS), wherein measures of similarity are defined between objects in a data set (e.g., automobiles, books in a library, characters in a play). MDS attempts to create a space of a prescribed number of dimensions, and to find locations for objects in that space, such that the distances between pairs of locations in the space are as closely correlated as possible with the measures of similarity. The output of the program can be displayed graphically.

This convergence between concepts of space and IT means that, increasingly, problems will be posed in and solved within spatial frameworks (Goodchild, 2001). In turn, people will be presented with opportunities to and faced with the need to think spatially in everyday life (using MapQuest to generate driving directions), in the workplace (using a display system to route traffic or control aircraft), and in science (using the visual output of a data mining program).

5.3 PROVIDING SKILLED SPATIAL THINKERS

A strong component of the drive for K–12 educational reform since the 1989 Charlottesville Education Summit has been a concern about the capacity of the American workforce to compete successfully in a context defined by intense international competition in global markets and rapid technological change in the nature of the work process. These concerns are part of the rationale for two of the National Education Goals: Goal 3 ("all students will leave grades 4, 8, and 12 having demonstrated competency over challenging subject matter . . . and every school in America will ensure that all students learn to use their minds well, so that they may be prepared for responsible citizenship, further learning, and productive employment in our Nations' modern economy") and Goal 6 ("every adult American will be literate and will possess the knowledge and skills necessary to compete in a global economy and exercise the rights and responsibilities of citizenship").

The thrust of the Secretary of Labor's Commission on Achieving Necessary Skills (SCANS) report (U.S. Department of Labor, 1991, p. 2) was that "for most of this century, as this nation took its goods and know-how to the world, America did not have to worry about competition from abroad. At home, the technology of mass production emphasized discipline to the assembly line. Today, the demands on business and workers are different. Firms must meet world class standards and so must workers." The report emphasized the need to reform American education in order to foster "five competencies which, in conjunction with a three-part foundation of skills and personal qualities, lie at the heart of job performance today. These eight areas represent essential preparation for all students, both those going directly to work and those planning further education. All eight must be an integral part of every young person's school life." The five competencies included the productive use of resources, interpersonal skills, information, systems, and technology. The skills comprise basic skills (reading, writing, arithmetic and mathematics, speaking, and listening), thinking skills, and the diligent application of personal qualities. Taken together, these eight competencies and skills comprise the needed "workplace know-how."

American employers are increasingly concerned about the knowledge and skills of high school graduates. They perceive a mismatch between their needs for a skilled, knowledgeable, and flexible workforce and the products of the K–12 education system. On-the-job training is expensive and disruptive to employers and workers alike. From the perspective of potential workers, the nature of work is changing. Not only are workers facing greater expectations in terms of knowledge and skills, but they are expected to participate in what is essentially a lifelong learning process. Knowledge and skills must be maintained, upgraded, and replaced. Thus, on average, American workers can expect to change employment seven times during a career. With each change come new demands—and opportunities—for work-related knowledge and skills. With each change comes the possibility of obsolescence.

At the heart of the necessary workplace skills are those of critical thinking. Halpern (1999, p. 74) identifies these as comprising (1) verbal reasoning, (2) argument analysis, (3) thinking as hypothesis testing, (4) using likelihood and uncertainty, and (5) decision making and problem solving. The SCANS (U.S. Department of Labor, 1991, p. 3) report argued that "employers and employees share the belief that all workplaces must 'work smarter'" and, in the title of his report to the Russell Sage Foundation, Hunt (1995) posed the question: *Will We Be Smart Enough?* His subtitle, *A Cognitive Analysis of the Coming Workforce*, captures his approach to the question. Hunt linked cognitive theory, psychometric approaches, and demographic projections to analyze workforce needs over the next decades. His focus on cognitive skills (such as problem solving and flexibility) reflects the emergence of the concept of knowledge workers in the information economy. Halpern (1998) defines knowledge workers as people who can carry out multistep operations, manipulate abstract and complex symbols and ideas, efficiently acquire new information, and remain flexible enough to recognize the need for continuing change and for new paradigms for lifelong learning. Knowledge workers are central to the rapidly emerging IT sector of the U.S. economy. By some estimates, 60 percent of the American workforce can currently be classified as knowledge workers. Even if that is an overestimate, IT will increasingly dominate workforce needs over the next decades.

One segment of the IT market, the geospatial information and technology sector, is projected to have annual revenues of $30 billion dollars by 2005 (Gaudet and Annulis, under review), with a job growth rate in related professions of 10–20 percent between 2000 and 2010 (Gaudet et al., 2003). As Gaudet and Annulis (under review) noted, "there is a serious shortfall of professionals and trained specialists who can utilize geospatial technologies in their jobs. The growth of this market demands support of the education, training, and development of geospatial professionals and specialists." Funded by NASA, the National Workforce Development Education and Training Initiative has developed a Geospatial Technology Competency Model (http://geowdc.com/assessment/) (see Table 5.1). It is built on an industry definition: Geospatial technology is an information technology field of practice that acquires, manages, interprets, integrates, displays, analyzes, or otherwise uses data focusing on the geographic, temporal, and spatial context. In effect, the

TABLE 5.1 The Geospatial Technology Competency Model

Technical Competencies	Business Competencies
Ability to assess relationships among geospatial technologies	**Ability to see the "big picture"**
Cartography	Business understanding
Computer programming skills	Buy-in, advocacy
Environmental applications	**Change management**
GIS theory and applications	**Cost-benefit analysis, Return on Investment**
Geology applications	Ethics modeling
Geospatial data processing tools	Industry understanding
Photogrammetry	Legal understanding
Remote-sensing theory and applications	Organization understanding
Spatial information processing	Performance analysis and evaluation
Technical writing	**Visioning**
Technological literacy	
Topology	
Analytical Competencies	**Interpersonal Competencies**
Creative thinking	Coaching
Knowledge management	**Communication**
Model building skills	Conflict management
Problem-solving skills	**Feedback skills**
Research skills	Group process understanding
Systems thinking	**Leadership skills**
	Questioning
	Relationship building skills
	Self-knowledge, Self-management

NOTE: Core competencies are shown in bold.
SOURCE: http://geowdc.com/assessment/.

Geospatial Technology Competency Model establishes a link between competencies—the knowledge, skills, and abilities that an individual needs to do a job—and roles, which are groupings of work-related competencies. Many of the technical and analytical competencies listed in the model are directly related to the process of spatial thinking.

In short, therefore, workforce demands are changing; those demands can be met only if the K–12 education system produces graduates with the requisite skills and knowledge, with a commitment to lifelong learning, and with flexibility to adapt to change. Central to changing workforce needs are knowledge workers for the rapidly growing IT sector. Central to the IT sector and many other sectors is spatial thinking. To what extent does the K–12 educational system generate graduates with these spatial thinking skills? One answer can be found in the most recent international comparative survey of mathematics and science performance.

5.4 THE 1999 TRENDS IN INTERNATIONAL MATHEMATICS AND SCIENCE STUDY (TIMSS)

The Trends in International Mathematics and Science Study (formerly known as the Third International Mathematics and Science Study) is the international parallel to the National Assessment of Educational Progress. Sponsored by the U.S. Department of Education through the National Center for Education Statistics (NCES), TIMSS compares the performance of American students (at the end of the eighth grade) with those of other countries in five major content areas of mathematics and six content areas in science. TIMSS has been offered in 1995 and 1999 (the 2003 results are not yet available). Therefore, TIMSS provides the most reliable and comprehensive assessment of trends in student achievement from an international perspective.

The TIMMS 1999 results do not speak directly about spatial thinking as such. However, there are content areas in which performance would seem to be directly related to skill in spatial thinking. In the case of mathematics, performance in geometry is defined as understanding points, lines, planes, angles, visualization, triangles, polygons, circles, transformations, symmetry, congruence, similarity, and constructions (Mullis et al., 2000, p. 93). Although the average U.S. scale score for geometry was 473 and not statistically significantly different from the international average of 487 (range 575–335), U.S. students did rank 27 out of 38 countries. Thus, "the United States performed significantly above the international average in fractions and number sense; data representation, analysis, and probability; and algebra. In contrast, however, it performed similarly to the international average in measurement and geometry (a shift in ranking from 16th in data representation, analysis, and probability to 27th in geometry)" (Mullis et al., 2000, p. 94).

U.S. students showed a small but not statistically significant increase in achievement between 1995 and 1999. As the NCES (2000b, p. 108) report notes: "Changes in average achievement at a national level are not easy to bring about and inevitably take place over several years. Amending official curricula, producing relevant supporting resources, and changing teacher practice all take time, even under the most favorable conditions."

In the case of science, two content areas—Earth science (includes Earth features, Earth processes, and Earth in the universe) and physics (includes physical properties and transformations, energy and physical processes, and forces and motion)—appear to have strong connections to spatial thinking. With the notable exception of physics, the average achievement of U.S. students was significantly higher than the international average. The ranking of U.S. students ranged from 13th out of 38 in the case of scientific inquiry and the nature of science to 20th for physics. U.S. students ranked 16th out of 38 in achievement in Earth science. For the four areas for which trend data are available (Earth science, life science, physics, and chemistry), there was no significant difference between 1995 and 1999.

Given the importance of science and mathematics achievement and the significant investment in those areas of education, the TIMSS results are neither impressive nor satisfactory. While it is true that changing average levels of achievement is difficult, current educational policy, as exemplified by the No Child Left Behind Act of 2001 (Public Law 107-110), is committed to fostering academic achievement in core subjects (defined as English, reading or language arts, mathematics, science, foreign languages, civics and government, economics, arts, history, and geography). For at least three of the TIMSS content areas (geometry, physics, and Earth science), achievement is related to competence in spatial thinking, and to the extent that spatial thinking is taught with adequate supports, the committee believes that achievement in mathematics and science understanding will improve. However, that improvement will come about only if the educational system focuses its attention on spatial thinking. To what extent is that happening?

5.5 SPATIAL THINKING IN THE NATIONAL EDUCATION STANDARDS

5.5.1 The Role of Spatial Thinking in the Mathematics and Science Standards

In the current educational environment one important place to look for attention to spatial thinking is in the educational standards for various disciplines. These discipline-based standards, developed in the middle to late 1990s, provide statements of what K–12 students should know, understand, and be able to do; they are intended to serve as a basis for the development of curricula, assessment procedures, teacher-training programs, and supplementary instructional material.

The committee focused on two sets of standards:

1. *Principles and Standards for School Mathematics*, prepared by the National Council of Teachers of Mathematics in 2000. This is an update of the first-ever set of standards, those published for mathematics in 1989.

2. *National Science Education Standards*, prepared by the National Research Council in 1996.

Several sets of standards were examined, including those for geography (Geography Education Standards Project, 1994), but the mathematics and science standards offer a direct connection to spatial thinking and reasoning and they are fundamental to the process of education and to the idea of a technologically skilled workforce. (Spatial thinking is integral to geography as a discipline and, thus, figures prominently throughout the national geography standards. The first 3 of the 18 standards and all five of the sets of geographic skills are a primer in thinking spatially about geographic data; see Box 5.1).

As is the case for most education standards, these two sets of standards are organized in terms of intellectual themes with progressively more challenging standards of performance established for different grade levels along each theme. For example, the science standards are built around eight intellectual categories: unifying concepts and processes in science, science as inquiry, physical science, life science, Earth and space science, science and technology, science in personal and social perspectives, and the history and nature of science. For each category there is a content standard and "as a result of activities provided for all students in those grade levels, the content of the standard is to be understood or certain abilities are to be developed" (NRC, 1996, p. 6). In the case of the first category, there is no distinction by grade level; for the other seven categories, understanding is organized into three grade clusters: K–4, 5–8, and 9–12. The eight standards are to be used as a whole in order to achieve scientific literacy.

There are two questions about the relationship between spatial thinking and the sets of content standards: (1) Are the basic tenets of spatial thinking an explicit part of the expectations established by various standards? (2) Are spatial thinking concepts implicitly contained within the standards? To answer these questions, the committee considers the two sets of standards in sequence, beginning with mathematics because it has been in place since 1989 in its original form.

5.5.2 Spatial Thinking and the *Principles and Standards for School Mathematics*

The mathematics standards are built around five content standards—number and operations, algebra, geometry, measurement, and data analysis and probability—and five process standards—problem solving, reasoning and proof, communication, connections, and representation (NCTM, 2000). For each standard, there are two to four statements of what students should be able to do as a consequence of instruction, with specific expectations keyed to grade levels K–2, 3–5, 6–8, and 9–12. These expectations are summarized in Table 5.2.

In Table 5.2, only the geometry standard uses the language of spatial thinking (two and three dimensions, shapes, relationships, locations, spatial reasoning, etc.). However, in reading the detailed discussions, grade by grade, for each of the ten mathematics standards, it is clear that spatial thinking pervades and permeates the detailed articulation of what is expected of students. There are explicit references to spatial concepts in the geometry, measurement, data analysis and probability, and representation standards. Although the term spatial thinking is not used explicitly in the text of Table 5.2, the underlying concepts are implicit throughout. Thus, an understanding of spatial relations is presumed but never discussed explicitly. For many of the statements in Table 5.2,

BOX 5.1
Spatial Thinking and the *National Geography Standards*

As the opening definition of geography suggests, the discipline and spatial thinking are inextricably interwoven: "Geography is the science of space and place on Earth's surface" (Geography Education Standards Project, 1994, p. 1). The definition is extended to argue that "geography means a sensitivity to location, to scale, to movement, to patterns, to resources and conflicts, to maps and geographics" (Geography Education Standards Project, 1994, p. 18).

The standards are built around three components: subject matter (in the form of 18 content standards), skills (in the form of five sets of skills), and perspectives (in the form of two major perspectives [the spatial and the ecological] and two supporting perspectives [the historical and the economic]). The first three content standards are grouped under the idea of "the world in spatial terms":

Standard 1: How to use maps and other geographic representations, tools, and technologies to acquire, process, and report information from a spatial perspective
Standard 2: How to use mental maps to organize information about people, places, and environments in a spatial context
Standard 3: How to analyze the spatial organization of people, places, and environments on Earth's surface

Geographic skills provide the necessary tools and techniques for students to think geographically (or, as is clear, think spatially). This set of five skills makes an explicit link among three elements: the process of doing science, the process of problem solving, and the process of thinking spatially. The five skill sets are (1) asking geographic questions, (2) acquiring geographic information, (3) organizing geographic information, (4) analyzing geographic information, and (5) answering geographic questions. Thus, at the end of the fourth grade, students would be expected to prepare maps, graphs, tables, and diagrams to display geographic information (skill set 3). They would be able to analyze Earth's surface in terms of its spatial elements of point, line, area, and volume (Standard 3). They would be able to locate Earth's continents in relation to each other and to principal parallels and meridians (Standard 2). They would be able to use a map grid (e.g., latitude and longitude or alphanumeric system) to answer the question—What is this location? (Standard 1).

The cumulative structure of increasingly demanding standards, skills, and perspectives is aimed at a high school graduate who is geographically informed, seeing meaning in the arrangement of things in space; seeing relations between people, places, and environments; using geographic skills; and applying spatial and ecological perspectives to life situations.

Spatial thinking underpins the intellectual structure of the geography standards. Interestingly, however, these standards are also stand-alone. Although there is a direct connection with the discipline of history through one content standard, there is no explicit connection with either the mathematics or the science standards. Given the way geography is taught in elementary school—as part of social studies—there is a very low probability that students would enjoy the benefits of coordination between, say, mathematics and geography teaching and learning. The geography standards demonstrate the possibility and power of infusing spatial thinking into a discipline. They also show the need for a coordinated approach to spatial thinking standards across the curriculum. Ironically, they illustrate the rapid change in technology, as well: GIS as a support system for geographical thinking was relegated to an appendix rather than being integrated into the structure of the geography standards. The geography standards, therefore, exemplify the possibility of developing standards for spatial thinking across the curriculum.

spatial concepts could be applicable. In numbers and operations, ways of representing numbers could include a number line, which is a spatialization. In communication, spatializations in graphs could support the process. In data analysis, graphs could be used. However, in this most fundamental statement of what students should know and be able to do in mathematics, space and spatial thinking do not play a prominent role.

The geometry standard provides explicit connections to the concepts of spatial thinking. In fact, the opening paragraph of the broad discussion of geometry states:

TABLE 5.2 Table of Standards and Expectations for School Mathematics

Number and operations	• Understand numbers, ways of representing numbers, relationships among numbers, and number systems
	• Understand meanings of operations and how they relate to one another
	• Compute fluently and make reasonable estimates
Algebra	• Understand patterns, relations, and functions
	• Represent and analyze mathematical situations and structures using algebraic symbols
	• Use mathematical models to represent and understand quantitative relationships
	• Analyze change in various contexts
Geometry	• Analyze characteristics and properties of two- and three-dimensional geometric shapes and develop mathematical arguments about geometric relationships
	• Specify locations and describe spatial relationships using coordinate geometry and other representational systems
	• Apply transformations and use symmetry to analyze mathematical situations
	• Use visualization, spatial reasoning, and geometric modeling to solve problems
Measurement	• Understand measurable attributes of objects and the units, systems, and processes of measurement
	• Apply appropriate techniques, tools, and formulas to determine measurements
Data analysis and probability	• Formulate questions that can be addressed with data, and collect, organize, and display relevant data to answer them
	• Select and use appropriate statistical methods to analyze data
	• Develop and evaluate inferences and predictions that are based on data
	• Understand and apply basic concepts of probability
Problem solving	• Build new mathematical knowledge through problem solving
	• Solve problems that arise in mathematics and in other contexts
	• Apply and adapt a variety of appropriate strategies to solve problems
	• Monitor and reflect on the process of mathematical problem solving
Reasoning and proof	• Recognize reasoning and proof as fundamental aspects of mathematics
	• Make and investigate mathematical conjectures
	• Develop and evaluate mathematical arguments and proofs
	• Select and use various types of reasoning and methods of proof
Communication	• Organize and consolidate mathematical thinking through communication
	• Communicate mathematical thinking coherently and clearly to peers, teachers, and others
	• Analyze and evaluate the mathematical thinking and strategies of others
	• Use the language of mathematics to express mathematical ideas precisely

continued

TABLE 5.2 Continued

Connections	• Recognize and use connections among mathematical ideas • Understand how mathematical ideas interconnect and build on one another to produce a coherent whole • Recognize and apply mathematics in contexts outside of mathematics
Representation	• Create and use representations to organize, record, and communicate mathematical ideas • Select, apply, and translate among mathematical representations to solve problems • Use representations to model and interpret physical, social, and mathematical phenomena

> Spatial visualization—building and manipulating mental representations of two-and three-dimensional objects and perceiving an object from different perspectives—is an important aspect of geometric thinking. (NCTM, 2000, p. 41)

In many ways, this statement parallels part of the committee's definition of spatial thinking. The discussion of the standard goes on to make the point that "geometric modeling and spatial reasoning offer ways to interpret and describe physical environments and can be important tools in problem solving" (NCTM, 2000, p. 41).

The second and third parts of the geometry standard, which refer to the specification of location and the use of transformations, are strongly connected to the spatial concepts discussed in Chapter 2. The importance of spatial concepts is clear from the detailed discussion of the standard at each grade level. For example, a succession of activities that require spatial thinking can be found in progressing through the first two grade groups.

- Grades K–2

— Describe, name, and interpret relative positions in space and apply ideas about relative position.
— Describe, name, and interpret direction and distance in navigating space and apply ideas about directions and distance.
— Find and name locations with simple relationships such as "near to" and in coordinate systems such as maps.

- Grades 3–5

— Describe location and movement using common language and geometric vocabulary.
— Make and use coordinate systems to specify locations and to describe paths.
— Find the distance between points along horizontal and vertical lines of a coordinate system.

In light of one of the charges to the committee—to address the utility of GIS in supporting education—there are two interesting aspects to the mathematics standards.

The first is contained in the representation standard, which calls for the ability to "use representations to model and interpret physical, social, and mathematical phenomena" (NCTM, 2000, p. 67). The detailed explication of this standard asks what a representation should look like and what the role of the teacher should be in developing representations. Thus, the introductory explanation of the representation standard for grades 9–12 begins:

> If mathematics is the "science of patterns" (Steen, 1988), representations are the means by which those patterns are recorded and analyzed. As students become mathematically sophisticated, they develop an increasingly large repertoire of mathematical representations and the knowledge of how to use them productively. This knowledge includes choosing specific representations in order to gain particular insights or achieve particular ends. (NCTM, 2000, p. 360)

In one respect, the mathematicians have an even broader concept of representation than is embodied in the committee's approach to spatial thinking. For example, their view includes the discussion of numbers as representations. GIS is a system for generating multiple representations of spatial information, especially numerical information.

Second, the mathematics standards address the role of technology in the principles that serve as a preface to the standards and cover such matters as equity, assessment, and teaching. The technology principle states: "Technology is essential in teaching and learning mathematics; it influences the mathematics that is taught and enhances students' learning" (NCTM, 2000, p. 11). In the detailed discussion of this principle, several points have bearing on the committee's consideration of GIS as a support for spatial thinking: technology enhances mathematics learning, technology supports effective mathematics teaching, and technology influences what mathematics is taught.

Spatial thinking is, therefore, very much part of the mathematics standards. It is central to one content standard and incorporated in several others. The idea of GIS as a support system is implicit in one process standard, and the concept of a support system is endorsed in one of the principles—"describe particular features of high-quality mathematics education" (NCTM, 2000, p. 11). To what extent is this the case for the science standards?

5.5.3 Spatial Thinking and the *National Science Education Standards*

The relationship of the science standards to the basic concepts of spatial thinking is by no means as explicit as it is in the mathematics standards (NRC, 1996). A detailed reading of the science standards suggests that there is spatial thinking and spatial reasoning content, but neither phrase appears in the text, nor are the concepts addressed explicitly and systematically.

The science standards are similar in structure to those for mathematics. The one exception is that while the mathematics standards speak of "standards and principles," the science standards broadly apply the concept of standards to every element of the educational system that touches the student-teacher relationship. So in the science standards there are standards for teaching, assessment, teacher preparation, and content, while the mathematics standards handle many of these topics in the principles.

The science content standards contain six basic themes, for which standards are elaborated in each of three grade intervals (K–4, 5–8, and 9–12). These themes are unifying concepts and processes; science as inquiry; physical science, life science, Earth and space science; science and technology; science in personal and social perspective; and history and nature of science.

The content standards for physical, life, Earth, and space sciences build on a theme associated with spatial thinking. This theme is one of an orderly progression from naming and locating objects, to placing objects in relationship to each other, naming those relationships, and then progressing to explanations of the spatial and functional structure of objects and their relationships. This parallels the discussion in Chapter 3 of the historical process that astronomy has taken from first locating and naming objects in the sky to inferring the structure and evolution of the universe. These steps are recapitulated in the Earth science standard, which begins with finding and describing Earth materials and culminates with the origin and evolution of the Earth system at level 9–12, including explicitly in level 5–8 the spatial structure of the Earth system. In the life sciences standard a similar constructivist approach culminates at 9–12 with an understanding of matter, energy, and organization of living systems, progressing in grades 5–8 through the study of structure and function in living systems.

The science content standards necessarily reflect spatial thinking and reasoning in an implicit way because many of the objects of study for science exist in the real world. Thus, it is necessary to place things in that world, to speak to their relationships, and to make inferences about their structure and function. The question of how an explicit focus on spatial thinking might enhance that process of study remains unanswered in the science standards, with one possible exception in the program standards for the design and implementation of science programs at the school and district levels. Standard C of the program standards states that "the science program should be coordinated with the mathematics program to enhance student use and understanding of mathematics in the study of science and to improve student understanding of mathematics" (NRC, 1996, p. 214).

The discussion speaks to the value of mathematics, broadly referring to its use primarily in the display and analysis of data. While the science program standard implies a two-way street between mathematics and science, the narrative states:

> Science requires the use of mathematics in the collection and treatment of data and in the reasoning used to develop concepts, laws, and theories. School science and mathematics programs should be coordinated so that students learn the necessary mathematical skills and concepts before and during their use in the science program. (NRC, 1996, p. 214)

This suggests that mathematical knowledge is a precondition for the development of scientific inquiry. Perhaps if spatial thinking is important to science education, there is a sense that students may have learned it as part of mathematics before they are expected to apply it in learning science.

Spatial thinking is, therefore, only an implicit but nevertheless essential part of the process of doing science, as articulated in the science standards. It is central to science, but it is not explicitly presented as part of the responsibility of science educators in fostering scientific literacy in K–12 students. To what extent are the two sets of standards coupled such that the prerequisite knowledge and skills are available to students?

5.5.4 The Role of Spatial Thinking in the Coupling Between the Mathematics and Science Standards

Several questions arise from this overview of the national standards for mathematics and science. Where exactly in the course of K–12 standards-based education are the fundamental concepts of space, representation, and spatial reasoning taught, exercised, and developed? Who— as in teachers of which school subject(s)—is responsible for ensuring that students develop increasing mastery of these ideas? Is this mastery available for transfer across the curriculum?

As noted above, the mathematics standards are constructivist, building to higher levels of abstraction as the student progresses through the grades to the level of understanding and competency expected of a graduating senior. Chapter 3 of the *Principles and Standards for School Mathematics* provides an integrated view of the progression of understanding and competency for all ten mathematics standards. Figures 5.1 and 5.2 are excerpts from two parts of the geometry standard: (1) specify locations and describe spatial relationships using coordinate geometry and other representational systems, and (2) use visualization, spatial reasoning, and geometric modeling to solve problems. These two parts are closely tied to concepts of space, representation, and spatial reasoning. Each of these parts has clearly stated outcomes with respect to mathematical understanding and contains clear examples of their application to real-world problems.

Chapters 4 through 7 of the mathematics standards describe how the goals are accomplished in

Specify locations and describe spatial relationships using coordinate geometry and other representational systems

Students should gain experience in using a variety of visual and coordinate representations to analyze problems and study mathematics.

At first, young children learn concepts of relative position, such as above, behind, near, and between. Later they can make and use rectangular grids to locate objects and measure the distance between points along vertical or horizontal lines. Experiences with the rectangular coordinate plane will be useful as they solve a wider array of problems in geometry and algebra. In the middle and secondary grades, the coordinate plane can be helpful as students work on discovering and analyzing properties of shapes. Finding distances between points in the plane by using scales on maps or the Pythagorean relationship is important in the middle grades. Geometric figures, such as lines in the middle grades or triangles and circles in high school, can be represented analytically, thus establishing a fundamental connection between algebra and geometry.

Students should gain experience in using a variety of visual and coordinate representations to analyze problems and study mathematics. In the elementary grades, for example, an interpretation of whole-number addition can be demonstrated on the number line. In later years, stu-

FIGURE 5.1 Specify locations and describe spatial relationships using coordinate geometry and other representational systems. SOURCE: NCTM, 2000. Reprinted with permission from *Principles and Standards for School Mathematics*, copyright 2000 by the National Council of Teachers of Mathematics. All rights reserved.

Use visualization, spatial reasoning, and geometric modeling to solve problems

Beginning in the early years of schooling, students should develop visualization skills through hands-on experiences with a variety of geometric objects and through the use of technology that allows them to turn, shrink, and deform two- and three-dimensional objects. Later, they should become comfortable analyzing and drawing perspective views, counting component parts, and describing attributes that cannot be seen but can be inferred. Students need to learn to physically and mentally change the position, orientation, and size of objects in systematic ways as they develop their understandings about congruence, similarity, and transformations.

One aspect of spatial visualization involves moving between two- and three-dimensional shapes and their representations. Elementary school students can wrap blocks in nets—two dimensional figures, usually made of paper, that can be folded to form three-dimensional objects—as a step toward learning to predict whether certain nets match certain solids. By the middle grades, they should be able to interpret and create top or side views of objects. This skill can be developed by challenging them to build a structure given only the side view and the front view, as in figure 3.4. In grades 3–5, students can determine if it is possible to build more than one structure satisfying both conditions. Middle-grades and secondary school students can be asked to find the minimum number of blocks needed to build the structure. High school students should be able to visualize and draw other cross-sections of the structures and of a range of geometric solids.

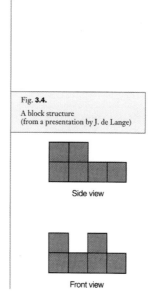

Fig. **3.4.**
A block structure
(from a presentation by J. de Lange)

Side view

Front view

FIGURE 5.2 Use visualization, spatial reasoning, and geometric modeling to solve problems. SOURCE: NCTM, 2000. Reprinted with permission from *Principles and Standards for School Mathematics*, copyright 2000 by the National Council of Teachers of Mathematics. All rights reserved.

four developmental levels (pre-K–2, 3–5, 6–8, and 9–12). The progression for the geometry standard starts with the identification of points and coordinate systems, clearly oriented toward maps and other graphic representations, and the visualization of two- and three-dimensional objects. These basic concepts are developed in the corresponding sections of grade levels K–2 (Figure 5.3) and 3–5 (Figure 5.4) standards. In Figure 5.3 the idea of placing things in space begins a process of

Specify locations and describe spatial relationships using coordinate geometry and other representational systems

Four types of mathematical questions regarding navigation and maps can help students develop a variety of spatial understandings: direction (which way?), distance (how far?), location (where?), and representation (what objects?). In answering these questions, students need to develop a variety of skills that relate to direction, distance, and position in space. Students develop the ability to navigate first by noticing landmarks, then by building knowledge of a route (a connected series of landmarks), and finally by putting many routes and locations into a kind of mental map (Clements 1999b).

Teachers should extend young students' knowledge of relative position in space through conversations, demonstrations, and stories. When students act out the story of the three billy goats and illustrate *over* and

under, *near* and *far*, and *between*, they are learning about location, space, and shape. Gradually students should distinguish navigation ideas such as *left* and *right* along with the concepts of distance and measurement. As they build three-dimensional models and read maps of their own environments, students can discuss which blocks are used to represent various objects like a desk or a file cabinet. They can mark paths on the model, such as from a table to the wastebasket, with masking tape to emphasize the shape of the path. Teachers should help students relate their models to other representations by drawing a map of the same room that includes the path. In similar activities, older students should develop map skills that include making route maps and using simple coordinates to locate their school on a city map (Liben and Downs 1989).

FIGURE 5.3 Specify locations and describe spatial relationships using coordinate geometry and other representational systems. SOURCE: NCTM, 2000. Reprinted with permission from *Principles and Standards for School Mathematics*, copyright 2000 by the National Council of Teachers of Mathematics. All rights reserved.

Computers can help students abstract, generalize, and symbolize their experiences with navigating. For example, students might "walk out" objects such as a rectangular-shaped rug and then use a computer program to make a rectangle on the computer screen. When students measure the rug with footprints and create a computer-generated rectangle with the same relative dimensions, they are exploring scaling and similarity. Some computer programs allow students to navigate through mazes or maps. Teachers should encourage students to move beyond trial and error as a strategy for moving through desired paths to visualizing, describing, and justifying the moves they need to make. Using these programs, students can learn orientation, direction, and measurement concepts.

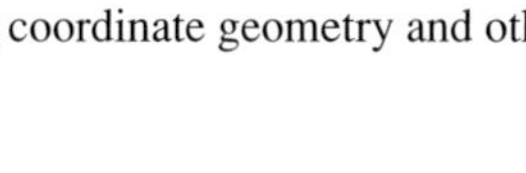

E-example 4.3

Navigating Paths and Mazes (Part 1)

FIGURE 5.4 Specify locations and describe spatial relationships using coordinate geometry and other representational systems. SOURCE: NCTM, 2000.

constructing the ability to deal with more complicated spatial concepts that grows to ideas of distance and direction, part of a progression of increasingly complicated spatial concepts. In Figure 5.4 not only are these concepts developed further, enabling navigation for example, but also basic computer technology is used to support and enhance the learning process.

In Figure 5.5 the focus is on developing spatial thinking as a skill in young learners, explicitly in terms of navigation and visualization. By the time students are in grades 3–5, the geometry standard calls not only for the building of additional spatial thinking skills (Figure 5.6), but also for the teacher to explicitly tie those skills to other areas of mathematics *and* to other disciplines such as science.

How well is the mathematicians' call for making ties to other disciplines reflected in and supported by the science standards? The simple concepts of position and shape (Figures 5.3 and 5.4) are nicely mirrored in the science standards. The science standards provide a guide to the specific science content at each grade level (K–4, 5–8, and 9–12) for each area of science covered (physical, life, Earth, and space). The content guide for the physical science standard for grades K–4 is shown in Figure 5.7. The sections on the physical properties of objects and materials and the position and motion of objects both use the spatial concepts being developed in the mathematics standard (Figure 5.3). Objects have position and shape in the science standard. In the geometry standard the concepts of position and shape are explicitly taught and reinforced. Similarly there are connections to other parts of the mathematics standards, and therefore the connection between the mathematics and science standards seems clear. At these early grades, the assumptions on the part of the writers of the science standards that mathematics will provide a prerequisite basis of knowledge that can be drawn on by science teachers and students seems appropriate.

Given this close connection between the science and mathematics standards based on similar words and concepts in the early grades, is this connection maintained in the higher grade levels?

Figures 5.8 and 5.9 contain the content guide to the physical science and the Earth and space science standards, respectively, for grade levels 9–12. The physical science standard focuses on atomic structure and the complex geometry of molecules, and the role of shape in chemical reactions (Figure 5.8). The Earth and space science standard talks about how the heating of Earth's surface drives the ocean currents and winds (Figure 5.9). Achieving the understanding called for in each of these science content areas would be greatly enhanced by abilities in spatial representation, visualization, and spatial reasoning. Both sets of science concepts contain critical scientific content that requires the ability to visualize structures and to keep in mind complex physical relationships that vary over space and time.

For example, understanding how the energy of the Sun drives oceanic currents and atmospheric winds is complicated. In particular, the poleward transport of energy in both the atmosphere and the ocean is modified by the rotation of Earth. Understanding the space-time dynamics requires an ability to take concepts derived from a two-dimensional treatment of rotating frames of reference and adding the idea of the Coriolis effect to explain the more complex motion on the surface of a sphere that is required to explain phenomena such as the trade winds.

The geometry standard for middle school and high school requires students to "specify locations and describe spatial relationships using coordinate geometry and other representational systems" and to engage in "visualization, spatial reasoning, and geometric modeling" (Figures 5.10 and 5.11). The geometry standard does not appear to be developing the associated spatial thinking concepts in a fashion that is tightly coupled to the requirements implicit in the science standards for the parallel grades.

The expectation "specify locations" is moving into formal Euclidean geometry, a logical outcome for the geometry standard (Figure 5.12). There is some development of the concepts of coordinate systems on spheres and polar coordinates (Figure 5.13), which could be drawn upon by a science teacher in the Earth science activity relating to winds and ocean currents. The understanding of coordinate systems could be used to facilitate the projection of the three-dimensional sphere into two dimensions, but the science teacher would have to add the complicating factors of thinking about what is happening in a rotating coordinate system, something not addressed in the geometry standard.

Similarly, the "visualization" sections of the geometry standard for middle and high school students are not providing content that ties to the science standards. The standards for these grades emphasize networks (Figure 5.14) and the concept of perspective. In grade levels 6–8 there is additional work on two- and three-dimensional representations. All three concepts—networks, perspective, and representation—are important domains of knowledge for students to learn and

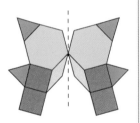

Line symmetry

Use visualization, spatial reasoning, and geometric modeling to solve problems

Spatial visualization can be developed by building and manipulating first concrete and then mental representations of shapes, relationships, and transformations. Teachers should plan instruction so that students can explore the relationships of different attributes or change one characteristic of a shape while preserving others. In the activity in figure 4.17, students are holding a long loop of yarn so that each student's hand serves as a vertex of the triangle. In this arrangement, students experiment with changing a shape by increasing the number of sides while the perimeter is unchanged. Conversations about what they notice and how to change from one shape to another allow students to hear different points of view and at the same time give teachers insight into their students' understanding. Work with concrete shapes, illustrated in this activity, lays a valuable foundation for spatial sense. To further develop students' abilities, teachers might ask them to see in their "mind's eye" the shapes that would result when a shape is flipped or when a square is cut diagonally from corner to corner. Thus, many shape and transformation activities build spatial reasoning if students are asked to imagine,

Fig. **4.17.**

Making a string triangle

FIGURE 5.5 Continues

could be applied to science examples. However, in the specific case of winds and currents, only the content on representations appears relevant, and the development of an understanding of rotating frames of reference appears to be left to the science teacher.

As part of the grades 9–12 experience, the physical science standard involves developing an understanding of the geometry of molecules. An examination of the geometry standard (Figure 5.14) for the corresponding grade grouping does not yield any material that is closely connected to the kind of spatial thinking required for understanding the examples of molecules. However the geometry standards for pre-K–2 and grades 3–5 do contain material useful in developing spatial predict, experiment, and check the results of the work themselves (see fig. 4.18).

Classroom activities that enhance visualization, such as asking students to recall the configuration of the dots on dominoes and determine the number of dots without counting, can promote spatial memory. A teacher could place objects (such as scissors, a pen, a leaf, a paper clip, and a block) on the overhead projector, show the objects briefly, and ask students to name the objects they glimpsed. Or the teacher might have students close their eyes; she could then take one object away and ask which one was removed.

In another "quick image" activity, students can be briefly shown a simple configuration such as the one in figure 4.19 projected on a screen and then asked to reproduce it. The configuration is shown again for a couple of seconds, and they are encouraged to modify their drawings. The process may be repeated several times so that they have opportunities to evaluate and self-correct their work (Yackel and Wheatley 1990). Asking, "What did you see? How did you decide what to draw?" is likely to elicit different explanations, such as "three triangles," "a sailboat sinking," "a square with two lines through it," "a y in a box," and "a sandwich that has been cut into three pieces." Students who can see the configuration in several ways may have more mathematical knowledge and power than those who are limited to one perspective.

Spatial visualization and reasoning can be fostered in navigation activities when teachers ask students to visualize the path they just walked from the library and describe it by specifying landmarks along the route or when students talk about how solid geometric shapes look from different perspectives. Teachers should ask students to identify structures from various viewpoints and to match views of the same structure portrayed from different perspectives. Using a variety of magazine photographs, older students might discuss the location of the photographers when they took each one.

Teachers should help students forge links among geometry, measurement, and number by choosing activities that encourage them to use knowledge from previous lessons to solve new problems. The story of second graders estimating cranberries to fill a jar, described in the "Connections" section of this chapter, illustrates a lesson in which students use their understanding of number, measurement, geometry, and data to complete the tasks. When teachers point out geometric shapes in nature or in architecture, students' awareness of geometry in the environment is increased. When teachers invite students to discover why most fire hydrants have pentagonal caps rather than square or hexagonal ones or why balls can roll in straight lines but cones roll to one side, they are encouraging them to apply their geometric understandings. When students are asked to visualize numbers geometrically by modeling various arrangements of the same number with square tiles, they also are making connections to area. Making and drawing such rectangular arrays of squares help primary-grades students learn to organize space and shape, which is important to their later understanding of grids and coordinate systems (Battista et al. 1998).

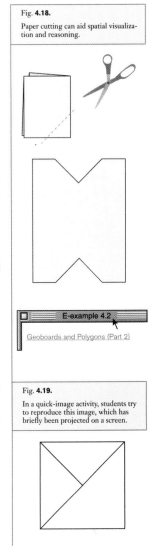

Fig. 4.18.
Paper cutting can aid spatial visualization and reasoning.

E-example 4.2

Geoboards and Polygons (Part 2)

Fig. 4.19.
In a quick-image activity, students try to reproduce this image, which has briefly been projected on a screen.

FIGURE 5.5 Use visualization, spatial reasoning, and geometric modeling to solve problems: developing spatial thinking. SOURCE: NCTM, 2000. Reprinted with permission from *Principles and Standards for School Mathematics*, copyright 2000 by the National Council of Teachers of Mathematics. All rights reserved.

thinking skills that could be used to understand three-dimensional molecular structures. Specifically, the visualization standard (Figure 5.6) for grades 3–5 has a focus on building up three-dimensional structures from blocks. In the pre-K–2 standards, students are asked to apply transformations and to use symmetry to analyze mathematical situations, skills that could again be useful in describing molecular structures. However, in sharp contrast to the strong links between K–4 mathematics and science, the necessary concepts in geometry are not introduced concurrently with science content that might use them. Therefore, the tight coordination of simple spatial concepts in the early years is not retained through high school.

Use visualization, spatial reasoning, and geometric modeling to solve problems

Students in grades 3–5 should examine the properties of two- and three-dimensional shapes and the relationships among shapes. They should be encouraged to reason about these properties by using spatial relationships. For instance, they might reason about the area of a triangle by visualizing its relationship to a corresponding rectangle or other corresponding parallelogram. In addition to studying physical models of these geometric shapes, they should also develop and use mental images. Students at this age are ready to mentally manipulate shapes, and they can benefit from experiences that challenge them and that can also be verified physically. For example, "Draw a star in the upper right-hand corner of a piece of paper. If you flip the paper horizontally and then turn it 180°, where will the star be?"

Much of the work students do with three-dimensional shapes involves visualization. By representing three-dimensional shapes in two dimensions and constructing three-dimensional shapes from two-dimensional representations, students learn about the characteristics of shapes. For example, in order to determine if the two-dimensional shape in figure 5.15 is a net that can be folded into a cube, students need to pay attention to the number, shape, and relative positions of its faces.

Students should become experienced in using a variety of representations for three-dimensional shapes, for example, making a freehand drawing of a cylinder or cone or constructing a building out of cubes from a set of views (i.e., front, top, and side) like those shown in figure 5.16.

Technology affords additional opportunities for students to expand their spatial reasoning ability. Software such as Logo enables students to draw objects with specified attributes and to test and modify the results. Computer games such as Tetris (Pajithov 1996) can help develop spatial orientation and eye-hand coordination. Dynamic geometry software provides an environment in which students can explore relationships and make and test conjectures.

Students should have the opportunity to apply geometric ideas and relationships to other areas of mathematics, to other disciplines, and to problems that arise from their everyday experiences. There are many ways to make these connections. For example, measurement and geometry are closely linked, as illustrated in the problem in figure 5.11, where geometric properties are used to relate the areas of two figures of different shapes. Geometric models are also important in investigating number relationships. Number lines, arrays, and many manipulatives used for modeling number concepts are geometric realizations of arithmetic relationships. In algebra, students in grades 3–5 often work with geometric problems to explore patterns and functions (see, for example, the "tower of cubes" problem in fig. 5.5).

In addition to its utility in exploring and understanding other areas of mathematics, geometry is closely associated with other subjects, such as art, science, and social studies. For example, students' work on symmetry can enhance their creation and appreciation of art, and their work on coordinate geometry is related to the maps they create or use in their study of the world. The study of geometry promotes a deeper understanding of many aspects of mathematics, improves students' abstract reasoning, and highlights relationships between mathematics and the sciences.

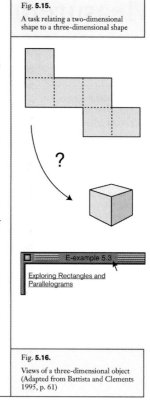

Fig. **5.15.**
A task relating a two-dimensional shape to a three-dimensional shape

?

E-example 5.3
Exploring Rectangles and Parallelograms

Fig. **5.16.**
Views of a three-dimensional object (Adapted from Battista and Clements 1995, p. 61)

FIGURE 5.6 Use visualization, spatial reasoning, and geometric modeling to solve problems: building additional spatial thinking skills. SOURCE: NCTM, 2000. Reprinted with permission from *Principles and Standards for School Mathematics*, copyright 2000 by the National Council of Teachers of Mathematics. All rights reserved.

speed of an object as fast, faster, or fastest in the earliest grades. As students get older, they can represent motion on simple grids and graphs and describe speed as the distance traveled in a given unit of time.

GUIDE TO THE CONTENT STANDARD
Fundamental concepts and principles that underlie this standard include

PROPERTIES OF OBJECTS AND MATERIALS

- Objects have many observable properties, including size, weight, shape, color, temperature, and the ability to react with other substances. Those properties can be measured using tools, such as rulers, balances, and thermometers.
- Objects are made of one or more materials, such as paper, wood, and metal. Objects can be described by the properties of the materials from which they are made, and those properties can be used to separate or sort a group of objects or materials.
- Materials can exist in different states—solid, liquid, and gas. Some common materials, such as water, can be changed from one state to another by heating or cooling.

POSITION AND MOTION OF OBJECTS

- The position of an object can be described by locating it relative to another object or the background.
- An object's motion can be described by tracing and measuring its position over time.
- The position and motion of objects can be changed by pushing or pulling. The size of the change is related to the strength of the push or pull.

- Sound is produced by vibrating objects. The pitch of the sound can be varied by changing the rate of vibration.

LIGHT, HEAT, ELECTRICITY, AND MAGNETISM

- Light travels in a straight line until it strikes an object. Light can be reflected by a mirror, refracted by a lens, or absorbed by the object.
- Heat can be produced in many ways, such as burning, rubbing, or mixing one substance with another. Heat can move from one object to another by conduction.
- Electricity in circuits can produce light, heat, sound, and magnetic effects. Electrical circuits require a complete loop through which an electrical current can pass.
- Magnets attract and repel each other and certain kinds of other materials.

Life Science

CONTENT STANDARD C:
As a result of activities in grades K-4, all students should develop understanding of
- The characteristics of organisms
- Life cycles of organisms
- Organisms and environments

DEVELOPING STUDENT UNDERSTANDING

During the elementary grades, children build understanding of biological concepts through direct experience with living things, their life cycles, and their habitats. These experiences emerge from the sense of won-

FIGURE 5.7 Guide to the content standard for physical science for grades K–4. SOURCE: NRC, 1996.

STRUCTURE AND PROPERTIES OF MATTER

- Atoms interact with one another by transferring or sharing electrons that are furthest from the nucleus. These outer electrons govern the chemical properties of the element.

- An element is composed of a single type of atom. When elements are listed in order according to the number of protons (called the atomic number), repeating patterns of physical and chemical properties identify families of elements with similar properties. This "Periodic Table" is a consequence of the repeating pattern of outermost electrons and their permitted energies.

- Bonds between atoms are created when electrons are paired up by being transferred or shared. A substance composed of a single kind of atom is called an element. The atoms may be bonded together into molecules or crystalline solids. A compound is formed when two or more kinds of atoms bind together chemically.

- The physical properties of compounds reflect the nature of the interactions among its molecules. These interactions are determined by the structure of the molecule, including the constituent atoms and the distances and angles between them.

- Solids, liquids, and gases differ in the distances and angles between molecules or atoms and therefore the energy that binds them together. In solids the structure is nearly rigid; in liquids molecules or atoms move around each other but do not move apart; and in gases molecules or atoms move almost independently of each other and are mostly far apart.

- Carbon atoms can bond to one another in chains, rings, and branching networks to form a variety of structures, including synthetic polymers, oils, and the large molecules essential to life.

FIGURE 5.8 Guide to the content standard for physical science in grades 9–12. SOURCE: NRC, 1996.

GUIDE TO THE CONTENT STANDARD
Fundamental concepts and principles that underlie this standard include

ENERGY IN THE EARTH SYSTEM

- Earth systems have internal and external sources of energy, both of which create heat. The sun is the major external source of energy. Two primary sources of internal energy are the decay of radioactive isotopes and the gravitational energy from the earth's original formation.

- The outward transfer of earth's internal heat drives convection circulation in the mantle that propels the plates comprising earth's surface across the face of the globe.

- Heating of earth's surface and atmosphere by the sun drives convection within the atmosphere and oceans, producing winds and ocean currents.

- Global climate is determined by energy transfer from the sun at and near the earth's surface. This energy transfer is influenced by dynamic processes such as cloud cover and the earth's rotation, and static conditions such as the position of mountain ranges and oceans.

FIGURE 5.9 Guide to the content standard for Earth science in grades 9–12. SOURCE: NRC, 1996.

The lack of connection takes two forms. In the first case, that of grades 9–12 chemistry, the spatial thinking concepts that would allow the student to grasp the structure of atoms and molecules are introduced well ahead of need; therefore both students and teachers may not recall the relevant material from earlier grades. In the second case, that of the Earth and space science standard, other than the discussion of coordinate geometry, the committee could not find anything in the mathematics standards that supported the complex spatial thinking process associated with the description of the motion of fluids (wind and ocean currents) on a rotating sphere. It is interesting to note that the examples and explicit ties from the mathematics to the science standards that were so noticeable for early education (Figure 5.4) have largely disappeared.

There are several conclusions about the coupling of the use of spatial thinking and reasoning in the mathematics and science standards. First, there is a close connection between the mathematics (pre-K–2 and 3–5) and the science standards (K–4) in early education. Second, the development of

Specify locations and describe spatial relationships using coordinate geometry and other representational systems

Geometric and algebraic representations of problems can be linked using coordinate geometry. Students could draw on the coordinate plane examples of the parallelograms discussed previously, examine their characteristic features using coordinates, and then interpret their properties algebraically. Such an investigation might include finding the slopes of the lines containing the segments that compose the shapes. From many examples of these shapes, students could make important observations about the slopes of parallel lines and perpendicular lines. Figure 6.18 helps to illustrate for one specific rhombus what might be observed in general: the slopes of parallel lines (in this instance, the opposite sides of the rhombus) are equal and the slopes of perpendicular lines (in this instance, the diagonals of the rhombus) are negative reciprocals. The slopes of the diagonals are

$$\frac{19-(-5)}{11-(-5)} = \frac{24}{16} = \frac{3}{2}$$

and

$$\frac{11-3}{-3-9} = \frac{8}{-12} = -\frac{2}{3}.$$

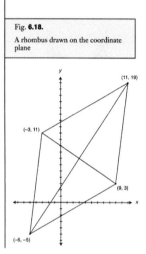

Fig. **6.18.**

A rhombus drawn on the coordinate plane

Apply transformations and use symmetry to analyze mathematical situations

Transformational geometry offers another lens through which to investigate and interpret geometric objects. To help them form images of shapes through different transformations, students can use physical objects, figures traced on tissue paper, mirrors or other reflective surfaces, figures drawn on graph paper, and dynamic geometry software. They should explore the characteristics of flips, turns, and slides and should investigate relationships among compositions of transformations. These experiences should help students develop a strong understanding of line and rotational symmetry, scaling, and properties of polygons.

From their experiences in grades 3–5, students should know that rotations, slides, and flips produce congruent shapes. By exploring the positions, side lengths, and angle measures of the original and resulting figures, middle-grades students can gain new insights into congruence. They could, for example, note that the images resulting from transformations have different positions and sometimes different orientations

FIGURE 5.10 Specify locations and describe spatial relationships using coordinate geometry and other representational systems. SOURCE: NCTM, 2000. Reprinted with permission from *Principles and Standards for School Mathematics*, copyright 2000 by the National Council of Teachers of Mathematics. All rights reserved.

spatial thinking and reasoning in the early years is, in the mathematics standards, aided by computer-based support systems. Third, this close coupling is not present during the grades 9–12 experience. Specifically, the science standards continue to presume, but do not make explicit, the use of spatial thinking and reasoning. Further, the presumed spatial thinking skills are more sophisticated than those being emphasized in the mathematics standards. Fourth, higher-level ability for spatial thinking is central to many key science education outcomes such as the analysis of situations in rotating frames of reference. Finally, the science standards seem to presume a very sophisticated skill set in spatial thinking, reasoning, and representation, and it is unclear where in the education system that skill set has been developed. To the extent that spatial thinking skills are explicitly taught, the process occurs under the rubric of geometry, which is only one of ten standards that are to be met by mathematics teaching and learning. Therefore, there is currently no significant, systematic treatment of spatial thinking as part of standards-based instruction in the United States.

Use visualization, spatial reasoning, and geometric modeling to solve problems

Students' skills in visualizing and reasoning about spatial relationships are fundamental in geometry. Some students may have difficulty finding the surface area of three-dimensional shapes using two-dimensional representations because they cannot visualize the unseen faces of the shapes. Experience with models of three-dimensional shapes and their two-dimensional "nets" is useful in such visualization (see fig. 6.25 in the "Measurement" section for an example of a net). Students also need to examine, build, compose, and decompose complex two- and three-dimensional objects, which they can do with a variety of media, including paper-and-pencil sketches, geometric models, and dynamic geometry software. Interpreting or drawing different views of buildings, such as the base floor plan and front and back views, using dot paper can be useful in developing visualization. Students should build three-dimensional objects from two-dimensional representations; draw objects from a geometric description; and write a description, including its geometric properties, for a given object.

Students can also benefit from experience with other visual models, such as networks, to use in analyzing and solving real problems, such as those concerned with efficiency. To illustrate the utility of networks, students might consider the problem and the networks given in figure 6.21 (adapted from Roberts [1997, pp. 106–7]). The teacher could ask students to determine one or several efficient routes that Caroline might use for the streets on map A, share their solutions with the class, and describe how they found them. Students should note the start-end point of each route and the number of different routes that they find. Students could then find an efficient route for map B. They should eventually conclude that no routes in map B satisfy the conditions of the problem. They should discuss why no such route can be found; the teacher might suggest that students count the number of paths attached to each node and look at where they "get stuck" in order to better

FIGURE 5.11 Use visualization, spatial reasoning, and geometric modeling to solve problems. SOURCE: NCTM, 2000. Reprinted with permission from *Principles and Standards for School Mathematics*, copyright 2000 by the National Council of Teachers of Mathematics. All rights reserved.

5.6 SPATIAL THINKING AND EDUCATION FOR THE NEXT GENERATION

Spatial thinking is a pervasive and powerful way of thinking that operates across the sciences, social sciences, and even the humanities. For example:

> . . . chemical education demands so much from students. It requires them to understand abstract theories (sometimes two to explain one phenomenon!), to have mathematical skills, to have experimental skills, to be able to communicate orally and in writing, and to visualize in three dimensions given information in two dimensions. And that is just the start. (Molecular Visualization in Science Education Workshop Advisory Board, 2001, p. iv)

Spatial thinking underpins many of the standards documents, yet it is not explicitly mentioned in any of them. Spatial thinking is presumed in many if not all of the sets of national K–12 standards. Despite its apparent predominance in geometry, it is *not* limited to any one discipline (Box 5.1).

Spatial thinking *is* the start of successful thinking and problem solving. Skill in spatial thinking is presumed throughout the K–12 curriculum but is formally and systematically taught nowhere. This leads to an educational blind spot. Formal, systematic instruction in spatial ideas is not part of the mainstream educational program. Therefore, although many of the general concepts under the rubric of spatial thinking are not novel, the committee believes that spatial thinking is under appreciated and under instructed in a systematic and coordinated way.

The committee's experience in reviewing the literature and examining the curriculum leads to a strong recommendation that we remedy the blind spot in the educational system by infusing and integrating diverse spatial thinking activities throughout the pre-college curriculum. Students could, for example, explore perspective in art; the perfect triangle in geometry; three-dimensional model-

Specify locations and describe spatial relationships using coordinate geometry and other representational systems

Geometric problems can be presented and approached in various ways. For example, many problems from Euclidean geometry, such as showing that the medians of any triangle intersect at a point, can be

approached through coordinate geometry. Although it is possible to use a different variable for the coordinates of each vertex (especially if a CAS package is effectively used), a "without loss of generality" argument can be used to lower the level of symbolic complexity. This type of argument relies on conveniently placing a coordinate plane over a general triangle (or other figure), often so that the coordinate axis coincides with a side of the triangle. By making clever choices about naming the coordinates of the vertices, taking care, of course, to be sure that the choices do not introduce unintended conditions, the calculations can be quite reasonable. Once they have obtained a representation like that in figure 7.16, students could determine the equations of two of the medians, find the point at which they intersect, and show that the third median passes through that point. Although proofs of this kind can be difficult for high school students, grappling with them may stimulate growth in students' understanding of geometry, algebraic variables, and generality.

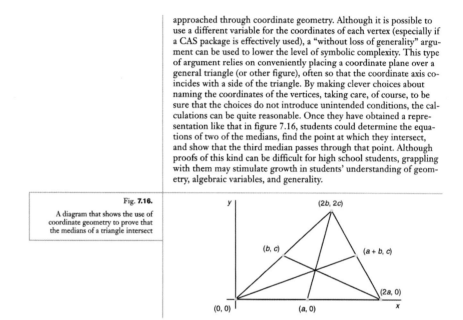

Fig. 7.16.

A diagram that shows the use of coordinate geometry to prove that the medians of a triangle intersect

FIGURE 5.12 Specify locations and describe spatial relationships using coordinate geometry and other representational systems. SOURCE: NCTM, 2000. Reprinted with permission from *Principles and Standards for School Mathematics*, copyright 2000 by the National Council of Teachers of Mathematics. All rights reserved.

In grades 9–12 students should also explore problems for which using other coordinate systems is helpful. They should have some familiarity with spherical and simple polar coordinate systems, as well as with systems used in navigation. Using rectangular coordinates, for example, students should learn to represent points that lie on a circle of radius 3 centered at the origin as

$$\left(x, \ \pm\sqrt{9-x^2}\right)$$

for $-3 \leq x \leq 3$. With polar coordinates, these pairs are represented more simply as $(3, \theta)$ for $0 \leq \theta \leq 2\pi$, where θ is measured in radians. Students should be able to explain why both of these forms describe the points on a circle. The polar-coordinate representation is simpler in this example and may be more useful for solving certain problems.

FIGURE 5.13 Geometry Standard: Specify locations and describe spatial relationships using coordinate geometry and other representational systems. SOURCE: NCTM, 2000. Reprinted with permission from *Principles and Standards for School Mathematics*, copyright 2000 by the National Council of Teachers of Mathematics. All rights reserved.

Use visualization, spatial reasoning, and geometric modeling to solve problems

Creating and analyzing perspective drawings, thinking about how lines or angles are formed on a spherical surface, and working to understand orientation and drawings in a three-dimensional rectangular coordinate system all afford opportunities for students to think and reason spatially. With the expanding role of computer graphics in the workplace, students will have increased needs and opportunities to use visualization as a problem-solving tool. Schooling should provide rich mathematical settings in which they can hone their visualization skills. Visualizing a building represented in architectural plans, the shape of a cross section formed when a plane slices through a cone (a conic section) or another solid object, or the shape of the solid swept out when a plane figure is rotated about an axis become easier when students work with physical models, drawings, and software capable of manipulating three-dimensional representations.

Geometric relationships explain procedures used by artists for drawing in perspective (see Smith [1995]), as demonstrated by the following perspective problem adapted from *Consortium for Mathematics and Its Applications* (1999, pp. 65–67):

Fig. 7.18.

Locating telephone poles so that they appear equidistant in a perspective drawing

An artist wants to draw a set of evenly spaced telephone poles along the side of a straight road, starting with two telephone poles as shown in figure 7.18a below. Where should the third telephone pole be placed so that it appears as far from the second as the second is from the first?

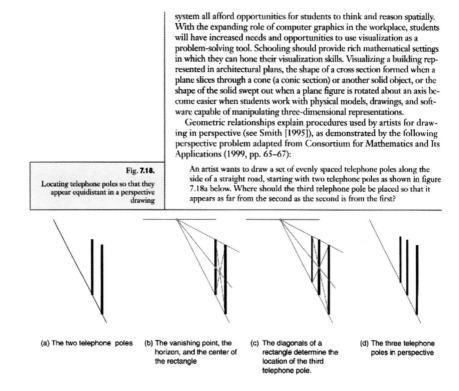

(a) The two telephone poles

(b) The vanishing point, the horizon, and the center of the rectangle

(c) The diagonals of a rectangle determine the location of the third telephone pole.

(d) The three telephone poles in perspective

FIGURE 5.14 Use visualization, spatial reasoning, and geometric modeling to solve problems. SOURCE: NCTM, 2000. Reprinted with permission from *Principles and Standards for School Mathematics*, copyright 2000 by the National Council of Teachers of Mathematics. All rights reserved.

ing in biology, chemistry and physics; and multidimensional reasoning in design aesthetics, literature, and psychology. They should have an opportunity to see connections between the use of graphs in economics and phase diagrams in physics. They should be able to understand the connection between changes in point of view as a function of degree of rotation in the horizontal and vertical planes. They should be able to practice skills in paper-and-pencil mapping, physical model building, and computer representation.

Teaching about spatial thinking is of particular significance now because, on the one hand, the capacity to support spatial thinking is increasing through the prevalence, power, and opportunities available from computers and software and, on the other hand, there is an increasingly urgent need to make sense of the increasing volumes of spatialized or spatializable data that are readily available.

Spatial thinking is also significant now because of changes in the process of education and in the ways in which we characterize knowledge. Increasingly, teachers are adopting the inquiry approach, which leads to fundamental changes in the relationship between teacher and student. The teacher becomes a facilitator or guide for the student's own process of exploration, discovery, and understanding. The teacher relinquishes the role of expert authority and instead models and supports the learning process of students. Learning is no longer the accumulation of a specific body of knowledge or the memorization of correct answers—it is a process of exploration and discovery driven by curiosity (the students in Bruner's study described in Chapter 1 [Bruner, 1959]). At the same time, there is a premium on connectivity and interdisciplinarity. Despite the power of the disciplinary approach to knowledge, real-world problems and the challenges of the workforce transcend traditional disciplinary boundaries. Multidisciplinary, collaborative approaches to problems are increasingly important. Again, spatial thinking is integral to these changes because it is a fundamental means of inquiry and because it connects across and adds coherence to the curriculum.

Therefore the committee believes that (1) we must recognize that spatial thinking is a fundamental and necessary mode of thought applicable across the life span in everyday life, in work situations, and in science; (2) we must foster a generation of students who are spatially literate; and (3) we must facilitate the transfer of generalizable spatial thinking skills across domains of knowledge in the K–12 curriculum, thus enhancing learning across the curriculum.

Spatial thinking can and should be taught in American schools. Students need formal training in specific spatial thinking skills (e.g., using point and cross-sectional data to create a three-dimensional model in anatomy or geology). There are many such spatial thinking skills, some of which may be specifically "tuned" to the needs of a particular disciplinary community.

We also need an educational process that leads to a fundamental understanding of spatial thinking in general, something that is more than a set of specific skills tailored to a particular discipline or school subject. Currently there are no standards for how we should think or learn spatially and no standards for how spatial thinking can be taught and assessed.

Recommendations for change in education encounter many problems, not the least of which is the understandable resistance of teachers who face increasing public demands for accountability on the one hand and demands for depth of coverage in specified knowledge domains on the other. Examples of such demands are those present in the No Child Left Behind Act of 2001 (Public Law 107-110), which mandates coverage of core areas of knowledge and regular assessment of student achievement in those areas. Adding another set of stand-alone standards to an already overcrowded curriculum would be unwelcome to say the least.

The breadth and variety of spatial thinking and of spatial thinkers pose an educational challenge. How can we design instructional programs to fit such a rich, diverse, complex, and intriguing set of learning tasks and domains? Clearly, education in spatial thinking must be strengthened. However, this should not add another layer to an increasingly complex and congested curriculum structure or overburden teachers. Spatial thinking is a missing link *across* the curriculum and it will help to make the curriculum more coherent. It is an invaluable approach to achieving existing curricular objectives. Spatial thinking is a fundamental process skill that transcends the bounds of particular disciplines. While it is central to the sciences, it is applicable in most, if not all, subject areas. It runs across the curriculum and extends from kindergarten through to twelfth grade (and beyond). It is increasingly possible to support the training of specific skills in spatial thinking and to foster a generation of students who are educated to think spatially. Moreover, because of emerging technologies, spatial thinking is more readily possible, and more challenging skills are being demanded and used because of the rapid evolution and widespread diffusion of technology. Technical systems for support leverage the human capacity for spatial thinking in many ways. They can speed up routine operations, manage massive data sets, generate alternatives, allow easy communication between people, and display results. Therefore, in Chapter 6, the committee develops a position statement about the nature and role of support systems in the K–12 context.

6

Tools for Thought: The Concept of a Support System

6.1 INTRODUCTION

A support system provides tools and technologies to leverage the power of the human capacity to think and to solve problems (Figure 6.1). In so doing, a support system augments and enhances selected mental capacities involving memory, computation, analysis, visualization, representation, reasoning, and evaluation. Levels of technology can range from simple pencil-and-paper tools to high-performance digital computing systems with scanners, printers, flat screens, voice and gesture interfaces, and projection systems. In the K–12 context, a support system comprises multiple elements: materials and technology, logistics, teachers, and curricula.

The chapter consists of nine sections. Section 6.2, using two detailed examples, establishes the two roles of a support system and emphasizes that its role is as a support, not as a substitute for human thought. Section 6.3, specifies the five principal functions of a support system in general. Section 6.4 identifies major problems in the design of a high-tech support system Section 6.5 focuses on criteria for the design of a high-tech support system in the context of K–12 education. Building from this base, Section 6.6 makes the case for a support system for spatial thinking, and Section 6.7 establishes requirements for the design of a support system for spatial thinking. Section 6.8 presents the need for a suite of tools, both high tech and low tech, for the support of spatial thinking in the K–12 context. Section 6.9 identifies five interlocking components essential for the implementation of a support system in the K–12 context.

6.2 THE NATURE OF A SUPPORT SYSTEM

The key to a support system is not technology as such. This is best illustrated by looking at a ubiquitous human spatial task, navigation, and drawing a contrast between two case studies. The first case (Box 6.1) is a description of the now famous navigational prowess of the Puluwatan islanders of the southern Pacific Ocean. The second case (Box 6.2) is an analysis of the typical vehicle navigation systems that are available in cars in the United States.

FIGURE 6.1 Using a calculator to solve a mathematical problem. SOURCE: http://pics.tech4learning.com/ details.php?img=calculator1.jpg. Reprinted by permission from Tech4Learning, Inc.

The parallels between Puluwatan voyagers and car drivers are striking: navigation is a function of knowledge structures and databases to which are applied rules and heuristics for selecting and following routes under a variety of environmental conditions. The differences are equally striking: in one case, most of the work is done "in the head" by a skilled navigator, whereas in the other a computer and a GPS unit do most of the work. The technological supports are minimal in one case and extensive in the other. But in both cases, it is the mind of the navigator or driver that determines the success of the operation. Navigators and drivers have learned how to navigate in a continuously changing and somewhat unpredictable environment. The Puluwatans have learned enormous amounts of highly specific information on land (from models and sketches drawn in the sand) and have practiced and mastered their skills at sea. Drivers have learned to operate the navigation system from the manual provided and then practiced and mastered their skills on the highway. It is the human power to think that is crucial: to the extent that the knowledge structures and display screens are functional (that is, user friendly and reliable), the in-vehicle navigation system (IVNS) works. In this way, support systems augment and leverage human problem solving.

Support systems play two principal roles, one practical and one conceptual. First, they enable us to do things more efficiently and more effectively in contexts ranging from everyday life to careers in all domains of knowledge: support systems are tools for thought and for lifelong learning. Second, they can change the process of education in fundamental ways for both students and teachers. In the case of spatial thinking, students can learn to understand and use the underlying thinking processes and they can learn to understand content areas whose concepts and data can be made more accessible through the application of spatial thinking. From a teacher's perspective,

BOX 6.1
Ocean Navigation in Micronesia

One of the classics of social science is Thomas Gladwin's (1970) *East Is a Big Bird*. The subtitle, *Navigation and Logic on Puluwat Atoll*, captures the thrust of this work. It is spatial thinking in its purest and perhaps most remarkable form. The culture of this group of Micronesian islanders values ocean navigation in outrigger canoes (Figure 6.2). Voyages are undertaken over hundreds of miles and many days, but they use none of the navigational equipment that is common to Western culture. There are no maps, compasses, sextants, or GPS units, at least in the classic form of this way of life.

The voyages are guided by highly trained and skilled navigators who have mastered a system of knowledge that is rich, complex, efficient, and non-Western in organization and principle. It is complete, in that every conceivable situation at sea is accounted for; it is strategic, built on a vast amount of detailed information and employing a series of heuristics; it is specific, tailored to the environment in the

FIGURE 6.2 A Puluwatan canoe. SOURCE: The Pacific Trust Territory of the Pacific Islands. Reprinted with permission of the Trust Territory Archives, Pacific Collection, University of Hawaii Library.

continued

BOX 6.1 Continued

immediate locality. The training takes years, linking on-land instruction to apprenticeship at sea. The on-land portion makes use of diagrams, drawn in the sand with shells as symbols, and the *mattang* or stick charts, depicting typical patterns of waves and currents (Figure 6.3).

The core of the system is an intricate and highly detailed knowledge of the physical environment: stars and their seasonal appearances in rising and setting positions; clouds and water color and their relationships to land; and birds and their typical foraging distances from land. The navigational process links star courses, sequences of rising and setting stars, with a system of dead reckoning. The canoes are steered by the "shape of the sky" as it relates to rigging of the canoe. The dead reckoning system depends on the continuous integration and updating of a mass of information, itself a remarkable feat of spatial thinking.

Star courses are memorized lists of sailing directions between islands, a list that must accommodate the rising and setting positions of stars at different times of the year. Because no single set of phenomena is sufficient to guide the canoe under all conditions, the system relies on backup procedures that vary in their ease of use and their accuracy and reliability. For people without clocks or compasses, it is much less accurate to sail using the constantly changing position of the Sun than it is to follow a sequence of stars, each for a short period of time.

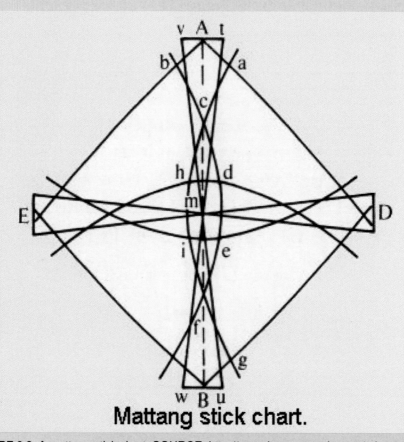

Mattang stick chart.

FIGURE 6.3 A mattang stick chart. SOURCE: http://www.janesoceania.com/micronesian_stick_chart/. Reprinted with permission from Dr. Jane Resture.

Nothing captures the power of spatial thinking better than one component of the dead reckoning system, known as *etak*. Gladwin (1970, p. 181) describes etak as an abstraction:

> . . . of a rather high order. The concept in etak of a specific but invisible island moving under often invisible navigation stars is not only an abstraction. It is also a purposefully devised logical construct by the use of which data inputs (rate and time) can be processed to yield a useful output, proportion of the journey completed.

While that description is analytical and framed to meet our technical understanding of cognitive processes, the remarkable nature of etak is best captured by these passages from Gladwin's book:

> Picture yourself on a Puluwat canoe at night. . . . On either side of the canoe water streams past, a line of turbulence and bubbles merging into a wake and disappearing in the darkness. Overhead there are stars, immovable, immutable. They swing in their paths across and out of the sky but invariably come up again in the same places. You may travel for days on the canoe but the stars will not go away or change their positions aside from their nightly trajectories from horizon to horizon. Hours go by, miles of water have flowed past. Yet the canoe is still underneath and the stars are still above. Back along the wake, however, the island you left falls farther and farther behind, while the one toward which you are heading is hopefully drawing closer. You can see neither of them, but you know this is happening. You know too that there are islands on either side of you, some near, some far, some ahead, some behind. The ones that are ahead will in due course fall behind. Everything passes by the little canoe—everything except the stars by night and the Sun in the day. (Gladwin, 1970, p. 182)

Thus, the canoe and the sky are seen as fixed in relation to each other: the world is seen as moving or flowing past the canoe. To track the canoe's position in this moving world requires an etak island (Figure 6.4).

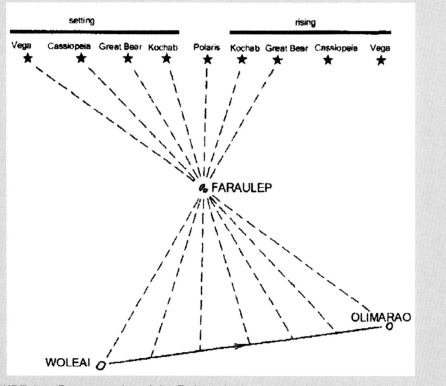

FIGURE 6.4 Representation of the Etak method, a system for tracking position at sea. SOURCE: Rainbird, 2004, p. 54. Reprinted with the permission of Cambridge University Press.

continued

BOX 6.1 Continued

It is the passage of the islands under the stars which is used for etak, the reckoning of distance traveled on a voyage. More specifically, one island is selected for each seaway and used throughout every voyage as a reference. . . . Ideally this island is fifty or so miles to one side of the line of travel and roughly opposite the midpoint of the seaway which stretches between the islands of origin and destination. The star bearings of the reference island from both the starting and ending points of the trip are known, since on another occasion the reference island may become a destination. In between there are other navigation star positions under which the reference island will pass as it "moves" backward. Its passage under each of these stars marks the end of one etak and the beginning of another. Thus the number of star positions which lie between the bearing of the reference island as seen from the island of origin and its bearing as seen from the island of destination determines the number of etak, which can here be called segments, into which the voyage is conceptually divided. When the navigator envisions in his mind's eye that the reference island is passing under a particular star he notes that a certain number of segments have been completed and a certain proportion of the voyage has therefore been accomplished. (Gladwin, 1970, p. 184)

This mental structure integrates speed and distance:

In sum, the contribution of etak is not to generate new primary information, but to provide a framework into which the navigator's knowledge of rate, time, geography, and astronomy can be integrated to provide a conveniently expressed and comprehended statement of distance traveled. . . . It is a useful and deliberate logical tool for bringing together raw information and converting it into the solution of an essential navigational question: "How far away is our destination?" (Gladwin, 1970, p. 186)

While we advocate the development and use of tools and technologies to support spatial thinking, the Puluwatan navigators illustrate the remarkable power of spatial thinking without modern technology. They show the way in which spatial thinking is woven into the culture of a group of people. They also show the remarkable ingenuity and inventiveness of those predecessors who "invented" the system. Although the regular use of the system does not generate new primary information, those sailors who developed the suite of strategies were indeed generators of new, primary knowledge.

---

support systems allow for the orderly and sequenced introduction of basic concepts and skills and for the guidance of the inquiry process.

Support systems cannot and should not substitute for thought. Therefore, a support system does *not* replace the human process of thinking, automating it by means of a "machine." It cannot provide a substitute for an understanding of what to do, when, how, and why. Instead, a support system provides an interactive environment within which thinking can take place. It is supportive in a variety of ways: it performs tasks that would otherwise be time-consuming and demanding in terms of effort and attention; it offers guidance in terms of options and alternatives; it provides checks and feedback; and it manages the flow of work. It is enhancing in that it allows access to a range of problem-solving strategies (heuristics and algorithms) that might otherwise be inaccessible, it fosters collaborative work by externalizing otherwise "private" processes, and it generates a range of possible answers to a question.

6.3 THE FUNCTIONS OF A SUPPORT SYSTEM

A support system for thinking in any domain of knowledge performs some or all of five functions:

1. *Database construction and management*: provides a capacity for data acquisition, entry, formatting, storage, and management (the functional equivalent of long-term memory)
2. *Data analysis*: performs operations and functions for data manipulation, analysis, interpretation, representation, and evaluation
3. *Memory*: provides working memory for tracking the flow of computations and the storage

of working and final results (the functional equivalent of short-term memory)

4. *Assistance*: provides prompts, feedback, hints, and suggestions to guide the choice of data analysis steps and to manage the flow of work

5. *Display*: provides a flexible display system for the representation of working and final results to oneself and to others—in physical form (e.g., a graph on paper, a three-dimensional model of molecular structure) or in virtual form (e.g., on-screen, for hard-copy printing, for export to other software packages)

For example, throughout history, we have developed, taught, and used a suite of tools—abacuses, compasses, Cuisenaire rods, protractors, graph paper, measuring and slide rules, and mechanical and electronic calculators—to facilitate calculations in the process of mathematical problem solving. Today, with the advent of sophisticated computer technologies, we are beginning to teach students to use software such as spreadsheets, database management programs, computer programming languages, and statistical analysis programs to perform calculations and to solve mathematical problems.

By routinizing basic mathematical operations (simple—such as addition, subtraction, multiplication, and division, complex—such as percentages, square roots, exponentiation, or generating trigonometric functions), tools and technologies provide ways of performing calculations and tracking the flow of sequences of chained operations. They can speed up the process of problem solving and increase the chances of arriving at a correct answer. They also provide ways of representing the working and final results to oneself and to others. Similar suites of tools and technologies can support spatial thinking in other knowledge domains (e.g., in architecture: pencil sketches, colored perspective drawings, sections [plans, elevations, etc.], balsa wood and cardboard models, CAD systems, virtual reality displays; in sea navigation; portolan charts, astrolabes, compasses, sextants, modified Mercator projection maps, chronometers, celestial tables, Loran, GPS).

In any knowledge domain, the components of a suite of support systems serve different functions in different contexts, for example, trading off speed and simplicity (in terms of data needs and the execution of operations) for depth and complexity. The elements of a suite of tools are not necessarily built in a coordinated fashion, either in terms of a division of functions or in terms of common design principles: they are assembled over time, with new tools adding to or replacing existing ones. However, their alignment along a low- to high-technology continuum is *not* necessarily synonymous with worse to better. Because of their simplicity, transparency, and intuitive nature, low-technology tools are often taught and used as precursors for understanding the complex, nontransparent, and non-intuitive operations of high-technology tools. Indeed, in many instances, the "back-of-the-envelope" answers generated by low-technology tools are perfectly adequate to the task at hand. However, with the increasing link between workforce demands and digital information technology, familiarity with and indeed mastery over high-technology tools is increasingly important.

6.4 TOOLS FOR THOUGHT: THE LIMITS TO POWER

Support systems, especially those that are computer based, are the cognitive equivalent of power tools. With the promise of access to such power comes costs and challenges. These include the time and committed effort it takes to learn to use a support system (and continuously upgrade to new versions), the need to understand the system's range of appropriate and inappropriate uses, and the need to appreciate the system's characteristic limits and idiosyncrasies.

There is a wide range of support systems available in science, mathematics, and design (see Box 7.1 for a description of hi-tech support systems for spatial thinking). These support systems can be a boon or a bane to the learner. Experts in a knowledge domain start with an understanding

BOX 6.2
Vehicle Navigation Systems in the United States

Becoming "lost" implies disorientation, a consequence of the failure to recognize one's current location, the failure to recognize local or distant landmarks, the failure to understand (or interpret) local signage, the inability to retrace the current path, the breakdown of cognitive processing (such as path integration or ability to define a homing vector), and the resultant emotional stress.

Not only do some drivers in the United States get lost when departing from a habitual travel route, but they cannot recover from the error. They have not developed the spatial thinking skills (including map reading) to be able to recover positional and orientational information from memory or from examining their proximate environment. Obviously this situation is not universal, and many highly skilled wayfinders and navigators are also present in the general population. However, a thriving technology, in-vehicle navigation systems (IVNS), has been developed to

• aid those who are lost directly by telling them where they are and giving directions in a spatialized natural language suitable for interpretation by spatially naive or unskilled travelers (e.g., the General Motors *Onstar System*) or
• provide in-vehicle visual or verbal instructions about a route to be traveled (e.g., screen-based road maps or verbal descriptions of routes).

Drivers have the luxury of choosing to be a navigator or a wayfinder. To navigate implies following a pre-planned route without departure except for unexpected emergencies (e.g., congestion, accidents, construction.). Wayfinding involves searching out a path rather than exactly following a pre-planned route. In the former case, the navigator has to recognize the presence of defined choice points where actions such as changing direction are involved. It is often referred to as "piloting," where the driver proceeds from landmark to landmark in a prescribed sequence. Wayfinders often choose their own routes, incorporating local knowledge of road systems plus select path segments by using their spatial skills (e.g., general orientational, directional, and distance knowledge or knowledge of environmental layout and its geometry). Strategies such as shortcutting through familiar or unfamiliar areas can be incorporated into the wayfinding strategy on both the outward and return journey.

Research on human navigation and wayfinding indicates that females often prefer the "piloting" system for local navigation, using a landmark to landmark (or choice point to choice point) decision support system. Males prefer to use their understanding of the geometry of layouts as a primary support system, enabling tactics such as shortcutting and minimizing travel time or travel distance (described as a "homing vector" or "path integration" procedure) (Montello et al., 1999; Saucier et al., 2002). The in-vehicle support system to accommodate this activity can be visual (map based), minimally verbally descriptive, or reliant only on a simple device such as a dashboard compass (Battista, 1990; Beatty and Tröster, 1987; Ferguson and Hegarty, 1993; Lawton, 1994; Loomis et. al., 1999; O'Laughlin and Brubaker, 1998).

In-vehicle navigation support systems can be low tech in design: a dashboard compass, a hand-held cartographic road map (e.g., topographic sheet), or a simplified and linearized route map (as in an AAA *Trip-Tik*). Because the bulk of daily travel is regularly episodic and habitual, relying on people's cognitive maps (or environmental knowledge stored in long-term memory), drivers in most situations have little need for an in-vehicle navigation support system. Exceptions occur when (1) a well-known route is obstructed, requiring a change of travel plans to bypass the obstruction; (2) one is required to travel to an unfamiliar destination; (3) one is exploring new places for, say, recreational or aesthetic purposes; and (4) one has become lost. In most of these cases, a low-tech system can be replaced by (or supplemented with) a high-tech IVNS.

of the nature of the data, the ways of thinking, and the problems characteristic of the field within which the system could be used. They develop a working understanding of the tool—especially its glitches and quirks—as they use it. In using systems for calculating, for example, they appreciate the difference between truncating and rounding, the necessity for appreciating the number of significant digits, the differences in the effects of error on addition and subtraction versus multipli-

When a driver becomes lost, a navigation system could perform a range of functions: (1) automatically call for help if an airbag is deployed; (2) if the vehicle is stolen, give the authorities the vehicle's current location from GPS tracking; (3) summon emergency services on request; and (4) provide concierge services such as making restaurant reservations. This system is both a navigation and a communication aid and is based on speech interaction with a home base. Vehicle location and tracking is done via a GPS, which uses radio signals from a selection of satellites orbiting at 10,900 nautical miles above Earth. Location is defined by the time taken for a satellite signal to reach a vehicle receiver. Input from four or more satellites enables triangulation of vehicle location in a georeferenced frame (latitude and longitude), which is downloaded and matched with the coordinate frame used in the vehicle's base map.

A more advanced IVNS might have all or most of the basic features in addition to an in-vehicle heads-up display of the travel environment. Early versions displayed only a screen-based two-dimensional road map with the current location identified and with a bird's-eye view of the travel environment, including destination location and perhaps a navigable route overlain on the road system. Current versions provide bird's-eye views of the total environment for "you are here" fixing, then enable zooming of scale and visualization from an eye-level perspective that obviates the need for abstract map reading, replacing this process with a more common local visual experience in which three-dimensional presentations of buildings and landmarks replace the two-dimensional flat maps that require abstract map reading skills.

An IVNS consists of (1) a computer; (2) a detailed, geocoded electronic base map covering road and/or highway systems; (3) a GPS for determining current location and/or for vehicle tracking; (4) a spatial (geocoded) supporting database (a GIS) that contains the locations of landmarks and other features such as commercial entities and a set of analytical tools that can use current location and a given destination to develop a route plan or to provide location-based services such as details of the location and types of restaurants; and (5) an appropriate in-vehicle interface that does not distract the driver's attention away from road and traffic conditions for any appreciable time. The latter implies using a simplified rather than a cluttered or complex visualization (e.g., a strip road map rather than a more complex land-use map), auditory description and instructions, or a combination of visual and auditory inputs.

The design of an IVNS should take account of the properties of spatial thinking including (1) the level of detail given in any visual or auditory portrayal of a relevant environmental representation; (2) the degree to which an IVNS distracts perceptual attention away from the primary task of driving safely; (3) the modality chosen to provide necessary information, usually sight or speech; (4) the nature of a visualization, particularly in terms of scale, continuous zooming capacity, use of color, feature simplification, information complexity, and time taken to interpret information; and (5) determining optimal in-vehicle location of an IVNS (e.g., on the ceiling, above the steering wheel, on the dashboard, on the console between the front seats) such that it requires minimal head-turning and optical scanning away from the road and traffic.

IVNS are important for commercial vehicles such as taxis, delivery systems such as FedEx or UPS, and mail delivery. Via GPS tracking, fleet vehicle locations can be monitored (e.g., for sending the closest taxi, police car, or emergency vehicle to a specific destination or for knowing current locations of members of a local or interstate trucking fleet). IVNS are still considered to be a luxury item in all but high-end private vehicles. However their use and acceptance are growing. IVNS reduce the cognitive load for drivers by substituting information from a spatial support system for the cognitive process of navigation while simultaneously providing a spatial support system for wayfinders, explorers, and independent and skillful spatial thinkers.

cation and division versus exponentiation, the problems of estimating rather than reporting a divide by zero as an error, and the difference between statistical significance and meaningful difference. Even for experts, there can be negative transfer in going, for example, from one word processing software system to another, with function keys having different meanings, identical patterns of keystrokes activating different operations, and identical operations being given different names.

Naive users, those who are not expert in a knowledge domain, face a dual problem: that of learning to use the support system in the context of an underdeveloped understanding of the knowledge domain. Appreciating the nature of data, understanding the characteristic ways of thinking (i.e., doing things), and sharing the sense of characteristic problems are skills that are, at best, partially and incompletely developed or, at worst, based on intuitive and often erroneous understandings of the knowledge domain.

In the case of someone engaged in the process of mathematical thinking, tools for thought provide support and challenges by (1) decreasing or increasing the cognitive demands (e.g., in terms of the performance of specific calculating tasks that might or might not be the most appropriate given the nature of the data); (2) decreasing or increasing the memory demands (in the use of short- and long-term memory capacity to recall how specific subroutines work or the meaning of conventions chosen by the system designer); (3) increasing or decreasing flexibility (by providing access to alternative sets of operations or making some apparently simple operations difficult to access or perform); (4) increasing or decreasing problem-solving skills (by offering access to model analysis sequences that could be illuminating or obscure); and (5) increasing or decreasing applicability (by enabling the person to make generalizations in the application of mathematical thinking across different problem domains that might or might not be appropriate).

Therefore, in the design of a support system, the implementation and instruction process, and the use of a support system, there are inevitably tensions that can lead to significant problems for learners and teachers. For each issue, there is no simple resolution.

1. *The end-means issue*: learning about the nature of a support system as an end in itself versus learning to use a support system as a means of solving problems. The more complex a system, the greater are the time and effort that must be invested in learning about the system. That investment, while necessary, does not of itself entail success in a particular domain of thinking. Tools are means, not ends, and the goal is successful problem solving. There is a significant risk of a disconnect between students learning about a support tool and students learning how to apply that tool in a variety of contexts. Support systems must be presented as working tools in the context of domain knowledge and domain problems.

The educational challenge is to ensure that there is a balance between learning about and learning to use the support system to solve problems.

2. *The opacity-transparency issue*: learning to perform operations that remain opaque versus having those operations become transparent through understanding what happens, how, and why. The so-called calculator wars in mathematics education exemplify this tension (Alkhateeb, 2002; Alkhateeb and Taha, 2002; NRC, 1991). In the absence of a support system, individuals must perform all of the steps in the process "by hand," as it were; thus, they are more likely to understand the meaning of the calculations. In a computer-based support system, most of the individual steps not only are hidden from view but often are inaccessible to the user.

The educational challenge is to ensure that a student has a good grasp of the fundamentals of problem solving in a domain before learning about and then using a support system that necessarily presumes an understanding of the fundamentals.

3. *The rote learning-comprehension issue*: learning the right sequence of buttons to push (the concept of "buttonology" in the e-domain) or the right sequence of things to do versus understanding what to do and why to do those things in that particular way in this particular problem context. This issue is an extension of the opacity-transparency issue. Learning to use a tool for thought is *not* the same as learning to think. It is relatively easy to reinforce a facile but inflexible command of, say, sequences of key strokes or the rote learning of a series of actions that lead to correct results if and only if the problem context remains the same. Problem solving can be reduced to

stereotypical and reflexive patterns of "this is how you do it." There is no transfer to other domains of knowledge.

The educational challenge is to ensure that a student understands why particular ways of doing things are appropriate for particular problem contexts. Problem solving must be reflective.

4. *The power-limitations issue*: learning and understanding what the system is versus is not capable of doing or what the system can versus should be used to do. Of necessity, any system privileges some ways of doing things at the expense of others. To the extent that the system design reflects best practices in a particular knowledge domain, especially as reflected in the thinking processes of domain experts, then the support system can be very powerful.

However, in the hands of an unwary user, support systems can do things that may be misleading, counterproductive, and wrong (Figure 6.5). Thus, cartographic mapping packages can generate a remarkable range of maps, based on different projections. Selection of the wrong projection can lead a user to make comparisons between data values plotted on a map that does not preserve area, thus resulting in inappropriate inferences (as exemplified by the so-called Greenland versus South America effect seen on an inappropriately used modified Mercator projection). Support systems have defaults, pre-set ways of operating that are taken as standard in a domain, but whose implications and use must be understood before they are applied automatically.

This general problem is compounded in the K–12 context because as the concepts of developmental and educational appropriateness make clear, data management, data analysis, and display functions must be matched to the student's cognitive capacities. Expert practices may not match the capacities and needs of beginning or even intermediate students.

The educational challenge is to build and deploy support systems that are educationally and developmentally appropriate. The committee believes: (1) that a successful support system should be a means to an end, that of problem solving, helping to frame problems and providing ways of responding to them; (2) that components of the system should be transparent wherever possible; and (3) that the system should be comprehensible to the full range of students. The ultimate goal in learning to use a support system is understanding and flexibility in problem solving, *not* necessarily enhancing speed and efficiency by minimizing error and increasing accuracy, desirable though those characteristics might be.

Therefore, a support system should be viewed not as a prosthesis that substitutes for and replaces thought but as an enabling device that facilitates and enhances the process of thinking. It should enable students to engage in thinking more consciously, more willingly, more effectively, more reflectively, and with more confidence in as wide a range of contexts as possible (i.e., integrating across the curriculum).

6.5 GENERAL CRITERIA FOR THE DESIGN OF A SUPPORT SYSTEM IN THE K–12 EDUCATIONAL CONTEXT

The design of a support system should (a) meet specific educational goals, (b) be appropriate to student needs, and (c) match the educational context. Given its analyses in Chapters 2 through 5, the committee has identified 10 general criteria for the design of a support system in K–12 education.

Meeting Educational Goals

1. Be *supportive of the inquiry process* in at least five basic ways:
    (a) providing prompts, feedback, and helpful hints to guide the flow of work and to encourage critical reflection;

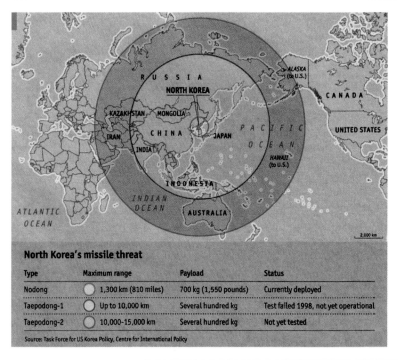

North Korea's missile threat

Type	Maximum range		Payload	Status
Nodong	⬤	1,300 km (810 miles)	700 kg (1,550 pounds)	Currently deployed
Taepodong-1	⬤	Up to 10,000 km	Several hundred kg	Test failed 1998, not yet operational
Taepodong-2	⬤	10,000-15,000 km	Several hundred kg	Not yet tested

Source: Task Force for US Korea Policy, Centre for International Policy

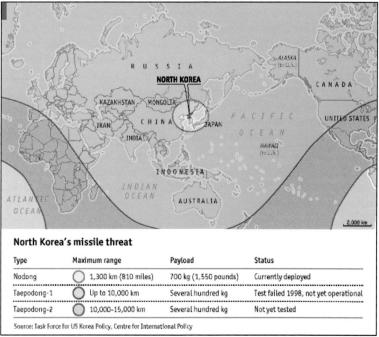

North Korea's missile threat

Type	Maximum range		Payload	Status
Nodong	⬤	1,300 km (810 miles)	700 kg (1,550 pounds)	Currently deployed
Taepodong-1	⬤	Up to 10,000 km	Several hundred kg	Test failed 1998, not yet operational
Taepodong-2	⬤	10,000-15,000 km	Several hundred kg	Not yet tested

Source: Task Force for US Korea Policy, Centre for International Policy

FIGURE 6.5 The dangers of an inappropriate map projection: (a) In this map, published in the *Economist* on May 3, 2003, concentric circles are erroneously superimposed on a Mercator map. As a result, the map incorrectly identifies regions that could be reached by missiles of various ranges launched from North Korea. (b) In the corrected map, published in the *Economist* on May 17, 2003, all of the United States and Canada are within range of the Taepodong-1 or Taepodong-2 missile. Reproduced with permission from Task Force on U.S. Korea Policy, Center for International Policy.

    (b) keeping track of the flow of work;

    (c) modeling ways of performing operations and analyses;

    (d) finding an exact or correct answer to a problem or presenting a range of alternate problem-solving scenarios (as in a decision support system for community planning); and

    (e) providing ways of representing data and results to oneself and to others.

  2. Be *useful in solving problems in a wide range of real-world contexts*

  3. *Facilitate learning transfer* across a range of school subjects

  4. Provide a *rich, generative, inviting, and challenging problem-solving environment* for the users of the support system

Being Appropriate to Student Needs

  5. Be *developmentally and educationally appropriate*, tailored for use by novice learners, not expert users, and graded to support increasing levels of skill and experience

  6. Be *accessible to and supportive of the full range of learners* (i.e., including those who are differently abled)

  7. Be *customizable* to meet the needs of specific groups of learners working on particular tasks in specific contexts

Matching the Educational Context

  8. Be *flexible enough to be effective in a variety of school contexts* (e.g., infused versus subject-based curricula; elementary versus high school) and to *enable a range of modes of use* (e.g., individual and stand-alone; collaborative and networked, locally and globally)

  9. Be *quick and intuitive for students and teachers to learn to use*

  10. Be *robust and realistic* in terms of the expectations placed on teachers and the demands on school infrastructure (in terms of hardware and software)

These 10 criteria are *desiderata* rather than immediately attainable goals. No support system can be expected to meet all of the criteria simultaneously and to the maximum extent. Indeed, systems can be successful without necessarily fulfilling all 10 criteria. In some contexts, criteria may pose contradictory demands. Thus, something that satisfies criterion 6 (ease of learning) may indeed meet criterion 8 (utility across a range of contexts) but do so only because it meets criterion 1 (support inquiry) and criterion 4 (a rich environment) in relatively superficial and shallow ways. Nevertheless, these 10 criteria provide working guidelines for the design and implementation of a support system.

6.6 THE NEED FOR SUPPORT SYSTEMS FOR SPATIAL THINKING (SSST)

The committee advocates the design, development, testing, and implementation of systems— low tech and high tech—for the support of spatial thinking. These systems can facilitate the inquiry approach (hypothesis generating and testing) to problem solving in real-world contexts. They can be fine-tuned to accommodate the needs of different disciplinary traditions and problem-solving contexts, and they can be structured to reflect individual performance differences as a function of age and ability (the concepts of developmental and educational appropriateness).

Support systems for spatial thinking are necessary for two reasons:

1. *Spatial thinking is a complex and challenging process.* Support systems can help to manage this complexity by
- storing and handling multiple and often large data sets;
- routinizing repetitious and laborious elemental parts of the process (akin to the development of macros in word processing programs);
- keeping track of the results of chained sequences of operations;
- providing in-process feedback and assistance; and
- providing a means for the display and communication of results, working and final, for oneself and for others.

2. *Spatial thinking is a powerful process.* Support systems can help to ensure the appropriate use of this power by
- making its roles clear;
- making its practice accessible to a wide range of users;
- making its instruction and application successful in a wide range of contexts;
- drawing on the experiences of as broad a range of disciplines as possible and on the expertise of members of those disciplines (the idea of best practices);
- providing multiple, alternative formats for representing data and results;
- providing access to key activities (in terms of transformations, operations, and analyses); and
- recognizing the roles of incompleteness and error in data, uncertainty in analysis, and therefore ambiguity in results.

Given the different forms that spatial thinking can take and the diverse range of contexts within which it can be applied, there is no single system that can be a universal support for spatial thinking. Chapters 8 and 9 analyze one exemplar system, GIS, in terms of its design and implementation in the K–12 context, and Chapter 10 presents recommendations for improving its design and implementation.

However, it is the committee's belief that a mix of support systems must be brought to bear on the teaching of spatial thinking. Although GIS is evaluated in detail as one such system, the committee recognizes that the fundamental challenge is first and foremost to appreciate the practical power and educational importance of spatial thinking. The problem that we face in American schools today is not one of inadequate tools as such but the need to appreciate and understand the process of spatial thinking. We can only teach people to do what we recognize, understand, and value.

6.7 THE REQUIREMENTS OF A SUPPORT SYSTEM FOR SPATIAL THINKING

Spatial thinking is built on a constructive amalgam of an understanding of space, representation, and reasoning (see Chapters 1 and 2). These three elements shape the specific characteristics of a support system for spatial thinking that must have the capacity to do the following:

1. *Spatialize data sets* by providing spatial data structures and coding systems (see Chapter 2) for spatial and nonspatial data.

Data sets that are spatial in form (e.g., containing positional data expressed in terms of latitude and longitude coordinates) must be registered and projected into a geographic space (e.g., on a map projection using the State Plane Coordinate System [SPCS]). With numerous ways of expressing spatial data, a support system must be able to integrate heterogeneous data sets by registering and projecting them onto a common framework for analysis and display.

Data sets that are not necessarily spatial in their original form can be spatialized by adding geo- or spatial coordinates. Temporal and attribute data can be spatialized. For a single data set, identities of objects can become locations in one or more spaces; pairwise relationships between objects located in that space (based on the degrees of similarity, difference, and connection, where those relationships can reflect function, genesis, history, appearance, properties, etc.) can become distances; sets of multiple relationships between the locations of objects can become patterns (permitting the identification of spatial structures, deviations, and exceptions); and patterns can be explained in terms of the processes that generated them. Multiple spatialized data sets can be overlain and combined in different spaces. All spaces can be restructured along different axes with different distance metrics and different dimensionalities.

The capacity to spatialize is what motivates the process of spatial thinking.

2. *Visualize working and final results* by creating representations that capture the structure of spaces and the locations, relationships, and patterns of objects depicted in them.

There are numerous general classes of representations—maps, graphs, diagrams, charts, cross sections, drawings, photographs, animations, models, remotely sensed images, etc.—that can be adapted to meet the needs characteristic of a particular knowledge domain (see Chapter 3).

Similarly, there are numerous forms for representations. Representations can be static or dynamic (either cross-sectional or continuous); they can be still images or animations; they can be visual-graphic or expressed in a variety of sensory modes (e.g., three-dimensional tabletop models, globes, plastic maps with raised relief, braille maps); they can be in black and white or in color; they can be presented via a range of media (e.g., video, sound, vibrotactile) that can be converted to other media forms (e.g., voice-recognition and text-to-speech software).

The capacity to represent is integral to the process of spatial thinking.

3. *Perform functions* that manipulate the structural relations of spatialized data sets. These functions include the following:

Transformations

- Symbolizing (use of graphic markers [point, lines, and areas] and sensory media-appropriate variables [e.g., in the visual graphic case: size, shape, orientation, hue, value, chroma] to capture the identity of objects; similar variables can be created for sensory media such as touch [force feedback, tactile, and vibrotactile mapping symbols] and sound)
- Scale change (zooming in [magnification] and zooming out [minification] in either a continuous or a discrete stepwise manner)
- Replotting into different frames of reference (from projections using one coordinate system to another [e.g., abstract as in azimuthal versus Cartesian or specific as in cartographic mapping systems such as latitude and longitude, the universal transverse Mercator zones, the SPCS])
- Reprojecting (within families of map projections that preserve properties such as area, shape, direction, and distance [e.g., the Molleweide equal area, which is used for world statistical maps where the areas of particular interest are in the midlatitudes])
- Rescaling (converting from one distance metric to another [e.g., Euclidean versus Manhattan])
- Perspective change (adopting different viewing azimuths [from 0° to 360° around an arbitrary reference] and viewing angles [from 0° to 90°, eye-level to orthogonal])
- Spatial transformations (movements of objects in terms of translations and rotations in the plane, etc.)
- Dimensional change (e.g., converting three-dimensional to two-dimensional depictions)

Operations

• Set theoretic relations between data sets (union, intersection, etc.) leading to aggregation and disaggregation
• Interpolation and extrapolation
• Abstraction (e.g., converting numerical point data to a surface with contour lines)
• Generalization (e.g., classification, smoothing, simplification, exaggeration [as in different scales for horizontal versus vertical distances on a map])

Analyses

• Descriptions of the properties of spatial distributions in terms of density, dispersion, centroids, regions, outliers
• Pattern analysis (e.g., differentiating random patterns from systematic patterns; classifying systematic patterns in terms of regularity [as in grids or other tessellations] or clustering; identifying deviations; identifying relations between patterns [positive and negative correlations])
• Structural analysis (e.g., for patterns, calculation of nearest neighbors, or spatial autocorrelation; for networks, calculations of centrality, connectivity, and various paths [shortest, the traveling salesman route, etc.]; for hierarchies, calculation of tree structures)
• Process modeling (e.g., developing explanations of spatial patterns as a function of time and/or distance [Boxes 1.1 and 1.2])

The capacity to manipulate structural relationships is the essence of spatial thinking.

6.8 SUPPORT SYSTEMS FOR SPATIAL THINKING IN THE K–12 CONTEXT

With the increasing availability of powerful IT systems, it is tempting to see the development of support systems for spatial thinking as necessarily being computer based and, therefore, high tech in nature. This is *not* the case.

Spatial thinking can also be supported with low-tech systems, essentially involving paper-and-pencil systems allied to the use of simple graphic representations (as in the case of Jerome Bruner's work using simple outline maps, cited in Chapter 1). Such low-tech systems are important for the following reasons:

• Despite the increasing penetration of IT into American schools, access to hardware and software remains limited. To build supports for spatial thinking only around IT would be a mistake; it would restrict the opportunities for both teachers and students to learn about and use spatial thinking across the curriculum.
• Understanding many of the fundamental building blocks of spatial thinking can be more readily achieved through simple, low-tech systems (see Box 6.3). These place fewer demands on teachers, students, and schools. They are easily adapted for use across the curriculum. They have immediacy and face validity that permit students to understand the basic components of spatial thinking. Specific skills can be isolated and practiced. For example, students can use simple transparencies to overlay maps and to understand correlations between patterns of data. They can use graph paper to learn about rescaling and transformations of data.

BOX 6.3
Thinking Inside the Box

As an example of a very effective and imaginative low-tech system for supporting spatial thinking, a class of 9-year-olds was presented with a box. The contents were unknown to them: their challenge was to find out what was inside the box through an ingenious adaptation of spatial sampling. The top of the box was perforated with 100 holes, arranged in a 10 × 10 grid. The two axes were labeled from 1 to 10 and from A to J, thus ensuring that each hole could be given a unique spatial identifier. Next to the box was a sheet of paper, also laid out with an identical 10 × 10 grid with the same axis identifiers. The children were given knitting needles and first had to calibrate them to provide "depth" readings below the surface of the box when the needle was inserted into a hole and it touched whatever object was in the box. They created summary tables of their data (in effect, x-y-z coordinates) and then transferred the coordinate data onto the paper using Lego blocks for the Z coordinate. When they finished creating a Lego shape and surface, they were allowed to open the box. Inside was a three-dimensional model of a mountain range which they had, much to their excitement, recreated through a classic example of spatial thinking.

6.9 THE IMPLEMENTATION OF A SUPPORT SYSTEM FOR SPATIAL THINKING IN THE K–12 EDUCATIONAL CONTEXT

In the K–12 educational context, the implementation of a support system for spatial thinking entails an awareness of a series of five interlocking components, all of which must be addressed for the system to be implemented successfully. There should be programs to provide

1. *material* support in the form of computer hardware, software, high-speed network access, tools, and supplies (e.g., disks, paper, pencils);
2. *logistical* support in the form of technical support for the installation, maintenance, and upgrading of hardware and software;
3. *instructional* support in the form of pre-service and in-service training programs for teachers;
4. *curriculum* support in the form of educational goals, knowledge and performance standards, assessment procedures, unit and lesson plans, and supporting materials; and
5. *community* support in the form of the recognition of the educational value of the support system and, therefore, the collaboration by stakeholders in providing students with opportunities for problem solving in real-world contexts (e.g., requests for assistance, internships, access to data).

Designed and implemented appropriately, systems for supporting spatial thinking can have three major effects in the K–12 education context. First, they can change how things are taught, which is important in itself, but more importantly, they can change what can be taught. Second, they can offer students a critical awareness of a crucial thought process that is either unknown or poorly understood because it is largely hidden from view and insufficiently appreciated at present. Third, they can be mind-enhancing: students can learn to use a powerful way of thinking, one that can have lifelong implications for problem solving in life and career contexts. If we are successful in the design and implementation of support systems, we can help to foster a generation of students who will become spatially literate (see Chapter 11).

A support system facilitates the process of spatial thinking: it empowers students. However, we have to distinguish clearly between two goals: (1) that of learning to think spatially and (2) that of learning to use a support system for spatial thinking per se.

In Part 1 of this report, the committee has presented the case for teaching spatial thinking to all students. It is important to understand what spatial thinking is and how it works. It is equally important to understand how expertise in spatial thinking develops in general and differently among different people. Both sets of understandings are necessary precursors for developing systematic educational programs to teach American students how to think spatially. In Part II of this report, the committee shows how support systems, particularly those that are technologically based, can facilitate the teaching and practice of spatial thinking. Chapter 7 reviews a series of high-tech support systems for spatial thinking, providing a context for the detailed analysis of GIS. Chapter 8 presents a critical analysis of the design, implementation, and use of GIS. The current use and potential development of GIS are evaluated in terms of the ten general criteria for the design of a support system and in terms of the three specific characteristics of a support system for spatial thinking. Chapter 9 summarizes the findings of the analysis of GIS. In Chapter 10, the committee presents recommendations directed at the goal of fostering spatial thinking in general and at the specific goal of enhancing the design and implementation of one support system, GIS.

Part II

Support for Spatial Thinking

7

High-Tech Support Systems for Spatial Thinking

7.1 INTRODUCTION

Spatial thinking underpins problem solving in everyday life, the workplace, and science. While much spatial thinking occurs unaided, there are numerous support systems for spatial thinking. In everyday life, for example, we can use *MapQuest* to find routes for driving; in the workplace, architects use CAD systems for designing structures; and in science, statisticians use the visualization powers of *Data Explorer* to understand complex relationships among variables.

Support systems range from low to high tech in character. Although we appreciate the value and indispensability of low-tech support systems for spatial thinking, we also recognize the significance of a rapidly developing suite of powerful high-tech tools for supporting spatial thinking. Given the links among changing twenty-first century workforce demands, the burgeoning IT industry, and the increasing use of IT in schools, the committee was charged to examine the incorporation of GIS as a support system for spatial thinking across the K–12 curriculum.

With respect to GIS, the committee was asked to examine two questions:

1. How might current versions of GIS be incorporated into existing standards-based instruction in all knowledge domains across the school curriculum?
2. How can cognitive developmental and educational theory be used to develop new versions of GIS that are age appropriate in their design and to implement new GIS curricula that are age appropriate in their scope and sequence?

The committee answers these questions in Chapters 8 and 9 by using the frameworks laid out in Chapter 6 for assessing support systems in the K–12 educational context: (1) the three requirements of a support system for spatial thinking; (2) the 10 criteria for the design of a support system for spatial thinking; and (3) the five components for the implementation of a support system for spatial thinking.

This chapter, however, sets GIS into the context of a range of systems for supporting spatial thinking. The chapter is divided into three sections: Section 7.2 sets GIS in the context of a suite of

---

BOX 7.1
High-Tech Systems to Support Spatial Thinking

Geospatial Data Systems

GIS and remote-sensing analysis systems (e.g., *ArcView, MapInfo, Idrisi, Erdas, Imagine*) provide advanced data management and analysis capabilities along with the means to generate maps, graphs, surfaces, and tables. They support a wide variety of spatial data types, have elaborate tools for geo-registering and integrating data, and typically provide high-quality cartographic tools. Their major drawbacks are poor support for the vertical dimension, poor support for the time dimension, complexity of the application program interfaces (APIs), and limited support for spatializing nonspatial information.

Geoscience analytical systems (e.g., *Surpac, Vulcan, Micromine, Fractal Technologies*), which are commonly used to manage geological exploration and mining activities, provide support for spatial thinking. Some of these products represent data in three dimensions, as opposed to two. Some of them explicitly model the change in a region through time (e.g., due to erosion, mining activities, etc.). Typically, these systems have strong analysis and geostatistical capabilities, but they are more limited cartographically than GIS.

Computer-assisted design systems (e.g., *AutoCAD, MicroStation*), which have an engineering and architectural heritage, provide strong graphics capabilities. They offer good support for vector-based data, complete support for the third dimension, and a high level of interoperation (data exchange) between systems. They offer no support for raster data or for geographic projections. They have limited spatial analysis and statistical capabilities.

Mathematical and Statistical Analysis Systems

Mathematical and statistical analysis systems (e.g., *Mathematica, Maple*) were developed to provide integrated environments for the analysis and transformation of scientific data. Consequently, they offer a strong selection of mathematical and statistical tools. Recently, they have been augmented with graphing tools that allow for the spatialization and visualization of data. Typically, they are limited in their ability to handle explicitly geographic data and to support high-quality cartographic output.

---

high-tech tools for supporting spatial thinking. The committee identifies the types of tools, their functions, and their strengths and weaknesses as supports for spatial thinking and shows how these systems are converging toward common goals, driven primarily by user expectations. Section 7.3 provides an introduction to the nature and functions of GIS. Section 7.4 assesses the current status of GIS, especially with respect to K–12 education.

7.2 HIGH-TECH SYSTEMS FOR SUPPORTING SPATIAL THINKING

A number of software tools have been developed to represent and manipulate objects in geographical space or in some other information space via spatialization. In the geospatial context, there are eight sets of tools: GIS and remote-sensing analysis systems; geoscience analytical systems; CAD systems; mathematical and statistical analysis systems; production graphics environments; animation environments; information visualization systems; and concept mapping tools (see Appendix E for web addresses that provide details of these tools). (There are also high-tech systems for spatial thinking in fields as diverse as protein analysis, medical imaging, and mapping star systems.) Each one of the eight high-tech tools offers different capabilities. For example, GIS and related satellite-based systems, such as GPS, have revolutionized geospatial data collection, analysis, and display.

Box 7.1 provides a description and assessment of these high-tech tools, which are divided into

Graphics Generators

Production graphics environments (e.g., *Photoshop, Freehand*) offer the most comprehensive set of tools to make attractive graphics, but are limited to two dimensions. More important, their content is not directly addressable (i.e., the image produced does not consist of individual features that can be selected and manipulated at will).

Animation environments (e.g., *Director, Flash*) are becoming popular as a means to bring interactive, animated graphics into a web environment (usually via the web plug-in). Analytically, they are limited and they are time-consuming to use. Nonetheless, they can produce effective, specialized teaching and learning aids that deal directly with time, thus allowing descriptions of processes to be animated, and they allow unimportant interface details to be hidden from the end user. Examples of *Flash* applications for K–12 education are available on the web from http://www.geovista.psu.edu/grants/MapStatsKids/pubs.html.

Visual Exploration Systems

Information visualization systems (e.g., *Data Explorer [DX], Advanced Visualization System [AVS]*) can sustain the greatest variety of data types. They provide support for the third dimension and often for time as well. They permit a high degree of flexibility in the way that data are displayed. However, they offer limited analysis capability. In information visualization systems, spatial variables have no special status and no predefined assignment because any data value can be assigned to any visual variable. Thus, whereas in a GIS only data that are specifically spatial can be used as the location of an object, information visualization systems enable users to assign any data to be represented by, say, location or height.

Concept mapping tools (e.g., *TouchGraph, ThemeRiver*) spatialize data that are not inherently spatial, relying typically on an algorithm to order the position and displacements between components of the display (Figures 2.4 and 2.5). Like information visualization methods, concept graphing tools are usually geared toward visual exploration rather than analysis. They do not address any of the explicitly geographical aspects of spatial information.

---

four groups. Table 7.1 compares these eight high-tech tools in relation to their ability to spatialize, visualize, and perform functions (see Chapter 6.7).

Currently, none of the high-tech tools listed in Box 7.1 and Table 7.1 meet all of the necessary requirements to support spatial thinking. Instead, each system meets some of the requirements. For example, information visualization systems offer great flexibility in the way data are displayed, but provide limited analytical capability. Concept graphing tools support the spatialization and visual exploration of data, but do not reference objects in geographic space. Although animation environments deal well with time, they are cartographically and analytically weak. GIS support a wide variety of data types, integrate and geo-register data, provide high-quality cartographic output, and support spatial analysis. However, they offer poor support for time, the vertical dimension, and multimedia. At best, GIS provide limited support for spatializing nonspatial data. However, when set in the context of alternative hi-tech systems, GIS fares as well as, if not better than, other high-tech systems (see Table 7.1) as a tool for the support of spatial thinking.

All of the high-tech systems in Table 7.1 are becoming more powerful by (1) adding analytical capabilities; (2) providing flexible and visually appealing graphic and cartographic presentations; (3) supporting multimedia and multiformat data; (4) supporting tools such as APIs that can generate specialized but easy-to-use applications; (5) providing easier-to-use functionality, supported by context-sensitive help and software wizards; and (6) offering better integration with other information system products via emerging middleware standards, possibly leading to the embedding of

TABLE 7.1 Comparison of the Current Capabilities of High-Tech Systems That Can Support Spatial Thinking

	Geospatial Data Systems		
	GIS and remote-sensing analysis systems	Geoscience analytical systems	Computer-assisted design systems
Spatialization			
Projection and registration in geographic space	√	√	O
Integrates heterogeneous data by registering or transforming them to a common spatial position and projection	√	√	√
Allows spatialization of nonspatial data	O	O	X
Visualization			
Provides tools for high cartographic quality production	√	O	O
Supports explicit modeling of time, animation	X	O	X
Support for full multimedia (e.g., sound, video)	X	X	X
Performing Functions			
Supports transformations	O	O	O
Supports operations	√	√	X
Supports spatial analysis	√	√	X

KEY: √ yes, in most cases; O yes, for some systems or to some extent; X no, in most cases.

explicitly geographic data handling and processing capacities in many of the systems. Although software vendors seem to have no coordinated plan, systems are converging toward common goals because of the needs of business, industry, and government. Users want flexible systems to handle data sets that come from multiple sources, at different scales, and with different accuracies.

As these systems become functionally more powerful and converge toward common goals, their capabilities will offer greater support for spatial thinking. Because of the diverse forms spatial thinking can take and the diverse contexts in which spatial thinking can occur, it is unlikely that a single system will be able to accommodate spatial thinking in all of its forms and contexts.

Even though spatial thinking may be too complex, challenging, and powerful for a single system to offer universal support, most current GIS software systems provide more support for spatial thinking than K–12 students will probably ever need. Indeed, estimates suggest that the range of functions available in GIS products is so extensive that even most professional GIS users access only 10 percent of their software's functionality (Tomlinson, 2003).

7.3 THE NATURE AND FUNCTIONS OF GIS

In the 1970s and 1980s, GIS were viewed as computer-based toolboxes—as mapping tools (Burrough, 1986), spatial databases (Arnoff, 1989), decision support tools (Carter, 1989; Cowen, 1988), or spatial analytical tools (Parker, 1988). However, rapid developments of GIS technology have rendered the traditional, instrumental definitions of GIS inadequate to capture the essence of the technology and its social implications. GIS technology is becoming increasingly part of our daily lives (e.g., providing navigation aids for driving, walking, or public transport; generating location-specific delivery services such as local weather, traffic conditions, cultural events) (Cowen,

Mathematical and Statistical Analysis Systems	Graphics Generators		Visual Exploration Systems	
Mathematical and statistical analysis systems	Production graphics environments	Animation environments	Information visualization systems	Concept mapping tools
O	X	X	O	X
√	√	√	√	X
X	X	X	√	√
X	√	O	√	O
X	X	√	O	O
X	X	√	O	X
X	X	X	O	X
X	X	X	X	X
√	X	X	O	X

1994), thus suggesting that GIS should be seen as media or a medium for the communication of geographic information in digital form (Sui and Goodchild, 2001). While GIS is a practical tool, GIScience, (Appendix F), addresses some fundamental questions about the relationships among data, space, and the digital world.

Whether viewed as a tool or as media, GIS can be defined as integrated software systems for the handling of geospatial information: for its acquisition, editing, storage, transformation, analysis, visualization, and indeed, virtually any task that one might want to perform with this particular information type (Figure 7.1). In the case of GIS, the information is georeferenced to locations on Earth's curved surface. As such, GIS stand in much the same relationship to geographic information as spreadsheet packages do to tabular information, word processors to text, or statistical packages to statistical data. All of these systems rely on a basic economy of scale: once the foundation has been established for storing a particular data type, it is possible to add a vast array of functions and to serve a similarly vast array of applications with a single software package. The potential of GIS for geographic data storage, analysis, and display is described in introductory texts (Burrough and MacDonnell, 1998; Clarke, 2002, Heywood et al., 2002; Longley et al., 2001), and in more comprehensive surveys of the field (Bossler, 2001; DeMers, 2000; Longley et al., 1999).

The geospatial data that are the focus of GIS can be defined as information about places on, just above, or just below Earth's surface. Geographic data link three elements: place, time, and attributes. For example, consider the statement that the temperature at noon on August 22, 2003, at latitude 44 degrees 58 minutes north, longitude 93 degrees 15 minutes west, was 30°C. The statement ties place and time to the attribute of atmospheric temperature. Geospatial data are acquired from a wide range of sources, including data obtained from fieldwork, maps, images of Earth obtained from satellites, and videofilm of Earth taken from low-flying aircraft.

Parts of a geographic information system

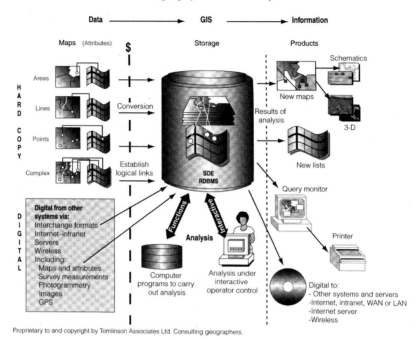

Proprietary to and copyright by Tomlinson Associates Ltd. Consulting geographers.

FIGURE 7.1 Components of a GIS. The diagram shows that a GIS stores geospatial data in a GIS storage database where analytical functions are controlled interactively by an operator to generate the needed information. SOURCE: Tomlinson, 2003, p. 3. Reprinted with permission from Dr. Roger Tomlinson.

The range of possible generalizations and structures for storing geospatial data is large, and this powerful flexibility is one explanation for the complexity of GIS and, therefore, the difficulties many people experience in learning how to use these systems. The methods used to structure data are called data models. A data model is a set of constructs for describing and representing selected aspects of the real world in a computer. Data models are vitally important in a GIS because they control the way data are stored and have an impact on the type of analytical operations that can be performed (Burrough and Frank, 1996; Molenaar, 1998; Rigaux et al., 2002; Shekar and Chawla, 2003; Worboys, 1995; Zeiler, 1999).

For two-dimensional geographic data, the most common data models used in a GIS are the raster data model and the vector data model. Figure 7.2 shows an example of raster data displayed in a GIS, and Figure 7.3 shows an example of vector data displayed in a GIS.

Raster models capture geographic variation on the basis of a grid of values assigned to equal-sized rectangular cells, just as a digital camera captures an image. Relative location is defined in terms of the order of the cells, and the grid is positioned with respect to Earth's surface by assigning coordinates to its corners. Raster models are useful as a backdrop display because they can communicate a lot of information rapidly. They are also widely used for analytical operations such as disease dispersion modeling, surface water flow analysis, and store location modeling.

Vector data represent phenomena as discrete points, lines, and areas and capture location by assigning coordinates to these individual geometric objects. For example, a road might be represented as a sequence of points forming a line in a vector database, whereas in a raster database, the road would be a string of connected cells. Vector models have been widely implemented in GIS

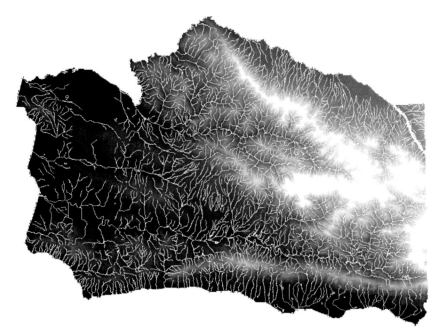

FIGURE 7.2 A raster-based map of Santa Barbara County. Relief ranges from black (low) to white (high), and streams are recorded as a raster of cells in which each cell is associated with one gray level.

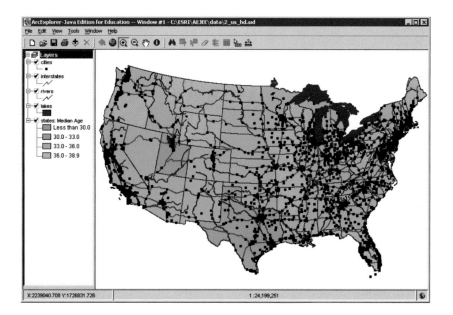

FIGURE 7.3 Map of the United States recorded on a vector GIS of polygons, lines, and points. It was created using *ArcExplorer* Java Edition for Education. It depicts lakes (in blue), states (in shades of green to gray showing median age), lines (rivers in blue and interstate highways in red), and points (cities are black squares).

FIGURE 7.4 A geographic information system. A GIS consists of a number of geographic data layers that are linked to one another in a common geographic coordinate system (such as latitude and longitude). In this example, the various thematic layers consist of remotely sensed data (from Landsat Thematic Mapper), the hydrologic network, digital elevation, road network, and watershed boundaries. SOURCE: NRC, 2002b, p. 14.

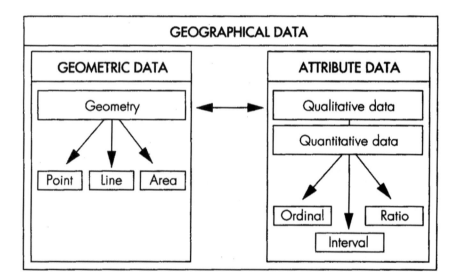

FIGURE 7.5 Geographical data can be divided into geometric data and attribute data. Attribute data can in turn be subdivided into qualitative data and quantitative data. SOURCE: Bernhardsen, 1999, p. 40. From *Geographic Information Systems: An Introduction*; Copyright 1999 T. Bernhardsen. This material is used by permission of John Wiley & Sons, Inc.

because of their storage efficiency, the quality of their cartographic output, and the availability of functional tools for operations such as overlay, analysis, and modeling.

A GIS stores geographic data as a collection of thematic layers (e.g., overlays of a map showing, for example, human population distribution, hydrology, transportation, soils, geology, land cover) that are linked to a common georeferencing system (Figure 7.4). Each thematic layer

ATTRIBUTE DATA

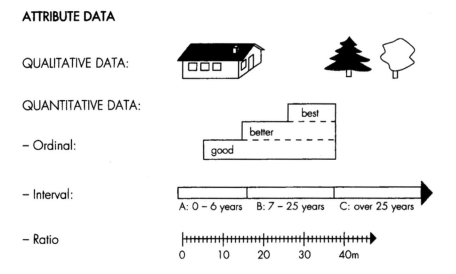

QUALITATIVE DATA:

QUANTITATIVE DATA:

– Ordinal:

    good   better   best

– Interval:

A: 0 – 6 years   B: 7 – 25 years   C: over 25 years

– Ratio

0   10   20   30   40m

FIGURE 7.6 Attribute data consist of qualitative or quantitative data. Qualitative data specify the type of object, whereas quantitative data can be categorized into ordinal, interval, and ratio data. SOURCE: Berhardsen, 1999, p. 40. From *Geographic Information Systems: An Introduction*; Copyright 1999 T. Bernhardsen. This material is used by permission of John Wiley & Sons, Inc.

has two information components: one is the location of a place in geometrical terms and the other is a description of the attributes of that place (Figures 7.5 and 7.6). Currently, paper maps and other hard-copy records supply much of the input data for these layers. For use in a GIS, hard-copy records must be digitized. Increasingly, more and more geographic data originate in digital form.

Storing data in multiple thematic layers is a simple but powerful concept that has proven valuable for solving problems. The power of a GIS is that it enables us to ask questions of a database, perform spatial operations on databases, and generate graphic output that would be laborious or impossible to do manually. A GIS can answer five generic questions (Rhind, 1992):

Question:	**Type of Task**
1. What is at . . . ?	Inventory
2. Where is . . . ?	Monitoring
3. What has changed since . . . ?	Inventory and monitoring
4. What spatial pattern exists . . . ?	Spatial analysis
5. What if . . . ?	Modeling

The first three questions are simple queries. Question 1 seeks to find out what exists at a particular location. Question 2 is the converse of Question 1 and asks where certain conditions are satisfied (e.g., the presence or absence of some phenomenon at particular locations). Question 3 seeks to find differences between the results to Questions 1 and 2 at two moments in time. Questions 4 and 5 are analytical. In asking Question 4, we may wish to know the spatial pattern of deaths due to cancer among residents around a nuclear power station and, if there are anomalies to the pattern, where the anomalies occur. Question 5 seeks to determine what happens, for example, if we build a model of cancer deaths in relation to distance from the power station and test the model's predictions against patterns of deaths at other power stations.

As a software system for data analysis and automated cartography, GIS is used in a vast range of applications, covering virtually any industry or agency concerned with the surface of Earth and with the human activities and physical processes that occur on or near Earth's surface. These include scientific research in the physical and social sciences and in the humanities; management of land and natural resources; modeling of environmental and ecological processes; routing and scheduling of vehicles; and management of urban, utility, and transportation assets. The introductory textbooks cited earlier provide abundant examples of GIS applications, and there are specialized books on the role of GIS in most major application areas.

7.4 THE CURRENT STATUS OF GIS

Currently, GIS is the accumulative result of continual additions and occasional restructurings, over a 30-year period, to a complex architecture. It is expert driven and, therefore, oriented to the needs of professional practitioners (Foresman, 1998). Designed for solving practical problems, GIS is used primarily by high-tech practitioners in industry, business, government, and research. For these practitioners, GIS provides an excellent vehicle for integrating and analyzing large amounts of geographic data rapidly, accurately, and reliably. It also provides a basis for decision support systems to facilitate management and planning decisions in both the public and the private sectors. A GIS supports decision-making by providing ways to examine and choose among alternative solutions to problems.

GIS was not designed with either children or learning in mind. Since it was introduced to schools in the 1980s, there has been very little adaptation of GIS for K–12 education. Moreover, the rate of adoption of GIS by schools has lagged far behind the rates for business and government. By 2003, GIS was used in only 1 percent of American high schools (Kerski, 2003, p. 128). This minimal level of adoption may be attributed in part to the name GIS. Because geography is such a small component of the K–12 curriculum, GIS may be marginalized. To be sure, the low level of

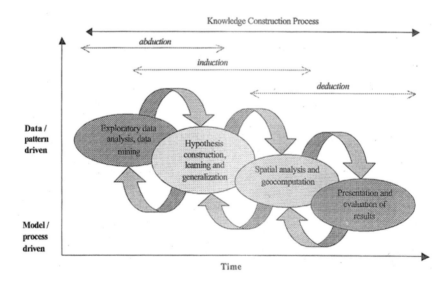

FIGURE 7.7 Phases in the scientific method. SOURCE: Gahegan et al., 2001, p. 2. First published in *Cartography and Geographic Information Science* 28(1):29–44. Reprinted by permission from the American Congress on Surveying and Mapping.

adoption can also be attributed to a number of structural limitations—access to hardware and software, intimidating software, insufficient time to learn how to use the software, and levels of technology training for teachers.

GIS has the capability to create an environment in which students learn science by doing (NRC, 1999). It can, therefore, extend the ability of students to do scientific inquiry as envisaged by the *Curriculum and Evaluation Standards for School Mathematics* (National Council of Teachers of Mathematics, 1989), *National Science Education Standards* (NRC, 1996), and *Geography for Life: The National Geography Standards 1994* (Geography Education Standards Project, 1994). These standards emphasize approaching scientific tasks using the scientific method (Figure 7.7).

GIS can expand the data available for student use, the scope and sophistication of their analyses, and the range of graphic representations, allowing students to uncover and understand real-world patterns and processes. To what extent can the potential of GIS be realized?

8

An Assessment of GIS as a System for Supporting Spatial Thinking in the K–12 Context

8.1 INTRODUCTION

An analysis of GIS as a high-tech support system for spatial thinking in K–12 education is timely because, given the increasing use of GIS in the workplace (government, industry, business, and academia), education and training in GIS is also increasingly important, especially at higher grades. Given efforts to incorporate GIS into the K–12 context (Appendix G), there are some data and experiences with which to assess GIS against the design and implementation criteria for support systems for spatial thinking.

Using the frameworks laid out in Chapter 6, this chapter addresses the question of whether GIS can provide an effective foundation for teaching and practicing spatial thinking in K–12 education. The committee appraises the current status of GIS in terms of (1) the requirements of a system for supporting spatial thinking, (2) the criteria for the design of a support system in the K–12 context, and (3) the criteria for the implementation of a support system in the K–12 context. This assessment is based on readily available versions of GIS. Readily available versions are products that are available off the shelf, not those extended by various scripts, third-party software, or *Visual Basic*, *Avenue*, or *AML* programming. These off-the-shelf systems are the ones that schools and teachers are most likely to use. Software products that are commonly used in K–12 education are listed in Table 8.1.

The products of ESRI dominate the K–12 market and dominate the assessment that follows. However, the results of the committee's analysis are reflective of the general issues of the design and implementation of a GIS for the K–12 context. The strengths and weaknesses of ESRI products, while specific to those products, would be matched by another set of different but sometimes overlapping strengths and weaknesses reflecting the particularities of another software package. Our purpose is to illustrate the challenges and potentials of implementing GIS in K–12 education and, thus, to answer the charge posed to the committee.

Software changes rapidly, with new releases replacing prior versions and offering increased functionality, capacity, and performance. Thus, this analysis is based primarily on ESRI's *ArcView 3,* although the committee recognizes that subsequent releases of *ArcView* (e.g., *ArcGIS, ArcView*

TABLE 8.1 Major GIS Software Products Used in K–12 Education

Programs	World Wide Web Address
ArcExplorer[a]	http://www.esri.com/arcexplorer
ArcView	http://www.esri.com/software/arcview
ArcVoyager[a]	http://www.esri.com/industries/K–12/voyager.html
Atlas GIS	http://rpmconsulting.com/
Autodesk Map	http://usa.autodesk.com/adsk/servlet/index?siteID=123112&id=3081357
GeoMedia	http://imgs.intergraph.com/geomedia/default.asp
GRASS	http://openosx.com/grass/
Idrisi	http://www.clarklabs.org
Mac GIS	http://dslmac.uoregon.edu/macGISinfo.html
MapInfo	http://www.mapinfo.com
Maptitude	http://www.caliper.com/
Mfworks	http://www.keigansystems.com/Products/Mfworks/Mfworks3.html
My World[a]	http://www.worldwatcher.northwestern.edu/MyWorld

[a]Software programs customized for K–12.

9) have addressed some of the design and implementation problems identified here. The point remains, however, that the frameworks for analysis, presented in Chapter 6, are an appropriate way for analyzing *any* high-tech support system for spatial thinking. Moreover, the types of problems identified by the committee will probably exist until GIS is designed from scratch with students and teachers in mind.

It must be stressed that GIS was not designed with educational applications in mind. It is a working system for the handling and analysis of geospatial data, designed by and for experts. It is an "industrial-strength" system that far exceeds the needs and capabilities of most teachers and students (indeed, most users). Nevertheless, GIS has been and is being used in educational settings, and ESRI itself has been very supportive of such efforts. Thus, the committee's analysis reflects a transitional stage in the evolution of GIS software. Just as specialized versions have been developed for specific user communities, such as business logistics or infrastructure design, the committee fully expects that versions will be developed with education in mind. These analyses are intended to aid in such development.

This chapter examines the strengths and weaknesses of currently available off-the-shelf versions of GIS as a learning environment. In making its judgment on the capacity (Section 8.2), design (Section 8.3), and implementation (Section 8.4) of GIS as a support system for spatial thinking in the K–12 environment, the committee relies on primarily oral presentations and written statements from system designers, researchers, and school and university educators (Appendix B). Each section follows a similar format. In the case of system capabilities, for example, there are three requirements: the capacity to spatialize, to visualize, and to perform functions. Each requirement is analyzed, and the committee's observations are summarized in two ways: (1) by means of a list of observations and (2) by means of an assessment table at the end of each section. Based on the results of this analysis of the current status of GIS in K–12 education, Section 8.5 examines organizational models for redesigning GIS software to fit the needs, constraints, and opportunities of the K–12 context.

8.2 THE CAPACITY OF GIS AS A SUPPORT SYSTEM FOR SPATIAL THINKING

For current GIS software products to support the teaching and learning of spatial thinking in the K–12 context, they must have the capacity to (1) spatialize data sets by providing spatial data structures and coding systems for nonspatial data, (2) visualize working and final results by providing multiple forms of representation, and (3) perform functions that manipulate the structural relations of data sets. The capacity to spatialize data sets motivates the process of spatial thinking, the capacity to visualize is integral to the process of spatial thinking, and the capacity to manipulate structural relations is the essence of spatial thinking. The following sections discuss the extent to which current GIS software products meet each of these three specific requirements of a support system for spatial thinking.

8.2.1 Capacity to Spatialize

Inside a typical GIS, space is defined by a combination of geometry, projection, and registration data. The structures of space and geographic data are so tightly bound in the software that they are inseparable at the application level. This strong bond sets a GIS apart from most other kinds of information systems by providing the infrastructure necessary for the direct support of geographic operations that can be performed on that space (e.g., registration, re-projection, neighborhood and distance calculations, network analysis, spatial interpolation).

Because of the bonds between space and geography, a GIS is a system that is designed to handle geographic data, but in principle, data defined in any spatial domain are also amenable to handling with GIS. The adjective *geographic* refers specifically to Earth's surface and near-surface, and the more general adjective *spatial* refers to any space, including the space of Earth's surface. Thus, GIS methods have been applied to nongeographic spaces, including the surfaces of other planets, the space of the cosmos, and the space of the human body. GIS has also been applied to the analysis of genome sequences of DNA.

Attempts have been made to estimate the amount of data that are geographic. It is estimated that between 70 to 80 percent of the data generated and used by local government organizations are geographic (Longley et al., 2001). Local governments use geographic data to improve the quality of their products, processes, and services. Typical GIS applications of geographic data include inventorying resources and infrastructure, planning transportation routing, improving service response time, managing land development, monitoring public health risk, and tracking crime. These applications of GIS often require databases that can easily reach a gigabyte or more in size (Table 8.2).

To be used in a GIS, data must be spatialized. Spatialization is the process of attaching coordinate codes to each data item (e.g., *x* and *y* in the case of two-dimensional spatial data, or latitude and longitude in the case of two-dimensional geographic data). A GIS does a fine job of spatializing spatial data. Once spatialized, these data can be presented in a visual representation such as a thematic map.

In contrast to spatial data, GIS give limited support for the spatialization of nonspatial data. For example, a GIS can draw a map of the Internet in which nodes are mapped by their geographic location. However, current versions of GIS cannot draw a map of the Internet based on bandwidth

TABLE 8.2 Potential GIS Database Volumes for Some Typical Applications

Database	Volume	Application
1 megabyte	1,000,000	Single data set in a small project database
1 gigabyte	1,000,000,000	Entire street network of a large city or a small country
1 terabyte	1,000,000,000,000	Elevation of entire Earth surface recorded at 30 m intervals
1 petabyte	1,000,000,000,000,000	Satellite image of entire Earth surface at 1 m resolution

NOTE: Volumes estimated to the nearest order of magnitude. Bytes are counted in powers of 2.
SOURCE: Longley et al., 2001, p. 6. Reprinted by permission of John Wiley & Sons, Inc.

accessibility or connection speed without "fooling" the GIS into thinking that bandwidth connections are actually "on" Earth's surface. Unlike GIS, however, visual exploration systems can readily spatialize nonspatial data. For example, they can draw a map of Internet bandwidth connections where nodes with low-bandwidth connections would be far apart and nodes with high-bandwidth connections would be close together. Thus, a GIS can produce a map of the Internet where space is defined geographically, whereas a visualization exploration system can produce a map of the Internet where space is defined by accessibility or connection speed.

Although GIS does support the x and y dimensions, it gives limited support to the z (or vertical) dimension because it uses only two-dimensional surfaces as a data type. For example, GIS cannot represent an overhanging cliff because some points in the x and y dimensions would require more than two z values. Likewise, a GIS cannot represent layered models of the solid Earth, atmosphere, or oceans because z values would be required for each x,y location. Many applications in science and geography also involve the representation and analysis of the vertical dimension in ways that cannot be represented adequately by a two-dimensional surface. This limitation of GIS does not occur, however, in many of the children's software games that fully support the construction and exploration of three-dimensional structures. For example, using the video game *The Sims Superstars*, children can design houses with multiple floors and connecting corridors and stairs, promoting the understanding of true three-dimensional structures.

From this analysis, three observations can be made about the capacity of current versions of GIS to spatialize data sets and, hence, motivate spatial thinking:

1. GIS does a fine job if the data are geospatial;
2. GIS provides limited support for the spatialization of nonspatial data; and
3. GIS does not support a true three-dimensional model of space.

8.2.2 Capacity to Visualize

The advent of GIS and computer displays of geographic data has reinvigorated the ancient field of cartography (Longley et al., 1999; NRC, 2002a).They give map designers new potential to express knowledge of Earth's surface and new powers to display aspects of this knowledge that were previously beyond the powers of traditional graphic visualizations. The term *geovisualization* captures this new potential and is the focus of an active and growing research community (NRC, 1997, pp. 63–65; http://www.geovista.psu.edu//sites/icavis/).

A GIS is, however, far more than a computer-based map-making machine. It can supplement maps with textual information, digital images, diagrams, and other graphical information. However, the portrayal of information in a GIS need not be limited to visual display. It could, but currently does not, provide full media support (e.g., sound, hyperlinks) to enhance the learning experience by creating an engaging and challenging environment. Full media support would provide more opportunities for self-paced exploration and support for distance or asynchronous learning.

Nonetheless, maps are the primary GIS products. One task of a GIS user is to transform geographic data in digital form into a visual product, a map, that is accurate, informative, and user-friendly. The appearance of data displayed as a map by a GIS is governed by several factors, including

- the types of display geometry provided (e.g., symbols, line styles, polygonal regions, images);
- the visual variables that these geometries can support (e.g., size, density, color, shape, texture, orientation; Bertin, 1983) (see Figure 8.1); and

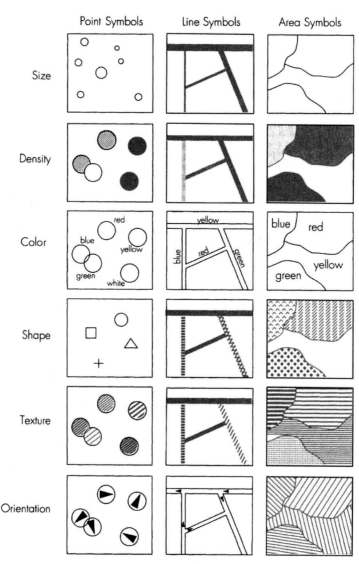

FIGURE 8.1 Six graphic variables that can be used to symbolize geographic phenomena. SOURCE: Bernhardsen, 1999, p. 275. From *Geographic Information Systems: An Introduction*; Copyright 1999 T. Bernhardsen. This material is used by permission of John Wiley & Sons, Inc.

• the mapping tools used to assign values in the data to these visual variables (e.g., line thickness, symbol size, color hue).

The cartographic capabilities of most GIS are quite advanced, providing users with perceptually valid color spaces and symbology. Yet GIS are not yet as graphically advanced as information visualization systems (e.g., *Advanced Visualization System, Data Explorer)* because not all visual variables are under the direct control of the user. GIS provide only a partial set of visual variables to communicate meaning. Some representational techniques are not supported (e.g., transparency, movement, height); others are accessible only via predefined, hard-coded paths. On the positive side, these paths constrain the options available to users to those that, in the judgments of system designers, make the most cartographic sense in practice. It is, therefore, difficult or even impossible for users to do things to the data that are inappropriate cartographically. By contrast, information visualization systems do not have the geospatial option constraints of GIS. Typically, systems such as *Advanced Visualization System* or *Data Explorer* do not enforce projection and registration constraints, thus providing flexibility but also allowing for the problems of misplaced data in the display.

A GIS has the capability to produce high-quality graphical representations, especially maps, making it a potentially valuable support system for the process of spatial thinking in the K–12 context. However, users must be aware of and understand the importance of data quality. Professional-looking final products may conceal data errors. These errors may be referential (i.e., an error in specifying something such as a street address), topological (i.e., a linkage error in spatial data such as an unclosed polygon), relative (i.e., an error in the position of two objects relative to each other), or absolute (i.e., an error in the true position of something such as a floodplain boundary not aligned with property boundaries) (Tomlinson, 2003). Currently, no GIS can automatically handle data error problems in a satisfactory manner. Moreover, products may be graphically misleading. No GIS can guide K–12 operators in the choice of map symbols and other graphic effects.

The process of exploring data on a GIS-produced map could be enhanced if users had real-time control over the visual display. Most information visualization systems provide user interface controls that remain "live" after the display is constructed. This enables users to change the appearance of features in the display interactively (e.g., a color ramp, a size control for point symbols, a transparency control for an image layer). Currently, GIS lack such a capability.

GIS provides poor support for the modeling of time (Peuquet, 2002) and related presentations via animation (MacEachren, 1994). Unlike animation systems such as *Director* and *Flash* that explicitly represent time (t) values, existing versions of GIS have no temporal "coordinate" as in x,y,t. Although there are ways to work around this problem, achieved by stacking map layers in a temporal sequence of cross sections that can be refreshed several times per second (Goodchild, 1988), they lead to a noncontinuous sense of time for users. Many important aspects of science and geography revolve around processes occurring through time (e.g., carbon and water cycles, glacial change, migration, urban expansion).

Although GIS lacks the capability to examine processes that occur continuously through time, technology exists for large-scale geospatial virtual representations of the entire Earth over time and in three dimensions. Keyhole Inc. Images (http://www.earthviewer.com) provides users, even those with legacy computers, with access to terabytes of imagery and GIS files to view Earth as a three-dimensional object. Figure 8.2 shows screenshots of *Earthviewer* (http://www.earthviewer.com), which allows users to zoom smoothly from a whole-Earth view to resolutions as detailed as 1 m and to "fly" over a realistic rendering of Earth's topography. The data to support these views are fed over the Internet, so a broadband connection is required for adequate performance. *Earthviewer* and similar developments come close to the vision of "Digital Earth" outlined by former Vice President Al Gore in *Earth in the Balance* (Gore, 1992). *Earthviewer* accommodates varying spatial resolutions, building its views dynamically from a patchwork of data obtained from various sources.

8.2.3 Capacity to Perform Functions

As an engine for performing transformations, operations, and analyses, GIS displays its full power for supporting spatial thinking. The earliest GIS was developed in response to the need to make accurate measurements of the size, shape, and characteristics of areas from large numbers of paper maps (Foresman, 1998), a task that is inaccurate, tedious, and expensive when performed by hand. This vision of a GIS as a calculating machine dominated thinking well into the 1990s, and

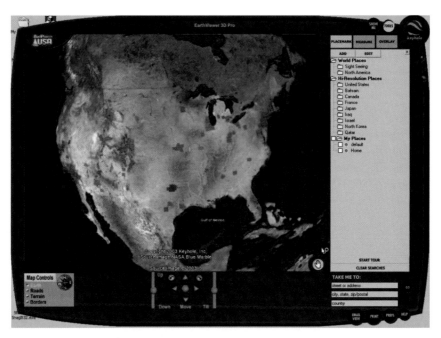

FIGURE 8.2 Two screenshots from *Earthviewer*. This web site allows users to zoom smoothly from global to submeter resolutions and to combine data from a patchwork of coverages. (a) A continental view, showing the patchwork of higher-resolution data available for U.S. cities. (b) An oblique view of the Santa Barbara coastline, combining high-resolution imagery with terrain. SOURCE: http://www.earthviewer.com/.

by that time, a vast array of techniques had been implemented, either as part of the basic GIS products offered by vendors or as extensions developed by users. Several texts describe the advanced analytic capabilities of GIS (Burrough and MacDonnell, 1998; Fotheringham and Rogerson, 1994; Lee and Wong, 2001). In principle, there is no limit to the range of functions that can be implemented in a GIS, but in practice, priorities are established by the demands of different user communities.

There have been several efforts to systematize the often overwhelming range of functions and to make it easier for users to navigate through them. These efforts range from simplifying schema to interface formats. Tomlin (1990) devised a schema termed *cartographic modeling* that has been widely adopted as the basis for spatial querying and analysis, despite the fact that it is limited in scope to operations on raster data. The schema classifies GIS transformations into four classes and is used in several raster GIS as the basis for their analysis languages: (1) local operations, which examine rasters cell by cell; (2) focal operations, which compare the value in each cell with the values in its proximate cells; (3) global operations, which produce results that are true of the entire layer, such as its mean value; and (4) zonal operations, which compute results for blocks of contiguous cells that share the same value. The development of so-called *WIMP interfaces*—based on windows, icons, menus, and pointers—has also helped user interaction, allowing spatial querying and analysis through pointing, clicking, and dragging windows and icons (Egenhofer and Kuhn 1999; Figure 8.3). Nonetheless, navigating through the multitude of capabilities of a modern GIS remains challenging, especially given the lack of a standard nomenclature for operations. Much work remains to be done to simplify user interfaces, standardize terminology, and hide irrelevant detail if GIS is to be adopted widely for use in K–12 education.

A typical GIS can be expected to perform a wide range of transformations, operations, and analyses. Transformations include changes in the map projection or coordinate system. For example, one can change the familiar Mercator projection to one more suitable for areal comparisons, such as the Albers Equal Area, which unlike the Mercator does not distort areas. Transformations might also include conversion from a raster to vector data model, or the reverse. An example of an operation is the point-in-polygon operation, which identifies whether a given area contains a given point. Operations in a GIS may be performed on points, lines, or areas and may involve considerations of spatial proximity or of changes over time. These operations, often highly complex, enable the analysis of spatial data. They can be used to detect whether clustering exists in patterns of points, to select optimal locations for new roads or businesses, and a host of other tasks. More specifically, the major operational functions of a GIS include (1) query, (2) buffer, (3) overlay, (4) proximity, (5) connectivity, and (6) modeling (Box 8.1). Various combinations of these functions are commonly used during the data analysis process.

By and large, the analysis capabilities of a GIS are more advanced than those that will probably be needed in most K–12 education applications. For students, the software's functionality is generally more complex than is necessary. However, system designers could help students perform analyses with the provision of age- and task-appropriate assistance in the form of wizards, which would guide students through the morass of functionality and options exposed on standard user interfaces.

There is one potential exception to the statement that GIS has more analytical capabilities than most students will ever need. In some desktop GIS, such as *ArcView* and *MapInfo,* there is a lack of support for topology, which is the science and mathematics of relationships and is one of the most important parts of geometry. Although topology is a difficult subject, it does present an excellent opportunity to explore and motivate logic-mathematical skills (such as reflexive, transitive, and symmetric relationships).

Where special-purpose analysis capability is missing in GIS, it can usually be added via the API that exposes some of the basic product functionality to a conventional programming language

POINTER   DROP DOWN MENU   ICONS

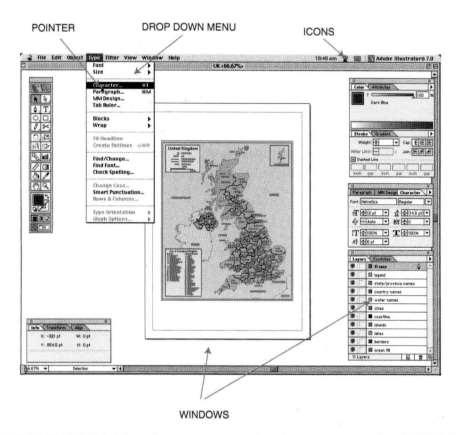

WINDOWS

FIGURE 8.3 The WIMP (windows, icons, menus, pointers) environment for computing. SOURCE: Longley et al., 2001, p. 266. John Wiley & Sons, Ltd. Reproduced with permission.

(e.g., *Visual Basic* in the case of *ArcView* and *MapInfo*). Using existing functionality as the building blocks, a programmer can develop special-purpose methods. Both *ArcView* and *MapInfo* connect to *Visual Basic* at the interface level, but the core of the GIS software is not directly accessible. Once new functionality is constructed, it can be made accessible by connecting it with menu items added to the interface. By contrast, a GIS such as *Smallworld* has a much smaller core, with most of the functionality and interface being developed using a custom-built programming language called *Magic*. Using *Magic*, developers can engage in "deep editing" in which the core functionality can be changed or augmented in major ways. The ability to customize software with the use of programming languages to meet the specific needs of students would be valuable in the K–12 context. Customization does, however, place significant demands on the curriculum developer or teacher.

From this analysis, four points can be made about the capacity of GIS to perform functions.

1. GIS is a very powerful tool for performing transformations, operations, and analyses.

2. The capacity of most GIS software to perform functions is greater than K–12 students require.

3. The complexity of existing product functionality is greater than is desirable for the K–12 context.

4. The flexibility to add functionality, although attractive and desirable, may be too challenging in most educational settings.

BOX 8.1
Functions of a GIS

Query. A query is a question asked of the support system. For example, a GIS could be asked to show all primary schools, water wells, or markets within a specified geographic area. Queries with more specific conditions might include the following:

- Where are all the lateritic soils?
- Where are croplands that are at risk from high erosion?
- Where are all the paved roads in an administrative area?

Buffer. Buffer analysis is a geographically or temporally constrained version of query analysis. The GIS creates a buffer or boundary of a specified distance (measured in units of length or time) around an object represented as a point, line, or polygon. The buffer is then used to constrain the queries to within that specified distance. The types of questions that might be asked using buffer analysis include the following:

- Where are all the people that fall within a specified distance of a clinic (a point)?
- Or within a specified distance of a river (line) (e.g., to determine a region's dependence on a particular water system)?
- Or within a specified distance of a city boundary (polygon)?

Overlay. This analysis involves the "electronic stacking" of thematic layers of spatial data (e.g., human population, land cover, soils, hydrology) on "top" of each other so that the geographic positions within each layer are precisely registered to all the other data layers in the database (Figure 7.4). Queries that might be answered using overlay analysis include the following:

- Show all locations where a particular vegetation type is growing on a specified soil type (vegetation layer and soil-type layer).
- Determine the distribution of people exposed to disease-vector (e.g., mosquito) habitats to show populations at greatest risk of health problems (population layer, hydrography layer, elevation layer, health center layer).
- Identify those areas where agricultural production may be most feasible and provides the greatest benefits (soil-type layer, vegetation-type layer, population density layer).

Proximity. This determines the characteristics of features that are in close proximity (neighboring) to an object or an area of interest. A moving window is used to define proximity; for example, a window might be moved systematically across a data layer to determine the statistical characteristics of the pixels within the window.

Connectivity. This is used on vector-based data sets to determine such network characteristics as the shortest route to a clinic.

Modeling. GIS can serve as a tool for analyzing processes, analyzing the results of trends, or projecting the possible results of decisions. Changes in the geographic characteristics of features such as size or shape can be modeled over time. For example, land-use changes, such as changing farming practices, can be modeled to predict per-hectare loss of soil over time.

SOURCE: NRC, 2002b.

TABLE 8.3 Assessment of the Capacity of GIS to Spatialize, Visualize, and Perform Functions

Requirements	High	Medium	Low
Capacity to spatialize data sets		+	
Capacity to visualize		+	
Capacity to perform functions		+	

8.2.4 Discussion Summary

Table 8.3 gives the committee's assessment of the capacity of GIS to spatialize data sets, visualize, and perform functions. Overall, GIS software products possess many of the requirements of a powerful support system for thinking spatially in general and in the K–12 context in particular. However, whether GIS does so in practice in the K–12 context is a function of two additional sets of criteria for its design and implementation. The next section turns to a discussion of the ten general criteria for the design of a K–12 support system and measures GIS against them.

8.3 THE DESIGN OF GIS AS A SUPPORT SYSTEM FOR SPATIAL THINKING IN THE K–12 EDUCATIONAL CONTEXT

Chapter 6 identifies 10 general criteria considered as *desiderata* for the design of a support system to aid spatial thinking in K–12 education. Here, the committee examines each of these criteria and assesses the extent to which current versions of GIS satisfy them. In essence, this section explores what GIS does well and not so well with respect to each criterion. To organize this assessment, the committee uses the framework established in Chapter 6 in which the 10 criteria are grouped under the headings of (1) meeting educational goals, (2) fitting student needs, and (3) adapted to the educational context.

8.3.1 Meeting Educational Goals

This subsection considers the ability of GIS to meet four educational goals: (1) be supportive of the inquiry process; (2) be useful in solving problems in a wide range of real-world contexts; (3) facilitate learning transfer across a range of school subjects; and (4) provide a rich, generative, inviting, and challenging problem-solving environment for the users of the support system. After considering each goal in turn, the committee provides a summary and an overall assessment of the ability of GIS to meet the four educational goals.

1. Be Supportive of the Inquiry Process. Learning is a process of exploration and discovery driven by curiosity (see the Jerome Bruner example in Chapter 1). Whether in the science or social studies classroom, the inquiry process is the same. Students are expected to

- develop questions based on their curiosity and interests;
- acquire data relevant to the questions they have asked;
- observe and explore patterns and relations within the data;
- analyze and draw inferences from observed patterns and relations; and
- generate possible answers and act upon their new understanding.

To be supportive of this process, a GIS analysis would involve several stages: initial assembly of data; addressing issues of transformation to achieve data compatibility; analysis using one or more functions; and preparation of the results for dissemination. As such, GIS has the potential to become an effective vehicle for accommodating the stages of scientific problem formulation and solution. The user, who is able to change direction and retrace steps based on interim results, directs the process of solution. In principle, then, GIS use can reflect many of the ideals of exploration-driven, discovery-based, student-centered inquiry.

In reality, however, current versions of GIS pose problems for student-centered inquiry in the following ways:

• GIS programs have a tendency to concentrate on the later stages of the inquiry process—analysis, presentation, and communication. They offer limited support for the data exploration stage—hypothesis generation and concept synthesis—upon which the later activities of the inquiry process are predicated. This situation is beginning to change with the inclusion of exploratory visualization techniques into GIS (Gahegan, 1999). These techniques allow the linking together of maps and charts to simultaneously explore spatial and nonspatial patterns in data.

• Student-centered inquiry benefits from guidance and feedback. GIS software lacks reflective wizards to provide directed feedback. Presently, there are scripting wizards that provide students with prescriptive guidance, but only in the sense of "here's how to get things done." Reflective wizards are needed to help students reflect on what is being done, why it is being done in those ways, and what is not being—but might be—done in other ways.

• Data for use in projects tend to be stored in more than one file. For example, three separate files are needed to view and work with a project in *ArcView*. These files are .shp (shape file), .dbf (attribute file), and .shx (index file). Lacking appropriate feedback, students tend to copy only one file (.shp) and forget that the other two files are also needed. This situation is beginning to change in ESRI's new data format where, for clarity, much of the necessary data are contained in a single file.

• GIS application interfaces do not facilitate multistage inquiry. Two styles of user interface design have dominated the field: the command-line style in which all commands are typed in text form and the WIMP. Both require a substantial commitment on the part of the user to choose and invoke relevant operations. Recently, there has been a movement to a more visual approach, which uses a pictorial interface to design and implement a process of multistage analysis (Figure 8.4). In pictorial interfaces, a box represents every intermediate data set, and arrows represent operations. Interacting with the diagram can lead to change in analyses, and intermediate steps can be recovered when it is necessary to replace one line of approach with another. Pictorial interfaces could make the process of inquiry more explicit and therefore more suited to the K–12 context. There is a clear need to promote pictorial user interfaces for the support of multistage inquiry.

2. Be Useful in Solving Problems in a Wide Range of Real-World Contexts. There is probably no better high-tech support system for addressing spatially explicit real-world problems than GIS. GIS succeeds as a tool for both curiosity-driven scientific research and context-driven problem-solving work because it supports functions that are useful in both situations. For example, ecologists use the perspective provided by GIS both to advance understanding of how organisms interact with each other and with their physical environment and to develop improved plans for wildlife management, based on principles identified by research scientists. Thus, GIS can provide the vital link between science and policy (application). At the most general level, science is interested in principles and laws that are true everywhere, independent of geographic context, and science can be presented as a process for abstracting such truths from their geographic setting.

FIGURE 8.4 Multistage analysis in a pictorially based GIS. SOURCE: Hemphill and Herold, 2003.

Policy, on the other hand, takes such principles and laws and puts them back in specific geographic contexts, in order to predict the outcomes of proposed developments or achieve better management of resources. The great bulk of GIS applications are about problem solving in particular contexts rather than elucidating general theories or laws.

In K–12 education, GIS can help students to appreciate and understand both curiosity-driven research and context-driven problem-solving approaches to science. Any tool that serves as a means to such intellectual ends is valuable. Even more valuable these days, when society expects K–12 education to devote attention to social ends, is a tool that can help students address real-world problems.

GIS can enable students to address real-world issues and, at the same time, help to break down boundaries and barriers between schools and local communities. The *Environmental and Spatial Technology* (EAST) initiative (http://www.cast.uark.edu/east/) has built on this philosophy by supporting schools with GIS software, data, training, and advice and has achieved success in involving K–12 students in public arenas. The initiative, which encourages spatial thinking through the use of a range of technologies (e.g., geospatial data systems, graphics generators, visual exploration systems) began in 1995 with 20 at-risk students at Greenbrier High School in Arkansas. Through the support of government and corporate partners, the EAST initiative has continued to flourish. More than 200 schools in seven states now participate, involving some 20,000 students in the higher grades. The EAST project is designed to serve a diverse population of students from those who are disadvantaged to those who are gifted. It provides a performance-based learning environment that utilizes problem-based service learning and advanced technological applications. Students, who are trained on-line to use a range of technologies including Intergraph's *GeoMedia*, work on real-world problems that can benefit their own schools and communities. To realize the full potential of new technology while enhancing opportunities for students, the EAST project strives to transform the classrooms of schools into information era learning centers.

Recent publications showcase how highly trained and motivated teachers have connected GIS and problem-based learning techniques to address real-world problems (Audet and Ludwig, 2000; English and Feaster, 2003; Malone et al., 2002). For example, *Community Geography: GIS in Action* (English and Feaster, 2003) presents community projects carried out by middle and high school students. The case studies include mapping and analyzing the patterns of an invasive weed species, mapping the patterns of crime in an urban school neighborhood, mapping the dangers presented by abandoned landfills in the school neighborhood, mapping the characteristics and potential problems of a school's tree population, mapping seasonal water quality variation in a local river, identifying students eligible to ride on school buses, and selecting potential sites for a parking lot in a wildlife preserve. Teachers served as resource guides and learning facilitators to students who asked questions, acquired the needed resources to study their environment, explored geographic information, and analyzed geographic data. The students presented their results and, in some cases, their recommendations to public officials (Box 8.2). These projects, therefore, provided students with a first-hand demonstration of the link between science and application.

Although GIS can enable students to analyze and understand issues at all scales, the local and state levels offer the greatest opportunity for personal involvement. When students, for example, provide recommendations for community forest planning to their town council, they know that their work made a difference. Students come away from such an experience having acquired not only academic content knowledge, but essential problem-solving skills and practical career skills as well.

There are two qualifications concerning the successful application of GIS to real-world issues in the K–12 context. First, very few teachers and students actually do use GIS in problem-solving contexts because of the still formidable barriers to the use of technology in the classroom (e.g., unreliable computers, lack of time for teachers to learn how to use the software, lack of time in the schedule for students to use computers in class). Second, secondary school students undertake the majority of the problem-solving projects because software developers and educational professionals have failed, for the most part, to provide GIS programs and curriculum materials that are developmentally appropriate for elementary students. The absence of GIS in the elementary grades means that for most students, their first exposure to the capacity of GIS to support spatial thinking may be delayed until their teenage years.

3. Facilitate Learning Transfer Across a Range of School Subjects. The first view of GIS that many users and learners encounter is the layer-cake model (Figure 7.4), reflecting the notion that geography can be expressed as a series of layers: the map of soils, the map of vegetation, the

BOX 8.2
Students Analyzing a Real-World Problem with GIS:
Characteristics and Potential Problems of a School's Tree Population

Students from 10 Rhode Island communities used an *ArcView* extension, *CITYgreen,* to map and analyze trees at their schools. American Forests, a nonprofit citizen conservation organization, developed *CITYgreen.*

Changes in Rhode Island's state planning guidelines in the late 1990s required every Rhode Island town to include an urban forestry component in its comprehensive plan, but few communities were prepared to do so. Students used GIS to help their own communities meet this state mandate as they simultaneously learned about the urban ecosystem, trees, and the power of spatial analysis in addressing community issues.

For example, students at Barrington Middle School prepared a map of trees conflicting with utility lines by digitizing the school building and trees on an orthophotograph of the school's property. Trees in conflict with utility lines were assigned a different color from other trees to create a thematic map (Figure 8.5).

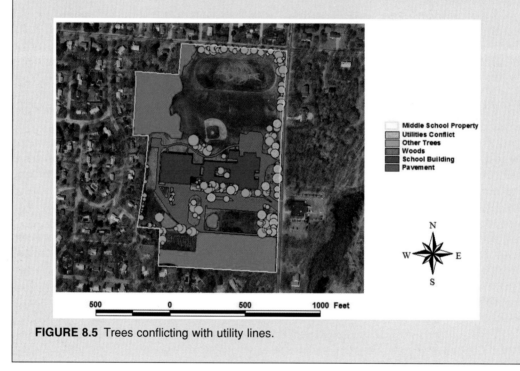

FIGURE 8.5 Trees conflicting with utility lines.

map of population, and so forth. GIS is often seen, therefore, as an integrating technology, capable of bringing together disparate knowledge domains by means of a common georeferencing system. By overlaying maps, one can investigate the impact of groundwater contamination on residential populations or the influence of soils on vegetation and habitat. The concept of overlay integration can be applied as a metaphor for the processes studied by the different social sciences (Goodchild et al., 2000) Thus, GIS can be a software system to integrate knowledge of economic processes and demographic processes as they simultaneously impact an area or influence its future. However, although GIS can, in principle, facilitate learning transfer across school subjects, there is insuffi-

They also queried the data to select all trees that were in poor or dying condition and that conflicted with utility lines or the school building. They converted the selected trees to a new category called "hazardous trees." With their symbol color changed to purple, the hazardous trees were easily visible on the map (Figure 8.6).

The students presented their observations in class, but they also presented the results and made recommendations to the Barrington Town Council. With a new database of tree information and a list of recommendations, the Barrington Public Works Department came a step closer to developing a program of tree maintenance and replanting in the town.

SOURCE: English and Feaster, 2003, pp.179–199.

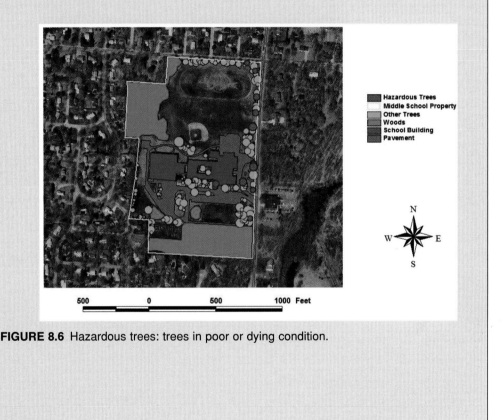

FIGURE 8.6 Hazardous trees: trees in poor or dying condition.

cient research for us to make a definitive statement about the efficacy of GIS in fostering learning transfer from one subject to another (see also Chapter 4).

GIS has the potential to be a useful tool for learning in a surprisingly large range of disciplines, some of which apparently have no immediate link to Earth's surface. For example, a chemistry teacher could use a GIS to make chemistry relevant to everyday life, through analysis of maps of hazardous chemicals and the impacts of spills and releases on human populations. Perhaps more powerful, however, is the lesson that students can learn through GIS about the value of interdisciplinary perspectives, as they integrate information from different disciplines. Because GIS are a means to facilitate interdisciplinary and multidisciplinary learning, they have the potential to be a mainstay cross-disciplinary educational tool like the calculator or word processor.

4. Provide a Rich, Generative, Inviting, and Challenging Problem-Solving Environment. GIS has the potential to provide students in all grades with a rich, inviting, and challenging problem-solving environment. However, existing, professional-level GIS software packages, which take a long time to learn to use to their fullest extent, are too rich as a general tool for the K–12 context. Most of the activities that schools need to support, especially through the elementary and middle grades, could be achieved with software systems that are more lightweight, easier to deploy, easier to use, and free from distracting details. Above all, qualitatively different software packages that are easy to customize would enrich the K–12 learning environment. GIS can be inviting to students because of its potential for display and exploration. However, the lack of support for animation, which helps to illustrate important spatial processes, and the limited support for spatialization of nonspatial data may reduce the ability of GIS to captivate students. Twenty-first century students have grown up in a world of television, video games, and digital images; they are comfortable in the digital world and gravitate toward it. These students are used to computers that provide a high degree of interaction in terms of the display of geographic space (from computer gaming), and for them, GIS may pale in comparison. Educational applications of GIS that use animation software such as *Flash* or *Director* would likely have great appeal to many students. Unquestionably, the use of GIS can, with well-trained teachers and well-equipped schools, foster critical thinking and problem-solving skills among students especially when linked with other media and fieldwork. Of equal importance, GIS can also provide students with the IT skills needed in the twenty-first-century workplace (Chapter 5).

Discussion Summary

From this analysis, the committee can make the following observations about the ability of current versions of GIS to meet educational goals:

1. In principle, GIS reflects many of the ideals of exploration-driven, discovery-based, student-centered inquiry. Nonetheless, current GIS is less well equipped for data exploration and hypothesis generation than for data analysis and presenting information. In addition, current GIS is too cumbersome and inaccessible for effective use in K–12 education. User interfaces, the lack of reflective wizards, and multiple files contributing to a single data source are among concerns that diminish the ability of GIS to support inquiry.
2. GIS can enable K–12 students to address a broad range of real-world issues. Although GIS allows students to analyze and understand issues at all scales, it is probably the local and state levels that offer students the greatest opportunity for personal involvement and action.
3. In principle, GIS can foster learning transfer across subjects. However, insufficient research has been conducted to make a definitive statement about learning transfer from one subject to another.
4. GIS has the potential to provide students in all grades with a rich, inviting, and challenging problem-solving environment. However, existing, industrial-strength GIS software packages are too rich as a general tool for the K–12 context.

Table 8.4 gives the committee's assessment of GIS as a support system for spatial thinking through its capacity to meet educational goals. Overall, GIS rates very well as a tool for students to address a wide range of real-world contexts. It rates least well as a software system that supports the

TABLE 8.4 Assessment of the Design of GIS to Meet Educational Goals

Criteria	High	Medium	Low
Be supportive of the inquiry process			+
Be useful in solving problems in a wide range of real-world contexts	+		
Facilitate learning transfer across a range of school subjects		+	
Provide a rich, generative, inviting, and challenging problem-solving environment for the users of the support system		+	

inquiry process. In principle, GIS is supportive of the inquiry process, but it will become a more effective technology for that purpose when the user interface facilitates multistage GIS analysis.

8.3.2 Being Appropriate to Student Needs

This subsection considers the capacity of GIS to be appropriate to student needs (see Section 6.5): (5) be developmentally and educationally appropriate; (6) be accessible to and supportive of the full range of learners; and (7) be customizable. After considering each in turn, a summary and an overall assessment of the ability of GIS to meet these three needs are presented.

5.   Be Developmentally and Educationally Appropriate. The GIS software built by the vendor community is industrial-strength. Designed almost entirely for and by experts, this professional-level software draws from many diverse, powerful technologies and sophisticated knowledge domains that include geography, database design, programming, statistics, remote sensing, geodesy, surveying, spatial analysis, and geometry. As a direct consequence of the history of its design, GIS software has been difficult to learn, complex to use, and difficult and expensive to customize. Appropriate use of GIS often requires at least a rudimentary understanding of many of these knowledge domains, explaining why many users take at least one higher-education course in GIS and many have degrees or certificates in GIS. Therefore, it is no wonder that initial access to, let alone attainment of proficiency in, GIS technology can seem daunting to the novice user. The learning curve to become a proficient user of industrial-strength GIS software is steep.

GIS education is, in many respects, an introduction to a language of specialized concepts. GIS trainees learn to decode such acronyms as DEM (digital elevation model) or DRG (digital raster graphic), and they learn the basis of common coordinate systems such as UTM (Universal Transverse Mercator) or SPC (State Plane Coordinate). While K–12 learners would not necessarily need to know all of these concepts to take advantage of the power of GIS to support thinking spatially, current GIS designs do little to protect users from them.

Developers and designers have thought long and hard about how to simplify GIS user interfaces, and the results are evident in special-purpose, GIS-based products designed for the general public. Consider, for example, ways to handle the idea of spatial scale. Users of *MapQuest* are shielded from any interaction with map projections or coordinate systems. They encounter scale not in the relatively complex and convention-bound sense of representative fraction (the ratio of distance on the map to distance on the ground), but as a simple point-and-click stepwise gradation from coarse to fine, labeled "zoom out" and "zoom in." Microsoft's *Encarta* implements the metaphor of a helicopter, inviting the user to raise the helicopter to reduce detail and lower the helicopter to increase it. Scale can also be implemented in terms of familiar objects by presenting the user with an ordered range, from detailed ("enough to see individual cars on the street") to coarse ("enough to see major cities or lakes"). What is needed, then, is a GIS with a user interface that is built for "ease of learning and ease of use." To provide a basis for the design of a user-friendly system, research is needed on the functions most frequently employed by teachers and students and on the ways in which those functions are best understood by students of different ages and different skill levels.

If GIS is to move beyond the preserve of the highly trained few, the geographic information software industry needs to respond to a wide range of potential users by developing software tools that are easy, flexible, and interesting to use. Ideally, a GIS designed for the K–12 community would manage, behind the scenes, all details except those of current interest to the user.

In addition to the ideal, at least three other options are possible:

• A GIS that is a lightweight version of the industrial strength model, one that is specifically targeted to the needs of teachers and students: It would be stripped down in terms of the range of functions presented and the interface would be simplified and more supportive (e.g., through the addition of wizards). This option is unlikely to materialize because the K–12 education market, as currently constituted, is not a significant revenue producer for geographic information software developers.

• A GIS that enables teachers to hide and expose functionality as needed: A GIS can be customized to remove details that might cause confusion to novice users. At the moment, customization technology (e.g., APIs) is not geared toward the needs of educators, and it is not easy to use without advanced training. However, customization is a place on which to focus future efforts. An example of a software product that is customized to gradually expose the functionality of the user interface is ESRI's *ArcVoyager* system (see Box 8.3). This scalable system provides four graded levels of exposure to the user interface, progressively adding more functionality and more complexity in the analysis and display activities.

• A GIS that uses a component-based system or open system architecture: In this option, applications would be composed of only the most frequently used functions identified by GIS practitioner educators, and data would be developed and deployed separately from the main product. The component-oriented approach offers potential for teachers or students to package GIS functionality into a series of separate miniprograms to meet specific needs. (See Box 8.4 for a description of some advantages of component-based system architectures.)

The component-oriented approach may make it easier to design developmentally and educationally appropriate GIS software for the K–12 context. Ideally, a component-oriented version of GIS would provide a self-contained software application complete with data, documentation, and assessment materials that can be easily accessed, deployed, and evaluated. It could be tailored for use by teachers and students and graded to support increasing levels of skill and experience. Also, it would have to be suitable for use by both secondary and primary school students. Currently, the use of GIS at the elementary level lags far behind its adoption in the middle and upper grades. Software designers should explore alternative interfaces that would be developmentally and educationally appropriate for elementary students. The problem is not that GIS is inherently too complex for younger learners, but that GIS designers have not addressed the needs of this audience. Appropriately designed GIS, which are capable of analyses from the most simple to the most complex, could facilitate the process of thinking spatially from the early through the upper grades.

BOX 8.3
ArcVoyager

ArcVoyager was created by the K–12 Education Group at ESRI in the mid-1990s, at a time when many teachers had little or no experience with computers. The *ArcVoyager* software program (http://www.esri.com/industries/K–12/voyager.html) is an application of *ArcView GIS*. Literally, it is a stripped-down version of the industrial-strength *ArcView*. It is customized in terms of its functionality to give novice users a graduated experience with some of the capabilities of GIS. Consisting of four ramped levels, *ArcVoyager* takes users from a simple beginner interface called "Exploring Key Concepts: Teach Me" to a fully functional GIS program called "Creating New Worlds: Turn Me Loose." The program interface and its GIS functionality become gradually more complex as students move through the four levels, allowing learners the opportunity to increase their mastery and comfort level before progressing to the next level.

ArcVoyager's levels differ in terms of the number of buttons or options as well as the freedom users have to see maps versus create their own maps.

• *Level 1.* "Exploring Key Concepts: Teach Me" is a hyperlinked help file. It offers no capacity for starting projects. It introduces people to geographic concepts, GIS concepts, and data and computer issues through a hotlinked progression of text and images. It is a text that also allows users to practice or demonstrate mouse skills.
• *Level 2.* "Viewing World Snapshots: Show Me" is an *ArcView* project with a heavily customized interface, which has a few buttons, a few tools, a few menus, and 20 layers of world-level data classified and symbolized in an unchangeable manner. At this level, visualization and identification are possible, but analysis is not possible at least on screen.
• *Level 3.* "Designing Global Adventures: Point Me" has more tools, buttons, menus, and data than Level 2. It also has an open-ended ability to add data sets. The preexisting data sets provide starting points for exploration, analysis, and presentations at world and regional scales.
• *Level 4.* "Creating New Worlds: Turn Me Loose" has the same interface as Level 3 but with no starting data. Users are on their own to create their own maps from scratch (Figure 8.7).

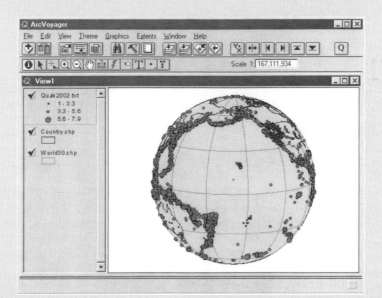

FIGURE 8.7 A screen display from a user-built map generated from Level 4 of *ArcVoyager*. The user has chosen to display the world data in an orthographic view, centered on 10 degrees north and 160 degrees west; earthquakes have been brought in as a text file and classified and symbolized.

continued

BOX 8.3 Continued

ArcVoyager requires the prior installation of *ArcView GIS*, although ESRI made a version—*ArcVoyager Special Edition*—that can be installed without having *ArcView*. The major disadvantage of *ArcVoyager Special Edition* is that it does not permit students to save their work.

Although it is a relatively simple process, program installation has sometimes presented obstacles to the classroom use of *ArcVoyager*. Both versions of *ArcVoyager* are installed from ESRI's GIS for Schools and Libraries CD that also includes extensive links and resources for teachers. Teachers with

(a)

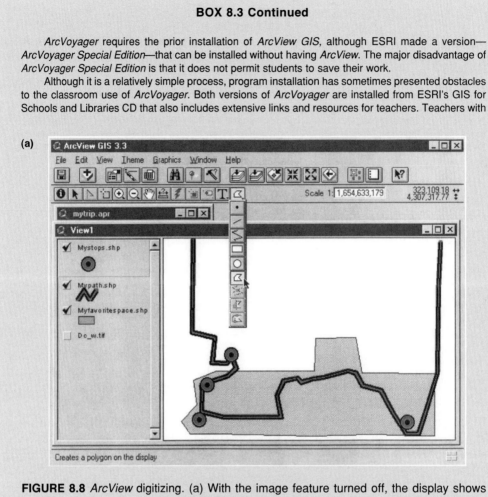

FIGURE 8.8 *ArcView* digitizing. (a) With the image feature turned off, the display shows point, line, and polygon features and the pull-down tool selections from which the appropriate tool was selected to accomplish the digitizing. (b) With the image feature turned on, the graphic shows what the display looks like after a student digitizes point, line, and polygon features.

6. Be Accessible to and Supportive of the Full Range of Learners. GIS use in K–12 education is minimal. However, although the adoption of GIS in schools is in its very early stages, all students—in keeping with the purpose of the No Child Left Behind Act of 2001 (Public Law 107-110)—should have a fair, equal, and significant opportunity to use technology as it becomes available to them.

The general purpose of Public Law 107-110 is "to ensure equal educational opportunity for all children regardless of socioeconomic background and to close the achievement gap between poor and affluent children by providing additional resources for schools serving disadvantaged students" (Public Law 107-110, section 1001). Section 2402 of Public Law 107-110 focuses on improving the academic achievement of differently-abled students through the effective use of technology. The minimal computer skills often have difficulty distinguishing the software installation component of the CD from its HTML-formatted directories of resources, links, and documents.

Nonetheless, *ArcVoyager* was developed as a tool for those K–12 teachers with minimal computer skills. It is "GIS for the masses," with a large number of potential users but limited functionality. It introduces users to some of the capabilities of GIS and permits them to conduct simple analyses. However, unlike its heavyweight parent, *ArcView*, *ArcVoyager* does not introduce users to many of the key GIS terms and concepts (e.g., shapefile, theme, view, table, chart, project) that are needed to understand the operations of a GIS. Thus, for work in the higher grades, students need to know that shapefiles store geographic features digitally as points, lines, and areas (polygons) if they are to use the on-screen tools to digitize real-world features. When advanced students start to use the data capture functionality of *ArcView*, they can create their own data for analysis and display (Figure 8.8) and then they can begin to use GIS as a powerful support system for spatial thinking.

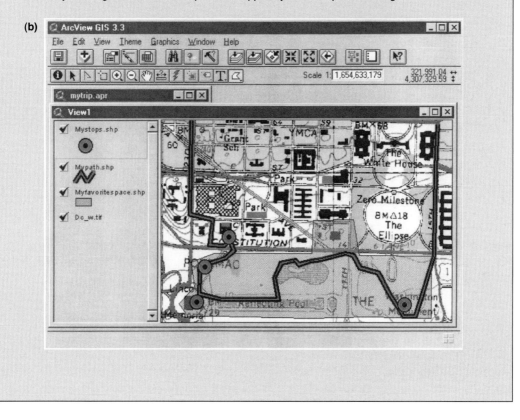

primary goal is "to improve student academic achievement through the use of technology in elementary and secondary schools" (Public Law 107-110, section 2402). An additional goal of the act is "to assist every student in crossing the digital divide by ensuring that every student is technologically literate by the time the student finishes the eighth grade, regardless of the student's race, ethnicity, gender, family income, geographic location, or disability" (Public Law 107-110, section 2402).

The challenge of making GIS accessible to the full range of learners is daunting in its complexity and will require many initiatives including those that "provide school teachers, principals, and administrators with the capacity to integrate technology effectively into curricula and instruction that are aligned with challenging State academic content and student academic achievement stan-

---

BOX 8.4
Open Versus Closed Software System Architectures

GIS and most other software systems that can support spatial thinking are industrial-strength, monolithic systems. As such, they are designed as stand-alone systems, perhaps with add-ons, but with tightly coupled data structures and control structures. It is usually not possible to break such systems apart into a number of independent components, because each piece is highly dependent on the other pieces.

GIS are generally seen as having reached a critical point in their development. They now offer so much functionality and, like many other support systems, are trying to address an ever-broadening set of issues and application domains. Although this functionality allows broad support for a huge number of application areas, it also results in ever more complex APIs, steep learning curves for developers and users alike, and problems with legacy systems. Yet most users of these monolithic systems access only a small percentage of the functions available to them.

Throughout the software industry there is a movement away from such monolithic engineering, where the resultant system is a single self-contained program, to a component model where functionality is broken down into small, independently deployable pieces that communicate through well-defined interfaces. This component-oriented model offers two advantages for the design, customization, and implementation of GIS. First, if interfaces are made public (i.e., published), it becomes easier for the value added reseller (VAR) to use the services that the components offer and to construct specific, focused applications that extend the basic functionality. Second, it offers the possibility, for vendors and resellers, to substitute one component for another as long as the new component adheres to the interface specification. Consequently it might be possible, for example, to swap the current map display tool for a new component that produces a highly stylized map or even a synthesized spoken description for the visually impaired. The new version of *ArcGIS* (9) takes this kind of component-oriented approach (http://www.esri.com), as does *GeoVISTA Studio* (http://www.geovistastudio.psu.edu).

---

dards, through such means as high-quality professional development programs" (Public Law 107-110, section 2402). Nonetheless, progress toward meeting the accessibility goal can be made along several fronts. For example:

• **Assisting Visually Impaired Learners.** Current GIS rely heavily on visualization at all stages—from input to output. They are not yet amenable for use without sight. To enable such use, alternative access modes—touch, haptics, speech, and hearing—must be incorporated into the GIS interface. The most accessible technologies to facilitate interaction include a haptic mouse, software that converts text to speech, and voice input. Haptic mice, developed mostly for video game use, work on the principle of force-feedback. For example, a simple outline map of a country and its political divisions can be constructed using virtual boundaries consisting of lines of resistance (electronic "forces") that act both as guides for shape tracing, and therefore learning, and as buffers to inhibit entry into an enclosed area. Therefore, force would have to be exerted on the haptic mouse to enter or exit a region (polygon). Interiors of polygons can be filled with vibratory or tactual shading (hachures, diagonal lines, and different densities of dots). The user feels the surface via the haptic mouse and compares the shading textures and patterns to a legend to identify the information being shown. This is a haptic version of the visual choropleth or isopleth map (Figure 8.9). Text-to-speech conversion software allows a user to listen to written descriptions of materials or to follow sequences of descriptions for comprehending what is being visually represented on screen. Voice interaction relies on speech recognition software that has become commonly available. This provides an alternative to using the keyboard or mouse to enter commands for search and exploration. For example, speech can be used to find locations using simple "up-down-left-right" instructions, or it can initiate requests such as "take me to place *x*."

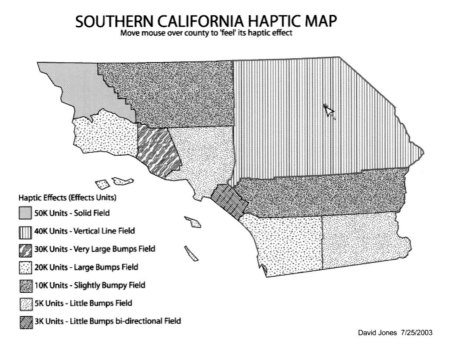

FIGURE 8.9 "On-screen" representation of a haptic choropleth map of southern California. County boundaries (dark lines) are defined by virtual walls to help locate them and to identify size and shape. Interiors are represented by different types of tactile surfaces, which provide vibratory feedback to the user via a haptic mouse. SOURCE: Generated by David Jones as part of the Haptic Soundscapes Project funded by NSF Grant #HRD-0099261. Principal Investigators R. Golledge and D. Jacobson.

Although both the hardware and the software to enable these nonvisual interfaces exist, no current GIS incorporate anything but keyboard or standard mouse interfaces or provide anything but tabular, numerical, text, or visual map-diagram output. Thus the potential exists to make GIS more accessible to the visually impaired. Research and development efforts should explore the capacity and complementarity of text, sound, and other communication channels as GIS input and output modes for those who are visually impaired. Everybody can use these channels, but they are indispensable for the visually impaired.

• **Meeting the Needs of English Language Learners.** While GIS is rigorous enough to challenge the most gifted students, it is also potentially accessible to students who are non-English speakers. As students whose first language is not English improve their proficiency in English, they are also learning academic content in subjects such as science and mathematics and can learn how to use technology such as GIS. However, if GIS technology is to support students whose command of English is limited, they might benefit from some changes in interface design. For example, first language guides could be provided on what buttons to push. Teachers of Spanish-speaking children in Conroe, Texas, who were introduced to *Mapping Our World: GIS Lessons for Educators* (Malone et al., 2002) did *not* want the book itself translated into Spanish. They wanted their students to become fluent in English and technologically literate. In their view, the right level of assistance for

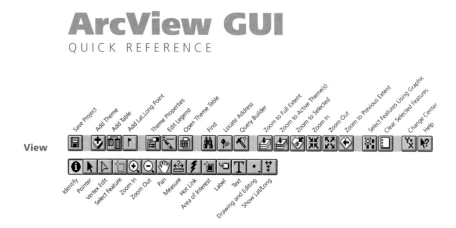

FIGURE 8.10 *ArcView* Quick Reference Graphical User Interface. SOURCE: ESRI *ArcView* Software. *ArcView* Graphical User Interface is the intellectual property of ESRI and is used herein with permission. Copyright © 2002 ESRI. All rights reserved.

students learning English and learning to use GIS is to translate only the *ArcView* Graphical User Interface (GUI) Quick Reference (Figure 8.10). The translation helped the Spanish-speaking students to know what a button would do and whether they were on the right track. For teachers who use *Mapping Our World: GIS Lessons for Educators*, this simple interface aid can provide English language learners with an opportunity to use GIS effectively as a support to the inquiry process.

Currently, GIS is not accessible to and supportive of the full range of learners. Few students in the primary grades use GIS. Most students with learning disabilities do not have opportunities to use GIS. In addition, there is an unequal distribution of computing resources among schools, and a critical lack of pre-service teacher training in areas such as spatial literacy, problem-based teaching techniques, and computer skills. Nonetheless, GIS does have the potential to accommodate the full range of learners and to do so in some creative and interesting ways.

7. Be Customizable. Current GIS software products were developed as specialist tools for use in government, industry, and higher education. In such environments, software vendors could assume that sophisticated users were willing to invest considerable time and money in learning how to use a software product and how to customize its interface and functionality as needed. These conditions do not hold generally in K–12 education. In the K–12 context, there is a lack of time and money to learn how to use industrial-strength GIS.

Out of necessity, however, most GIS software used in the K–12 context involves industrial-strength, heavyweight applications that were not designed with students and learning in mind. Exceptions include *ArcVoyager* (see Box 8.3), a customized version of *ArcView*, which is designed to help students begin to navigate the world of maps and geographic inquiry through GIS. Another exception is *CITYgreen,* which is a community forestry application for *ArcView* developed by American Forests (see Box 8.2). This customized program, which has built-in modeling, statistical, and analytical functions, provides learners with an opportunity to engage in ecological analyses that affect their communities: development, planning, alternative land-use proposals, and the preservation of green spaces.

To help K–12 teachers use *ArcView* in their classes, ESRI published *Mapping Our World: GIS*

Lessons for Educators (Malone et al., 2002). It provides customized lessons that lead students step-by-step to create maps. (See Appendix H for an example of students using GIS to understand spatial and temporal variations in rainfall in India.) Students are directed to hypothesize, investigate, analyze, and so on during the procedure of creating a series of maps. However, there is no explicit help for either teachers or students to complete the analysis of the maps and data. Evidence suggests that eighth-grade students, when given proper scaffolding and support, can make effective use of GIS (Baker and White, 2003).

The committee suggests that GIS software products be better adapted to users—both students and teachers—if they are to meet the needs of K–12 education. At present, the onus is on teachers to adapt to software products such as *ArcView*. If they have considerable knowledge of GIS, they can customize *ArcView* using its customizing options. If they can apply *Avenue*, *ArcView*'s object-oriented programming language, they can also customize *ArcView*'s GUI. However, the vast majority of teachers do not have the expertise, let alone the time, to use *ArcView*'s customization functions or *Avenue*.

Teachers and students would be better served by GIS software tools that are easy, flexible, and interesting to use. This view was shared by those who worked on the Technology in Education Research Consortium's (TERC) *Mapping Our City* in the late 1990s. The objective was to apply GIS in various middle school settings. The project leaders concluded that the "out-of-the box" functionality of *ArcView* should be reorganized to meet the needs of the education community. They recommended organizing tools into three categories—drawing, questioning, and movement—using more intuitive naming conventions and visual cues to aid recognition. The *Mapping Our City* project employed a tiered format that gradually exposed all of the functionality, not unlike *ArcVoyager*.

For teachers and students to use GIS effectively, the industrial-strength technology should be simplified by vendors rather than users and third parties. In the committee's view, the development of a component software application is an attractive option. Software developers in collaboration with the education community should investigate this option. The software must be designed for easy adoption by K–12 users with minimal training. Current versions of GIS, like much software, are too rich for teachers to integrate easily into their classes. Software should be designed to meet two needs. First it must accommodate what teachers need to know in order to feel comfortable teaching GIS. Second it must present what students need to be able to do in using GIS to solve problems. In both cases, the key is selectivity: software designers must distinguish between what is possible and what is necessary in the design of GIS for the K–12 context.

Discussion Summary

From this analysis, the following observations can be made about the capacity of current versions of GIS to fit student needs.

1. Existing professional-level GIS software products are not developmentally and educationally appropriate for the K–12 context. They are too complicated to use throughout all K–12 grades. The software industry should develop tools that teachers and different students find easy, flexible, and interesting to use.

2. Currently, GIS is not accessible to and supportive of the full range of learners, and making it so is daunting in its complexity. Nonetheless, GIS does have the potential to reach all learners, including the differently abled.

3. Existing professional-level GIS is customizable for the K–12 setting. For example, *ArcView* can be customized to fit student needs. With the use of *Avenue*, it is possible to customize *ArcView*'s interface, which opens up opportunities for organizing the data entry process, streamlining related

TABLE 8.5 Assessment of GIS in Terms of Its Appropriateness to Meet Student Needs

Criteria	High	Medium	Low
Be developmentally and educationally appropriate			+
Be accessible to and supportive of the full range of learners		+	
Be customizable		+	

functionality, and creating a more intuitive interface. However, teachers have neither the time nor the expertise to undertake such major customization efforts to meet the needs of their students. Even if teachers had the time and expertise to customize the GIS software, customization would be occurring at the wrong scale, at the retail or school scale, not the wholesale or vendor scale. For wholesale, systemic change, GIS vendors have to develop products that can be readily deployed by the K–12 community.

Table 8.5 gives the committee's assessment of GIS as a support system for spatial thinking in terms of its appropriateness to meet student needs. Existing GIS rate poorly on the criterion "be developmentally and educationally appropriate." Because users can in principle customize GIS and because GIS has the potential to reach the full range of learners, it fares better on the other two criteria.

8.3.3 Matching the Educational Context

This subsection considers the capacity of GIS to match the needs and constraints of the educational context. The criteria considered are (see Section 6.5): (8) be flexible enough to be effective in a variety of school contexts and enable a range of modes of use; (9) be quick and intuitive for students and teachers to learn to use; and (10) be robust and realistic in terms of the expectations placed on teachers and the demands on school infrastructure. A summary and an overall assessment of the capacity of GIS to match the educational context follow the discussion.

8. Be Flexible Enough to Be Effective in a Variety of School Contexts and Enable a Range of Modes of Use. A system to support spatial thinking in the K–12 context must have the flexibility to be effective in a variety of configurations because there is no common or universal mode of use. While some students find themselves learning in classrooms with only one computer, others report to classrooms with multiple computer stations. Many schools have computer laboratories where teachers can take their classes for a single lesson, whereas other schools restrict laboratories for use by certain departments. With so many different possibilities, an effective support system must be adaptable in terms of delivery and use. GIS has this essential quality.

Before the popularization of the Internet and the web in the mid-1990s, the traditional mode of GIS use was a single user seated at a desk. The user treated the GIS as a calculating machine designed to perform the kinds of analyses that the user found too difficult, tedious, or time-consuming to perform by hand. However, collaborative technologies are now available to support the widespread sharing of spatial data, map views, and projects via the Internet.

Collaborative technologies raise interesting prospects for the support of interactions at a distance, between students in different locations, or between students and stakeholders interested in particular problems. Students can exchange data or results and work collaboratively on large-scale projects. For example, one might think of supporting interaction between students and city officials, between students in different parts of the world sharing an interest in a particular environmental problem, or between students in the United States and students in countries that are the subject of instruction. In today's global and interconnected economy, it would be prudent to consider the use of GIS in collaborative learning projects among geographically dispersed students, as is the case for KanCRN (http://www.pathfinderscience.org) and GLOBE (http://www.globe.gov). Such efforts would enable students to practice valuable workforce skills.

9. Be Quick and Intuitive for Students and Teachers to Learn to Use. An apparent obstacle to the implementation of GIS in American schools is the perception that the tool is a high-end software program requiring a heavy investment of time to learn to use in inquiry-based instruction. Although there is some truth to that perception, this impediment need not necessarily prevent the integration of GIS into the K–12 curriculum. There is a difference between the *perception* and the *reality* of the time it takes to learn how to use GIS.

The perception versus reality issue comes down to the question of whether or not a teacher has to have "mastered" GIS before integrating it into the curriculum. Many teachers feel uncomfortable teaching an industrial-strength technology—or any technology, for that matter—that they are just beginning to learn. They look at the range and capability of GIS software, and they find its power appealing. They look at its design, its interface, its specialized language, and they find them intimidating and confusing. They infer that because the learning curve is so steep, it will take them a long time—too long—to pick up the skills to use it on their own.

In reality, few GIS users—in education or any other field—would describe themselves as having mastered this technology. Instead, they would say that they have learned the particular skills they need to know in order to use GIS in a specific context, whether the context is municipal government, real estate, public health, or transportation. If teachers could adopt a similar need-to-know approach to learning to use GIS (and if we could guide them in this process), they would realize that they do not have to be GIS aficionados to use it in the classroom. They just need to know the specific GIS skills and functionalities required of a particular lesson or task. The challenge for designers of education-oriented GIS is to identify those skills and functionalities.

For the successful use of GIS in the classroom, teachers have to know the basic procedures of file navigation and management. In addition to these technical skills, they need to know how to use the basic tools (zoom, pan, identify, find, etc.) and functions (legend editing, querying, buffering, selecting by theme, etc.) of a GIS program. Taken one at a time, each of these skills can be learned rather quickly. Teacher training in GIS has to capitalize on this fact by dividing the many skills and functions into manageable and coherent subsets for teachers to use as a basis for meaningful analysis and problem solving in the classroom. With appropriately sequenced training, teachers can develop discrete GIS skill sets and feel confident that they have the expertise needed to teach a lesson based on those skills. Teachers must be liberated from the anxiety generated by the perception that GIS is a monolithic, highly technical, and very demanding software program that they do not have the time to learn.

At the same time, however, vendors should develop new GIS software packages that are more easily adopted with minimal training by teachers. With more intuitive and user-friendly software, teachers should grow more comfortable with using GIS to support inquiry-based instruction.

Students, like teachers, run into difficulties in using GIS (Box 8.5). Many of the problems involve computer file management. Some difficulties arise because of interferences between what the Microsoft operating system wants and what GIS wants. A systematic research program should be launched to identify the problems that teachers and students face when using GIS and to find

BOX 8.5
Illustrative Difficulties That Teachers and Students Confront
When Working with GIS

Four examples illustrate situations in which teachers and/or students encounter problems while working with *ArcView* software. Each example is keyed to a particular part of the software. A brief explanation of what goes wrong and why is presented, followed by a suggestion on how the problem has been or can be remedied.

1. **On or Off Themes.** *ArcView 3* uses a "View" frame composed of a map space and a "Table of Contents" (TOC). Layers of data, known as themes in *ArcView,* are either on (and accessible) or off, according to a checkbox in the TOC. Newly added themes are not turned on automatically. Novice users will often wonder what they did wrong or why something fails to work, when all they have to do is turn on the data layer. Figure 8.11 shows the result of adding a theme in *ArcView 3.* It appears atop the TOC but is not turned on by default. For adults, this sometimes means that they will re-add the theme several times before saying, "Oh, I need to turn it on . . . duh!" with which students do not have nearly as much trouble. This problem is remedied in *ArcView 8,* which automatically turns on added features.

2. **Active and Inactive Themes.** In its mapping space, *ArcView 3* relies on a concept of "active theme" (i.e., a data layer against which a process is to be accomplished). The active theme is estab- lished by clicking one time anywhere on the name or symbols of that data set within the TOC; an active theme looks somewhat raised or embossed. Novice users attempt to run a process without remember- ing to specify the active theme. When an unexpected result occurs, users are often baffled until they are reminded by more experienced users to check which theme is active. Figures 8.11, 8.12, and 8.13 show the condition of having 0, 1, or 2 specific themes active. Notice that many buttons and tools are grayed out when there is no active theme, because a process cannot be applied to nothing. *ArcView 8* resolves this problem by introducing "right-click" operations, which require users first to identify a theme and then to choose an activity. Figures 8.12 and 8.13 show *ArcView 3* after the user has made one theme (Figure 8.12) or two themes (Figure 8.13) active by clicking on their names.

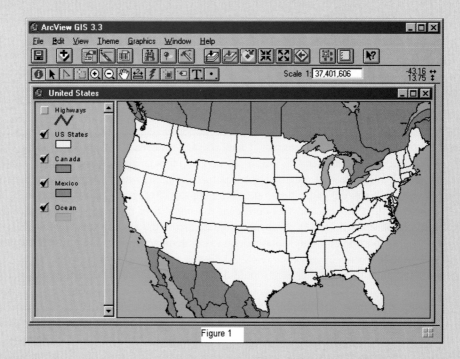

FIGURE 8.11 On or off themes: adding a theme in *ArcView 3.* The "Highway" theme has been added but is not turned on. No themes are active in this display.

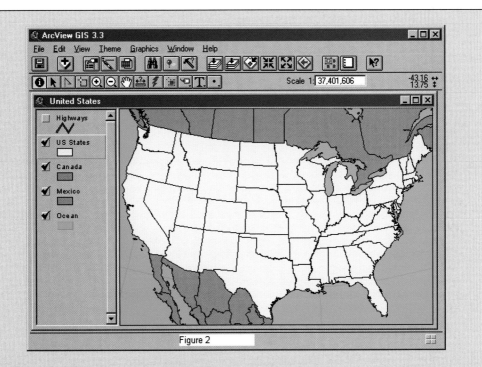

FIGURE 8.12 Active and inactive themes: one active theme.

FIGURE 8.13 Active and inactive themes: two active themes.

continued

BOX 8.5 Continued

3. Logical Queries. In *ArcView*, a query is a logical statement used to select features or records. A simple query contains a field name, an operation, and a value. In constructing a logical query (e.g., highlight all countries with a birthrate above two per thousand), *ArcView 3* provides a query builder tool that relies on carefully constructed independent clauses, in which precise use of punctuation and conjunctions is critical. The procedure typically involves selecting a field from the left column, an operation from the center column, and a value from the right column, thus building a statement in the box below the columns. Users often highlight fields and values without paying attention to the sequence of the phrase being constructed below. Efforts to repair the phrase through typing by hand, rather than selection, are often inaccurate, leading to a signal of "syntax error." When this happens, novice users try to identify the "single tweak necessary," even when they may have inappropriately specified logic statements. The recommended approach is always to do as much selection as possible with the mouse and to watch the box being filled in with a text statement. This problem is difficult to remedy without introducing even more opportunities for error. Logical queries can be complex and syntax is critical. Figure 8.14 shows an *ArcView 3* logical query window that provides no formal assistance in construction of the query; in this case, the user has single-clicked in the field column at the left, generating the suite of alternative values at right, but there is no firm clue about the nature of the statement desired in the space below. Figure 8.15 shows an *ArcView 8* logical query window that operates in a similar fashion but at least provides a modicum of formal assistance with the statement immediately above the box where the query is to be constructed. Contrast these options with a window such as Figure 8.16, in which the user is guided by the window to construct a logical sentence, in this case, "select features of active themes (here, highways) that <<intersect>> the selected features of <<choose: U.S. States>>" (which will generate a selection of highways in Texas). Because logical queries can range from extremely simple to extremely complex, with multiple conditionals and nested elements, attempting to program for simplicity may actually end up introducing confusion or reducing capacity. The *ArcView 8* strategy of "beginning the English translation of the sentence" seems a reasonable compromise.

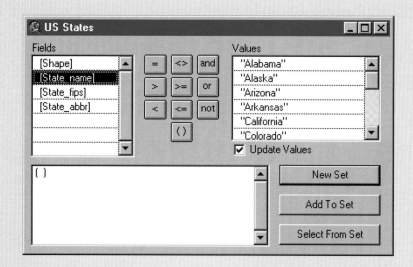

FIGURE 8.14 Logical queries: query window in *ArcView 3*.

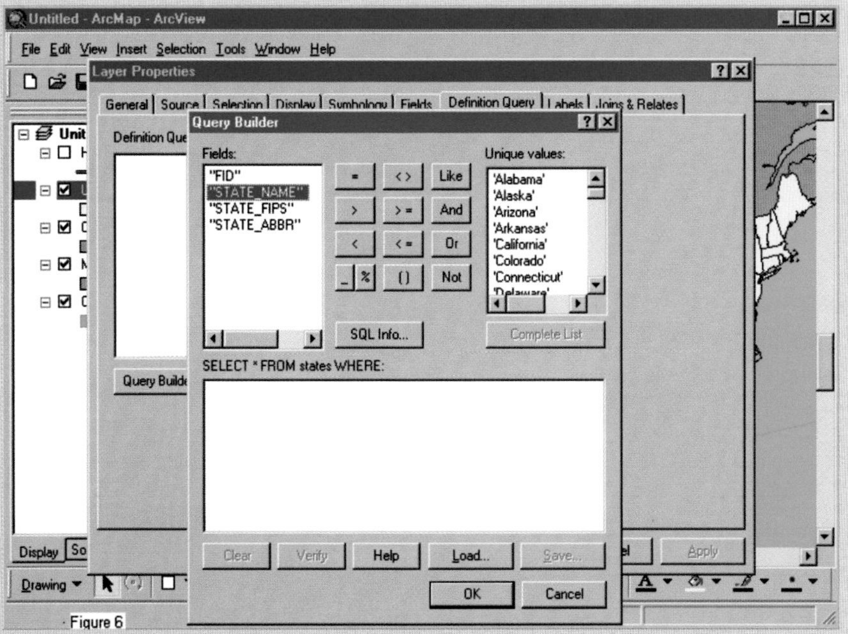

FIGURE 8.15 Logical queries: query windows in *ArcView 8*.

FIGURE 8.16 Logical queries: select by theme.

continued

BOX 8.5 Continued

4. Zooming In. The "magnify/plus" tool in *ArcView 3* operates like a zoom tool in many other software packages. Thus, users click once in the map space to zoom in a specified amount and move the clicked spot into the center. Users can also "click-hold-drag diagonally" to define a box into which to zoom. Attempting to use the "single-click" method, novice zoomers frequently "click-and-wiggle," unknowingly creating a tiny square that becomes the whole of the rescaled map space, and wonder where their map went, or they create a zoom box nearly matching the size of the original map space, and wonder why no zooming takes place. To remedy this problem, some software packages permit zooms only in specified amounts, perhaps requiring use of a "pan" tool to select a desired site. However, the best remedy seems to be practice or familiarity with the zoom tool. Figure 8.17 shows the *ArcView 3* zooming tool, and Figure 8.18 shows the standard procedure. Figure 8.19 shows what happens when a user clicks in a site (such as the center of a state) and accidentally wiggles before releasing the mouse, creating a tiny box, telling the software in effect to zoom into the tiny square.

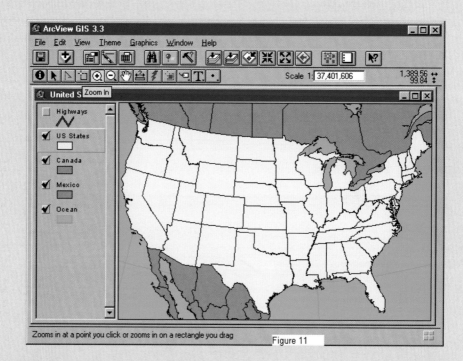

FIGURE 8.17 Zooming in: *ArcView 3* zooming tool.

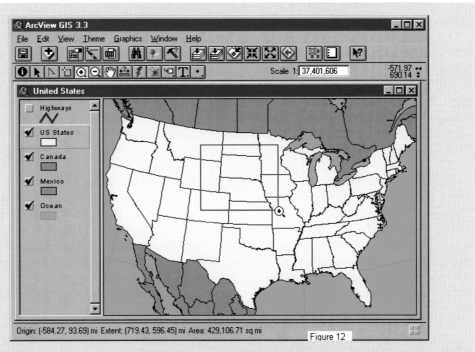

FIGURE 8.18 Zooming in: standard procedure for defining a box to create a rescaled map.

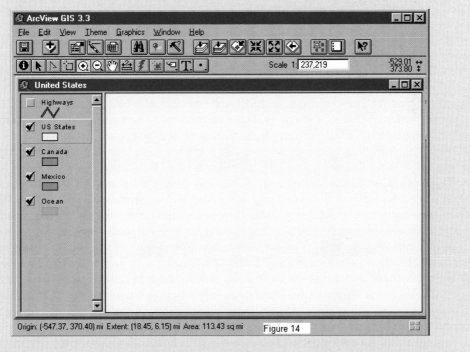

FIGURE 8.19 Zooming in: what happens when a user clicks in a site and accidentally wiggles before releasing the mouse?

solutions to these problems that are sensitive to the different needs and abilities of teachers and students.

An essential way to spur the learning of GIS by teachers is to devise training programs that will enable them to learn fundamental GIS skills and integrate those skills into their classroom lessons. Such training should be built on teaching a sequence of basic GIS skill sets. Then, combined with the availability of lesson materials that utilize those basic skill sets, teachers would be able to import GIS into their classrooms. However, since the majority of teachers receive little or no training in either basic technology skills (NRC, 2002c) and integrating technology into the curriculum (Fatemi, 1999), it is not surprising that many teachers find out-of-the-box, industrial-strength GIS too complex to use effectively in K–12 education.

10.   Be Robust and Realistic in Terms of the Demands Placed on Teachers and on the School Infrastructure. Today's professional GIS is fully compatible with the standard office computer. However, the majority of schools tend to be considerably behind the cutting edge of computing technology and to have difficulty implementing the kinds of network connectivity typical of the modern office or even of many homes. GIS designers have responded quickly to new computing power, taking advantage of every increase in speed and capacity to increase the power of their products. Thus, there is a significant gap between the capacity of the computing environment available in the typical K–12 setting and the system demands of the latest generation of professional GIS.

A GIS designed to support thinking spatially in the K–12 context would have to address this issue. It would have to be able to run on earlier versions of operating systems that are less demanding of computer resources. It would also have to run on the outdated hardware that is prevalent in all but wealthy schools. Learning modules would have to be compatible with the kinds of network connectivity found in schools and the kinds of Internet access restrictions (for content and security) that schools have put in place.

GIS designers also have to deal with the problem of Windows versus Macintosh operating platforms. (To exemplify the differences between the two operating platforms, the computational requirements of Windows and Macintosh platforms for *Idrisi* and ESRI's *ArcView* family of software are summarized in Table 8.6.) As with most software, the GIS industry favors the Windows platform, so that the latest versions of ESRI software and *MapInfo* are not available for the Macintosh platform. This is a major problem because many schools are still equipped with Macintosh computers. (ESRI supports both Macintosh and Windows platforms for the older *ArcView 3.x* system, which requires less computational resources, but offers less functionality.) One solution is to run Windows emulation software on the Macintosh, but this adversely affects system performance. Another option is to move away from locally hosted GIS software and to access GIS functionality via an Internet plug-in working with a remote application server. (ESRI's Internet *Mapping System* and MapInfo's *MapExtreme* are relevant examples.) Although expensive, remote application servers could be purchased at local or regional school levels.

Besides infrastructure needs, a support system has to be robust and realistic in terms of teacher expectations. In American schools today, several factors combine to impede the implementation of GIS in the classroom and across the curriculum. Among these impediments are ever-increasing expectations about teacher performance and frequently inflexible school infrastructures. Unless the GIS community can successfully address these impediments, the educational use of GIS will continue to be sporadic and unsystematic.

The movement to develop national content standards in core disciplines led to the identification and assessment of benchmark achievement levels at different grades—typically fourth, eighth, and tenth or twelfth grades. In many states and communities, such assessments have become high-stakes tests that can determine school funding, school accreditation, and even the jobs of adminis-

TABLE 8.6 Computational Requirements for *Idrisi* and *ArcView* Software

Software	Requirements
Clark Labs' *Idrisi* Software (Kilimanjaro Edition) (http://www.clarklabs.org/IdrisiSoftware.asp?cat=2)	**Windows (*Idrisi Kilimanjaro*):** Pentium III or faster PC computer, 128+ MB RAM, minimum XGA (1024 × 768) graphics resolution with 64,000+ colors, running Windows XP/2000/NT4/ME/98/95, 600 MB hard drive space for *Idrisi* software and data
ESRI's *ArcView* Software (http://www.esri.com/industries/k-12/bundle.html)	**Windows (*ArcView 8.3*):** Pentium III or faster PC computer, 128+ MB RAM (recommend 256+), running Windows 2000/NT4/XP, 1 GB or more hard drive space for *ArcView* software and data
	Windows (*ArcView 3.3*): PC computer, Pentium (recommend Pentium III or better), with 32+ MB physical RAM (recommend 64+), running Windows 95 or higher, 200+ MB hard drive space for *ArcView* software and data
	Macintosh (*ArcView 3.0a*): G3, G4, or iMac computer, with 32+ MB physical RAM (recommend 64+ MB RAM), running MacOS 7.1 or higher, 200+ MB hard drive space for *ArcView* software and data

trators and teachers. In such an atmosphere, teachers are under pressure to prepare their students for these tests and often feel that they cannot add GIS (or anything else) to the curriculum because it will take time away from essential test preparation tasks. It is imperative, therefore, that we find out whether GIS—in fact, all support systems for spatial thinking—enhance student learning across the curriculum. Thus, the committee advocates that a rigorous study be undertaken by the U.S. Department of Education's Institute for Educational Sciences to determine whether or not the use of GIS in primary and secondary schools improves academic achievement across the curriculum.

Another issue for teachers is the increasing amount of time taken up with out-of-class responsibilities such as individual education plans, record keeping, conferences with guidance counselors and social workers, and student evaluations. These responsibilities consume nonteaching hours and leave little time for learning GIS or other support systems and for developing appropriate instructional applications. If GIS is to be implemented in school classrooms, teachers will need release time for training and curriculum development. Thus, a supportive professional development structure is essential if teachers are going to be able to incorporate GIS into their classrooms.

The concept of school infrastructure includes physical components such as school buildings, classroom configuration, computer labs, computer software and hardware, local area networks (LAN), wide area networks (WAN), and the Internet, as well as other technology support systems such as printers, scanners, and multimedia stations. It can also include nonstructural and intangible components such as technology support structures, school scheduling, and professional development practices and procedures. Because there are so many variations, it is difficult to generalize about school infrastructure. Thus, it is also difficult to generalize about the school infrastructure needed for the implementation of GIS.

A decade ago, problems related to the physical components of infrastructure were a major obstacle to the implementation of GIS in many schools; there were problems such as inadequate wiring for computer use and Internet access and lack of adequate computers to run the software programs. Although these physical infrastructural problems have not completely disappeared, they do not pose an insuperable problem to the implementation of GIS in schools. To be sure, some configurations of physical infrastructure are better than others in making it possible for a school to realize the potential of GIS. Physical components that can enhance a school's GIS capability, such as computer laboratories or plotters, may be beyond the reach of start-up users, but their absence should not prevent the school from the initial implementation of GIS. From the standpoint of physical infrastructure, GIS implementation is now a realistic possibility in most schools in the country. At the least, most schools have the hardware to run software systems such as *ArcView 3*. However, because of a major digital divide in technology investment, with poorer schools spending far less on technology than richer ones, it will be years before schools with high concentrations of lower-income students can be expected to invest in the hardware to run higher-end software tools. Without initiatives to bring appropriate hardware to schools in lower-income districts, students in poorer schools will continue to be left behind (PCAST, 1997).

If schools have appropriate high-speed access to the Internet, implementation of GIS in the K–12 context is unlikely, in most instances, to be stymied by issues of scalability. In situations where large numbers of students are engaged in collaborative work and are geographically dispersed, the Internet achieves scalability by linking users across a densely connected network, using protocols that ensure messages will pass along links with available capacity. Similarly, small groups of students collaborating over the Internet will not find their communications substantially affected. More problematic, however, are scalability issues associated with large numbers of students at-tempting to obtain service from a single host GIS or a single data archive, but such problems might arise only if the number of simultaneous users ran into the hundreds of thousands.

Today, it is the intangible part of a school's infrastructure that is a key to the successful implementation of GIS. Administrative and institutional support is crucial to the integration of GIS into American K–12 education. All too often, GIS implementation in a school comes about because of an enterprising, pioneering teacher, who has invested personal time and effort to make this happen. This teacher becomes the school's GIS expert, the one who trains and encourages other teachers to adopt the technology, and the one that other teachers look to for data, for solutions to technical problems, and for help in developing projects and lessons. In many instances, the imple-mentation of GIS in a school is dependent totally on the support and guidance of one teacher. The positive benefits of peer support are counterbalanced by the fragility of the situation. If that teacher leaves the school, those roles are vacated and the use of GIS is apt to disappear. Lasting systemic integration of GIS in the school curriculum must be supported and fostered administratively at levels beyond the lone pioneering teacher.

Administrative support means making spatial technologies a priority for the school's technol-ogy support system—from personnel to purchasing. Technology coordinators must be conversant with GIS technology, its requirements, and its use so they can provide the expertise and support that the pioneer teacher once provided and more. Administrative support means exploring flexible scheduling options to provide blocks of time for GIS implementation other than the traditional 45-minute period. Finally, administrative support means providing meaningful, ongoing professional development rather than one-shot training events. Professional development may take the form of peer coaching, released time for curriculum development, funding for on- and off-site training, or hiring spatial technology consultants to mentor new users. School administrators are the decision makers whose support means the difference between real and lasting change or temporary change that is wholly dependent on one or two individuals. Such real and lasting change is entirely possible if GIS proponents can educate administrators about the potential of GIS to enhance student learning.

TABLE 8.7 Assessment of GIS to Match the Educational Context

Criteria	High	Medium	Low
Be flexible enough to be effective in a variety of school contexts and enable a range of modes of uses	+		
Be quick and intuitive for students and teachers to learn to use			+
Be robust and realistic in terms of the demands placed on teachers and on school infrastructure			+

Discussion Summary

From this analysis, the following observations can be made about the capacity of GIS to be adapted to the educational context.

1. GIS is flexible and scalable enough to be used in a wide variety of school contexts from the one-computer classroom to classrooms or laboratories with multiple computer stations. The support system can serve the needs of a single user seated at a desk or act as a medium for collaborative networked learning among geographically dispersed students.

2. Professional-level GIS is neither quick nor intuitive for students and teachers to use as a support tool for spatial thinking. Teachers, more often than students, have a hard time learning how to use the software.

3. Most schools are behind the cutting edge of computing technology. Therefore, a GIS designed to support spatial thinking in the K–12 context would have to run on the types of hardware often found in schools. Besides the existing gap between the computing environment available in the typical K–12 setting and the demands of the latest generation of professional GIS, stumbling blocks to the implementation of GIS are the ever-increasing expectations about teacher performance and frequently inflexible school infrastructures. Increased demands placed on teachers leave them with little time to learn GIS and develop applications. All too often, GIS is implemented in a school because of a pioneering teacher rather than a supportive school administration.

Table 8.7 gives the committee's assessment of GIS as a support system for spatial thinking through its ability to match the needs and constraints of the educational context. GIS rates well as a tool that can be used in a variety of school contexts and enable a range of uses, but it rates less well on the other two criteria. GIS is not a tool that is quick and intuitive to use. GIS is not robust and realistic in terms of the demands placed on teachers and the demands placed on the school infrastructure system.

8.4 THE IMPLEMENTATION OF GIS AS A SUPPORT SYSTEM FOR SPATIAL THINKING

Chapter 6 identifies five tightly linked and interdependent components that must be addressed if GIS is to be implemented successfully as a support system for spatial thinking. The five components are material support, logistical support, instructional support, curriculum support, and community support.

8.4.1 Material Support

Access to computers and telecommunication networks is essential for both teachers and students to make use of GIS as a learning tool for spatial thinking in K–12 education. Although instructional computers have been present in most American schools for nearly 20 years, their use was limited by the small number of computers compared to the number of students. Today, public schools have an average of one instructional computer for every six students, which is close to the ratio of four to five students per computer that "many experts consider to represent a reasonable level for the effective use of computers within the schools" (PCAST, 1997, p. 21). Nearly every public school—regardless of level, poverty concentration, and metropolitan status—is connected to the Internet, and two-thirds of them are connected to the Internet by dedicated-line network connections (NCES, 2000a). However, the use of these lines may well be for administrative rather than academic support.

Although nearly all public schools have access to instructional computers and the Internet, there is much variation in their availability. For example, medium to large schools have a greater number of students per computer with Internet access than small schools, and urban schools have a greater number of students per computer than rural schools. The largest variations occur in schools with varying degrees of poverty. Schools with the highest concentration of poverty have the most students per instructional computer (NCES, 2000a). Moreover, poorer schools spend far less on computer technology than richer ones, making them less likely to be able to acquire the latest computers as they emerge in the future (Anderson and Becker, 2001).

As the availability of computers and network connections in schools and classrooms has grown, so has the number of teachers and students using them and the frequency with which they use them (Levin et al., 1999). Despite such increases, only about 50 percent of the teachers with instructional computers available in their schools use digital software for instruction (Smerdon et al., 2000). This modest figure is attributed to the relative neglect of spending for software and technology support (Anderson and Becker, 2001). The types of software that teachers use most in their classes are word processing software for composing and editing text, CD-ROM reference software, and World Wide Web browsing software (Becker et al., 1999). Only the more computer-skilled and enterprising teachers in schools with above-average computing environments use technology in more innovative ways (e.g., using software to solve problems and to analyze and display data) (Becker et al., 1999).

For teachers to integrate GIS into instruction, they must have adequate numbers and types of computers. The majority of schools have adequate hardware and network connections to run current versions of GIS and the connectivity to download data. However, only a handful of schools have a laboratory dedicated to GIS. The majority of schools have dedicated writing laboratories or computer science laboratories, but it is difficult for classes in other subjects to gain access to them. With the growing importance of geospatial technologies in the workplace and in everyday life, consideration should be given to the creation of laboratories in schools that are dedicated to tools such as GIS.

If schools are to implement more than stripped-down versions of GIS, software designers have to depart from their normal assumptions. Typically, their assumptions are based on the ability of the user community to afford the latest computers and their willingness to replace existing ones every two to four years. These assumptions are invalid in the K–12 context for all but the wealthiest schools; so a change in mind-set will be needed if GIS is to be implemented in an equitable manner.

Most software packages (e.g., *Idrisi, MapInfo, ArcView*) have been developed for professionals in business and government and, in education, for the higher education market. The lack of GIS software designed for the K–12 market is perhaps not surprising given the relative lack of penetration of GIS into school education. Yet without the provision of software packages that are developmentally and educationally appropriate for K–12 students, the effective use of GIS in and across the school curriculum will be stymied at all levels, especially the elementary level.

However, much learning about GIS—and indeed spatial thinking—can be achieved without the support of computers, network connections, and software. As argued in Chapter 6, spatial thinking must be supported by tools that range in character from low to high tech. Indeed, it can be asserted that tasks are learned better when first performed by hand (Linn and Hsi, 2000). Instructors in statistics and mathematics have commonly made this contention. They would insist that all calculations first be performed by hand in order to encourage students to learn and understand all aspects of the process. In principle, there is nothing a computer can do that a person cannot do by hand given enough time. Complex tasks such as inverting a matrix can be scaled down to be possible by hand within reasonable time limits (e.g., invert nothing larger than a 3×3 matrix to learn the process, and use a computer to invert everything larger).

On this same basis, all GIS operations can be emulated and should be learned without computers, but the full power of GIS will be evident only to students who can experience the real thing. Some GIS concepts and some aspects of thinking spatially can be learned with pencil and paper, and with overhead projectors and transparent maps. To date, however, little research has been conducted to identify such concepts and to design appropriate teaching materials.

8.4.2 Logistical Support

Computing equipment requires continuous maintenance, particularly in educational settings where it is often outdated and unreliable and where stress on it is greater than in the single-user professional office. Students are also, perhaps, less tolerant than professionals of the inevitable malfunctions and computer crashes, but instructors often assert that such failures are a valuable part of the learning experience. In principle, GIS applications should not be any more stressful on hardware than any other technology a school might implement.

However, in many school systems, the logistical support network is spread dangerously thin, with one or two people expected to provide assistance to multiple schools or designated classroom teachers expected to provide assistance to their building colleagues in one or two nonteaching periods during the school day. All too frequently, frustrated teachers cannot get a GIS program started because they do not have the appropriate technical support. In addition, security concerns result in delays and rules. For example, some teachers have to obtain permission to install GIS software and students must apply for permission to use certain directories on the computer in order to complete their work and save their personal settings. These kinds of stumbling blocks create barriers to the adoption and integration of technology into the school curriculum.

For successful GIS implementation, each school requires a technical support team that addresses two needs. One need is for a "nuts-and-bolts" technician, who is charged to make sure that hardware, software, and networks are operating correctly. The other need is for an educator to help teachers teach with technology through activities such as team teaching, peer coaching, software training, and resource management. A school that meets these needs will likely foster successful GIS implementation.

Technical support for GIS in schools is problematical. Industry pays hefty maintenance fees for access to graded service contracts for technical support. This support is labor intensive and, thus, expensive for vendors to provide. Schools cannot afford the maintenance fees that businesses can afford to pay. Consideration has to be given to increasing per-student technical support expenditures in American schools. Presently, an average of 20 percent of the technology budget is spent on support, compared to 73 percent for hardware and 7 percent for software (Anderson and Becker, 2001).

GIS vendors (especially ESRI through on-line training sessions, conferences, and the promotion of "GIS Day") provide considerable logistical support to schools. Traditionally, they have been highly active in encouraging schools to adopt GIS and in offering heavy discounts on software. Several statewide agreements have been made to provide access to proprietary software and data for any school in the state. However, such agreements have occurred in the absence of GIS designed specifically for schools. A specialized GIS to support thinking spatially in K–12 would require a specialized business plan and continuous technical support that would provide an adequate return to the designers and developers and adequate performance for schools at affordable prices.

8.4.3 Instructional Support

Teacher training is fundamental to the successful implementation of GIS as a support system for spatial thinking. Pre-service and in-service teachers should acquire training in basic GIS skills (see Box 8.6) and how to use the technology effectively in the classroom. With this training, teachers are more likely to be comfortable using the technology in their instruction.

Given appropriate technical support and training, we can imagine the characteristics of a

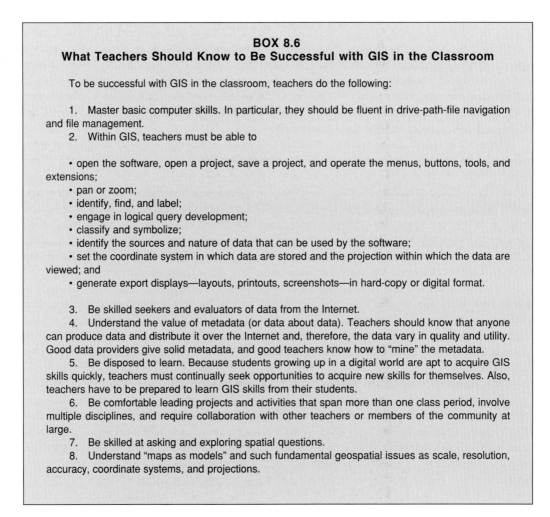

BOX 8.6
What Teachers Should Know to Be Successful with GIS in the Classroom

To be successful with GIS in the classroom, teachers do the following:

1.   Master basic computer skills. In particular, they should be fluent in drive-path-file navigation and file management.
2.   Within GIS, teachers must be able to

• open the software, open a project, save a project, and operate the menus, buttons, tools, and extensions;
• pan or zoom;
• identify, find, and label;
• engage in logical query development;
• classify and symbolize;
• identify the sources and nature of data that can be used by the software;
• set the coordinate system in which data are stored and the projection within which the data are viewed; and
• generate export displays—layouts, printouts, screenshots—in hard-copy or digital format.

3.   Be skilled seekers and evaluators of data from the Internet.
4.   Understand the value of metadata (or data about data). Teachers should know that anyone can produce data and distribute it over the Internet and, therefore, the data vary in quality and utility. Good data providers give solid metadata, and good teachers know how to "mine" the metadata.
5.   Be disposed to learn. Because students growing up in a digital world are apt to acquire GIS skills quickly, teachers must continually seek opportunities to acquire new skills for themselves. Also, teachers have to be prepared to learn GIS skills from their students.
6.   Be comfortable leading projects and activities that span more than one class period, involve multiple disciplines, and require collaboration with other teachers or members of the community at large.
7.   Be skilled at asking and exploring spatial questions.
8.   Understand "maps as models" and such fundamental geospatial issues as scale, resolution, accuracy, coordinate systems, and projections.

successful GIS classroom teacher. Ideally, such teachers infuse the technology into the curriculum rather than making the technology an end in itself. They have training in both curriculum integration and basic technical skills. These well-trained teachers, who use GIS regularly in their classes, are comfortable with problem-based learning and inquiry-based learning and they are knowledgeable about the subject matter they teach. (GIS is not restricted to the geography classroom: indeed its greatest impact will be in school subjects such as science and mathematics.) In addition to appropriate teaching methods and subject matter competency, these teachers have acquired basic GIS skills. They are comfortable with file navigation and management and with databases. They are adept at visualizing, sorting, classifying, querying, selecting, subsetting, and combining data. They know about important GIScience issues such as data currency, data accuracy, data format, projection, scale, and representation issues. These teachers also appreciate that many students, even in early grades, may have more computing skills than they do.

Rarely do pre-service teachers have an opportunity to learn GIS and how to use it in class. Only about 10 percent of pre-service teachers are even introduced to GIS, and only a few institutions such as the University of Minnesota's School of Education offer a teacher training course in GIS (Bednarz and Audet, 1999). Consequently, the most common way for teachers to learn GIS is through in-service teacher training courses. Although there is as yet no formula for successful professional development in GIS, there are lessons to be learned from the experiences of teachers who have become GIS users and from GIS teacher trainers. Teachers who have a one- or two-day GIS training experience and then return to their schools without receiving subsequent contact or support are unlikely to use GIS with their students. In one or two days, trainers can provide hands-on practice in basic GIS operations and can demonstrate examples of the power and potential of GIS in the classroom. However, trainers cannot provide the foundation that most teachers need in order to integrate GIS into the curriculum. To be successful, teacher-training courses in GIS have to combine training in basic technical skills with curriculum integration in content areas. Moreover, the training should be ongoing. Whether the initial experience is a short introduction to the technology or a lengthy training in GIS and curriculum integration, a key to successful teacher training is for participants to know that there will be instructional support for implementation and opportunities to address procedures and problems after the course ends.

Without effective teacher-training courses, most teachers are ill-prepared to incorporate GIS and other digital technologies into their classrooms. According to a survey conducted by the National Center for Education Statistics, only 1 in 10 teachers felt very well prepared to integrate technology into his or her teaching methods (NCES, 1999). Slightly more than half (53 percent) of the teachers surveyed felt somewhat prepared to integrate technology into their classes, and 13 percent stated that they were not at all prepared (NCES, 1999) (Figure 8.20). Whether teachers use GIS or other digital technologies in their classrooms depends heavily on the amount and type of professional development they receive. Teachers who receive 11 or more hours of curriculum integration training feel much better prepared to integrate technology into their lessons than do teachers who receive fewer hours of training. Teachers who receive both basic technology skills training and integration training tend to feel better prepared than those who receive only one type of training (Fatemi, 1999). While teacher training has a big impact on the use of computers in the classroom, the number of years of teaching experience appears to make little difference. Teachers with 5 or fewer years of teaching experience are no more likely to use computers in the classroom than teachers with 20 or more years of teaching experience (Fatemi, 1999).

In recent years, many efforts have been made to provide professional development opportunities for teachers and support for GIS use in the classroom. For example, the Earth System Science Internet Project (ESSIP) at the University of Wyoming provides teacher-training courses in the use of GIS technology. GIS vendors have been active in providing opportunities for K–12 teachers to acquire and use their software, and to present their results. Intergraph (http://

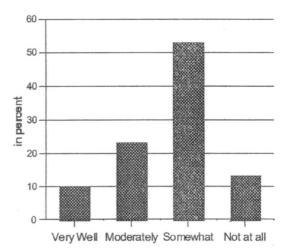

FIGURE 8.20 Teachers' feelings of preparedness to incorporate digital content into their classrooms. SOURCE: NCES, 1999.

www.intergraph.com/schools/), *Idrisi* (http://www.clarklabs.org/), and ESRI (http://www.esri.com/industries/k-12/atp/courses.html) are among software vendors that offer GIS teacher training courses. Organizations such as the National Center for Geographic Information and Analysis (NCGIA) (http://www.ncgia.ucsb.edu/) provide teacher workshops. The National Science Foundation (http://www.nsf.gov/) has a history of funding educational initiatives such as the Technology in Education Research Consortium (TERC) (http://www.terc.edu/) *Mapping Our City* project and the Extending Scientific Inquiry Through Collaborative Geographic Information Systems (http://www.gis.kuscied.org/) program to promote the use of geotechnologies in K–12 science education. The National Geographic Alliance network (http://www.nationalgeographic.com/education/) has been active in enhancing GIS opportunities in many states.

The professional development effort, however, has serious shortcomings. It tends to concentrate on technical skills and pay insufficient attention to curriculum integration. The focus is on higher grades. The effort is minuscule in relation to the size of the K–12 sector and the number of subject areas with potential interest in GIS. Moreover, the effort is uncoordinated, haphazard, and based largely on a few enthusiastic, pioneering champions. Clearly, the vast majority of teachers and, therefore, children are being left behind in terms of their exposure to GIS as a tool to support spatial thinking.

8.4.4 Curriculum Support

At present, there are no voluntary national or state spatial thinking content standards. Consequently, there is no leverage to integrate a suite of low- and high-tech tools to support spatial thinking as part of a larger mechanism for systemic change in American schools. If written, spatial thinking standards would provide an opportunity for spatial thinking to be recognized as crucial across the curriculum in K–12 education and would specify what students must know and be able to do throughout their school careers. Standards would offer an educational goal toward which all students would strive and a benchmark against which teachers could measure student performance. The standards must also be linked with the development of tools for assessing levels of student performance in spatial thinking. Although the standards would provide the basis for a scope and sequence document, they would not constitute a curriculum. The committee urges that consideration be given to the development of spatial thinking standards and assessment tools. In their absence, the systematic incorporation of GIS and other support tools for spatial thinking across the K–12 curriculum will never occur.

Because of the absence of spatial thinking standards, there is little incentive to develop a curriculum and curriculum materials to support spatial thinking skills and abilities through the use of GIS. However, there are programs and projects that do generate GIS learning materials; these generally support the existing curriculum and are designed primarily for the middle and high school grades. These materials have come in part through a top-down process, in which experts develop and test learning modules, and in part from peer-to-peer exchange, in which teachers develop, test, and share materials among themselves. A sharing infrastructure exists to support both modes, through Access Excellence (http://www.accessexcellence.org) and the Digital Library for Earth System Education (DLESE; http://www.dlese.org). DLESE has more than 3,000 items indexed and described in terms of age applicability and subject, and most of the items are designed for K–12 education (Figure 8.21). In an initiative similar to DLESE, ESRI's Geography Network site (http://www.geographynetwork.com) links a large number of resources, including data sets and functionality, but it is not specifically organized around educational needs (Figure 8.22). A welcome addition to these initiatives would be the creation of a central clearinghouse for GIS educational materials.

A variety of GIS-based curriculum materials, courses, and competitions are available, and they offer some support to middle and high school teachers who have implemented GIS. Examples follow.

Curriculum Materials. Examples of GIS materials for teachers and students that can be integrated into the existing curriculum include those developed by the Saguaro Project (http://saguaro.geo.arizona.edu), Kansas Collaborative Research Network (KanCRN; http://kangis.org/lessons), Missouri Botanical Garden (http://www.mobot.org), and ESRI (http://gis.esri.com).

The Saguaro Project has developed modules on cyclones, the dynamic Earth, and hurricane hazards. KanCRN provides two modules, one that spatially relates tornadoes and average jet stream positions and another that analyzes leaf samples for ozone assessments. The Missouri Botanical Garden has developed six natural science modules. Each module comes with a tutorial and data set as well as instructions on how to view data and conduct analyses using GIS. ESRI has developed materials that both promote its GIS software and support the teaching of science, social studies, and community-based studies through GIS. ESRI's *ArcLessons* web site offers 110 downloadable lessons covering a range of topics from social studies to life sciences (http://gis.esri.com/industries/education/arclessons/titles_only.cfm), and the *Explore your World* web site offers 50 lesson plans for use in the classroom (http://www.esri.com/industries/k-12/download/docs/explore.pdf). *Mapping Our World: GIS Lessons for Educators* (Malone et al., 2002) teaches how to use GIS software through standards-based lesson plans. *Community Geography: GIS in Action* (English and Feaster, 2003), which assumes that teachers and students are already using *ArcView*, contains case studies of community projects completed by U.S. students.

Courses. Digital Quest's (http://www.digitalquest.com) SPACESTARS program and the Looking at the Environment (LATE) project (http://www.worldwatcher.nwu.edu/late/LATEpublicpage/index.html) have developed courses for the upper school grades.

Digital Quest's SPACESTARS curriculum consists of three turn-key GIS related courses for grades 9–12. The courses, which provide an introduction to GIS and working with GIS, are based on the terminology, key concepts, and core applications of social studies and science topics. The purpose of the SPACESTARS courses is to teach decision-making and problem-solving skills using GIS. The courses, which are tailored to the school and other regional contexts, are intended to

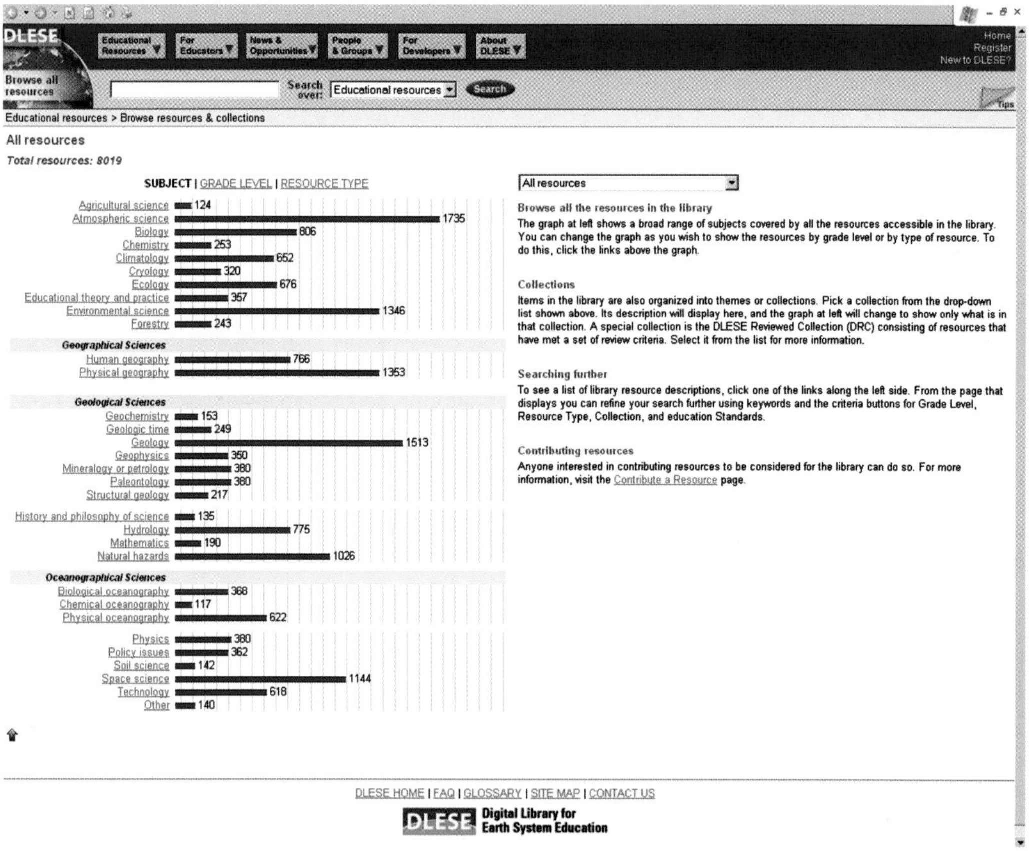

FIGURE 8.21 Browsing the DLESE library for educational resources by subject. The source of this material is the DLESE web site at http://www.dlese.org. All rights reserved.

prepare students for the "cross-curricular" world of work by implementing interdisciplinary teaching methods in three ways: through cross-disciplinary core subject matter, interoccupational skills instruction, and utilization of multidisciplinary data.

LATE has created and tested a one-year high school environmental science course that uses geographic visualization and data analysis tools to promote an inquiry-based approach to science education. The curriculum is designed to implement national content standards for science, geography, and technology. The curriculum is made up of four units that explore environmental issues at all scales. The first unit—populations, resources, and sustainability—introduces the techniques that students will use throughout the year. The second unit—meeting the demand for energy—focuses on electrical power generation, growing energy demand, and associated environmental consequences. The third unit deals with managing water resources. The final unit, investigating the local environment, provides students with an opportunity to conduct field work and to use geographic and attribute data from their own community to investigate a local environmental issue. Each unit has a culminating activity that allows students to analyze data and develop a set of recommendations using GIS.

Competitions. Community Atlas (http://www.esri.com/industries/k-12/atlas) and My Community,

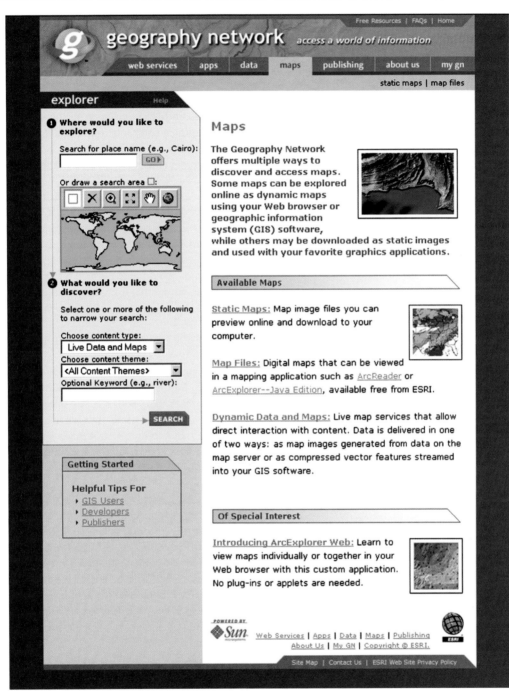

FIGURE 8.22 A page from ESRI's Geography Network web site from which users can access a huge collection of geospatial datasets.

Our Earth: Geographic Learning for Sustainable Development (MyCOE; http://www.geography.org/sustainable/) are projects designed to encourage students and teachers to use GIS in pursuit of curriculum-related goals.

This description of some of the largest and best-known GIS education efforts by the private sector and academic institutions illustrates the diversity and creativity of efforts to infuse GIS into the existing school curriculum. These much-needed efforts, though uncoordinated, have produced some high-quality and challenging learning materials that are helpful to pioneering teachers. Enthusiastic teachers who have implemented GIS have done so through a reorganization of their curriculum and a shift to problem-based learning (Bednarz, 2000; Donaldson, 2001). However, because of the current emphasis on high-stakes testing in only a few school subjects, most teachers are reluctant to reorganize the curriculum for their students.

Clearly, it will be difficult to integrate GIS and other support tools into the instructional process without the muscle of national spatial thinking standards and assessments. If spatial thinking standards were enhanced by the addition of GIS content and performance benchmarks or indicators, it would reinforce the concept of teaching with GIS instead of teaching about GIS. Spatial thinking standards would legitimize GIS as a support tool that can foster and strengthen critical thinking, analysis, and problem-solving skills. Standards would lead to the development of new curricula that are appropriate in terms of scope and sequence and that use GIS as part of a suite of tools to support spatial thinking across a range of subjects.

8.4.5 Community Support

Before there can be community recognition of the educational value of GIS, there must be community recognition of the universal practical value of GIS. GIS is not yet a household word and it is often confused with GPS. At best, most people think of GIS as "map stuff," a way of producing maps. A major task for proponents of GIS in K–12 education, then, is to find a way to raise awareness of the analytic power and utility of this technology among the general public.

One way to raise awareness of the power of GIS is for schools to undertake community service projects. The following examples illustrate how students working with GIS made a difference in their communities.

• **Reducing crime:** Students in grades 10 through 12 at Bishop Dunne Catholic School in Dallas, Texas, put GIS to work to answer the simple questions of where and when the Dallas Police Department should assign task force patrols in order to reduce crime. After acquiring robbery data from the police department, students geocoded robberies to create points, calculated robbery surfaces, identified hot-spot areas, digitized task force patrol zones, and created daily robbery maps. Next, the students analyzed the geographic patterns. The analysis indicated the most effective patrol areas and times. Finally, recommendations were provided to the police department, and when they were applied, there was a reduction in crime. As a result of the success of the project, the students continue to work with the Dallas Police Department.

• **Monitoring river water quality:** Students at Red River High School in Grand Forks, North Dakota, took part in a year-long study of the Turtle River to determine which parts of the river were healthy, which sites would support trout habitat restoration, and what influences the water quality of the river. The students obtained GPS locations for selected sites along the river, collected water quality data for each site throughout the year, and acquired base map data of the area. They explored the data by mapping water quality variables (e.g., alkalinity, hardness, dissolved oxygen, phosphates, turbidity). They analyzed the data to identify temporal and spatial trends. Following the analysis, students summarized the results and gave presentations to local television stations and campers in the Turtle River State Park. In their presentation to the campers, students explained why different parts of the river are better for fishing than others. This presentation caught the attention of the Red River Regional Council (RRRC), a government organization conducting environmental projects that benefit the local economy. The RRRC was interested in evaluating the student data for a possible trout habitat restoration project.

• **Identifying point-source pollution:** High school students at Crescent School in Toronto, Ontario, conducted a study of abandoned landfill sites in Toronto to answer the following questions: Is there a pattern to the location of abandoned landfill sites across the metropolitan region, and what levels of danger do these sites pose to public places and the environment and water resources? Students collected landfill location and attribute data. They also obtained base map data such as local street data for mapping major streets, rivers, lakes, landmarks (e.g., schools, hospitals), land use, and census information. They analyzed the proximity of abandoned landfills to rivers, schools, hospitals, and parks. Their analysis identified potential environmental hazards. The results of the study were presented to environmental groups such Lake Ontario Keeper, whose staff were interested in learning more from the school about how GIS can assist them in their own research.

These three studies demonstrate how GIS can be used by students to address community issues. Students asked questions. They gathered data, and they explored and analyzed them. Finally, they took the knowledge gained to their local communities. In this way, students learned how to use GIS to answer questions about real-world problems, and communities recognized that GIS is a tool that can be used by decision makers to make better decisions.

Community support in the form of recognition of the educational value of GIS is negligible in relation to the number of schools in the United States.

8.4.6 Discussion Summary

From this analysis, the following observations can be made about the implementation of GIS as a support system for spatial thinking (Table 8.8).

1. Nearly all schools have access to instructional computers and network connections to run some current versions of GIS and have the connectivity to download data. Most schools, especially poorer ones, have legacy computers and are in no position to upgrade their hardware every few years. Schools are forced to use software packages developed for the business, government, and higher education markets. Without software that suits the specific needs and constraints of K–12 education, the use of GIS in the curriculum will be severely limited.

TABLE 8.8 Assessment of Programs for the Implementation of GIS as a Support System

Criteria	High	Medium	Low
Material support		+	
Logistical support			+
Instructional support		+	
Curriculum support		+	
Community support			+

2. In nearly all school systems, the logistical support necessary to maintain computing equipment is spread dangerously thin. Successful implementation of GIS in schools requires a support team to ensure that the hardware, software, and networks are integrated and work properly.

3. A few pre-service teachers are taught how to teach GIS, but rarely are they taught how to teach with GIS. Professional development is the most common way in which teachers learn about GIS, and it is becoming more common through after-school classes, workshops, summer institutes, and on-line course work. Most of this training fails to develop spatial thinking skills for the participants. The professional development effort, which suffers from a lack of follow-through, is insignificant in relation to the size of the K–12 sector.

4. There is no standards-based approach to teaching spatial thinking, even though a suite of low- and high-tech tools is available. Consequently, there is no incentive to develop a curriculum or learning modules to guide the teaching of spatial thinking with GIS. Instead, there are many uncoordinated efforts that produce high-quality materials for use by teachers who wish to integrate GIS into the existing curriculum. These valuable efforts, though uncoordinated, have produced some challenging learning materials that are helpful to pioneering teachers. Clearly, it will be difficult for teachers to integrate GIS and other support tools into the instructional process without the muscle of national spatial thinking standards. Until there are spatial thinking standards, the implementation of GIS across the school curriculum will be unsystematic and unsuccessful.

Community support in the form of recognition of the educational value of GIS is negligible in relation to the number of schools in the United States. Because most communities are unfamiliar with GIS, they are unlikely to recognize the educational value of GIS before schools demonstrate what they can accomplish with GIS.

8.5 MECHANISMS FOR THE REDESIGN OF GIS EDUCATIONAL SOFTWARE

A redesign of GIS software is a key step if GIS is to succeed as a tool for supporting spatial thinking in the K–12 context. Among the GIS design issues that must be addressed are the following:

- broadening its accessibility to the full range of learners;
- strengthening the capacity to spatialize nonspatial data;
- overcoming the visualization weaknesses;
- providing graded systems of GIS that are age and/or experience appropriate;
- redesigning interfaces to be more intuitive and to provide help and guidance; and
- making the software customizable.

The committee recognizes that many of these design challenges are not specific to the K–12 context and that their solution may not occur with that context in mind. Should this be the case, then someone must take responsibility for adapting the solutions to the particular needs of teachers and students. Teachers and students should not be expected to adapt to a one-size-fits-all GIS that does not reflect their special needs.

In this section, the committee examines how a redesign of GIS to accommodate the needs of the K–12 education community might take place and suggests how it might be managed. The committee identified three mechanisms that led to the development of current versions of GIS software: the academic model, the commercial model, and the collaborative model. The academic model was based on researchers writing their own software. Changes in operating systems and hardware architectures led to the demise of many such systems, but *Idrisi* is one example that has flourished. It is priced for the academic market and for use by large classes at the college level. Its business model relies on sales as well as grants from agencies to pursue specific goals. The commercial model, exemplified by companies such as ESRI, Intergraph, and Autodesk, is market driven with a business model that reflects the need to balance the costs of software development and support against income from the open market. The educational market plays little or no role in this model. The collaborative model views GIS software development as a collaborative process, underpinned by an open foundation of standards and basic functions. Thus, in the 1980s the U.S. Army Corps of Engineers developed the *Geographic Resources Analysis Support System (GRASS)* package and fostered a community of users who contributed extensions to the package. In this model, there is no distinction between users and developers. *GRASS* was built as open software, with no proprietary restrictions on access or use. Despite its success, it was seen as competing unfairly with the commercial market and, therefore, its support was terminated in the early 1990s although a residual community continues to use it.

These three models offer distinct options for the redesign of GIS software for the K–12 context. For the collaborative mechanism to succeed, a community would have to be identified, comprising specialists with sufficient technical skills to share the development of appropriate software, and with sufficient scientific understanding of the needs in the K–12 context. An organization such as the University Consortium for Geographic Information Science (UCGIS) might be appropriate to facilitate collaboration, with sufficient funding from an appropriate federal agency. UCGIS has access to technical and intellectual expertise at each of its more than 60 member institutions and has sufficient experience in organizing large, distributed projects.

For the commercial mechanism to succeed, it would be necessary for an appropriate federal agency to request proposals and select a suitable developer. One major advantage of this mechanism is that much of the software foundation for a new GIS already exists in each vendor's products. Because educational support for spatial thinking is somewhat distant from the normal domain of commercial applications, there would have to be strong and robust mechanisms for oversight of the design and implementation of the software, and for practical testing. Contracts would have to deal with issues of long-term maintenance, intellectual property, and long-term support. A careful study would be necessary to determine whether the K–12 sector could generate sufficient funds to pay for long-term maintenance.

For the academic model to succeed there would have to be a similar proposal solicitation process: it would require an appropriate federal agency to select and contract with one or more academic institutions for the basic software development. This mechanism might be more successful than the commercial one in ensuring the appropriate intellectual content, but stringent oversight would be needed to ensure quality control in software development and to ensure that the designs were practical and scalable in the educational context.

All three mechanisms appear to have merit, as well as potential pitfalls. The choice between them, therefore, should be made by the appropriate funding agency. In the committee's view, the collaborative model appears to offer the most promise because it would involve all parties— software developers, government, academia, and the K–12 user community.

Based on the levels of investment being made by commercial vendors and on experience from many GIS development projects, it would be reasonable to assume that a suitable GIS could be developed over a period of three years by a team of ten programmers. Allowing for oversight and other costs, the initial development might require a total investment of $3 million to $5 million.

To coordinate the development of GIS software using the collaborative model, the committee recommends the creation of a "Federation of GIS Education Partners." A federation is a bottom-up association of autonomous partners that agree to abide by specified interface standards, business practices, and expectations to achieve a common goal (Handy, 1992). Federations, such as the National Center for Atmospheric Research (NCAR), NASA's Earth Science Information Partners (ESIPs), and the Association of Research Libraries, provide a means for representing the multiple interests of broad interest communities. In an ideal federation, partners come together to achieve ends they could not achieve alone. The federation should consist of GIS developer and user partners, drawn from academia, government, the private sector, and the K–12 user community.

To be successful, the following should be considered in the design of a GIS educational software federation (NRC, 1998):

1. The federation should be a grass-roots, community-driven effort.

2. A bottom-up (rather than a top-down approach) should be the governance basis of the federation to ensure that the priorities of the broader community are honored. However, some centralized management would be necessary for making major decisions on behalf of the federation's constituents, for representing the federation's interests, and for conducting day-to-day operations. The instrument of centralized management should be used sparingly.

3. The federation should be flexible. Thus, the initial rules and procedures should not be overspecified.

4. A significant part of the responsibility of a federation is managing the tensions that may arise from constituents with differing expectations (e.g., software companies, teachers).

8.6 CONCLUSION

As might be expected with any piece of complex software that has evolved over time, GIS has both strengths and weaknesses as a system for supporting spatial thinking. The sets of criteria developed in Chapter 6 have allowed the committee to do two things: (1) explore, in detail, the capacity, design, and implementation of GIS as a support system for spatial thinking in the K–12 context; and (2) identify mechanisms for the redesign of GIS. Chapter 9 presents an overall assessment as to whether GIS provides a useful foundation for spatial thinking in the K–12 context.

9

GIS as a Support System for Spatial Thinking

9.1 INTRODUCTION

A mix of support systems can be brought to bear on spatial thinking. These support systems form a suite that ranges from the simple to the most complex. Chapter 7 considers GIS as an exemplar of a high-tech support system for spatial thinking and compares GIS with other high-tech support systems. Chapter 8 examines the extent to which GIS fulfills the three necessary requirements of a support system for spatial thinking, assesses the capacity of GIS to meet the 10 criteria for the design of a support system in the K–12 context, and discusses the five components for the implementation of a support system for spatial thinking in the K–12 context. This chapter summarizes the committee's findings about whether GIS provides a useful foundation for spatial thinking in the K–12 context.

9.2 THE NECESSARY REQUIREMENTS OF A SUPPORT SYSTEM
FOR SPATIAL THINKING

Compared with other high-tech support systems, current versions of GIS rate well in terms of their ability to address the three fundamental requirements of a system to support spatial thinking across the curriculum, having the capacity (1) to spatialize data sets by providing spatial data structures and coding systems for spatial and nonspatial data; (2) to visualize by creating multiple forms of representation; and (3) to perform functions by manipulating the structural relations of spatialized data sets.

GIS is designed to handle geographic data, but in principle, data defined in any spatial domain are amenable to handling with GIS. Although GIS does a fine job spatializing geographic data, it provides only modest support for nonspatial data, and fails to support a true three-dimensional model of space.

As a visualization system, GIS provides tools for high-quality production of multiple forms of representation. Although GIS provides poor support for the modeling of continuous time, it has the capacity to illustrate change by stacking map layers in a temporal sequence of cross sections. GIS is not yet linked to multimedia in all of its variety, it cannot handle automatically the visualization of the quality of data, and it fails to provide user interface controls that remain "live" after the display is constructed.

As an engine for transformations, operations, and analyses, GIS reveals its full potential. However, the capacity of most current GIS software to perform functions is greater than K–12 students require. Moreover, the complexity of existing product functionality is greater than is desirable for the K–12 context.

GIS possesses many of the necessary requirements of a system for thinking spatially, although the committee notes that much of the initial learning about GIS—and indeed spatial thinking—can take place without the support of computers, network connections, and software.

9.3 THE DESIGN OF GIS AS A SUPPORT SYSTEM FOR SPATIAL THINKING IN THE K–12 EDUCATIONAL CONTEXT

In the committee's view, existing versions of GIS can meet 6 out of the 10 criteria for the design of a support system in K–12 education.

• GIS can facilitate the process of scientific problem formulation and solution, and therefore, it exemplifies many of the ideals of discovery-based, student-centered inquiry.

• GIS can be useful in solving problems in a wide range of real-world contexts. It can succeed as a tool for both scientific research and problem solving. Consequently, it provides a link between science and policy. At the most general level, science is interested in principles and laws that are true everywhere, independent of geographic context. Policy, on the other hand, often takes such principles and puts them back in specific geographic contexts in order to predict the outcomes of proposed developments or to achieve better management of resources. In the K–12 context, the link between science and policy is exemplified in GIS community projects.

• GIS has the potential to facilitate learning across a range of school subjects and to enhance interdisciplinary and multidisciplinary learning.

• GIS can provide a rich, generative, inviting, and challenging problem-solving environment. It can empower students to address significant issues with the same tools that professionals use to address issues in their work.

• GIS has the potential to accommodate and be accessible to the full range of learners, including the visually impaired. It is rigorous enough to challenge gifted students and accessible enough to reach many students who have difficulty learning in traditional ways.

• GIS can be used effectively in a variety of educational settings. This tool can be infused throughout the curriculum or used in traditional subject-based curricula. It can be employed in all grades. In addition, it enables a range of modes of use (e.g., individual and stand-alone, collaborative and networked).

GIS fares less well on the four criteria for the design of a support system for spatial thinking:

• Current versions of GIS are not developmentally and educationally appropriate. They are professional level and, therefore, tailored for use by expert users rather than novice learners. New versions of GIS should respond to the needs of the K–12 students. These new systems should be easy to learn, flexible, easy to use, and graded to support increasing levels of skill and experience.

• Current versions of GIS are not customized by vendors to meet the needs of specific groups of learners working on particular tasks in specific contexts. Existing versions of full-blown GIS are customizable by users, but in the K–12 context, teachers have neither the time nor the expertise to customize GIS software. New versions of GIS should be adapted to meet the needs of learners.

• Current versions of GIS are neither quick nor intuitive for students and teachers to use as a tool for spatial thinking. Teachers more than students find professional-level GIS software intimidating. Because the learning curve is steep, effective teacher-training programs should be devised.

• Current versions of GIS are not robust and realistic in terms of the demands placed on teachers and school infrastructure. Today's professional GIS is fully compatible with the standard office computer, but schools lag behind the cutting edge of computing technology. Therefore, a GIS designed to support spatial thinking in the K–12 context would have to run on the types of hardware typically found in schools. Major stumbling blocks to the implementation of GIS are the ever-increasing expectations about teacher performance and frequently inflexible school infrastructures. Increased demands placed on teachers leave them with little time to learn GIS and develop applications.

9.4 THE IMPLEMENTATION OF GIS AS A SUPPORT SYSTEM FOR SPATIAL THINKING

Five interlocking components must be in place to implement GIS successfully as a support system for spatial thinking: (1) material support, (2) logistical support, (3) instructional support, (4) curriculum support, and (5) community support. Currently, the level of support for GIS is weak.

The implementation of GIS requires material support in the form of a marked improvement in the quantity and quality of computing resources. Most schools possess instructional computers, but they lag behind the cutting edge of computing technology. Unlike the modern office, schools cannot respond to new computing opportunities and replace existing computers with new ones every few years. Thus, there is a significant gap between the computing environment available in most schools and the demands of the latest generation of GIS. A GIS designed to support spatial thinking in schools would have to address this issue. It would have to run on legacy systems and be less demanding of computing resources.

GIS software is designed largely for the expert user who is willing to commit to learning its use. Without the rapid development of software packages that are quick and intuitive for students and teachers to use and that are developmentally and educationally appropriate for K–12 students, the effective use of GIS in K–12 education will languish at all levels, especially the elementary level. What teachers want are flexible, easy-to-use systems. They would welcome, for example, simplified user interfaces and wizards that provide directed feedback. Students might find GIS more appealing if it were to give better support to three-dimensional structures and animation. The committee suggests that software designers give consideration to the development of a component-based GIS. A component-based model would enable teachers to package GIS functionality into a series of separate miniprograms. A model customized with learning in mind is also consistent with the committee's view that GIS should be adapted to users rather than vice versa.

Logistical support is vital if hardware, software, and networks are to run properly. In the K–12 context, logistical support is insufficient when one or two people are expected to provide assistance to multiple schools or when designated teachers are expected to provide assistance to their colleagues in nonteaching periods during the day. For successful GIS implementation, a school must have an appropriate technical support team. At the minimum, such a team would consist of a "nuts-and-bolts" technician charged to maintain the hardware, software, and networks on a continuous basis and an educator charged to help teachers teach with digital technologies, including GIS.

Teacher training is crucial if GIS is to be used to support spatial thinking. With an exception or two, learning about GIS and how to work with it in the classroom is not part of any pre-service program. Consequently, the most common way for teachers to learn about GIS is through in-service teacher training courses. Most of these courses provide training in what teachers need to know about GIS (e.g., operate the menus, buttons, tools, and extensions; pan or zoom; logical query;

classification and symbolization; generate export displays), but few of them provide training on how to integrate GIS into the content areas of the curriculum. Without effective teacher-training programs, most teachers will remain unaware of GIS and other digital technologies. Currently, the professional development effort is woefully inadequate given the size of the K–12 sector. Moreover, the effort is uncoordinated and haphazard. As a result, the vast majority of teachers and, therefore, students are being left behind in terms of their exposure to GIS as a tool to support spatial thinking.

Adoption of GIS as a support system for spatial thinking in K–12 education requires curriculum support and the development of high-quality, challenging learning modules. At present, there are uncoordinated efforts to produce modules to teach GIS software in the context of the existing curriculum. However, neither the curriculum nor the curriculum support materials designed to develop spatial thinking skills exist, even though a suite of support tools is available. Because spatial thinking is a skill that can and should be learned by all students, we need a systematic educational program that begins with the development of national spatial thinking standards. Spatial thinking content standards would specify the essential subject matter and skills that every student should have in order to attain high levels of competency. They would offer a goal toward which students would strive and an assessment benchmark against which teachers could measure performance. The standards would provide a basis for developing a curriculum for teaching spatial thinking across the range of school subjects. Such a curriculum should introduce GIS as part of a suite of low- and high-tech systems. Without the development of a standards-based curriculum on spatial thinking, there will be a problem of getting time to teach spatial thinking with GIS and there will be no incentive to develop learning materials.

Community support for the use of GIS in schools is negligible in relation to the size of the K–12 sector. In schools where GIS has been implemented, community recognition of the value of GIS is often a consequence of successful place-based studies that demonstrate a strong link between science and policy.

9.5 THE REDESIGN OF GIS EDUCATIONAL SOFTWARE

GIS software must be redesigned if GIS is to succeed as a tool for supporting spatial thinking. Redesign of software is a normal and continuous process. Thus, for example, during the lifetime of this committee, GIS in general and ESRI products in particular have changed at a rapid rate. The driving forces remain the same, for professional-level and expert users, although the newly designed software may have educational applications. Box 9.1 describes some of the changes that have taken place.

Three models—academic, commercial, and collaborative—offer options for the redesign of GIS to meet the needs of K–12 education. All three models appear to have merit as well as pitfalls. In the committee's view, the collaborative model is appealing because of its potential to involve software developers, government, academia, and the K–12 user community. With the establishment of a "Federation of GIS Education Partners," a suitable GIS could be developed within three years.

9.6 CONCLUSION

The current status of GIS as a support system for spatial thinking is as much cause for optimism as for pessimism among those who want to see GIS infused throughout the K–12 curriculum. The successful adoption of GIS as a support system will be an immense challenge. Because this tool is in its early adoption phase, widespread diffusion of GIS throughout the K–12 sector is not guaranteed. Much will depend on the will of potential stakeholders, including the willingness of federal agencies, especially the U.S. Department of Education, to recognize that spatial thinking is an essential skill that should be learned for productive employment in the twenty-first century. Unless there is well-articulated support among parents, teachers, curriculum developers, and business and policy leaders for national spatial thinking standards in this period of high-stakes testing, there will be little incentive to incorporate GIS across the K–12 curriculum. The widespread adoption of GIS is also contingent on the redesign of GIS to meet the particular needs of teachers and students.

GIS is a good—but not the perfect—tool for supporting spatial thinking. Therefore, it cannot and should not be *the* basis for teaching spatial thinking but *a* basis for doing so. The committee recognizes that GIS has a clearly demonstrated potential as a support system for spatial thinking, but that there are significant challenges if it is to be successfully integrated into the curriculum. Therefore, the committee urges the development of a systematic plan and mechanism for design changes and a program of implementation. That plan must also recognize the role of GIS as one part of a coordinated suite of tools.

In the committee's view, GIS

- has significant potential and some limitations as a system for supporting spatial thinking across a range of subjects in the K–12 curriculum, but for numerous reasons, that potential is not yet close to being realized;
- can and should be redesigned to accommodate the full range of learners and school contexts; and
- must be supported by a systematic implementation program.

Therefore, the committee sees GIS as exemplifying both the theoretical power of a system for supporting spatial thinking and the practical design and implementation problems that must be faced in the K–12 context. Although GIS does have the potential to make a significant impact on K–12 education, its impact will be greater if

- it is integrated into discipline-based standards and is itself standards based;
- it spans as wide a range of school subjects as possible; and
- it is part of a suite of supporting tools.

GIS alone is not the answer to the problem of teaching spatial thinking in American schools; however, it can be a significant part of the answer.

BOX 9.1
Technological Evolution in GIS

Technological Change in Computing

GIS software has changed in response to more users, more options, more analytical power, greater ease of use, and more and higher levels of capacity requiring more computing power. The changes are reflective of Moore's Law, which suggested that computer power doubles every 18 months. GIS has undergone a rapid evolution. *ArcGIS*—a suite of integrated products to provide ever more power and capacity to the surging number of GIS users—has eclipsed *ArcView 3*. *ArcView 3* was not rendered obsolete because it works on a great range of technology; there is still an important role that *ArcView 3* fills.

As the same time technology changes, so too do demands from users. More people are interested in viewing data spatially and in asking analytical questions about their data. However, few people are familiar with cartographic principles and crucial concepts such as projections and datums. At the same time, many software packages are more "intelligent," helping users make more sensible (or at least predictable) choices. Therefore, people expect GIS software to be more helpful and to make fewer demands on them in advance.

In the last five years, the Internet has grown in importance. It is now an essential part of daily life for millions. It is a critical delivery mechanism for geographic data and software. GIS technology can take advantage of additional and more complex formats, a wider variety of content, and data capacity that has increased by orders of magnitude. Data from the Internet can be downloaded and stored "permanently" or used "on the fly" without local storage. Likewise, the Internet can deliver software for downloading, installing, and using ("thick clients"), or one can rely on the Internet ("thin clients") as the access channel to GIS capacity.

These changes to technology and the audience generate enormous challenges. How do you create software that allows people greater power and more options while increasing ease of use? It is difficult to maximize all variables at once. Software standards have made the "look and feel" of interfaces more predictable. However, added benefits require clever programming, more wizards, better help files, and more testing.

With change come costs: software expands in terms of disk space consumed, and delivery modes shift from floppies to CDs and now to DVDs. Each new opportunity means new complexities, which require software integration and new instructions for users. Variation in and evolution of hardware and software mean that GIS technologies have to adapt. Widespread usage means that the adaptations have to be more broadly integrated. Patches and service packs are more common and more accepted.

Fortunately, storage has decreased in price and increased in availability. Recent computers are well equipped to handle larger packages of software and especially data. Internal disk drives are typically 10 times the size they were a few years ago, and external hard drives are even larger; disk space is cheap. Everything is faster than before.

Change in GIS

ArcGIS is a family of software products designed to provide a full range of GIS capacity to a wide range of users. It includes desktop GIS at several levels (*ArcReader, ArcView, ArcEditor,* and *ArcInfo,* with extensions to enhance capacity), mobile or handheld GIS (*ArcPad*), server-based GIS tools (*ArcIMS, ArcGIS* server, *ArcSDE*), and embeddable GIS (*ArcGIS* Engine). The products take advantage of new data storage formats (geodatabases). The result is a more scalable system for GIS across an entire "enterprise" (or "organization") or out to the general public.

There are opportunities for teachers to incorporate GIS.

1. Perhaps the most significant event has been the release of *Mapping Our World: GIS Lessons for Educators* (Malone et al., 2002). The book provides software, data, projects, instructions, and the support materials that teachers expect. While some teachers have trouble implementing the technology, the book has helped many teachers to be successful. Its tightly organized and well-constructed curriculum is the key for most teachers. The version engaging *ArcView 3* was released in spring of 2002; a version using *ArcView 9* was released in 2005.

2. Web-based interactive mapping has grown rapidly, giving teachers and students experience with (a) maps in general, (b) dynamic maps instead of static ones, (c) controlling the design and content of the map, and (d) access to more data of interest. On both Windows and Macintosh, with just a current web browser (preferably Java-enabled, though many work even on simple HTML browsers), teachers and students can examine an array of content from a global to a local level.

3. *ArcExplorer Java Edition for Education* (*AEJEE*) is a downloadable, lightweight GIS package for Windows and MacOSX computers (Figure 9.1). As a free tool, it can be installed at school and at home, making it easier for students and teachers to expand their GIS tinkering time. At first glance, it provides a modest set of capacities through a modest set of three toolbars with 20 tools in order to reduce confusion. Yet advanced users can accomplish surprisingly sophisticated analyses by combining the tools' powers creatively. *AEJEE* can use data delivered over the Internet via *ArcIMS* sites. *AEJEE* projects can also be saved and shared, unlike creations with *ArcVoyager Special Edition* (ESRI's previous free tool, with a runtime version of *ArcView 3*).

4. *ArcView 9* allows users to integrate appropriately documented geographic data that are stored in multiple coordinate systems. *ArcView 3* was able to project, on the fly, decimal degree vector data (raster could not be projected). However, *ArcView 9* can project, on the fly, both vector and raster data and integrate multiple data sets stored in any coordinate system, as long as the data contain appropriate projection information. This feature alone is enough to make some teachers shift to *ArcView 9* because it facilitates data integration. Such integration is not foolproof, because the software cannot perform the projection "magic" if the data do not include projection information, but the software does warn users if they try to integrate data lacking the critical information. Creating the all-important projection information file, for vector and raster data, is easy with *ArcToolbox*, once the user knows the simple procedure and knows the information for a given data set.

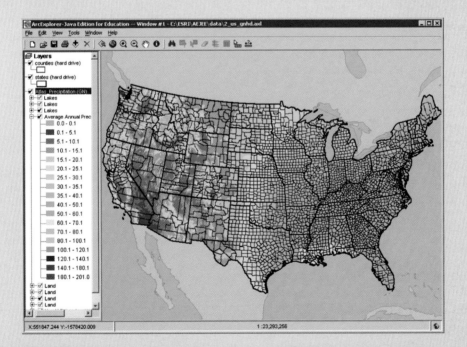

FIGURE 9.1 The U.S. map, showing average annual precipitation superimposed on county and state boundaries, is based on a built-in project in ESRI's *ArcExplorer Java Edition for Education.*

continued

BOX 9.1 Continued

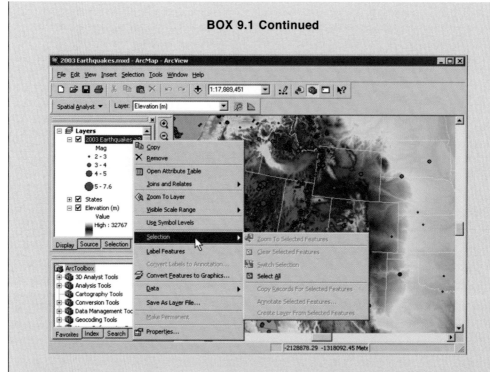

FIGURE 9.2 This map of elevation and earthquakes, superimposed on state borders, is part of a project generated by ESRI's *ArcView 9*. The user interface has been customized by adding a toolbar (Spatial Analyst) and moving the navigation toolbar into a vertical position between the Table of Contents (at left) and the map, facilitating the selection of commonly used tools. The ArcToolbox palette has been engaged and positioned below but in line with the Table of Contents.

    5. *ArcView 9* is a 100 percent Windows-compliant software package (see Figure 9.2). *ArcView 3* had been built with a code base designed to permit cross platform use, so idiosyncrasies crept in. *ArcView 9* adheres to dominant software standards for look and feel, with drag-and-drop operations, right-click options, movable toolbars, and so forth. Users who are knowledgeable about how current Windows applications work have an easy time figuring out how to accomplish a task in *ArcView 9*. (However, users who are not particularly comfortable with the multiwindow nature of sophisticated Windows software [with hierarchical options, cascading sub-menus, tabbed property windows leading to sequential dialog boxes, and stacks of toolbars] find the increased blizzard of options in *ArcView 9* even more intimidating than in *ArcView 3*.)

    6. *ArcView 9* includes a specific application, ArcCatalog, for exploring and managing geographic data. Rather than relying on the viewing and analysis tool to be both the exploration and the management tool, *ArcView 9* users can conduct more speedy layer-by-layer explorations of geographic data. ArcCatalog also facilitates creation of metadata.

    7. The *ArcView 9* three-dimensional Analyst extension includes a stunningly powerful application, *ArcGlobe*, (see Figure 9.3) which gives users a fast experience zooming from world display down to the local community. By integrating data sets, users can explore seamlessly over broad areas and represent data in a dazzling three-dimensional display. Users can also generate an animation with just a few clicks, customize it, and export it to video for sharing with others (see Figure 9.4).

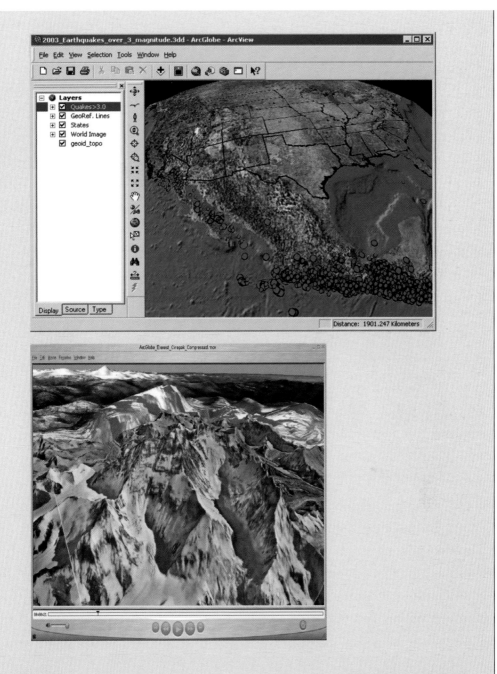

FIGURE 9.3 An oblique perspective view of North America showing earthquakes (greater than 3.0 on the Richter scale). Features can be displayed in more realistic combinations of size, shape, and orientation than with flat maps. Users can easily rotate the globe and "fly" within the view, and export their resulting experience to a video file. This capacity to create movement within the map is very alluring to student users and can help them build a more powerful understanding of relationships.

continued

BOX 9.1 Continued

FIGURE 9.4 A frame, showing Mount Everest, from a QuickTime video file exported from *ArcGlobe*. Viewers "travel" from the relatively flat plane of the Indian subcontinent up the steep slopes of the Himalayas before moving out onto the Tibetan Plateau.

8.   *ArcGIS* includes a new geodatabase format that can be thought of as a "project file cabinet," with rules affecting the nature of the stored data. The geodatabase can include multiple data types and incorporate large volumes of data, yet it remains a single file that can be easily moved. (However, geodatabases are not yet downward compatible, so *ArcView 8.3* cannot read an *ArcView 9* geodatabase, though *ArcView 9* could read an *ArcView 8.3* geodatabase. *ArcView 3* and *AEJEE* cannot read geodatabases at all.)

SOURCE: Charles Fitzpatrick, personal communication, 2005.

Part III

Supporting Spatial Thinking in the Future

10

Conclusions and Recommendations

10.1 INTRODUCTION

Chapters 10 and 11 form a pair. In Chapter 10, the committee derives six recommendations from its conclusions about the educational links between spatial thinking and GIS in the K–12 context. The thrust of the committee's position is simple: spatial thinking is not being taught systematically to K–12 students at present. We need to do so, across the curriculum and for all K–12 students, because it is fundamental to everyday life, the workplace, and science. If we are to teach how to think spatially, then we need to provide both low- and high-tech support systems for practicing and performing spatial thinking. The recommendations range from the setting of research agendas to guidelines for software redesign, but underpinning all of these recommendations is a goal—spatial literacy. We must foster a new generation of American students who are equipped to think spatially.

Chapter 11, therefore, paints a picture of spatial thinkers at work, in this case eighth-grade students who are using GIS as a support system to help answer questions about the causes of high infant mortality rates in sub-Saharan Africa. This picture represents the best of supporting spatial thinking through GIS. It does not reflect the situation in the vast majority of American classrooms. Students are not systematically being taught to think spatially because as a society, we do not yet recognize the pervasiveness of spatial thinking and appreciate its power and value.

It is the strong belief of the committee that these six recommendations are a way to ensure that the next generation of American students will have the opportunity to meet the goal of becoming spatially literate.

10.2 CHARGE TO THE COMMITTEE

The title of the proposal that led to the formation of the committee was *Support for Thinking Spatially: The Incorporation of Geographic Information Science Across the K–12 Curriculum*. The charge contained two questions that logically followed from the proposal title:

1. How might current versions of GIS be incorporated into existing standards-based instruction in all knowledge domains across the school curriculum?

2. How can cognitive developmental and educational theory be used to develop new versions of GIS that are age appropriate in their design and to implement new GIS curricula that are age appropriate in their scope and sequence?

The first question was intended to generate recommendations for levels of technology (hardware and software), system support (e.g., software, hardware, teaching materials), curriculum scope and sequence (i.e., the role of necessary precursors), and pre-service and in-service training. The second question was intended to generate recommendations, based on an assessment of theoretical and empirical approaches in psychology and education that are relevant to the development of knowledge and skills that underpin the use of GIS.

However, as explained in Section 1.3, the committee recognized that these two questions could not be answered without first addressing the educational role of spatial thinking itself. New and better support tools for education—such as GIS—may well be necessary and appropriate, but to what purpose and in what contexts? The answer might seem obvious from the title of this report: to support spatial thinking across the K–12 curriculum. However, such an answer raises some fundamental questions: Why do we *need* to support spatial thinking across the K–12 curriculum? Why should we invest in better GIS or any other support tools?

After coming to appreciate the fundamental importance of spatial thinking and realizing that it was not just undersupported, but underappreciated, undervalued, and therefore underinstructed, the committee came to a new understanding of the charge. The two original questions about the current role and future development of GIS as a support system could be answered satisfactorily only after two additional questions were addressed, one about the need for spatial thinking and the other about the ways in which we learn to think spatially. Therefore, the committee developed an understanding of the nature and character of spatial thinking, leading to a more coherent and comprehensive set of recommendations. With this reorganization of the task, Part I of this report, "The Nature and Functions of Spatial Thinking," led to Recommendation 1, and Part II, "Support for Spatial Thinking," led to Recommendations 2–6.

10.3 THE NATURE AND FUNCTIONS OF SPATIAL THINKING

The committee arrived at a position on the educational necessity for teaching and learning about spatial thinking:

• Spatial thinking is a collection of cognitive skills. The skills consist of declarative and perceptual forms of knowledge and some cognitive operations that can be used to transform, combine, or otherwise operate on this knowledge. The key to spatial thinking is a constructive amalgam of three elements: concepts of space, tools of representation, and processes of reasoning (see Section 1.2).

• Spatial thinking is integral to everyday life. People, natural objects, human-made objects, and human-made structures exist somewhere in space and the interactions of people and things must be understood in terms of locations, distances, directions, shapes, and patterns (see Chapter 2).

• Spatial thinking is powerful: it solves problems by managing, transforming, and analyzing data, especially complex and large data sets, and by communicating the results of those processes to one's self and to others (see Chapter 2).

• Spatial thinking is integral to the everyday work of scientists and engineers and it has underpinned many scientific and technical breakthroughs (see Chapter 3).

• Spatial thinking is a skill that can—and should—be learned by everyone, but there are significant individual and group differences in levels of performance (see Chapters 2 and 4 and Appendix C).

• Spatial thinking develops uniquely in individuals depending on their experience, education, and inclination (see Chapter 4 and Appendix C).

• Expertise in spatial thinking draws on both general spatial skills that cross many domains of knowledge and spatial skills that are particular to parts of a domain of knowledge (see Chapter 4).

• Expertise in spatial thinking develops in the context of specific disciplines and becomes transformed and refined through training and extensive practice (see Chapters 3 and 4).

• While transfer of spatial thinking skills from one domain of knowledge to another is neither automatic nor easy, appropriately designed curricula that encourage infusion across school subjects can facilitate transfer (see Chapter 4).

• Spatial thinking is currently not systematically instructed in the K–12 curriculum despite its fundamental importance and despite its significant role in the sets of national standards for science, mathematics, geography, etc. (see Chapter 5). There is a major blind spot in the American educational system.

• Support systems leverage the power of the human capacity to think and to solve problems (see Section 6.1).

• Spatial thinking is a complex, powerful, and challenging process, and support systems provide an interactive environment within which spatial thinking can take place by helping students to spatialize data sets, visualize working and final results, and perform analytic functions (see Section 6.6).

• Given the increasing need for lifelong learning skills in a technologically changing world, students need opportunities to learn a range of low- and high-tech support systems for spatial thinking (see Chapter 6).

• Implementing any support system in the K–12 context requires coordinated programs for material, logistical, instructional, curriculum, and community support (see Section 6.4).

Therefore, the committee views spatial thinking as a basic and essential skill that can be learned, that can be taught formally to all students, and that can be supported by appropriately designed tools, technologies, and curricula. With appropriate instruction and commensurate levels of low- and high-tech support, spatial thinking can become an invaluable, lifelong habit of mind.

However, the problem with respect to teaching and learning about spatial thinking is far deeper than simply a lack of adequate supporting tools. Tools are a means to an end: tools are therefore necessary but not sufficient. Schools teach what society values. Society values that for which there is a clear and explicit need and, therefore, educational rationale. Thus, two of the most valued school subjects are mathematics and science. As Chapter 5 makes clear, however, underpinning success in both mathematics and science is the capacity to think spatially. Also, as Chapter 3 makes clear, spatial thinking underpins many tasks in everyday life, the workplace, and science. Ironically, these underpinnings are not yet matched by either a deep scientific understanding of the process of spatial thinking or a broadly accepted educational rationale and therefore mandate for learning how to think spatially.

The committee believes that Chapters 3 and 5 provide a powerful educational rationale for teaching spatial thinking. Chapter 2 offers a first attempt to describe and understand the process of spatial thinking, and Chapter 4 and Appendixes C and D summarize what we know about the learning and teaching of spatial thinking, leading to a position statement on the fostering of expertise in spatial thinking (see Section 4.5).

Chapter 5 demonstrates that there is no systematic and comprehensive attempt to teach about spatial thinking as part of the national science and mathematics standards. Nowadays, school curricula are designed to meet subject-based content standards, of either national or state origin, that express what students should know and be able to do at various points throughout their school careers. Schools, and increasingly society at large, measure their success against benchmarks using standards-based assessments. As the educational saying goes, "We assess what we value and we value what we assess."

There are neither content standards nor valid and reliable assessments for spatial thinking. Without such standards and assessments, spatial thinking will remain locked in a curious educational twilight zone: extensively relied upon across the K–12 curriculum but not explicitly and systematically instructed in any part of the curriculum. No matter how well designed support tools for spatial thinking might be, they will not be effective without a societal recognition of the importance of spatial thinking and an educational commitment to teaching spatial thinking to all students in all grades.

However, spatial thinking itself is not a content-based discipline in the way that physics, biology, or economics are disciplines: it is not a stand-alone subject in its own right. Spatial thinking is a way of thinking that permeates those disciplines and, the committee would argue, virtually all other subject matter disciplines. Instruction in spatial thinking should play an equivalent role to that of the "writing across the curriculum" approach. Standards for spatial thinking, therefore, should be general guidelines for what students need to know about concepts of space, tools of representation, and processes of reasoning in order to be able to solve problems. These general guidelines—elements of which are illustrated in Chapter 2—must be correlated with and integrated into the particular content knowledge expectations for various subject matter disciplines. The guidelines should, therefore, be infused across the curriculum and supported in as many disciplines as possible.

Spatial thinking is *not* an add-on to an already crowded school curriculum but a missing link across the curriculum. Integration and infusion of spatial thinking can help to achieve existing curricular objectives. Spatial thinking is another lever to enable students to achieve a deeper and more insightful understanding of subjects across the curriculum.

Instruction in spatial thinking would help to foster a new generation of spatially literate students who are proficient in terms of spatial knowledge, spatial ways of thinking and acting, and spatial capabilities (see Section 1.4.1). With this proficiency, students will have established the habit of mind of thinking spatially, seeing opportunities for approaching problems by using their knowledge of concepts of space. They will be able to practice spatial thinking in an informed way, drawing on their knowledge of tools of representation. They will adopt a critical stance to spatial thinking, using the appropriate processes of spatial reasoning (see Section 1.4.2). Chapter 11 shows eighth-grade students practicing spatial thinking in a remarkably sophisticated way with the support of a tool, GIS, and with the guidance of an enlightened teacher.

The first recommendation is designed to help achieve the goal of spatial literacy for all American students.

Recommendation 1

Through the support of federal funding agencies (i.e., National Science Foundation [NSF], the National Institutes of Health, and the Department of Education), there should be a systematic research program into the nature, characteristics, and operations of spatial thinking. The NSF competition for "Science of Learning Centers" provides one program model for developing knowledge about spatial thinking.

The findings of this research program would be expected to highlight the importance of spatial thinking across the K–12 curriculum as well as to encourage the development of spatial thinking standards and curriculum materials to train K–12 students in spatial thinking.

The ultimate goal should be to foster a new generation of spatially literate students who have the habit of mind of thinking spatially, can practice spatial thinking in an informed way, and can adopt a critical stance to spatial thinking. Meeting this long-term goal will require careful articulation of the links between spatial thinking standards and existing disciplinary-based content standards. It will necessitate the development of innovative teaching methods and programs to train teachers, together with new ways to assess levels of spatial thinking and the performance of educational support programs. There should be a national commitment to the systemic educational efforts necessary to meet the goal of spatial literacy.

10.4 SUPPORT FOR SPATIAL THINKING

The committee arrived at a position on the educational challenges of providing systems for supporting spatial thinking in K–12 education:

- Spatial thinking can be supported and facilitated by the development of a coherent suite of supporting tools, ranging from low to high technology in nature, that can (1) address a range of types of problems, (2) use a range of types and amounts of data, and (3) require different levels of skill and experience (see Chapter 6).
- Support systems for spatial thinking must meet three requirements: they must (1) allow for the spatialization of data, (2) facilitate the visualization of working and final results, and (3) perform a range of functions (transformations, operations, and analyses) (see Chapter 6).
- The success of a support system in the K–12 context is a function of its design (see the 10 criteria in Chapter 6) and its implementation across the curriculum (see the five support needs in Chapter 6).
- GIS has significant but as yet unrealized potential for supporting spatial thinking across a range of subjects in the K–12 curriculum (see Chapters 7, 8, and 9).
- However, there are significant design and implementation challenges to be met before GIS can play a significant role alongside other tools for teaching standards-based spatial thinking across the curriculum. GIS should be redesigned to accommodate the full range of learners and school contexts, to be more developmentally and educationally appropriate, to be easier to teach and to learn, and to accommodate current levels of computing equipment in schools (see Chapters 8 and 9).
- GIS must be supported by a systematic implementation program that incorporates teacher training, curriculum development, and material support (see Chapters 8 and 9).

The committee sees GIS as exemplifying the theoretical power of a high-tech system for supporting spatial thinking and the practical design and implementation problems that must be faced in the K–12 context:

- The power of GIS lies in its ability to support the scientific research process and to provide policy-related answers to significant real-world problems arising in a variety of disciplinary contexts.
- The appeal of GIS lies in its direct connection to significant workforce opportunities in the information technology sector.
- The potential of GIS lies in its ability to accommodate the full range of learners and to be adapted to a range of educational settings.
- The practical problems of adapting GIS to the K–12 context are equally striking. As an expert-based, "industrial-strength" technology, it is, in one sense, too powerful for most K–12 needs. It is challenging and inviting, yet intimidating and difficult to learn. While the design issues can be addressed, the implementation challenges are immense. All of the essential implementation

supports—for materials, logistics, instruction, curriculum, and in the community—are either weak or nonexistent.

Therefore, while GIS can make a significant impact on teaching and learning about spatial thinking, it must be situated in a context wherein there is a systematic, standards-based approach to teaching spatial thinking and there is a suite of supporting tools available to do so. Taken alone, GIS is not *the* answer to the problem of teaching spatial thinking in American schools; however, it can play a significant role in *an* answer. For GIS to be able to play that significant role, the committee identified a set of five recommendations.

Recommendation 2

There should be a coordinated effort among GIS designers, psychologists, and educators to redesign GIS to accommodate the needs of the K–12 education community. Among the many design issues that must be addressed are

- broadening its accessibility to the full range of learners (e.g., adding alternative sensory input and output modes);
- strengthening the capacity to spatialize nonspatial data;
- overcoming the visualization limitations (e.g., with respect to time and to full 3-D capacity);
- providing graded versions of GIS that are age and/or experience appropriate (e.g., that are easy to learn, cumulative, and flexible);
- redesigning interfaces to be more intuitive and to provide help and guidance (e.g., providing reflective wizards);
- making the software customizable (e.g., adopting an open system architecture; making it possible for teachers to hide or expose functionality as needed); and
- making the software "teacher friendly" in terms of ease of installation, maintenance, and use.

The committee recognizes that many of these design challenges are not specific to the K–12 context and that their solution may not occur with this context in mind. Should that be the case, then someone must take responsibility for adapting the solutions to the particular needs of teachers and students. Teachers and students should not be expected to adapt to a "one-size-fits-all" GIS that does not reflect their special needs.

The committee identified three mechanisms that led to the development of GIS software: the academic model, the commercial model, and the collaborative model. These three models offer distinct options for the redesign of GIS software for the K–12 context. All three mechanisms appear to have merit, as well as potential pitfalls. The choice between them, therefore, should be made by the appropriate funding agencies.

Based on the levels of investment being made by commercial vendors, and on experience from GIS development projects, it would be reasonable to assume that a suitable GIS could be developed over a period of three years. Therefore:

Recommendation 3

To coordinate the development of GIS software, a "Federation of GIS Education Partners" should be established. The federation should consist of GIS developer and user partners, drawn from academia, government, the private sector, and the K–12 user community.

To be successful, the following should be considered in the design of a GIS educational software federation:

- The federation should be a grass-roots, community-driven effort.
- The governance basis of the federation should be a bottom-up (rather than a top-down approach) to ensure that the priorities of the broader community are honored. However, some centralized management would be necessary for making major decisions on behalf of the federation's constituents, for representing the federation's interests, and for conducting day-to-day operations. The instrument of centralized management should be used sparingly.
- The federation should be flexible. Thus, the initial rules and procedures should not be over specified.
- The federation should manage the tensions that may arise from constituents with differing expectations (e.g., software companies, teachers).

Recommendation 4

Working in collaboration, GIS system designers, educational IT specialists, and teachers should develop guidelines for a model GIS-enabled school.

The guidelines should address software and hardware needs (including schedules for up-grades), local and global network design and access requirements, classroom layouts for different modes of instruction, and levels of technical support for hardware and software.

Recommendation 5

Working in collaboration, representatives of colleges of education and GIS educators should

- establish guidelines for pre- and in-service teacher training programs for teaching spatial thinking using GIS; and
- develop a model standards-based curriculum for teaching about GIS.

Recommendation 6

With funding from either a government agency (e.g., NSF, the Department of Education) or a private philanthropy, a research program should be developed to see whether or not an understanding of GIS improves academic achievement across the curriculum. Without credible assessment of results, the value of GIS and other support systems for spatial thinking cannot be evaluated.

This set of recommendations (2–6) contains overlaps and critical interdependencies. Thus, for example, the GIS redesign process must inform the development of guidelines for GIS-enabled schools. The model curriculum must be linked to assessment procedures and to the research program on the impact of GIS on academic achievement. (See Figure 10.1 for an implementation timetable.)

10.5 CONCLUSION

The premise for this report is the need for systemic educational change. Fundamental to that change is a national commitment to the goal of spatial literacy. Spatial thinking must be recognized

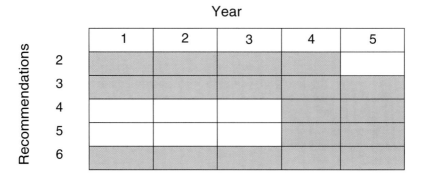

FIGURE 10.1 Timetable for implementing Recommendations 2–6.

as a fundamental and necessary part of the process of K–12 education. The committee does not view spatial thinking as one more piece to be added on to an already overburdened curricular structure. In contrast, spatial thinking is viewed as an integrator and a facilitator for problem solving across the curriculum. Spatial thinking does not and should not stand alone, but equally well, without explicit attention to it, we cannot meet our responsibility for equipping the next generation of students for life and work in the twenty-first century. Chapter 11 shows what can be achieved by using one high-tech support system, GIS, to engage students in scientific problem solving.

11

The Spatial Thinker

11.1 GIS AND THE CHALLENGE OF THINKING SPATIALLY

In 1958, Jerome Bruner challenged fifth-grade students to think spatially for themselves, using a paper outline map and a pencil (see Chapter 1). Today, students can be challenged to think spatially for themselves, using a database, a virtual map, and a mouse. In both cases, the responses from students are based on a spatial reasoning process that involves critical observation, exploration, posing questions, developing hypotheses, and generating answers. Both sets of tools offer the power to learn. As Chapters 7, 8, and 9 make clear, GIS is a tool for supporting spatial thinking, one with considerable potential but with genuine limitations, at least in its present incarnations.

Nevertheless, the power and potential of GIS can be seen in this example from Lyn Malone's eighth-grade world geography classroom (Lyn Malone, personal communication, June 2003). The similarities with Jerome Bruner's work are clear: the contrast between passive knowledge receipt versus active learning; the focus on describing and understanding spatial patterns; the search for multiple explanations; the process of collaborative learning; and above all, the excitement of success. The differences are equally clear: the richness of the data sources and the number of maps; the scale of the project; the low-tech support system versus the high-tech support system. Yet the intent remains the same in both cases: fostering the creative power of spatial thinking in young students. GIS certainly makes a significant difference in the process of learning but not necessarily *the* difference in the outcome. In both cases, there is a support system at work: material support, instructional support, and curriculum support combine to offer the opportunity to practice and develop spatial thinking skills. There is a creative juxtaposition between students and teachers, between tools and questions, and between learning and achievement.

11.2 AN EXAMPLE OF USING GIS TO THINK SPATIALLY

Our world geography curriculum is regional in approach. In the fall of 2000, we were beginning our study of sub-Saharan Africa. Traditionally, I would start the study of a new region by having the students draw and label maps under the assumption that place name recognition would

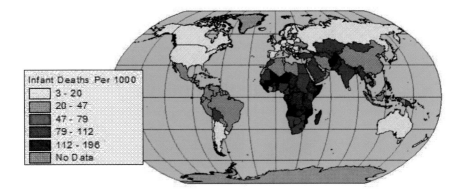

FIGURE 11.1 Map of infant mortality rates.

be essential to later activities and investigations in the unit. Following my own introduction to GIS, however, I decided to try a new approach and introduce sub-Saharan Africa in an altogether different way.

Our unit on sub-Saharan Africa began with the examination of a world map of infant mortality rates (IMR). Figure 11.1 clearly indicated that sub-Saharan Africa has some of the highest IMR rates in the world.

As we looked at the map, class discussion focused on the regional patterns of infant mortality rates that we observed. When I asked students to identify questions that were raised by those patterns, many asked why infant mortality rates in Africa were so high. The question became the springboard for a challenging activity—an investigation of the causes of and potential cures for the high rates of infant mortality in this region.

Before we began our investigation, I asked students to speculate about what might cause a region—any region—to have a high infant mortality rate. We listed possibilities on the board: not enough doctors, not enough hospitals, lack of food, disease, poverty, war. The preliminary list became the basis of our investigation.

I presented students with a scenario to shape their investigation. In the scenario, the students had been asked to serve on a World Health Organization (WHO) task force charged with recommending programs to address the high rates of infant mortality in sub-Saharan Africa (Figure 11.2). The WHO had several program options but, because of cost, they could not implement all of them. The WHO wanted the IMR Task Force to identify the programs that would be most likely to result in reductions in the high infant mortality rates. Among WHO's program options were providing immunization against preventable childhood diseases, creating public service messages on radio and television regarding key health issues, funding the construction of sanitation systems for water and sewage, training more doctors and nurses, and expanding opportunities for elementary and secondary education. The students' task was to discover the leading causes of infant mortality in sub-Saharan Africa and identify the programs that would most effectively target those causes.

The class was enthusiastic about the assignment and anxious to get underway. Our investigation began in the computer lab; GIS was to be the IMR Task Force's principal investigative tool. In a GIS project that I created for them, students began their search for a cause by looking for other indicators that correlated closely with patterns of infant mortality rates (Figure 11.2b). Using GIS, they compared spatial patterns of infant mortality rates with spatial patterns of the following variables: percent of the population with access to safe water, average number of calories consumed

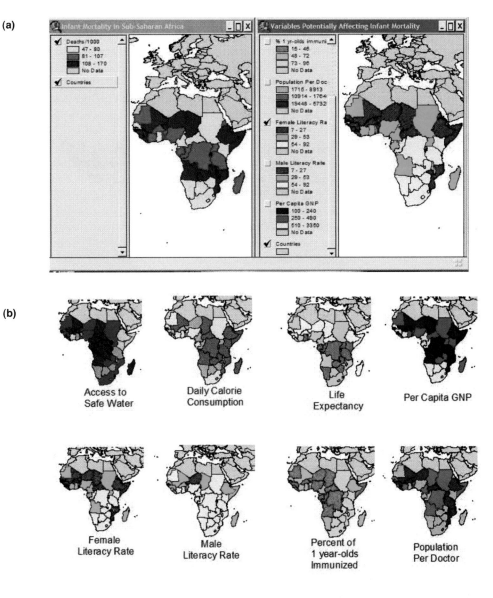

FIGURE 11.2 Maps of variables affecting infant mortality.

per day, percent of one-year-olds immunized against common childhood diseases, population per doctor, life expectancy, female literacy rate, male literacy rate, and per capita gross national product (GNP).

In this initial phase of investigation each student worked independently at his or her own computer although they were free to question one another or share observations while they worked. As they moved between on-screen maps in the project they made notes and listed observations about specific countries and regions, and about the relationships and patterns they detected. Each student was becoming an "expert" in preparation for their upcoming work as a Task Force member.

For the next phase of the investigation, I grouped the students into teams of four or five members. Each team would assume the responsibilities of the Task Force. They had to reach within-group consensus on the most important causal factors in sub-Saharan Africa's infant mortality rates and on program recommendations to the WHO to address those causal factors. The students had reading materials describing those programs and the costs associated with each. We worked in the classroom at this point, but each group had access to a computer with the GIS project to aid in their discussions and in the preparation of their final report. Each group was to prepare maps and an oral presentation to the WHO, supporting and explaining their decision.

The IMR Task Force groups got to work eagerly. They began to compare notes about the inferences they had drawn from their GIS investigation. It was obvious they were enthusiastic about the activity, but I was totally unprepared for the impassioned debates that ensued! As the teams began their discussions, the classroom erupted with the sounds of spirited argument and delibera-tion. "Television ads make no sense at all—just look at the per capita GNP. The countries with the highest infant mortality rates have the lowest GNP. These people don't have televisions—they're poor." "It's got to be education—look at the female literacy rate map. It's practically a mirror image of infant mortality. Besides, education will help people get better jobs." "Look how much it costs to train doctors—let's send in nurses to give vaccinations. The countries that aren't vaccinating babies have high rates of infant mortality. That program is inexpensive, and it will reduce infant mortality now, not ten years from now."

The GIS-based classroom presentations by each Task Force group provided clear evidence that the project had fostered appreciation for and new understanding about the complex and interrelated factors that contribute to high rates of infant mortality in sub-Saharan Africa. Not only did students appreciate the complexity of causal variables, but they also recognized the myriad obstacles and problems associated with eliminating those causes. The groups' conclusions and recommendations were not identical, but all were supported by maps and data from their GIS-based investigation. Some groups were convinced that health care initiatives—immunization programs and training doctors—offered the greatest possibility of reducing infant mortality rates. Others felt it was essen-tial to address at once the most basic human needs for food and safe water, while still others focused on education as the only way to bring about lasting and sustained change. Their arguments were eloquent, informed, and credible.

There were several unexpected benefits from this activity. Although I had decided to forgo my traditional map labeling activities, I found that the students had acquired place name recognition as a side effect of working with the project. They noted countries that were high or low in each variable and, in the process, began to learn their names. They'd ask questions like "What's going on in Mali (or Sierra Leone or Niger)—it's on practically every map?" Such questions set the stage for later investigations into subjects like desertification in Africa's Sahel or the legacy of colonialism in sub-Saharan Africa. Essentially, I discovered that the project not only accomplished its primary objective of teaching about infant mortality in sub-Saharan Africa, but it also provided a foundation for investigations and lessons yet to come.

The success of this project reinforced all my beliefs about the value of GIS in the classroom. GIS enabled me to be the facilitator of a learning process, not the disseminator of information. My students loved the sense of discovery they experienced with GIS and felt empowered by the opportunity to investigate and draw their own conclusions. Students experienced active learning through their own hands-on exploration and analysis of data rather than passively absorbing and restating information from secondary sources or information authority figures. Their powerful learning experience resulted from an inquiry process, not from being provided with "the right answer," and GIS was the engine that powered the inquiry process. (Lyn Malone, personal commu-nication, 2003).

11.3 MEETING THE CHALLENGE TO LEARN TO THINK SPATIALLY

As this example shows, GIS is a powerful support system that can, with well-trained and imaginative teachers and the appropriate school infrastructure, help to reshape learning across the curriculum.

These students did show a developing spatial literacy. They broadened and deepened their spatial knowledge (through, for example, the search for explanatory factors that would account for patterns of infant mortality). They showed an increasing command over spatial ways of thinking and acting (through the comparison of spatial patterns of infant mortality with the spatial patterns of the possible explanatory factors). They developed spatial capabilities (through the use of GIS). They also became more critical spatial thinkers. They had to find and then use spatial data. They had to construct, articulate, and defend a line of reasoning ("Television ads make no sense at all—just look at the per capita GNP. The countries with the highest infant mortality rates have the lowest GNP. These people don't have televisions—they're poor").

As Lyn Malone rightly concludes, the power of this learning experience is the result of an inquiry process that is supported by a tool (in this case GIS). However, GIS is *only* one of a suite of support systems, high and low tech in nature, that must be brought to bear in fostering an understanding for and appreciation of spatial thinking. All students deserve and need the opportunity to be challenged, to be supported, and to become critical spatial thinkers.

The premise for this report is the need for systemic change. Fundamental to that change is a national commitment to the goal of spatial literacy. Spatial thinking must be recognized as a fundamental and necessary part of the process of K–12 education.

The committee does not view spatial thinking as one more piece to be added on to an already overburdened curricular structure. Instead, spatial thinking is seen as an integrator and a facilitator for problem solving across the curriculum. Spatial thinking is not an add-on but a missing link across the curriculum. Thus, integration and infusion of spatial thinking can help to achieve existing curricular objectives. The idea of spatial thinking does not and should not stand alone, but equally well, without explicit attention to it, we cannot meet our responsibility for equipping the next generation of students for life and work in the twenty-first century.

References

Abell, G. 1969. Exploration of the Universe, 2nd edition. New York: Holt, Reinhart, Winston.

Access Excellence. Available at http://accessexcellence.org. Accessed on March 23, 2004.

Ackerman, P. L., and A. Cianciolo. 2002. Ability and task constraint determinants of complex task performance. Journal of Experimental Psychology: Applied 8:194–208.

Aguirre, G. K., E. Zarahn, and M. D'Esposito. 1998. Neural components of topographical representation. Proc. Natl. Acad. Sci. USA 95(3):839–846.

Alexander, G. M., and B. S. Peterson. 2001. Sex steroids and human behavior: Implications for developmental psychopathology. CNS Spectrums 6:75–88.

Alexandria Digital Library Collection. Available at http://www.alexandria.ucsb.edu. Accessed on January 5, 2004.

Alkhateeb, H. M. 2002. Special Issue: Correlations for Scores on Conceptions of Mathematics and Approaches to Learning Mathematics. Perceptual and Motor Skills 95(3):1251–1255.

Alkhateeb, H. M., and N. Taha. 2002. Mathematics self-concept and mathematics anxiety of undergraduate majors in education. Psychological Reports 91(3):1273–1276.

Amorim, M. A. 1999. A neurocognitive approach to human navigation. In R. G. Golledge, editor, Wayfinding Behavior: Cognitive Mapping and Other Spatial Processes, pp. 152–167. Baltimore and London: Johns Hopkins University Press.

Anderson, R. E., and H. J. Becker. 2001. School Investments in Instructional Technology. Report 8. Teaching, Learning, and Computing: 1998 National Survey. Irvine, Calif.: Center for Research on Information Technology and Organizations.

Annett, M. 1985. Left, Right, Hand, And Brain: The Right Shift Theory. Hillsdale, N.J.: Erlbaum Associates.

ArcGIS. Available at http://www.esri.com. Accessed on January 14, 2004.

ArcLesson. Available at http://gis.esri.com/industries/education/arclessons/titles_only.cfm. Accessed on March 29, 2004.

ArcVoyager. Available at http://www.esri.com/industries/k-12/voyager.html. Accessed on February 12, 2004.

Arnheim, R. 1977. The Dynamics of Architectural Form. Berkeley, Calif.: University of California Press.

Arnoff, S. 1989. Geographic Information Systems: A Management Perspective. Ottawa, Canada: WDL Publications.

Arnold, A. P., and S. M. Breedlove. 1985. Organizational and activational effects of sex steroid hormones on vertebrate brain and behavior: A re-analysis. Hormones and Behavior 19:469–498.

Audet, R., and G. Ludwig, editors. 2000. GIS in Schools. Redlands, Calif.: ESRI Press.

Baddeley, A. 1986. Working Memory. New York: Oxford University Press.

Baenninger, M., and N. Newcombe. 1989. The role of experience in spatial test performance: A meta-analysis. Sex Roles 20:327–344.

Baker, T. R., and S. H. White. 2003. The effects of G.I.S. on students' attitudes, self-efficacy, and achievement in middle school science classrooms. Journal of Geography 102(6):243–254.

Barsalou, L. W. 1999. Perceptual symbol systems. Behavioral and Brain Sciences 22(4):577–609.

Barsalou, L. W., W. K. Simmons, A. K. Barbey, and C. D. Wilson. 2003. Grounding conceptual knowledge in modality-specific systems. Trends in Cognitive Sciences 7(2):84–91.

Bartlett, F. C. 1932. Remembering: A Study in Experimental and Social Psychology. New York: Cambridge University Press.

Baskin, C. W. 1957. A Critique and Translation of Walter Christaller's Die zentralen Orte in Siiddeutschland. Unpublished Ph.D. dissertation, Department of Economics, University of Virginia.

Battista, M. T. 1990. Spatial visualization and gender differences in high-school geometry. Journal for Research in Mathematics Education 21(1):47–60.

Beatty, W. W., and A. I. Tröster. 1987. Gender differences in geographical knowledge. Sex Roles 16(11–12):565–589.

Becker, H. J., J. L. Ravitz, and Y. T. Wong. 1999. Teacher and Teacher-Directed Student Use of Computers and Software. Report 3. Teaching, Learning, and Computing: 1998 National Survey. Irvine, Calif.: Center for Research on Information Technology and Organizations.

Bednarz, S. W. 2000. Problem-based learning. In R. Audet and G. Ludwig, editors, GIS in Schools, pp. 89–101. Redlands, Calif.: ESRI Press.

Bednarz, S. W., and R. Audet. 1999. The status of GIS technology in teacher preparation programs. Journal of Geography 98(21):60–67.

Berenbaum, S. A., and M. Hines. 1992. Early androgens are related to childhood sex-typed toy preferences. Psychological Science 3:203–206.

Berenbaum, S. A., and E. Snyder. 1995. Early hormonal influences on childhood sex-typed activity and playmate preferences: Implications for the development of sexual orientation. Developmental Psychology 31(1):31–42.

Berenbaum, S. A., K. Korman, and C. Leveroni. 1995. Early hormones and sex differences in cognitive abilities. Learning and Individual Differences (74):303–321.

Bernhardsen, T. 1999. Geographic Information Systems: An Introduction. New York: John Wiley & Sons.

Bertin, J. 1983. Semiology of Graphics. Madison, Wisc.: University of Wisconsin Press.

Bethell-Fox, C. E., and R. N. Shepard. 1988. Mental rotation: Effects of stimulus complexity and familiarity. Journal of Experimental Psychology: Human Perception and Performance 14(1):12–23.

Biederman, I., and M. S. Shiffrar. 1987. Sexing day-old chicks: A case study and expert systems analysis of a difficult perceptual-learning task. Journal of Experimental Psychology: Learning, Memory, and Cognition 13(4):640–645.

Biswas, G., S. R. Goldman, D. Fisher, B. Bhuva, and G. Glewwe. 1995. Assessing design activity in complex CMOS circuit design. In P. Nichols and S. Chipman, editors, Cognitively Diagnostic Assessment, pp. 167–188. Hillsdale, N.J.: Erlbaum Associates.

Bjork, R. A., and A. Richardson-Klavehn. 1989. On the puzzling relationship between environmental context and human memory. In C. Izawa, editor, Current Issues in Cognitive Processes: The Tulane Flowerree Symposium on Cognition, pp. 313–344. Hillsdale, N.J.: Erlbaum Associates.

Bock, R. D., and D. Kolakowski. 1973. Further evidence of sex-linked major-gene influence on human spatial visualizing ability. American Journal of Human Genetics 25(1):1–14.

Bossler, J. D., editor. 2001. Manual of Geospatial Science and Technology. New York: Taylor and Francis.

Bower, G. H. 1973. How to ... uh ... remember. Psychology Today 7:63–70.

Bradford, M., C. Suplee, and N. Lubick. 2003. Science and engineering visualization challenge: Visualization and the communication of science. Science 301(5639):1472–1477.

Bransford, J. D., and D. L. Schwartz. 1999. Rethinking transfer: A simple proposal with multiple implications. Review of Research in Education 24:61–100.

Bransford, J. D., A. L. Brown, and R. R. Cocking, editors. 1999. How People Learn: Brain, Mind, Experience, and School. Washington, D.C.: National Academy Press.

Broecker, W. S. 1991. The great ocean conveyor. Oceanography 4:79–89.

Brooks, L. R. 1968. Spatial and verbal components of the act of recall. Canadian Journal of Psychology 22(5):349–368.

Brown, A. B. 1953. Watson and Crick with their DNA model. Science Photo Library, Ltd., London, England.

Brown, A., and J. S. DeLoache. 1978. Skills, plans, and self regulation. In R. Siegler, editor, Children's Thinking: What Develops, pp. 3–35. Hillsdale, N.J.: Erlbaum Associates.

Bruck, M., and S. Ceci. 1999. The suggestibility of children's memory. Annual Review of Psychology 50: 419–439.

Bruner, J. S. 1959. Learning and thinking. Harvard Educational Review 29(3):184–192.

Bruner, J. 1960. The Process of Education. Cambridge, Mass.: Harvard University Press.

Bunge, W. 1966. Theoretical Geography. Lund: Gleerup.

Burrough, P. A. 1986. Principles of Geographic Information Systems for Land Resource Assessment. Monographs on Soil and Resources Survey No. 12. New York: Oxford University Press.

Burrough, P. A., and A. U. Frank, editors. 1996. Geographic Objects with Indeterminate Boundaries. New York: Taylor and Francis.

Burrough, P. A., and R. MacDonnell. 1998. Principles of Geographical Information Systems. New York: Oxford University Press.

Cariglia-Bull, T., and M. Pressley. 1990. Short-term memory differences between children predict imagery effects when sentences are read. Journal of Experimental Child Psychology 49(3):384–398.

Carter, J. R. 1989. On defining the geographic information system. In W. J. Rippler, editor, Fundamentals of Geographical Information Systems: A Compendium, pp. 3–7. Falls Church, Va.: ASPRS/ACSM.

Casey, M. B. 1996. Understanding individual differences in spatial ability within females: A nature/nurture interactionist framework. Developmental Review 16(3):241–260.

Casson, L. 2001. Libraries in the Ancient World. New Haven: Yale University Press.

Catalano, J. F., and B. M. Kleiner. 1984. Distant transfer in coincident timing as a function of variability in practice. Perceptual and Motor Skills 58:851–856.

Chase, W. G., and H. A. Simon. 1973. Perception in chess. Cognitive Psychology 4(1):55–81.

Cheng, P. C. 2002. Electrifying diagrams for learning: Principles for complex representational systems. Cognitive Science 26(6):685–736.

Christaller, W. 1972. How I discovered the theory of central places: A report about the origin of central places. In P. W. English and R. C. Mayfield, editors, Man, Space and Environment, pp. 601–610. New York: Oxford University Press.

Clarke, K. C. 2002. Getting Started with Geographic Information Systems, 3rd edition. Upper Saddle River, N.J.: Prentice Hall.

Clement, J. 1998. Expert novice similarities and instruction using analogies. International Journal of Science Education 20(10):1271–1286.

Clement, J. 2000. Levels of causal knowledge in solving explanation problems in science. Paper presented at the Annual Meeting of the American Educational Research Association, New Orleans, April 2000.

Clement, J. 2003. Imagistic simulation in scientific model construction. Proceedings of the Twenty-Fifth Annual Conference of the Cognitive Science Society. Mahwah, N.J.: Erlbaum.

Clifford, C.E. Siccar Point. Available at http://www.geos.ed.ac.uk/undergraduate/field/siccarpoint/images.html. Accessed on October 15, 2004.

Collaer, M. L., and M. Hines. 1995. Human behavioral sex differences: A role for gonadal hormones during development? Psychological Bulletin 118(1):55–107.

Columbia University, Earth Institute. Marie Tharp. Available at http://www.earthinstitute.columbia.edu/library/MarieTharp.html. Accessed on January 12, 2004.

Community Atlas. Available at http://www.esri.com/industries/k–12/atlas/. Accessed on March 29, 2004.

Connor, J. M., and L. A. Serbin. 1977. Behaviorally based masculine- and feminine-activity-preference scales for preschoolers: Correlates with other classroom behaviors and cognitive tests. Child Development 48:1411–1416.

Connor, J. M., M. Schackman, and L. A. Serbin. 1978. Sex-related differences in response to practice on a visual-spatial test and generalization to a related test. Child Development 49:24–29.

Cornoldi, C., and T. Vecchi. 2003. Visuo-Spatial Working Memory and Individual Differences. New York: Psychology Press.

Cowan, N. 1997. The development of working memory. In N. Cowan, editor, The Development of Memory in Childhood, pp. 163–200. Hove, East Sussex, U.K.: Psychology Press.

Cowen, D. J. 1988. GIS versus CAD versus DBMS: What are the differences? Photogrammetric Engineering and Remote Sensing 54:1551–1554.

Cowen, D. J. 1994. The importance of GIS for the average person. In Proceedings of First Federal Geographic Technology Conference, pp. 7–11. Washington, D.C.: National Research Council.

Cuthbert, A. J., D. B. Clark, and M.C. Linn. 2002. WISE learning communities: Design considerations. In K. A. Renninger and W. Shumar, editors, Building Virtual Communities: Learning and Change in Cyberspace. Cambridge, U.K.: Cambridge University Press.

DataScape. Available at http://www.wri.org/enved/datascap.html. Accessed on March 29, 2004. (Discontinued)

Davis, E. A. 2003a. Prompting middle school science students for productive reflection: Generic and directed prompts. Journal of the Learning Sciences 12(1):91–142.

Davis, E. A. 2003b. Untangling dimensions of students' beliefs about scientific knowledge and science learning. International Journal of Science Education 25(4):439–468.

DeBeni, R., and C. Cornoldi. 1988. Imagery limitations in totally congenitally blind subjects. Journal of Experimental Psychology: Learning, Memory, and Cognition 14(4):650–655.

De Corte, E. 2003. Transfer as the productive use of acquired knowledge, skills, and motivations. Current Directions in Psychological Science 12(4):142–146.

de Groot, A. D. 1978. Thought and Choice in Chess, 2nd edition. The Hague: Mouton.

DeMers, M. N. 2000. Fundamentals of Geographic Information Systems, 2nd edition. New York: John Wiley & Sons.

de Souza, A. R. 1990. A Geography of World Economy. Columbus, Ohio: Merrill Publishing Company.

Digital Library for Earth System Education (DLESE). Available at http://www.dlese.org. Accessed on October 20, 2004.

diSessa, A. A. 2000. Changing Minds: Computers, Learning, and Literacy. Cambridge, Mass.: MIT Press.

Dobson, J., and P. F. Fisher. 2003. Geoslavery. Institute of Electrical and Electronics Engineers (IEEE) Technology and Society Magazine 22(1):47–52.

Donaldson, D. P. 2001. With a little help from our friends: Implementing geographic information systems (GIS) in K–12 schools. Social Education 65(3):147–150.

Downs, R. M., and L. S. Liben. 1991. The development of expertise in geography: A cognitive-developmental approach to geographic education. Annals of the Association of American Geographers 8(2):304–327.

Duncker, K. 1945. On problem solving. Psychological Monographs 58(270): 1–113.

Earthviewer. Available at http://www.earthviewer.com. Accessed on March 23, 2004.

Economist. May 3, 2003. North Korea's Missile Threat.

Economist. May 15, 2003. Correction: North Korea's missile threat.

Economist. 2003. The revenge of geography. 366(8315):19–22.

Edelson, D. C., D. N. Gordin, and R. D. Pea. 1999. Addressing the challenges of inquiry-based learning through technology and curriculum design. Journal of the Learning Sciences 8(3/4):391–450.

Educational Researcher. 2003. Issue on Expertise, 32(8). Available at http://www.aera.net/pubs/er/toc/er3208.htm. Accessed on April 16, 2004.

Egenhofer, M. J., and W. Kuhn. 1999. Interacting with GIS. In P. A. Longley, M. F. Goodchild, D. J. Maguire, and D. W. Rhind, editors, Geographical Information Systems: Principles, Techniques, Management, and Applications, Chapter 28. New York: John Wiley & Sons.

Ekstrom, R. B., J. W. French, and H. H. Harman. 1976. Manual for Kit of Factor Referenced Cognitive Tests. Princeton, N.J.: Educational Testing Service.

Eliot, J. 1987. Models of Psychological Space. New York: Springer-Verlag.

English, K. Z., and L. S. Feaster. 2003. Community Geography: GIS in Action. Redlands, Calif.: ESRI Press.

Environmental and Spatial Technology (EAST) initiative. Available at http://www.cast.uark.edu/east/. Accessed on January 11, 2004.

Eratosthenes Project. Available at http://www.physastro.sonoma.edu/observatory/eratosthenes/#original. Accessed on February 15, 2004.

Ericsson, K. A. 1996. The Road to Excellence: The Acquisition of Expert Performance in the Arts and Sciences, Sports, and Games. Mahwah, N.J.: Erlbaum Associates.

Ericsson, K. A., and N. Charness. 1994. Expert performance: Its structure and acquisition. American Psychologist 49(8):725–747.

ESRI Curriculum Materials. Available at http://gis.esri.com. Accessed on March 23, 2004.

ESRI Teacher Training Courses. Available at http://www.esri.com/industries/k-12/atp/courses.html. Accessed on March 22, 2004.

Ewing, M., and B. Heezen. 1956. Mid-Atlantic ridge seismic belt. Transactions of the American Geophysical Union 37:343.

Explore Your World. Available at http://www.esri.com/industries/k-12/download/docs/ explore.pdf. Accessed on March 29, 2004.

Fabrikant, S. I. 2000. Spatialized browsing in large data archives. Transactions in GIS 4(1):65–78.

Fabrikant, S. I., and B. P. Buttenfield. 1997. Envisioning User Access to a Large Data Archive. GIS/LIS '97 Annual Conference and Exposition Proceedings, Cincinnati, Ohio, October 28–30, 1997, p. 686–692.

Fabrikant, S .I., and B. P. Buttenfield. 2001. Formalizing semantic spaces for information access. Annals of the Association of American Geographers 91(2):263–280.

Fahle, M, and T. Poggio, editors. 2000. Perceptual Learning. Cambridge, Mass.: MIT Press.

Fahle, M., S. Edelman, and T. Poggio. 1995. Fast perceptual learning in hyperacuity. Vision Research 35:3003–3013.

Farah, J. J. 1989. The neural basis of mental imagery. Trends in Neurosciences 12:395–399.

Farah, M. J., K. D. Wilson, M. Drain, and J. N. Tanaka. 1998. What is "special" about face perception? Psychological Review 105(3):482–498.

Fatemi, E. 1999. Building the digital curriculum: Summary. In Technology Counts '99: Building the Digital Curriculum. Education Week 19(4):5.

Feldman, A., C. Konold, and B. Coulter. 2000. Network Science, A Decade Later: The Internet and Classroom Learning. Mahwah, N.J.: Erlbaum Associates.

Ferguson, E. L., and M. Hegarty. 1993. Constructing mental models of space from hierarchical texts. Paper presented at the annual meeting of the American Educational Research Association, San Francisco, April, and at the annual meeting of the American Psychological Society, San Diego, June.

Finke, R. 1989. Principles of Mental Imagery. Cambridge, Mass.: MIT Press.

Finke, R., and R. N. Shepard. 1986. Visual functions of mental imagery. In K. R. Boff, L. Kaufman, and J. P. Thomas, editors, Handbook of Perception and Human Performance, Vol. II., pp. 19–55. New York: John Wiley & Sons.

Fisher, R. P., R. E. Geiselman, and M. Amador. 1989. Field test of the cognitive interview: Enhancing the recollection of actual victims and witnesses of crime. Journal of Applied Psychology 74(5):722–727.

Fitch, R. H., and H. A. Bimonte. 2002. Hormones, brain, and behavior: Putative biological contributions to cognitive sex differences. In A. McGillicuddy-De Lisi and R. De Lisi, editors. Biology, Society, and Behavior: The Development of Sex Differences in Cognition. Advances in Applied Developmental Psychology, Vol. 21, pp. 55–91. Westport, Conn.: Ablex Publishing.

Fitzpatrick, C. 2005. Personal communication, May 2005.

Foresman, T. W. 1998. The History of Geographic Information Systems: Perspectives from the Pioneers. Upper Saddle River, N.J.: Prentice Hall.

Fotheringham A. S., and P. Rogerson, editors. 1994. Spatial Analysis and GIS. London: Taylor and Francis.

Franklin, N., and B. Tversky. 1990. Searching imagined environments. Journal of Experimental Psychology: General, 119(1):63–76.

French, J. W., R. B. Ekstrom, and L. A. Price. 1963. Manual for Kit of Reference Tests for Cognitive Factors, revised edition. Princeton, N.J.: Educational Testing Service.

Gahegan, M. 1999. Four barriers to the development of effective exploratory visualization tools for the geosciences. International Journal of Geographic Information Science 13(4):289–310.

Gahegan, M., M. Wachowicz, M. Harrower, and T.-M. Rhyne. 2001. The integration of geographic visualization with knowledge discovery in databases and geocomputation. ICA Commission on Visualization: Working Group on Database-Visualization Links, pp. 1–20.

Gardner, H. 1983. Frames of Mind: The Theory of Multiple Intelligences. New York: Basic Books.

Garling, T., and G. Evans. 1991. Environment, Cognition, and Action: An Integrated Approach. New York: Oxford University Press.

Gaudet, C., and H. Annulis. Under review. Geospatial Technology Competency Model. URISA Journal. Version 11/02/01. Available at http://www.urisa.org/Journal/Under_Review/gaudet/geospatial_technology_competency_model.htm. Accessed on January 22, 2004.

Gaudet, C., J. C. Carr, and H. Annulis. 2003. How to recruit, select, and manage geospatial technology professionals. Paper 0559 presented at Annual ESRI International User Conference, San Diego, July 8–12, 2002.

Geography Education Standards Project. 1994. Geography for Life: National Geography Standards 1994. Washington, D.C.: National Geographic Research and Exploration on behalf of the American Geographical Society, the Association of American Geographers, the National Council for Geographic Education, and the National Geographic Society.

Geography Network. Available at http://www.geographynetwork.com. Accessed on March 23, 2004.

Geospatial Technology Competency Model. Available at http://geowdc.com/assessment/. Accessed on January 22, 2004.

GeoVISTA Studio. Available at http://www.geovistastudio.psu.edu/. Accessed on December 17, 2003.

Geovisualization. Available at http://www.geovista.psu.edu/sites/icavis/. Accessed on December 15, 2003.

Gibson, E. J. 1969. Principles of Perceptual Learning and Development. Englewood Cliffs, N.J.: Prentice-Hall.

Gibson, E. J., and A. D. Pick. 2000. An Ecological Approach to Perceptual Learning and Development. New York: Oxford University Press.

Gibson, J. J. 1979. The Ecological Approach to Visual Perception. Boston: Houghton Mifflin.

Gick, M. L., and K. J. Holyoak. 1983. Schema induction and analogical transfer. Cognitive Psychology 15(1):1–28.

Gladwin, T. 1970. East Is a Big Bird: Navigation and Logic on Puluwat Atoll. Cambridge, Mass.: Harvard University Press.

GLOBE. Available at http://www.globe.gov/. Accessed on March 23, 2004.

Golbeck, S. L., editor. 2001. Psychological Perspectives on Early Childhood Education: Reframing Dilemmas in Research and Practice. Mahwah, N.J.: Erlbaum.

Goldschmidt, G. 1994. On visual design thinking: The vis kids of architecture. Design Studies 15(2):158–174.

Golledge, R. G. 1995. Primitives of spatial knowledge. In T. L. Nyergess, D. M. Mark, R. Laurini, and M. J. Egenhofer, editors, Cognitive Aspects of Human-Computer Interaction for Geographic Information Systems, pp. 29–44. Dordrecht: Kluwer Academic Publishers.

Golledge, R. G. 2002. The nature of geographic knowledge. Annals of the Association of American Geographers 92(1): 1–14.

Golledge, R. G., and R. J. Stimson. 1997. Spatial Behavior: A Geographic Perspective. New York: Guilford Press.

Golledge, R. G., G. D. Richardson, J. N. Rayner, and J. J. Parnicky. 1983. Procedures for defining and analyzing cognitive maps of the mildly and moderately mentally retarded. In H. L. Pick and L. P. Acredolo, editors, Spatial Orientation: Theory, Research, and Application, pp. 79–104. New York: Plenum Press.

Goodchild, M. F. 1988. Stepping over the line: Technological constraints and the new cartography. American Cartographer 15(3):311–319.

Goodchild, M. F. 2001. A geographer looks at spatial information theory. In D. R. Montello, editor, Spatial Information Theory: Foundations for Geographic Information Science: Proceedings of the International Conference COSIT, Morro Bay, Calif., pp.1–13. Lecture Notes in Computer Science 2205. Berlin: Springer.

Goodchild, M. F., L. Anselin, R. P. Appelbaum, and B. H. Harthorn. 2000. Toward spatially integrated social science. International Regional Science Review 23(2):139–159.

Gore, A. 1992. Earth in the Balance: Ecology and the Human Spirit. Boston: Houghton Mifflin.

Gould, P. R., and R. White. 1974. Mental Maps. New York: Penguin Books.

Greenfield, P. M., G. Brannon, and D. Lohr. 1994. Two-dimensional representation of movement through three-dimensional space: The role of video game expertise. Journal of Applied Developmental Psychology 15(1):87–103.

Haber, R. N. 1987. Why low-flying fighter planes crash: Perceptual and attentional factors in collisions with the ground. Human Factors 29(5):519–532.

Halpern, D. F. 1998. Teaching critical thinking for transfer across domains: Dispositions, skills, structure training, and metacognitive monitoring. American Psychologist 53(4):449–455.

Halpern, D. F. 1999. Teaching for critical thinking: Helping college students develop the skills and dispositions of a critical thinker. New Directions for Teaching and Learning 80:69–74.

Halpern, D. F. 2000. Sex differences in cognitive abilities, 3rd edition. Hillsdale, N.J.: Erlbaum Associates.

Hamblin, W. K. 1994. Introduction to Physical Geology, 2nd edition. New York: Macmillan Publishing Company.

Hampson, E. 1990. Variations in sex-related cognitive abilities across the menstrual cycle. Brain and Cognition 14(1): 26–43.

Hampson, E., J. F. Rovet, and D. Altmann. 1998. Spatial reasoning in children with congenital adrenal hyperplasia due to 21-hydroxylase deficiency. Developmental Neuropsychology 14:299–320.

Handy, C. 1992. Balancing corporate power: A new federalist paper. Harvard Business Review (November–December): 59–62.

Hanson, S., and P. Hanson. 1993. The geography of everyday life. In T. Gärling and R. G. Golledge, editors, Behavior and Environment, pp. 249–269. Amsterdam: Elsevier Science Publishers.

Hatano, G., and J. G. Greeno. 1999. Commentary: Alternative perspectives on transfer and transfer studies. International Journal of Educational Research 31(7):645–654.

Heezen, B. C., and M. Tharp. 1956. South Atlantic physiographic diagram. Geological Society of America Bulletin 69(12, Part 2):1579.

Heezen, B. C., and M. Tharp. 1977. World Ocean Floor. Washington, D.C.: U.S. Navy.

Hegarty, M. 1992. Mental animation: Inferring motion from static displays of mechanical systems. Journal of Experimental Psychology: Learning, Memory, & Cognition 18(5):1084–1102.

Hegarty, M., and M. A. Just. 1993. Constructing mental models of machines from text and diagrams. Journal of Memory and Language 32(6):717–742.

Hegarty, M., J. Quilici, N. H. Narayanan, S. Holmquist, and R. Moreno. 1999. Multimedia instruction: Lessons from evaluation of a theory-based design. Journal of Educational Multimedia and Hypermedia 8(2):119–150.

Heiser, J., and B. Tversky. 2002. Diagrams and descriptions in acquiring complex systems. In W. Gray and C. Schunn, editors, Proceedings of the Cognitive Science Society Meetings, 447–452. Hillsdale, N.J.: Erlbaum Associates.

Heiser, J., and B. Tversky. Manuscript. Mental models of complex systems: Structure and function.

Hemphill, J., and M. Herold. 2003. Multistage Analysis Graphic. University of California, Santa Barbara.

Heywood, I., S. Cornelius, and S. Carver. 2002. An Introduction to Geographical Information Systems, 2nd edition. New York: Prentice Hall.

Hines, M. 2000. Gonadal hormones and sexual differentiation of human behavior: Effects on psychosexual and cognitive development. In A. Matsumoto, editor, Sexual Differentiation of the Brain, pp. 257–278. Boca Raton, Fla.: CRC Press.

Hirshman, E., and Bjork, R. 1988. The generation effect: Support for a two-factor theory. Journal of Experimental Psychology: Learning, Memory and Cognition 14(3):484–494.

Hoadley, C. M. 2004. Fostering productive collaboration offline and online: Learning from each other. In M. Linn, E. Davis, and P. Bell, editors, Internet Environments for Science Education, pp. 145–174. Mahwah, N.J.: Erlbaum Associates.

Hobbs, B. E., W. D. Means, and P. F. Williams. 1976. An Outline of Structural Geology. New York: John Wiley & Sons.

Hochberg, J. 1978. Perception. Englewood Cliffs, N.J.: Prentice-Hall.

Homa, D., and J. Cultice. 1984. Role of feedback, category size, and stimulus distortion on the acquisition and utilization of ill-defined categories. Journal of Experimental Psychology: Learning, Memory, and Cognition 10:83–94.

Hubble, E. 1936. The Realm of the Nebula. New Haven, Conn.: Yale University Press.

Hunt, E. B. 1995. Will We Be Smart Enough: A Cognitive Analysis of the Coming Workforce. New York: Russell Sage Foundation.

Hurlbut, C. S. 1971. Dana's Manual of Mineralogy, 18th edition. New York: John Wiley & Sons.

Hutton, J. 1788. Theory of the Earth. Darien, Conn.: Hafner Pub. Co. (reprinted 1970).

Idrisi Teacher Training Courses. Available at http://www.clarklabs.org/. Accessed on March 23, 2004.

Inhelder, B., H. Sinclair, and M. Bovet. 1974. Learning and the Development of Cognition. Cambridge, Mass.: Harvard University Press.

Intergraph Teacher Training Courses. Available at http://www.intergraph.com/schools/. Accessed on March 23, 2004.

Janzen, G., and M. van Turennout. 2003. Navigational relevance of object location encoded in parahippocampal gyrus: An fMRI study. 9th International Conference on Functional Mapping of the Human Brain. Neuroimage 19(2).

Judd, C. H. 1908. The relation of special training and intelligence. Educational Review 36:28–42.

Kali, Y., N. Orion, and B. Eylon. 2003. The effect of knowledge integration activities on students' perception of the Earth's crust as a cyclic system. Journal of Research in Science Teaching 40(6):545–565.

Kansas Collaborative Research Network (KanCRN). Available at http://kangis.org/lessons/. Accessed on March 23, 2004.

Kennett, J. 1982. Marine Geology, 1st Edition. Englewood Cliffs, N.J.: Prentice-Hall, Inc.

Kerski, J. J. 2003. The implementation and effectiveness of geographic information systems technology and methods in secondary education. Journal of Geography 102(3):128–137.

Kimura, D. 1999. Sex and Cognition. Cambridge, Mass.: MIT Press.

Kitchin, R. M. 1994. Cognitive maps: What are they and why study them? Journal of Environmental Psychology 14(1):1–19.

Kitchin, R. M., and S. Freundschuh, editors. 2000. Cognitive Mapping: Past, Present, and Future. London and New York: Routledge.

Klahr, D., and S. M. Carver. 1988. Cognitive objectives in a LOGO debugging curriculum: Instruction, learning, and transfer. Cognitive Psychology 20:362–404.

Kosslyn, S. M. 1978. Measuring the visual angle of the mind's eye. Cognitive Psychology 10:356–389.

Kosslyn, S. M., and O. Koenig. 1992. Wet Mind: The New Cognitive Neuroscience. Cambridge, Mass.: MIT Press.

Kosslyn, S. M., J. A. Margolis, A. M. Barrett, E. J. Goldknopf and P. F. Daly. 1990. Age differences in imagery abilities. Child Development 61:995–1010.

Kusnick, J. 2002. Growing pebbles and conceptual prisms: Understanding the source of student misconceptions about rock formation. Journal of GeoScience Education 50(1):31–39.

Lakoff, G., and M. Johnson. 1980. Metaphors We Live By. Chicago: University of Chicago Press.

Lamont-Doherty Earth Observatory. 2001. Citation for Award of First Lamont Heritage Award. Available at http://www.earthinstitute.columbia.edu/news/aboutStory/about7_1_01.html. Accessed on January 7, 2004.

Lawrence, D. M. 1999. Mountains Under the Sea, Mercator's World. Available at http://www.mercatormag.com/article.php3?i=68. Accessed on January 7, 2004.

Lawrence, D. M. 2002. Upheaval from the Abyss: Ocean Floor Mapping and the Earth Science Revolution. New Brunswick, N.J.: Rutgers University Press.

Lawton, C. A. 1994. Gender differences in way-finding strategies: Relationship to spatial ability and spatial anxiety. Sex Roles 30(11–12):765–779.

Lee, J., and D. W. S. Wong. 2001. Spatial Analysis with *ArcView* GIS. New York: John Wiley & Sons.

Lesgold, A. M. 1988. Problem solving. In R. J. Sternberg and E. E. Smith, editors, The Psychology of Human Thought, pp. 188–213. New York: Cambridge University Press.

Levin, D., M. Stephens, R. Kirshstein, and B. Birman. 1999. Toward Assessing the Effectiveness of Using Technology in K–12 Education. U.S. Department of Education. Washington D.C.: Office of Educational Research and Improvement.

Levine, M., I. Marchon, and G. Hanley. 1984. The placement and misplacement of You-Are-Here maps. Environment and Behavior 16(2):139–158.

Lewis, E. L., and M. C. Linn. 1994. Heat energy and temperature concepts of adolescents, adults, and experts: Implications for curricular improvements. Journal of Research in Science Teaching 31(6):657–677.

Liben, L. S., and R. S. Bigler. 2002. The developmental course of gender differentiation: Conceptualizing, measuring, and evaluating constructs and pathways. Monographs of the Society for Research in Child Development 67(2):1–147.

Liben, L. S., and R. M. Downs. 1993. Understanding person-space-map relations: Cartographic and developmental perspectives. Developmental Psychology 29(4):739–752.

Liben, L. S., R. S. Bigler, and H. R. Krogh. 2002. Language at work: Children's gendered interpretations of occupational titles. Child Development 73(3):810–828.

Library of Congress. Mid-Atlantic Ridge. Available at http://www.loc.gov/exhibits/treasures/trr078.html. Accessed on February 18, 2004.

Linn, M. C., and S. Hsi. 2000. Computers, Teachers, and Peers: Science Learning Partners. Mahwah, N.J.: Erlbaum.

Linn, M. C., and A. C. Petersen. 1985. Emergence of characterization of sex differences in spatial ability: A meta-analysis. Child Development 56(6):1479–1498.

Linn, M. C., and A. C. Petersen. 1986. A meta-analysis of gender differences in spatial ability: Implications for mathematics and science achievement. In J. S. Hyde and M. C. Linn, editors, The Psychology of Gender: Advances Through Meta-Analysis, pp. 67–101. Baltimore, Md.: Johns Hopkins University Press.

Linn, M. C., E. A. Davis, and P. Bell. 2004. Internet Environments for Science Education. Mahwah, N.J.: Erlbaum.

Littlefield, J., and J. J. Rieser. 1993. Semantic features of similarity and children's strategies for identifying relevant information in mathematical story problems. Cognition and Instruction 11(2):133–188.

Lobato, J. 2003. How design experiments can inform a rethinking of transfer and vice versa. Educational Researcher 32(1):17–20.

Lohman, D. F. 1979. Spatial Ability: Review and Re-Analysis of the Correlational Literature. Technical Report 8. Stanford, Calif.: Stanford University.

Lohman, D. F, and P. D. Nichols. 1990. Training spatial abilities: Effects of practice on rotation and synthesis tasks. Learning and Individual Differences 2(1):67–93.

Longley, P. A, M. F. Goodchild, D. J. Maguire, and D. W. Rhind, editors. 1999. Geographical Information Systems: Principles, Techniques, Management and Applications. New York: John Wiley & Sons.

Longley, P.A., M. F. Goodchild, D. J. Maguire, and D. W. Rhind. 2001. Geographic Information Systems and Science. New York: John Wiley & Sons.

Looking at the Environment (LATE) project. Available at http://www.worldwatcher.nwu.edu/late/LATEpublicpage/index.html. Accessed on March 29, 2004.

Loomis, J. M. 1985. Digital Map and Navigation System for the Visually Impaired (unpublished white paper). Available at http://www.geog.ucsb.edu/pgs/papers/loomis_1985.pdf. Santa Barbara, Calif: Department of Psychology, University of California, Santa Barbara.

Loomis, J. M., R. L. Klatzky, R. G. Golledge, and J. W. Philbeck. 1999. Human navigation by path integration. In R. G. Golledge, editor, Wayfinding Behavior: Cognitive Mapping and Other Spatial Processes, pp. 125–151. Baltimore, Md.: Johns Hopkins University Press.

Lowe, R. K. 2001. Components of expertise in the perception and interpretation of meteorological charts. In R. R. Hoffman and A. B. Markman, editors, Interpreting Remote Sensing Imagery: Human Factors, pp. 185–206. Boca Raton, Fla.: CRC Press.

Lowe, R. K. 2003. Animation and learning: Selective processing of information in dynamic graphics. Learning and Instruction 13(2):157–176.

Luria, A. 1968. The Mind of a Mnemonist: A Little Book About a Vast Memory. Cambridge, Mass.: Harvard University Press.

Macaulay, D. 1976. Underground. Boston: Houghton Mifflin Co.

MacEachren, A. M. 1994. Time as a cartographic variable. In H. M. Hearnshaw and D. J. Unwin, editors, Visualization in Geographical Information Systems, pp. 64–81. Chichester, England: John Wiley & Sons.

Maguire, E. A., R. S. J. Frackowiak, and C. D. Frith. 1997. Recalling routes around London: Activation of the right hippocampus in taxi drivers. Journal of Neuroscience 17(18):7103–7110.

Malone, L. 2003. Personal communication, June 6, 2003.

Malone, L., A. M. Palmer, and C. L. Voight. 2002. Mapping Our World: GIS Lessons for Educators. Redlands, Calif.: ESRI Press.

Mannes, S. M., and W. Kintsch. 1987. Knowledge organization and text organization. Cognition and Instruction 4(2): 91–115.

Manning, D. J., and J. Leach. 2002. Perceptual and signal detection factors in radiography. Ergonomics 45(15):1103–1116.

Marshak, S. 2002. Earth Portrait of a Planet, Appendix B-2. New York: W.W. Norton & Co.

Mayer, R., and J. G. Greeno. 1972. Structural differences between learning outcomes produced by different instructional methods. Journal of Educational Psychology 63:165–173.

Mazullo, J. 1996. Investigations into Physical Geology: A Laboratory Manual. New York: Saunders College Publishing.

Mazur, A., and A. Booth. 1998. Testosterone and dominance in men. Behavioral and Brain Sciences 21(3):353–397.

McBeath, M. K., D. M. Shaffer, and M. K. Kaiser. 1995. How baseball outfielders determine where to run to catch fly balls. Science 268(5210):569–573.

McBurney, D. H., S. J. C. Gaulin, T. Devineni, and C. Adams. 1997. Superior spatial ability of women: Stronger evidence for the gathering hypothesis. Evolution and Human Behavior (Formerly, Ethology and Sociobiology) 18:165–174.

McCauley, M. R., and R. P. Fisher. 1995. Facilitating children's eyewitness recall with the revised cognitive interview. Journal of Applied Psychology 80(4):510–516.

Menard, H. W. 1986. The Ocean of Truth; A Personal History of Global Tectonics. Princeton, N.J.: Princeton University Press.

Merriwether, A. M., and L. S. Liben. 1997. Adults' failures on Euclidean and projective spatial tasks: Implications for characterizing spatial cognition. Journal of Adult Development 4:57–69.

Missouri Botanical Garden. Available at http://mobot.org. Accessed on March 23, 2004.

Molecular Visualization in Science Education Workshop Advisory Board. 2001. Molecular Visualization in Science Education Workshop Report. Arlington, Va.: National Science Foundation.

Molenaar, M. 1998. An Introduction to the Theory of Spatial Object Modeling for GIS. New York: Taylor and Francis.

Montello, D. R. 1993. Scale and multiple psychologies of space. In A. U. Frank and I. Campari, editors, Spatial Information Theory: A Theoretical Basis for GIS. Lecture Notes in Computer Science 716, Proceedings, European Conference, COSIT '93, pp. 312–321. New York: Springer-Verlag.

Montello, D. R., K. L. Lovelace, R. G. Golledge, and C. M. Self. 1999. Sex-related differences and similarities in geographic and environmental spatial abilities. Annals of the Association of American Geographers 89(3):515–534.

Morgan, W. W., A. E. Whitford, and A. D. Code. 1953. Studies in galactic structure. I. A preliminary determination of the space distribution of the blue giants. Astrophysical Journal 118:318.

Morrison, P., P. Morrison, and the Office of Charles and Ray Eames. 1982. Powers of Ten: About the Relative Size of Things in the Universe. New York: W. H. Freeman and Company.

Mullis, I. V. S., M. O. Martin, E. J. Gonzalez, K. D. Gregory, R. A. Garden, K. M. O'Connor, S. J. Chrostowski, and T. A. Smith. 2000. TIMSS 1999 International Mathematics Report: Finding from IEA's Repeat of the Third International Mathematics and Science Study at Eighth Grade. Boston, Mass: International Study Center, Lynch School of Education, Boston College.

My Community, Our Earth: Geographic Learning for Sustainable Development (My COE). 2002. Available at http://www.geography.org/sustainable/. Accessed on March 29, 2004.

NCES (National Center for Education Statistics). 1999. Teachers' feelings of preparedness. Indicator of the Month by the National Center for Education Statistics. U.S. Department of Education. Washington, D.C.: Office of Educational Research and Improvement.

NCES. 2000a. Internet access in U.S. public schools and classrooms: 1994–1999. NCES 2000-086. U.S. Department of Education. Washington, D.C.: Office of Educational Research and Improvement.

NCES. 2000b. T. Williams, D. Levine, L. Jocelyn, P. Butler, C. Heind, and J. Haynes, editors, Mathematics and Science in the Eighth Grade: Findings from the Third International Mathematics and Science Study (TIMMS). Washington, D.C.: U.S. Government Printing Office.

NCTM (National Council of Teachers of Mathematics). 1989. Curriculum and Evaluation Standards for School Mathematics. Reston, Va.: National Council of Teachers of Mathematics.

NCTM. 2000. Principles and Standards for School Mathematics. Reston, Va.: National Council of Teachers of Mathematics.

Newcombe, N., and J. Huttenlocher. 2000. Making Space: The Development of Spatial Representation and Reasoning. Cambridge, Mass.: MIT Press.

Newcombe, N., M. M. Bandura, and D. G. Taylor. 1983. Sex differences in spatial ability and spatial activities. Sex Roles, 9:377–386.

Nickerson, R. S., and M. J. Adams. 1979. Long-term memory for a common object. Cognitive Psychology 11(3):287–307.

Novick, L. R., and S. M. Hurley. 2001. To matrix, network, or hierarchy: that is the question. Cognitive Psychology 42(2):158–216.

Novick, L. R., and D. L. Morse. 2000. Folding a fish, making a mushroom: The role of diagrams in executing assembly procedures. Memory and Cognition 28(7):1242–1256.

Novick, L. R., and B. Tversky. 1987. Cognitive constraints on ordering operations: The case of geometric analogies. Journal of Experimental Psychology: General 116(1):50–67.

NRC (National Research Council). 1991. Adding It Up: Helping Children Learn Mathematics. Washington, D.C.: National Academy Press.

NRC. 1996. National Science Education Standards. Washington, D.C.: National Academy Press.

NRC. 1997. Rediscovering Geography: New Relevance for Science and Society. Washington, D.C.: National Academy Press.

NRC. 1998. Toward an Earth Science Enterprise Federation: Results from a Workshop. Washington, D.C.: National Academy Press.

NRC. 1999. How People Learn: Brain, Mind, Experience, and School. Washington, D.C.: National Academy Press.

NRC. 2002a. Research Opportunities in Geography at the U.S. Geological Survey. Washington, D.C.: National Academy Press.

NRC. 2002b. Down to Earth: Geographic Information for Sustainable Development in Africa. Washington, D.C.: National Academy Press.

NRC. 2002c. Technically Speaking: Why All Americans Need to Know More About Technology. Washington, D.C.: National Academy Press.

O'Brien, M. and A. C. Huston. 1985. Development of sex-typed play behavior in toddlers. Developmental Psychology 21(5):866–871.

O'Gorman, J. F. 1998. The ABC of Architecture. Philadelphia: University of Pennsylvania Press.

O'Laughlin, E. M., and B. S. Brubaker. 1998. Use of landmarks in cognitive mapping: Gender differences in self report versus performance. Person. Indiv. Diff. 24(5):595–601.

Packard, E. 1994. Imagining the Universe: A Visual Journey. New York: Perigee Books.

Pani, J. R., J. A. Jeffres, G. T. Shippey, and K. T. Schwartz. 1996. Imagining projective transformations: Aligned orientations in spatial organization. Cognitive Psychology 31(2):125–167.

Parker, H. D. 1988. The unique qualities of a geographic information system: A commentary. Photogrammetric Engineering and Remote Sensing 54(11):1547–1549.

PCAST (President's Council of Advisors on Science and Technology). 1997. Report to the President on the Use of Technology to Strengthen K–12 Education in the United States. Washington, D.C.: U.S. Government Printing Office.

Period-Luminosity Diagram. Available at http://www.astro.livjm.ac.uk/courses/one/NOTES/Garry%20Pilkington/cepinp1.htm. Accessed on February 18, 2004.

Peuquet, D. J. 2002. Representation of Space and Time. New York: Guilford.

Piaget, J. 1954. The Construction of Reality in the Child. New York: Ballantine Books.

Piaget, J. 1970. Science of Education and the Psychology of the Child. D. Coltman, translator. New York: Orion Press.

Piaget, J., and B. Inhelder. 1956. The Child's Conceptualization of Space. London: Routledge.

Pick, H. L., and J. J. Lockman. 1981. From frames of reference to spatial representations. In L. S. Liben, A. H. Patterson, and N. Newcombe, editors, Spatial Representation and Behavior Across the Life Span: Theory and Application, pp. 39–61. New York: Academic Press.

Pick, H. L., Jr., M. R. Heinrichs, D. R. Montello, K. Smith, C. N. Sullivan, and W. B. Thompson. 1995. Topographic map reading. In J. Flach, P. Hancock, J. Caird, and K. Vincente, editors, Global Perspectives on the Ecology of Human-Machine Systems, pp. 255–284. Hillsdale, N.J.: Erlbaum Associates.

Podgorny, P., and R. N. Shepard. 1978. Functional representations common to visual perception and imagination. Journal of Experimental Psychology: Human Perception and Performance 4(1):21–35.

Portugali, J., editor. 1996. The Construction of Cognitive Maps. Dordrecht: Kluwer Academic Publishers.

Rainbird, P. 2004. The Archaeology of Micronesia. Cambridge, U.K.: Cambridge University Press.

Ramsay, J. G., and M. I. Huber. 1987. The Techniques of Modern Structural Geology, Volume 2: Folds and Fractures. New York: Academic Press; Harcourt Brace Jovanovich.

Ray, S., and J. J. Rieser. 2003. Young children can generate dynamic spatial representations from listening to stories. Presentation to the Society for Research in Child Development, Tampa, Fla.

Rehault, J. P., J. Mascle, A. Fabbri, E. Moussat, and M. Thommeret. 1987. The Tyrrhenian Sea before Leg 107. In K. A. Kastens, J. Mascle, C. Auroux, et al., editors, Proceedings of the ODP, Initial Reports 107:23. College Station, Tex.: Ocean Drilling Program.

Reiser, B. J., I. Tabak, W. A. Sandoval, B. K. Smith, F. Steinmuller, and A. J. Leone. 2001. BGuILE: Strategic and conceptual scaffolds for scientific inquiry in biology classrooms. In S. M. Carver and D. Klahr, editors, Cognition and Instruction: Twenty Five Years of Progress, pp. 263–305. Mahwah, N.J.: Erlbaum.

Resnick, M. 1994. Turtles, Termites, and Traffic Jams: Explorations in Massively Parallel Microworlds. Cambridge, Mass.: MIT Press.

Resnick, S. M., S. A. Berenbaum, I. I. Gottesman., and T. J. Bouchard. 1986. Early hormonal influences on cognitive functioning in congenial adrenal hyperplasia. Developmental Psychology 22(2):191–198.

Rhind, D. 1992. Why GIS? ARC News 11(3):1–4.

Rieser, J. J. 2002. Perceptual learning. In J. Guthrie, editor, Encyclopedia of Education. New York: McMillan.

Rigaux, P., M. Scholl, and A. Voissard. 2002. Spatial Databases: With Applications to GIS. San Francisco: Morgan Kaufmann.

Robinson, A. H. 1982. Early Thematic Mapping in the History of Cartography. Chicago: University of Chicago Press.

Rodgers, J. 1990. Fold-and-thrust belts in sedimentary rocks. Part 1: Typical examples. American Journal of Science 290:321–359.

Rodgers, J. 2001. The company I kept, Autobiography of a geologist. Transactions of the Connecticut Academy of Arts & Sciences 58:1–224.

Rönnqvist, L., and C. von Hofsten. 1994. Neonatal finger and arm movements as determined by a social and an object context. Early Development and Parenting 3:81–94.

Rovee-Collier, C., K. Hartshorn, and M. DiRubbo. 1999. Long-term maintenance of infant memory. Developmental Psychobiology 35(2):91–102.

Rumelhart, D. E. 1980. Schemata: The building blocks of cognition. In R. J. Spiro, B. C. Bruce, and W. F. Brewer, editors, Theoretical Issues in Reading Comprehension: Perspectives from Cognitive Psychology, Linguistics, Artificial Intelligence, and Education. Hillsdale, N.J: Erlbaum Associates.

Saguaro Project. Available at http://saguaro.geo.arizona.edu. Accessed on March 23, 2004.

Salthouse, T. A., R. L. Babcock, E. Skovronek, D. R. D. Mitchell, and R. Palmon. 1990. Age and experience effects in spatial visualization. Developmental Psychology 26(1):128–136.

Sameroff, A. J. 1975. Early influences on development: Fact or fancy? Merrill-Palmer-Quarterly 21(4):267–294.

Saucier, D., S. M. Green, J. Leason, A. MacFadden, S. Bell, and L. J. Elias. 2002. Are sex differences in navigation caused by sexually dimorphic strategies or by differences in the ability to use the strategies? Behavioural Neuroscience 116(3):403-410.

Schon, D. A. 1983. The Reflective Practitioner. New York: Basic Books.

Schwartz, D. L. 1999. Physical imagery: Kinematic vs. dynamic models. Cognitive Psychology 38(3):433–464.

Schwartz, D. L., and J. B. Black. 1996. Analog imagery in mental model reasoning: Depictive models. Cognitive Psychology 30(2):154–219.

Schwartz, D. L., and J. D. Bransford. 1998. A time for telling. Cognition and Instruction 16(4):475–522.

Serbin, L.A., and J. M. Connor. 1979. Sex-typing of children's play preferences and patterns of cognitive performance. The Journal of Genetic Psychology 134(2):315–316.

Shea, J. B., and R. L. Morgan. 1979. Contextual interference effects on the acquisition, retention, and transfer of a motor skill. Journal of Experimental Psychology: Human Learning and Memory 5:179–187.

Shekhar S., and S. Chawla. 2003. Spatial Databases: A Tour. Upper Saddle River, N.J.: Prentice Hall.

Shepard, R. 1988. The imagination of the scientist. In K. Egan and D. Nadaner, editors, Imagination and Education, pp. 153–185. New York: Teachers' College Press.

Shepard, R. N. 1984. Ecological constraints on internal representations: Resonant kinematics of perceiving, imaging, thinking, and dreaming. Psychological Review 91:417–447.

Shepard, R. N., and L. A. Cooper. 1982. Mental images and their transformations. Cambridge, Mass.: MIT Press.

Shepard, R. N., and L. Cooper. 1986. Mental images and their transformations. Cambridge, Mass.: MIT Press.

Shepard, R. N., and J. Metzler. 1971. Mental rotation of three-dimensional objects. Science 171(972):701–703.

Shiffrar, M. M., and R. N. Shepard. 1991. Comparison of cube rotations around axes inclined relative to the environment or to the cube. Journal of Experimental Psychology: Human Perception and Performance 17(1):44–54.

Silverman, I., and M. Eals. 1992. Sex differences in spatial ablities: Evolutionary theory and data. In J. H. Barkow, L. Cosmides, and J. Tooby, editors, The Adapted Mind: Evolutionary Psychology and the Generation of Culture, pp. 533–549. Oxford: Oxford University Press.

Simon, H. A. 2001. Observations on the sciences of science learning. Journal of Applied Developmental Psychology 21(1):115–121.

Sims, V. K., and R. E. Mayer. 2002. Domain specificity of spatial expertise: The case of video game players. Applied Cognitive Psychology 16(1):97–115.

Skupin, A., and B. P. Buttenfield. 1996. Spatial Metaphors for Visualizing Very Large Data Archives, pp. 607–617. Proceedings GIS/LIS_96. Bethesda, Md.: American Society for Photogrammetry and Remote Sensing.

Skupin, A., and B. P. Buttenfield. 1997. Spatial Metaphors for Visualizing Information Spaces, pp. 116–125. Proceedings AUTO-CARTO 13. Bethesda, Md.: ACSM/ASPRS.

Slamecka, N. J., and P. Graf. 1978. The generation effect: Delineation of a phenomenon. Journal of Experimental Psychology: Human Learning and Memory 4:592–604.

Smerdon, B., S. Cronen, L. Lanahan, J. Anderson, N. Iannotti, and J. Angeles. 2000. Teachers' Tools for the 21st Century: A Report on Teachers' Use of Technology. NCES 2000–102. Washington, D.C.: National Center for Educational Statistics.

Smith, S., and E. Vela. 2001. Environmental context-dependent memory: A review and meta-analysis. Psychonomic Bulletin and Review 8:203–220.

Smith, S. M, A. M. Glenberg, and R. A. Bjork. 1978. Environmental context and human memory. Memory and Cognition 6(4):342–353.

Snow, J. 1855. On the Mode of Communication of Cholera, 2nd edition. London: Churchill.

Soloway, E., and J. Spohrer, editors. 1989. Studying the Novice Programmer. Hillsdale, N.J.: Erlbaum Associates.

SPACESTARS program. Available at http://www.digitalquest.com. Accessed on March 29, 2004.

Spelke, E. S., and E. L. Newport. 1998. Nativism, empiricism, and the development of knowledge. In R. M. Lerner, editor, Handbook of Child Psychology, Vol. 1: Theoretical Models of Human Development, 5th edition. (Editor-in-Chief: William Damon). New York: John Wiley & Sons.

Steen, L. A. 1988. The science of patterns. Science 240:611–616.

Stein, B. S., and J. D. Bransford. 1979. Constraints on effective elaboration: Effects of precision and subject generation. Journal of Verbal Learning and Verbal Behavior 18(6):769–777.

Sternberg, R. J., editor. 1994. Encyclopedia of Human Intelligence Vols. 1–2. New York: Macmillan.

Sui, D. Z., and M. F. Goodchild. 2001. GIS as media? International Journal of Geographic Information Science 15(5): 387–390.

Suwa, M., and B. Tversky. 1997. What do architects and students perceive in their design sketches? A protocol analysis. Design Studies 18(4):385–403.

Suwa, M., and B. Tversky. 2001. Constructive perception in design. In J. S. Gero and M. L. Maher, editors, Computational and Cognitive Models of Creative Design V, pp. 227–239. Sydney: University of Sydney.

Suwa, M., B. Tversky, J. Gero, and T. Purcell. 2001. Regrouping parts of an external representation as a source of insight. Proceedings of the 3rd International Conference on Cognitive Science, pp. 692–696. Beijing, China: Press of University of Science and Technology of China.

Tarr, M. J., and S. Pinker. 1989. Mental rotation and orientation-dependence in shape recognition. Cognitive Psychology 21(2):233–282.

Technology in Education Research Consortium. 2003. Completed Projects: Mapping Our City. Available at http://www.terc. edu/template/projects_completed/item.cfm?projectid=95. Accessed October 18, 2005.

Tharp, M. 2001. Interview as part of the Oral History Project of the John Heinz III Center for Science, Economics and the Environment. March.

Thomas, H. 1983. Familial correlational analyses, sex differences, and the X-linked gene hypothesis. Psychological Bulletin 93(3):427–440.

Thomas, H., and R. Kail. 1991. Sex differences in speed of mental rotation and the X-linked genetic hypothesis. Intelligence 15(1):17–32.

Tom, A., and M. Denis. 2004. Language and spatial cognition: Comparing the roles of landmarks and street names in route instructions. Applied Cognitive Psychology 18(9):1213–1230.

Tomlin, C. D. 1990. Geographic Information Systems and Cartographic Modeling. Englewood Cliffs, N.J.: Prentice Hall.

Tomlinson, R. 2003. Thinking About GIS: Geographic Information System Planning for Managers. Redlands, Calif.: ESRI Press.

Tversky, B. 1981. Distortions in memory for maps. Cognitive Psychology 13(3):407–433.

Tversky, B. 2000a. Levels and structure of cognitive mapping. In R. Kitchin and S. M. Freundschuh, editors, Cognitive Mapping: Past, Present and Future, pp. 24–43. London: Routledge.

Tversky, B. 2000b. Remembering space. In E. Tulving and F. I. M. Craik, editors, Handbook of Memory, pp. 363–378. New York: Oxford University Press.

Tversky, B. 2001. Spatial schemas in depictions. In M. Gattis, editor, Spatial Schemas and Abstract Thought, pp. 79–111. Cambridge: MIT Press.

Tversky, B. In press. Functional significance of visuospatial representations. In P. Shah and A. Miyake, editors, Handbook of Higher-Level Visuospatial Thinking. Cambridge, U.K.: Cambridge University Press.

Tversky, B. 2003. Navigating by mind and by body. In C. Freksa, W. Brauer, C. Habel, and K. F. Wender, editors, Spatial Cognition III: Routes and Navigation, Human Memory and Learning, Spatial Representation and Spatial Reasoning, pp. 1–10. Berlin: Springer Verlag.

Tversky, B. 2005. Visualspatial reasoning. In K. Holyoak and R. Morrison, editors, The Cambridge Handbook of Thinking and Reasoning, pp. 209–240. Cambridge, U.K.: Cambridge University Press.

Tversky, B., J. B. Morrison, and M. Betrancourt. 2002. Animation: Can it facilitate? International Journal of Human-Computer Studies 57(4):247–262.

University of North Carolina, Chapel Hill, Department of Geological Sciences. Mylonite. Available at http://www.geolab.unc.edu/Petunia/IgMetAtlas/metamicro/mylonite.X.html. Accessed on February 12, 2004.

Unsöld, A. 1969. The New Cosmos. New York: Springer-Verlag.

U.S. Department of Labor. 1991. Secretary's Commission on Achieving Necessary Skills (SCANS) Report for America 2000. Springfield, Va: National Technical Information Service, U.S. Department of Commerce.

Using a Calculator. Available at http://pics.tech4learning.com/details.php?img=calculator1.jpg. Accessed on January 26, 2004.

van Geen, A., Y. Zheng, R. Versteeg, M. Stute, A. Horneman, R. Dhar, M. Steckler, A. Gelman, C. Small, H. Ahsan, J. Graziano, I. Hussein, and K. M. Ahmed. 2003. Spatial variability of arsenic in 6000 tube wells in a 25 km^2 area of Bangladesh. Water Resources Research 39(5):3-1–3-16.

Vandenberg, S. G., and A. R. Kuse. 1979. Spatial ability: A critical review of the sex-linked major gene hypothesis. In M. A. Wittig and A. C. Petersen, editors, Sex-Related Differences in Cognitive Functioning, pp. 67–95. New York: Academic Press.

Von Thunen, J. H. 1826. Der Isolierte Staat in Beziehung auf Landwirtshaft und Nationalökonomie. English translation by C. M. Wartenberg as The Isolated State in Relation to Agriculture in 1966, P. G. Hall, editor. New York: Pergamon Press.

Vrettos, T. 2002. Alexandria: City of the Western Mind. New York: Simon and Schuster.

Vygotsky, L. S. 1978. Interaction between learning and development. In M. Cole, V. John-Steiner, S. Scribner, and E. Souberman, editors, Mind in Society: The Development of Higher Psychological Processes, pp. 79–91. Cambridge, Mass.: Harvard University Press. (Originally published in 1935.)

Ward, S. L., N. Newcombe, and W. F. Overton. 1986. Turn left at the church, or three miles north: A study of direction giving and sex differences. Environment and Behavior 18:192–213.

Watson, J. D., and F. H. C. Crick. 1953. Molecular structure of nucleic acids. Nature 171(4356):737–738.

Weber, A. 1909. Uber den Standort der Industrien. English translation by C. J. Friedrich as Alfred Weber's Theory of the Location of Industries in 1909. Chicago: University of Chicago Press.

Wechsler, D. 1992. Wechsler Intelligence Scale for Children—3rd edition (WISC-III). San Antonio, Tex.: Psychological Corporation.

Wegener, A. 1929. The Origin of Continents and Oceans. London: Methuen.

Wegner, M. V., and D. C. Girasek. 2003. How readable are child safety seat installation instructions? Pediatrics 111(3): 588–591.

Wertenbaker, W. 1974. The Floor of the Sea: Maurice Ewing and the Search to Understand the Earth, p. 144. New York: Little Brown and Company.

Wertheimer, M. 1959. Productive Thinking, enlarged edition. New York: Harper and Row.

Wickens, C. D. 1992. Engineering Psychology and Human Performance. New York: Harper Collins.

Wickens, C. D. 1998. The Future of Air Traffic Control Human Operators and Automation. Washington, D.C.: National Academy Press.

Wickens, C. D., and A. S. Mayor. 1997. Flight to the Future: Human Factors in Air Traffic Control. Washington, D.C.: National Academy Press.

Wills, T. W., S. A. Soraci, R. A. Chechile, and H. A. Taylor. 2000. "Aha" effects in the generation of pictures. Memory and Cognition 28(6):939–948.

Winchester, S. 2001. The Map that Changed the World: William Smith and the Birth of Modern Geology. New York: Harper Collins.

Wiser, M., S. Carey. 1983. When heat and temperature were one. In D. Gentner and A. L. Stevens, editors, Mental Models, pp. 267–298. Hillsdale, N.J.: Erlbaum Associates.

Witkin, H. A., and D. R. Goodenough. 1981. Cognitive Styles: Essence and Origins. New York: International Universities Press.

Witkin, H., P. Oltman, E. Raskin, and S. Karp. 1971. A Manual for the Embedded Figures Tests. Palo Alto, Calif.: Consulting Psychologists Press.

Wittig, M. A., M. Allen, and K. Butler. 1981. Comments on Thomas and Jamison's "A test of the X-linked genetic hypothesis for sex differences on Piaget's water level task." Developmental Review 1(3):284–288.

Worboys, M. F. 1995. GIS: A Computing Perspective. New York: Taylor and Francis.

Workforce Investment Act of 1998, Public Law 105-220, 105th Cong. 7. Title II, Section 203, Number 12, August, 1998.

Wudka, J. Epicycles. Available at http://abyss.uoregon.edu/~js/glossary/ptolemy.html. Accessed October 18, 2005.

Zeiler, M. 1999. Modeling Our World: The ESRI Guide to Geodatabase Design. Redlands, Calif.: ESRI Press.

Appendixes

Appendix A

Biographical Sketches of Committee Members and Staff

Roger M. Downs, *chair*, is currently professor of geography and head of the Department of Geography at The Pennsylvania State University. Previously, he has held a permanent position at the Johns Hopkins University and sabbatical positions at Colgate University, the University of Washington, and the National Geographical Society. He holds B.A. (first class) and Ph.D. degrees from the University of Bristol and has received honors from the National Geographic Society, the Association of American Geographers, and the National Council for Geographic Education. His research interests are in three areas: the development of spatial cognition in children, graphics and wayfinding, and the history and theory of geography education. He has published three books and nearly 100 articles, reports, and reviews.

Sarah Witham Bednarz received her A.B. from Mount Holyoke College, M.A.T. from the University of Chicago, and Ph.D. from Texas A&M University. Dr. Bednarz is associate professor of geography at Texas A&M University. Her research interests focus on learning and teaching geography and related disciplines, particularly on the ways people learn to think spatially using different technologies. In addition, she has published on the implementation of discipline-based education reform and on the application of research to the development of effective science and social science instruction. As one of the primary authors of the national geography standards, she developed the materials on geographic skills as well as other components of the project.

Robert A. Bjork is professor and chair of psychology at University of California, Los Angeles (UCLA). His research focuses on how humans learn and on the implications of that research for instruction. He co-edits *Psychological Science in the Public Interest,* and earlier, he edited *Psychological Review,* and *Memory & Cognition.* His other responsibilities include chairing a National Research Council Committee on Techniques for the Enhancement of Human Performance, serving as president of the American Psychological Society, and chairing the Psychonomic Society. He is a recipient of UCLA's Distinguished Teaching Award and the Distinguished Scientist Lecturer Award of the American Psychological Association.

Peter B. Dow's involvement in education has spanned four decades. He currently serves as president of a newly formed not-for-profit company, First Hand Learning, Inc., an organization dedicated to supporting the implementation of hands-on, experience-based learning environments in schools. He has developed and co-led a number of foundation-supported educational projects, including TEAM 2000, a five-year National Science Foundation Local Systemic Change project that is providing professional development in inquiry-based science to 1,400 K–8 teachers in the Buffalo Public Schools, and Object Lessons, a natural history-based curriculum program for elementary schools funded by the Howard Hughes Medical Institute. His work in educational innovation includes 10 years at the Education Development Center where he served as director of the Social Studies Curriculum Program, and 7 years at the Buffalo Museum of Science where he founded the Center for Science Education. Mr. Dow has served on a number of national advisory boards including the National Research Council's Committee on Science Education K–12, the California Institute of Technology PreCollege Science Initiative, the MACE Project in Las Vegas, the National Science Resources Center, and the Glenn T. Seaborg Center for Teaching and Learning Science and Mathematics in Marquette, Michigan. He has published articles for a variety of educational publications and a book entitled *Schoolhouse Politics: Lessons from the Sputnik Era*, published in 1991. He holds adjunct appointments in the Anthropology Departments at the State University of New York at Buffalo and at Buffalo State College. He attended Harvard University, where he earned a B.A. in history in 1954, a M.A.T. in 1960, and an Ed.D. in 1979.

Kenneth E. Foote is professor and chair of the Geography Department at the University of Colorado at Boulder where he also directs the Center for Geographic Education. He is vice president for research and external relations of the National Council for Geographic Education (NCGE), national councilor of the Association of American Geographers (AAG), NCGE editor of special publications, and a member of the Geography Education National Implementation Project. He is a past editor of the *Journal of Geography in Higher Education* and past chair of the AAG's Commission on College Geography.

J. Freeman Gilbert is a research professor at the Scripps Institution of Oceanography, University of California, San Diego. His research interests include theoretical, inferential, and computational geophysics. He is a member of the National Academy of Sciences, a fellow of the American Academy of Arts and Sciences, American Geophysical Union, and Geological Society of America, and a foreign member (Socio Straniero) of the Accademia Nazionale dei Lincei. He is one of the founders of the San Diego Supercomputer Center and the National Partnership for Advanced Computational Infrastructure, sponsored by the National Science Foundation.

Reginald G. Golledge is professor of geography at the University of California, Santa Barbara. His research interests are in behavioral geography, disaggregate transportation modeling, spatial cognition, cognitive mapping, individual decision making, household activity patterns, geographic education, and the acquisition and use of spatial knowledge across the life span. His research has included work on adults, children, teenagers, mentally retarded persons, and adventitious and congenitally blind people. He has published extensively in the literature of several fields including geography, regional science, and psychology. He was awarded an Association of American Geographers Academic Honors Award in 1981 and the Institute of Australian Geographers International gold medal in 1999. He was a Guggenheim fellow in 1987–1988. He is an honorary lifetime member of the Institute of Australian Geographers and a fellow of the American Association for the Advancement of Science. He has been associate editor and editor of *Geographical Analysis* and founding co-editor of *Urban Geography*. He has served on editorial boards of the *Annals of* *the Association of American Geographers*, the *Professional Geographer*, *Tijdschrift Voor Economische en Sociale Geografie*, *Environment and Behavior*, and the *Journal of Spatial Cognition and Computation*.

Kim A. Kastens is a senior research scientist at the Lamont-Doherty Earth Observatory of Columbia University. She holds a bachelor's degree in geology and geophysics from Yale University, and a Ph.D. in oceanography from the Scripps Institution of Oceanography (University of California at San Diego). Her training and early career were in marine geology. She participated in or led 27 oceanographic cruises, most of which involved mapping the seafloor and interpreting the tectonic and sedimentary processes that shaped it. She has published maps of the Tamayo Transform Fault, Clipperton Transform Fault, Vema Fracture Zone, Mississippi Fan, Ebro Fan, and Mediterranean Ridge. Over the past five years, Kastens' professional interests have shifted to geoscience education, geoscience education research, and instructional technology. She designed and produced *Where Are We?* educational software and curricula for helping elementary school children learn to "translate" from the visually perceived terrain around them to a map of that same terrain. She is currently leading the collection-building effort of the Digital Library for Earth System Education.

Gaea Leinhardt is senior scientist at the Learning Research and Development Center and professor, School of Education, University of Pittsburgh. She received her B.A. and M.S.T. from the University of Chicago and her Ph.D. from the University of Pittsburgh. Over the past 25 years she has conducted innovative and rigorous quantitative and qualitative research in classroom discourse, instructional processes, and subject-matter instruction and learning. She has engaged in fine-grained cognitive analysis of classroom phenomena that has led to the development of a model of instructional explanation, a model tested in both computer simulations and instruction in geography as well as mathematics and history. Her evaluation work has ranged from large-scale studies of federally funded programs (such as Title I) to state-level and local programs. Her current research interests focus on how people learn in museum-like settings; how learning best occurs in web-based environments; and how teachers can be supported in learning what they need to teach well in classrooms. As the lead evaluator for the Open Learning Initiative at CMU and consulting advisor to the evaluation of MIT's OCW she has been engaged in designing complex multilayered evaluations and developing models for innovative evaluation use. She has published over 150 articles in major educational research journals (e.g., *American Educational Research Journal*, *Cognition and Instruction*, *Journal of Geography*), and she is the co-editor of three books (*Analysis of Arithmetic for Mathematics Teaching*, 1992; *Teaching and Learning in History*, 1994; and *Learning Conversations in Museums*, 2002) and co-author of *Listening in on Museum Conversations* (2004). She has been a fellow at the Center for the Advanced Study in the Behavioral Sciences at Stanford and has won awards from the American Federation of Teachers, American Educational Research Association, and the National Council on Geographic Education; serves on several journals' editorial advisory boards; and has been a member of several National Research Council panels on education.

Lynn S. Liben is currently distinguished professor of psychology at The Pennsylvania State University, where she previously served as head of the Department of Psychology and director of the Child Study Center. She is a fellow of the American Psychological Association (APA) and the American Psychological Society, former president of the Developmental Psychology Division of APA, and former president of the Jean Piaget Society. Dr. Liben is former editor of the *Journal of Experimental Child Psychology*, and is currently the editor-in-chief of *Child Development*. She holds a B.A. from Cornell and a Ph.D. from the University of Michigan. Her work has focused on the development of spatial cognition and representational understanding, and the application of this work to formal and informal education in Earth sciences and in the graphic arts. She has also conducted research on sex-related differences in spatial skills and geographic knowledge and has directed research grants and published widely on these topics.

Marcia C. Linn is professor of cognition and education at the University of California at Berkeley. Her research focuses on the role of sex differences in cognition and the use of the web and the Internet to facilitate science education in school and museum contexts. She is a fellow of the American Association for the Advancement of Science, the American Psychological Association, and the Center for Advanced Study in Behavioral Sciences. She received the first Award for Excellence in Educational Research from the Council of Scientific Society Presidents.

John J. Rieser is currently professor in the Department of Psychology and Human Development at Vanderbilt University. He received his B.A. from Harvard, and after teaching secondary sciences and mathematics in Botswana, earned his Ph.D. from the University of Minnesota. A fellow of the American Psychological Association, he has served as associate editor of *Developmental Psychology*, and a member of the NSF's Review Panel on Cognition and Perception, and he recently finished two terms as chair of his department. His research is about dynamic space perception and spatial orientation of infants, children, and adults. It is aimed at understanding how objects and environments are perceived, imagined, and acted on in contexts that involve solutions to practical problems involving wayfinding, navigating in virtual environments, and understanding science and math problems.

Gerald M. Stokes is the director of the Joint Global Change Research Institute, a collaborative effort between the Pacific Northwest National Laboratory (PNNL) and the University of Maryland. Previously he served as an associate laboratory director at PNNL, responsible for the Environmental and Health Sciences Division, the basic research division of PNNL. He also has held a variety of other scientific and management positions during his 27-year tenure at PNNL. He served as the chief scientist of the Department of Energy's Atmospheric Radiation Measurement program from 1990 to 1998. He has served previously on the National Committee on Science Education Standards and Assessment. He holds a B.A. in physics from the University of California at Santa Cruz and both a Ph.D. and a Master's in astronomy and astrophysics from the University of Chicago. His research interests include climate and the design of large-scale field research facilities. He has authored or co-authored more than 80 book chapters, journal articles, and reports on topics ranging from the interstellar medium to atmospheric spectroscopy, energy utilization, and climate policy.

Barbara Tversky is professor of psychology at Stanford University. After completing a Ph.D. in cognitive psychology at the University of Michigan, she taught at Hebrew University in Jerusalem before coming to Stanford. Her research focuses on spatial thinking and language, event cognition, memory, and categorization with applications to education, Human-Computer Interaction, eyewitness testimony, and cross-cultural research. She is a fellow of the Cognitive Science Society, and the American Psychological Society, is on the Governing Board of the Psychonomic and Cognitive Science Societies, and is a member of NRC's U.S. National Committee for the International Union of Psychological Sciences. She designed a prize-winning package of classic experiments in cognition, received a Phi Beta Kappa Teaching Award, and has served on the editorial boards of eight journals.

National Research Council Staff

Anthony R. de Souza is currently director of the Board on Earth Sciences and Resources at the National Research Council in Washington, D.C. Previously, he was executive director of the National Geography Standards Project, secretary general of the 27th International Geographical Union Congress, editor of *National Geographic Research & Exploration*, and editor of the *Journal of Geography*. He has held positions as a professor and as a visiting teacher and scholar at the George Washington University, University of Wisconsin-Eau Claire, University of Minnesota, University of California-Berkeley, and University of Dar es Salaam in Tanzania. He has served as a member of NRC committees. He holds B.A. (honors) and Ph.D. degrees from the University of Reading in England and has received numerous honors and awards, including the Medalla al Benito Juarez in 1992 and the Gilbert Grosvenor honors award from the Association of American Geographers in 1996. His research interests include the processes and mechanisms of economic development and human-environment relationships. He has published several books and more than 100 articles, reports, and reviews.

Appendix B

Oral Presentations and Written Statements

Heather Annulis, School of Engineering Technology, The University of Southern Mississippi, Hattiesburg

Thomas J. Baerwald, Geography and Regional Science, The National Science Foundation, Arlington, Virginia

Thomas R. Baker, Geography Department, University of Kansas

Dan Barstow, Exploring Earth Project, Technology in Education Research Consortium, Cambridge, Massachusetts

Osa Brand, Educational Affairs, Association of American Geographers, Washington, D.C.

Ines Cifuentes, Carnegie Academy of Science Education, Washington, D.C.

Kimberly A. Crews, Census 2000 Publicity Office, U.S. Census Bureau, Washington, D.C.

Brian DeAtley, Workforce Development, Information Technology Association of America, Arlington, Virginia

Brendan Dooher, Lawrence Livermore National Laboratory, Livermore, California

Dick Farnsworth, Edward Teller Education Center, University of California, Davis, Livermore

Charlie Fitzpatrick, Environmental Systems Research Institute (ESRI) Schools and Libraries, St. Paul, Minneapolis

Ted Habermann, National Geophysical Data Center, National Oceanic and Atmospheric Administration, Boulder, Colorado

Michelle Hall-Wallace, Department of Geosciences, The University of Arizona, Tucson

Eddie Hanebuth, Digital Quest, Inc., Ridgeland, Mississippi

Mary Hegarty, Department of Psychology, University of California, Santa Barbara

J.J. Helly, San Diego Computing Center, University of California, San Diego

Joseph J. Kerski, U.S. Geological Survey, Denver, Colorado

Keith R. Krueger, Consortium for School Networking, Washington, D.C.

George Leggett, Workforce Development: Mississippi Space Commerce Initiative, Stennis Space Center, Mississippi

David Maguire, Environmental Systems Research Institute, Redlands, California

Bill Miller, Environmental Systems Research Institute, Redlands, California

Stephanie Powers, National School to Work Office, U.S. Department of Education, Washington, D.C.

Martha Sharma, The National Cathedral School, Washington, D.C.

Brigitte Valesey, Center to Advance the Teaching of Technology and Science, International Technology Education Association, Reston, Virginia

Ming-Ying Wei, Commercial and Educational Division, National Aeronautics and Space Administration, Headquarters, Washington, D.C.

White Paper Contributors

Thomas R. Baker, Center for Research on Learning, University of Kansas, Lawrence

Mark N. Gahegan, Department of Geography, The Pennsylvania State University, University Park

Carol Gersmehl, Department of Geography, Macalester College, St. Paul, Minnesota

Philip J. Gersmehl, Department of Geography, University of Minnesota, Minneapolis

Michael Goodchild, Department of Geography, University of California, Santa Barbara

Marilyn Malone, Barrington, Rhode Island

Anita Palmer, Dallas, Texas

Christine L. Voigt, McKinney, Texas

Appendix C

Individual Differences in Spatial Thinking: The Effects of Age, Development, and Sex

Differences in domain-specific expertise are not the only way of characterizing distinctions among learners. This appendix addresses other ways in which differences among learners are relevant for spatial thinking. It begins by discussing the notion of learner differences in general, and then considers the links between learner characteristics and spatial thinking. In turn the roles of three factors are discussed: chronological age, developmental level, and biological sex and cultural gender.

CONCEPTUALIZING DIFFERENCES AMONG LEARNERS

At any given moment, a learner approaches a learning situation with particular skills, knowledge, experience, talents, motivation, and so on. These factors may affect the degree to which—and perhaps even the *way* in which—the learner acquires new knowledge and skills, and thus develops expertise. How can we understand the basis for differences among learners in general?

First, and contrary to common interpretations of statements about such differences, to argue that individuals differ in what they bring to a learning situation at a particular moment in no way prejudges the origins or causal explanations of those differences. For example, consider the observation that Learner A has better mental rotation skills than Learner B, and the suggestion that, as a result, Learner A can more easily imagine what a rock formation seen from one vantage point would look like from another. This statement says nothing about *why* Learner A has better mental rotation skills as he or she encounters a new learning opportunity. Explanations might include (1) biological mechanisms (e.g., genetic inheritance of talent); (2) experiential mechanisms (e.g., a history of differential experience with building toys such as Tinker Toys or model airplanes, both of which would be expected to call upon and hence develop mental rotation skills); and (3) biological-environmental interactions (e.g., differential inherited talents that are channeled differently depending upon environmental socialization practices).

Second, and again contrary to common interpretations, statements about differences among individuals (e.g., in their performance on a spatial abilities test such as the Block Design test of the Wechsler Intelligence Scale for Children; see Wechsler, 1992) or between groups of individuals (e.g., relative performance of males versus females or of older versus younger children) in no way prejudge the *immutability* of those differences. To continue with the example of mental rotation, the statement that Learner A has better mental rotation skills than Learner B says nothing about whether or not Learner B's mental rotation skills might be improved (e.g., through repetition) to be just as good as Learner A's.

Third, a statement about a difference between two learners on one specific skill need not imply something about the availability of another skill. Thus, although Learner B may be less adept than Learner A with respect to rotating a visual image mentally, Learner B may be more skilled in using a different strategy that may be just as effective (e.g., reasoning verbally about the relative locations of different sections of the geological formation).

In short, a statement about differential abilities or strategies carries no implications that differences are inherent (the first point), fixed (the second point), or pervasive (the third point).

Fourth, differences among learners may be considered either at the level of "group differences" or at the level of "individual differences." The observation that there are group differences with respect to spatial learning means that—on average—groups differ in their level of or strategies for spatial thinking. Groups may be defined along a virtual infinity of dimensions: for example, biological sex (boys versus girls; men versus women), educational focus (e.g., engineering versus education majors), chronological age (e.g., elementary versus middle school students), or socioeconomic background (e.g., children from professional versus working class backgrounds). A statement that there are "significant group differences" merely means that, overall, one group performs differently than the other group, and that statistical analyses show the observed differences are unlikely to be attributed to chance, but are instead reliable differences.

Even when groups do differ significantly, it is almost never the case that every single member of one group differs from every single member of the other group on the relevant characteristic. In real life, distributions overlap. For example, consider group membership defined by biological sex with respect to two variables, first, a familiar and uncontroversial one, physical height. On average, men are taller than women. However, among the group of men, some are short; among the group of women, some are tall so that a particular man may well be shorter than a particular woman. Thus, if we want to know the relative heights of a pair comprised of one man and one woman, we would be better off actually measuring them than we would simply assuming that the man was the taller of the two.

The identical reasoning holds for a second, potentially more controversial, variable—the ability to rotate mental images of two- or three-dimensional shapes. Again, at the group level of analysis, on average, boys perform better on tests of mental rotation than do girls, on average (e.g., Linn and Petersen, 1985). Nevertheless, many individual girls perform better than many individual boys. Thus, if one were planning to teach some spatial concept that would be taught differently depending on the level of the learner's mental rotation skills, it would be misguided to assume that all boys should get one form of instruction and all girls should get another. Rather, different instructional methods should be assigned to children based on a direct measure of mental rotation ability, not on the basis of their biological sex.

Similar reasoning holds for other differences between or among groups, including those related to chronological age. For example, on average, first-grade children may be expected to find it more difficult than fifth-grade children to employ projective spatial concepts (see Piaget and Inhelder, 1956). Yet a given first-grader may be particularly advanced and a given fifth-grader may be particularly delayed with respect to that mastery. As a result, decisions about the best ways to teach individual learners are better informed by obtaining information about specific prerequisite skills or concepts than by knowing chronological age alone. Alternatively, one may find means of presenting material at multiple levels of complexity and with multiple strategies so that the material will be appropriate for learners who have a range of strengths.

Research on individual differences is focused on the variability in performance that exists across the members of any group. Within a group defined by one or more dimensions (e.g., all first-grade boys), not everyone performs identically. Furthermore, if more than one skill is relevant for a learning task, the profiles of skills may vary from child to child. One boy might have relatively poor mental rotation skills but an excellent sense of his body in physical space, whereas another boy might have the reverse profile.

THE CONCEPT OF GROUP DIFFERENCES

Given the variability among individuals within any kind of group (such as those defined by the learner's biological sex or age), why should one bother with identifying differences at the level of groups? There are several reasons why it is useful to identify patterns of skills and behaviors across groups, even though knowledge of these group differences can provide only probabilistic information about the characteristics of any given learner.

The first reason is practical and stems from the way educational systems are structured. In particular, the two dimensions along which spatial skills and abilities are most commonly examined in psychological research—chronological age and gender—are also the dimensions along which many educational opportunities are differentiated.

Of the two, chronological age is more pervasive in the American education system. With few exceptions (e.g., in very small school districts or home schooling), most education is delivered in age-segregated schools and classrooms. Educational distinctions also occur with respect to gender despite the fact that there are no longer divisions between required curricula for boys and girls as was once the case (girls were required to take home economics, boys were required to take shop, and neither group was allowed into the other's classes). Nevertheless, proportions of males and females enrolled in elective subjects (e.g., computer science) continue to differ. Furthermore, private and public schools may offer intentional opportunities for single-sex classes, and even in classrooms containing students of both sexes, educational experiences may differ if not by design then by practice (as when disproportionate numbers of boys are found at classroom computers).

Although group membership will not ensure that every member of the group has a particular set of characteristics, knowledge of group membership is useful, given that it is—for practical reasons—impossible to measure individuals on every relevant dimension. In the absence of individually administered assessments of relevant variables, knowledge of group characteristics can provide hints about what kinds of experiences and skills learners bring to a new educational situation. However, the predictive power of gender, for example, is insufficient to use gender alone as a basis for recommending differential educational opportunities (see Box C.1).

A second reason to identify group differences is that they may suggest factors that account for individuals' development of different or better spatial skills and strategies. This knowledge could, in turn, provide educational guidance as to learning strategies that might be easier and/or more effective. Thus, the finding that spatial skills or strategies are *not* randomly distributed across groups may be useful in identifying what kinds of factors account for differential outcomes. For example, if boys as a group do better than girls as a group in learning to assemble car motors, we can look for differences between boys and girls that are potentially relevant. We might find that boys, on average, have been given 10 times more model cars to put together during childhood than have girls. We might hypothesize that something that helps people figure out how pieces of motors fit together is "model experience." To test this hypothesis, we could examine whether those girls who were given model cars to assemble during childhood do better at assembling car motors than do girls who were not given model cars. Of course, an affirmative answer would not prove the causal connection because it could be that children with better spatial skills begged for, and

---

BOX C.1
Use of the Terms Sex and Gender

The words "sex" and "gender" are differentiated by some scholars. Those who make a distinction usually argue that the term sex should be used to refer to biological sex (i.e., whether an individual is biologically male or female), whereas gender should be used to refer to societal variables and influences (i.e., to culturally defined characteristics, such as masculine or feminine identity or the degree to which an individual endorses gender-related attitudes of the culture). At first glance, one might assume that the former is a clean, dichotomous distinction, whereas the latter is a fuzzy, continuous one. However, in actuality, both sex-related and gender-related characteristics fall along a continuum. At the biological level, within groups of genetically male or genetically female individuals (i.e., those who have XY versus XX sex chromosomes), there is, for example, variation with respect to the amount of exposure to androgen and estrogen experienced during prenatal development or with respect to the quantity of sex steroids circulating during adolescence (e.g., see Liben and Bigler, 2002). At the societal level, individuals within such groups vary in the degree to which they self-identify or are identified by others as being representative of societal gender roles, as illustrated by the concept of "tomboys." Typically, respondents self-report, or researchers judge, physical features of participants to assign them to categories variously labeled as "boy or girl," "man or woman," or "male or female." It is rare that either biological sex or cultural gender is actually *measured* (e.g., by assessing relative amounts of circulating sex hormones or asking respondents to complete some measure of self-endorsement of culturally masculine and feminine traits). Because it is rare that investigators actually use these measures and because there are complex interconnections between biological and social constructs, the distinction between the terms sex and gender is not always a clean one. In general, the word sex is used to distinguish between males and females, with gender reserved for distinctions linked to culturally defined roles, but the boundaries are admittedly not sharp ones.

---

received, more model cars than did children with worse spatial skills. Additional support for the hypothesized link could come from research demonstrating that individuals randomly assigned to receive model-building experience later perform better on motor-assembly tasks than do individuals not given that experience.

THE VALUE OF STUDYING GROUP AND INDIVIDUAL DIFFERENCES

In summary there are several reasons for studying group and individual differences. First, they remind us that different learners approach tasks with different skills and experience and, hence, it is important to provide a range of educational opportunities. Second, they are valuable for suggesting hypotheses about the kinds of experiences that might promote spatial skills, and results from testing those hypotheses would be useful for the basic scientific study of learning and for the application of that science to the design of educational interventions. Throughout these efforts, it is, of course, important to remember that acknowledging group or individual differences in no way implies anything about either their origins or their immutability. Thus, rather than shying away from the identification of differences in the ease with which learners develop and apply spatial thinking to new learning challenges or in the types of strategic approaches that are employed, we should catalogue and understand these differences. In keeping with this position, the committee turns first to discussions of group differences concerning age and sex. The former was selected because much of our educational system is age based; the latter, because gender differences in spatial skills have often been observed (Linn and Petersen, 1985).

THE ROLES OF CHRONOLOGICAL AGE AND DEVELOPMENTAL LEVEL, AND THE CONCEPT OF EDUCATIONAL APPROPRIATENESS

The Role of Chronological Age. As is apparent from our age-graded educational system, chronological age is an important characteristic for many aspects of thinking and learning. As a group, older children are generally better prepared for learning more complex ideas and skills than younger children. Indeed, one way of thinking about very young children is that they are "universal novices" (Brown and DeLoache, 1978, p. 14). Growing older translates into becoming increasingly better prepared to acquire knowledge and understanding. As a result, when exposed to the same lessons or experiences, older learners are generally prepared to learn more from the experience than are younger learners.

Conceptualizing Developmentally Appropriate Education. Many educators and scholars have used the term "developmentally appropriate" to capture the notion that educational efforts should take age-linked changes into account. At this level of generality, the committee endorses the importance of the notion (also captured by the phrase *"educationally appropriate"*). It is important to caution, however, that the term developmentally appropriate has often been assigned extremely narrow meanings in developmental psychology and education. Thus, we must clarify what we do and do not mean when we suggest that learners of different ages have typically moved to different points along the novice-to-expert path.

From the perspective of developmental psychology, the committee means that age is an excellent predictor of how advanced an individual is in a variety of arenas—physical, cognitive, and social. It does *not*, however, mean that simple chronological age itself *determines* that level of preparation. Thus, for example, the committee is not suggesting that every child of age *X* is unprepared to learn concept *Y*. It would argue that there are some developmental constraints to learning: some aspects of understanding evolve gradually and sequentially. However, there is usually a broad range of possibility within any given age. From the perspective of education, the committee does mean that a developmentally appropriate curriculum takes the learner's preparedness into account in what and how it teaches. It does *not* mean that structured, teacher-directed programs that follow a relatively fixed sequence (as opposed to child-directed, "discovery learning" approaches) are necessarily doomed to failure, a way in which developmentally appropriate has often been interpreted in education (see Golbeck, 2001, for a discussion of this controversy in early childhood education).

Developmental Theories and Learning. Of the theoretical perspectives that are useful for conceptualizing developmentally appropriate learning, the committee focuses on three that have the broadest application and impact: those of Vygotsky, Piaget, and Bruner.

Vygotsky (1935, 1978) focused on children's cognitive development within the broader social context. More specifically, he suggested that at any given point in development, a child might evidence one level of skill independently, but with appropriate supports by the surrounding social context, the same child could show a higher level of functioning than had first been evident. For example, parents, teachers, or even peers might act as supports to extend the child's functioning. Supports would help to push toward the higher end of what that child is positioned to accomplish— what Vygotsky called the *zone of proximal development*.

Piaget (1970) offered similar ideas in his concepts of assimilation and accommodation. He argued that as the child encounters new experiences that go beyond existing levels of understanding, the existing concepts are stretched. Later investigators demonstrated the viability of using these ideas to facilitate learning (e.g., Inhelder et al., 1974).

Bruner (1960) proposed a "spiral curriculum" that "respects the ways of thought of the growing child." Although he argued that instruction needed to be appropriate to the child's logical abilities available at any given time, he also argued that "any subject can be taught effectively in some intellectually honest form to any child at any stage of development." Thus, the same subject should be introduced early but reintroduced repeatedly in later grades. Again, consistent with the point about the imperfect relation between intellectual progress and chronological age was Bruner's point that

> [t]he intellectual development of the child is no clockwork sequence of events; it also responds to influences from the environment, notably the school environment. Thus instruction in scientific ideas, even at the elementary level, need not follow slavishly the natural course of cognitive development in the child. It can also lead to intellectual development by providing challenging but usable opportunities for the child to forge ahead in his development. (Bruner, 1960 p. 147)

These developmental theories converge on three points: (1) children engage their current levels of understanding as they encounter new material; (2) the process of encountering new material can result not only in the child's acquiring knowledge about the topic at hand (e.g., information about plate tectonics and earthquakes) but also in the child's coming to understand broader conceptual principles and skills (e.g., understanding how to interpret spatial representations to show sequential states of some phenomenon); and (3) although cognitive functioning increases with age, this increase is not some precise, fixed, overdetermined function of the child's chronological age, but rather the result of complex interactions among organismic and experiential factors.

Age-Linked Spatial Development. The argument concerning age-linked (but not chronologically locked) changes in cognitive growth also applies to changes in spatial thinking. Certain kinds of spatial thinking are exhibited more uniformly by children at older ages than by children at younger ages. Again, however, within any age group there can be vast differences among children with respect to how far they have progressed in their spatial development.

For example, children were asked to show where someone was standing in their classroom by placing stickers on a map of the classroom (Liben and Downs, 1993). Much as often occurs with "you-are-here" maps (Levine et al., 1984), in one condition the map was out of alignment with the room. In unaligned conditions, people must reconcile different frames of reference (one being their own bodily experience in the space; the other being the frame of reference as defined on the map). Based on six items, the average correct numbers for children in grades K, 1, 2, and 5, respectively, were 1.3, 3.2, 4.1, and 5.1. Clearly, performance improved with age. However, these summaries of mean performance at the group level obscure the marked range in performance within each age group. For example, 18 percent of kindergarten children performed perfectly or nearly perfectly (six or five correct items), despite the low average performance of the kindergarten group as a whole. There remain controversies about whether children of a given age who do not demonstrate some kind of spatial thinking (reconciling frames of reference in the map example) are actually incapable of that kind of thinking. An alternative is that they have the skill, but are unable to demonstrate it on some particular task. Examples of this issue abound in work on spatial thinking in infancy. To illustrate, some developmental psychologists (e.g., Piaget, 1954) suggested that it is only gradually and through self-directed interactions with the physical world that infants come to link self body space with external space. This view is compatible with observations that in the first months of life, infants have difficulty in reaching out for and grabbing objects accurately (e.g., Pick and Lockman, 1981). Others (e.g., Spelke and Newport, 1998), however, have argued that fundamental spatial concepts are part of human infants' biological endowment. Recent work has shown that infants' skills may indeed be demonstrated early once the motor (or physical) demands of the task are reduced. Rönnqvist and von Hofsen (1994) showed that 2-day-old infants are able to make sweeping motions toward moving objects that are in synchrony with the objects' trajectories, even though infants at this age are completely unable to grasp moving objects.

Despite the debate over the levels of spatial thinking available during infancy, well before they enter preschool, children have mastered basic spatial relations in physical space, understanding notions such as *on, in, and into*, and understanding how to effect skilled movements in space. What remains less well developed by school entry are skills in manipulating mental or graphic spatial representations. Again, ongoing research is aimed at learning whether young children are completely unable to use certain conceptual systems in their spatial thinking (such as flexibility in frame of reference in the mapping example) or instead they simply have difficulty implementing them in particular tasks. Irrespective of which position one endorses, or which ultimately turns out to be more widely accepted, many more younger children than older children find certain kinds of spatial thinking challenging. What are some of the ways in which spatial thinking develops during the K–12 period?

Theoretical Approaches to Spatial Development. There are many ways in which spatial thinking becomes increasingly advanced in most children as they move from early, to middle, to late childhood. There is no one theory of spatial development that captures all relevant progressions, and therefore, this appendix merely samples ways in which age-linked changes in spatial thinking have been conceptualized. When taken together, theory and empirical work have identified a number of general spatial thinking skills and concepts that are relevant for education in specific domains (including but not limited to GIS).

One of the earliest and most far-reaching ways of describing the development of spatial thinking is Piaget and Inhelder's (1956) book, *The Child's Conceptualization of Space*. Piaget and Inhelder focus on the spatial concepts that children are able to understand and think about. They suggest that children initially understand topological concepts such as *in, on, next to, between, open*, and *closed*. Children at this developmental level (generally preschoolers) are, for example, able to distinguish open from closed figures (e.g., a *U* from a circle) but cannot distinguish figures that differ only metrically (e.g., a square from a trapezoid). Children at this stage are unaware of point of view and, as a consequence, are unable to distinguish how a scene would appear if one approached it from one side rather than from the other side.

Beginning in early elementary school years, and developing gradually through adolescence, children are said to master projective and Euclidean concepts. With an understanding of point of view, children are able to understand projections (thus, for example, to understand and represent ways that cast shadows change as an object is rotated, or to predict the shapes of cross sections made by slicing three-dimensional objects) (see Box C.2). Likewise, children can understand Euclidean representations—for example, using a Cartesian coordinate system to represent physical phenomena (e.g., the surface of the liquid is horizontal). Although subsequent research has placed serious doubt on characterizing spatial cognition as following a fixed, age-linked trajectory from topological to projective and Euclidean thinking, it has confirmed that the kinds of concepts studied by Piaget and Inhelder do challenge individuals throughout childhood and adolescence.

Newcombe and Huttenlocher (2000) present a conceptualization of the development of spatial thinking. Their work focuses on spatial location, and they present data showing that even infants are sensitive to metric information about location. Furthermore, they suggest that the kinds of processes used by young children to represent locations are fundamentally similar to those used by adults. These processes include identifying locations in relation to some space or landmark (similar to the concepts of *near* or *next to* in the topological formulation by Piaget and Inhelder) and then fine-tuning precise location (similar to the metric concepts discussed under Euclidean spatial understanding).

Both Piaget and Inhelder and Newcombe and Huttenlocher, however, characterize the child's developing understanding of space as resting on a general, categorical system (e.g., in regions, or near landmarks) as well as on a fine-tuned metric system. Furthermore, embedded within the approaches is another important component of spatial development—the use of alternative frames of reference. In Piaget and Inhelder's formulation, frame of reference is most explicit in the discussion of projective spatial concepts. It is, for example, tapped by the "three-mountains task" in which children are asked to identify what is seen by someone observing the model mountains from a different vantage point. In Newcombe and Huttenlocher's work, frame of reference is tapped when a child must figure out where to search for an object after moving to the opposite side of the room from where the child was when the object was being hidden. Again, we have to resolve the question of how early children are able to put aside their egocentric frame of reference to answer questions such as these, but it is clear that tasks involving conflicts across frames of reference are more demanding and difficult, and lead to multiple errors. Thus, in the case of misaligned you-are-here maps (Levine et al., 1984), even adults commonly walk in the wrong direction when the maps are not aligned with the environment, a situation that requires an understanding of alternative frames of reference.

These examples of how spatial development has been conceptualized are based on conceptual analyses of what spatial tasks demand, and on theories that explore how abilities to meet such demands change with age in concert with general cognitive progressions. An alternative approach to characterizing spatial development is one in which individuals are given a wide-ranging, diverse assortment of spatial tasks and their responses are analyzed statistically to reveal the implicit, underlying structure of component spatial skills. Insofar as tasks are given to individuals of different ages, the data allow for cataloging age-linked differences in levels of performance as well as the underlying structure of component spatial skills.

An illustration of this approach is the "psychometric testing" movement (Eliot, 1987) that began in the early part of the twentieth century, inspired less by theoretical goals than by practical ones. The practical concerns focused on finding ways to make decisions such as which people should be allowed to enter the United States as immigrants, which children should be steered toward academic education and which toward vocational education, who should be institutionalized, and who should be inducted into the armed forces. Tests of intellectual capacity and functioning were developed, and by amassing large data sets from people who took various tests, psychometricians catalogued age norms against which an individual's performance could be judged. People's performance on these tasks was analyzed (e.g., via factor analysis) to identify subcomponents of intellectual functioning. Significant from the perspective of spatial thinking is that some kind of spatial component emerged from analyses of virtually every intelligence test (Sternberg, 1994). More recently, "spatial intelligence" is included in the "Theory of Multiple Intelligences" proposed by Gardner (1983) that serves as a foundation for many contemporary educational programs. Much of the psychometric study of spatial intelligence or spatial abilities has been directed to identifying specific components of the broader category (e.g., French et al., 1963; Lohman, 1979) and then linking the more specific abilities to specific educational and occupational decisions.

As a broad generalization, and as may be seen from age-reported normative data for performance on these tasks, overall, performance improves over the K–12 period. Patterns of performance on separate components of spatial skills may also be used to examine the second kind of group difference, that linked to sex of learners.

GROUP DIFFERENCES: BIOLOGICAL SEX AND CULTURAL GENDER

Sex Differences in Spatial Performance: Descriptions

As noted above, factor analytic studies typically reveal subcomponents of spatial skills. In a study addressed to both developmental and sex-related issues, Linn and Petersen (1985) combined an analytical approach of this kind (i.e., a data-driven approach) with a conceptual analysis of what particular spatial tasks appear to demand of the respondent. Their work has thus been seminal both in the identification of component spatial skills and in the identification of sex differences within

BOX C.2
Shadow Projection Task

A dramatic illustration of the incomplete association between chronological age and spatial performance comes from research using a "shadow projection task," originally developed by Piaget and Inhelder (1956) as one method to study children's developing projective spatial concepts. In this task, children were asked to predict (through drawings or via selections among response alternatives) the shadows that would be cast on a screen if a light source were directed at an object. Of particular interest were children's predictions about shadows as the object was systematically rotated. Illustrative is a pencil that was initially positioned so that the side of the pencil was in the path of the light (thus casting a rectangular, horizontal line-like shadow) and then gradually rotated toward the light source so that the shadow line became shorter, and eventually became a small circle (once the light source directly faced the pencil point or pencil eraser end). Protocols from children under 9 or 10 years of age were used to demonstrate that young children have difficulty in using projective geometry to represent spatial transformations. For example, "knowing" that pencils are long and thin made it difficult for young children ever to give up the idea that the shadow would be line like.

Although the original reports suggested that children gradually and universally mastered projective spatial concepts and hence performed well on the shadow projection task, later research with an adult college population (Merriwether and Liben, 1997) demonstrates that many adults (more women than men) have the same kinds of difficulties on the shadow projection task that Piaget and Inhelder (1956) had reported for children some 40 years earlier. For example, adults were asked to draw the cast shadow of 10-mm-thick plastic shapes—circular, triangular, and hexagonal—when the shape was rotated 30, 60, and 90 degrees towards and away from the screen. Adults of both sexes averaged only about one correct answer for the 30 and 60 degree rotations, and although most males were generally correct (in about five of the six trials) on the 90 degree rotation (which casts a simple thick line [rectangular] shadow), females fared far worse (averaging only about three of six correct). Furthermore, the errors were not trivial. Figure C.1, from Downs and Liben (1991), shows three participants' responses. These data provide a striking illustration of the point that just as some young children succeed especially well on spatial tasks (as in the classroom location and direction task), some adults appear to have difficulty in visualizing or representing events that draw on spatial concepts.

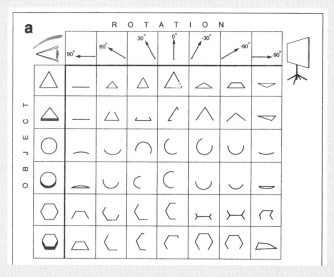

(a) Examples of college student's responses to the shadow projection drawing task. A response pattern characterized by (1) the use of incomplete outlines to depict the effect of rotation; (2) the preservation of defining features of the unrotated form; (3) an asymmetrical distinction based on the direction of rotation; and (4) a failure to depict the base of the thick form. The subject shows little understanding of shadows even in the upright case.

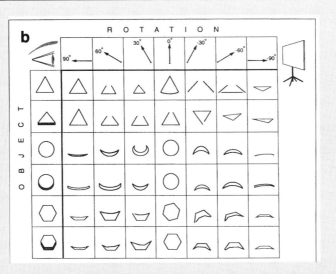

(b) A response pattern characterized by (1) the preservation of defining features of the unrotated form; (2) a largely symmetrical distinction based on the direction of rotation; and (3) a failure to depict the base of the thick form. The subject shows an understanding of the circle and hexagon shapes in the upright case but not the triangle shapes.

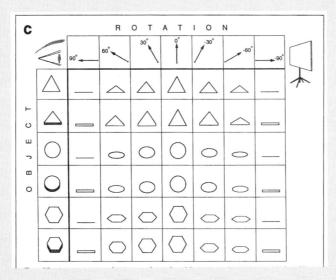

(c) A response pattern showing an understanding of the interaction between rotation angle and form. The subject differentiates between thin and thick forms, ignores the effect of direction of rotation, and appreciates the effect of the angle of rotation. Shadows are depicted by continuous outlines.

FIGURE C.1 Shadow projection drawing tasks. Source: Downs and Liben, 1991.

those skills. As Linn and Petersen (1985, p. 1480) argued, "explanations of sex differences in spatial ability depend, to some extent, on when these differences first occur." They addressed questions concerning first, the size of sex differences in spatial ability; second, whether the existence or size of sex differences varies among component spatial skills; and third, for any skill revealing sex differences, when in the life span differences emerge.

Based on psychometric studies and on their conceptual analysis of the tasks within empirically derived groups of abilities, Linn and Petersen (1985) identified three categories of spatial ability: spatial perception, mental rotation, and spatial visualization.

The first, spatial perception, refers to an individual's ability to identify spatial relations with respect to one's own bodily location or position in relation to something in the external space. One task falling into this category is the "rod and frame task, designed to study field-dependence/independence" (Witkin and Goodenough, 1981). In this task, people are asked to identify "vertical" in the face of conflicting spatial cues. A luminous square angled at 22 degrees appears in an otherwise darkened room, and the respondent is asked to adjust a rod (also positioned at 22 degrees and thus parallel to a side of the square) to vertical. Because the horizontal and vertical cues normally available are hidden from sight, the respondent must rely upon his or her own body position (gravitational upright) to solve the problem. Another illustrative spatial perception task is the "water-level task," which was originally designed by Piaget and Inhelder (1956) to assess children's developing ability to use a systematic coordinate system of horizontal and vertical axes with which to represent abstract or concrete phenomena. In a typical version, respondents are shown a picture of an empty, upright bottle and asked to draw a line to show how it would look if it were about half full. Even by kindergarten, children perform well, correctly drawing a horizontal line. Participants are then given a picture of the bottle in a tipped position (e.g., held at a 45 degree angle), told the bottle is being held steady in the position shown, and again asked to show the way the liquid would look in the bottle if it were about half full. Typically, children in early elementary grades err, at first placing the liquid line so it remains parallel to the base of the bottle. At slightly older ages they recognize that there is some change in position relative to the sides of the container, but do not yet recognize the invariance in relation to the context. Thus, for example, they may draw the line at a diagonal. Only later do they recognize the invariant horizontal position of the liquid, irrespective of the degree of bottle tilt.

The second component is mental rotation or the mental manipulation of an imagined figure or object. This skill permits one to imagine how something (a two-dimensional drawing such as a letter or a three-dimensional object such as a block construction) would look if rotated in the plane or in three-space (see Chapter 4). A classic mental rotation test is a block design task by Vandenberg and Kuse (1979), modeled after Shepard and Metzler (1971). A drawing of a construction made of blocks is shown as the model or standard (see Figure 4.1). Respondents are asked to look at additional drawings to decide whether or not they depict the same block construction except in a different position. Because respondents are given only a finite (and relatively brief) amount of time to work on the problems, the ease with which one can rotate images mentally is reflected in the total number answered correctly. Given limitless time, most people get the right answers, however.

Finally, the third component skill identified by Linn and Petersen, spatial visualization, involves the multistep manipulation of spatial information, which is thus conducive to the use of multiple solution strategies. Spatial visualization is tapped by "tasks that involve complicated, multistep manipulations of spatially presented information" (Linn and Petersen, 1985, p. 1484). This final component is less clear-cut and may be thought of as a conglomeration of strategies used in solving spatial tasks. An illustrative task is the Paper Folding Task developed by the Educational Testing Service (Ekstrom et al., 1976) in which respondents are shown a piece of paper that has been folded, and through which holes have been punched. Respondents must select from among five choices that show the way the paper would look once it is again unfolded. To solve the problem, one might use mental rotation strategies, verbal, logical strategies, and so on. Sample items from each of the three types of tasks are shown in Figure 2.1.

Sex Differences: Developmental Emergence

Having identified these three component skills, Linn and Petersen (1985) used meta-analyses to examine sex differences and their age of emergence. Specifically, they gathered data from prior investigations, calculated effect sizes, and then tested for homogeneity of effect sizes for groups of studies. The groupings began by including data from males and females and across broad ages. In cases in which homogeneity of effect sizes was not found, studies were partitioned into subgroups based on age and sex, and further partitioned into specialized groups until homogeneous or nearly homogeneous groups of studies were identified.

They identified sex differences—favoring males—in the first two skills—spatial perception and mental rotation—but not the third—spatial visualization. The sex difference on mental rotation was large, whereas that on spatial perception was small. For those skills that show sex differences, the differences appeared as early as the skill has been measured (e.g., at least as early as seven years of age). This suggests that at least some of the explanation for sex differences in spatial skills rests in factors that operate very early in life, potentially including early biological experiences such as differential exposure to hormones during the prenatal period.

Sex Differences in Memory for Spatial Location

In addition to the spatial abilities tested in the psychometric literature, there has been growing attention to another kind of spatial ability, namely the ability to remember spatial location. In a typical paradigm, participants are brought into a room that contains a desk on which are scattered miscellaneous objects (e.g., a stapler, scissors). Participants are asked to memorize the objects and are later asked to recall where the objects had been located. On such tasks, performance by females is typically better than performance by males (McBurney et al., 1997; Montello et al., 1999; Silverman and Eals, 1992).

In many of the tasks, performance may be arguably said to be "better" or "worse" in either males or females. There are, however, situations in which performance is probably best conceptualized as "different." For example, both women and men may be successful in getting from one location to another in a real environment, but they may use different strategies. Illustrative is the finding that as a group, men are more likely to invoke cardinal direction, whereas as a group, women are more likely to invoke relations to landmarks (Ward et al., 1996).

In summary, there is considerable evidence for spatial tasks on which males and females perform differently. In some cases, especially those involving mental rotation and spatial perception, males as a group perform better than females as a group. There are tasks on which the group difference is reversed and some in which the strategy or speed, but not the accuracy, of performance differs. Given that these findings, taken together, reveal at least some sex-related group differences, the next section reviews some of the explanations that have been offered for them.

Origins of Sex Differences

As in every other domain of sex-related differences, explanations for sex differences in spatial performance include experiential factors (nurture), biological factors (nature), and the interactive effects of both. The accumulated evidence suggests that all three factors play some role in the observed group differences.

The argument for nurture effects is a strong one, based on evidence showing different socialization patterns and different experiences encountered by boys and girls. Importantly, small differences in early years may have snowballing effects on choices and opportunities later in life, which in turn may have powerful effects on spatial outcomes. Only a sample of the research literature can be discussed here; detailed accounts are available (e.g., see Halpern, 2000).

At early ages, there is evidence that boys in Western cultures are given and encouraged to play with toys such as blocks and construction kits, whereas girls are given and encouraged to play with toys such as dolls and role play. The former are associated with physically more active play and with involvement in spatial actions (such as the need to rotate construction toy pieces to connect them). There are data showing that boys who engage in more culturally "masculine" play perform relatively better on spatial tasks (Connor and Serbin, 1977; O'Brien and Huston, 1985; Serbin and Connor, 1979). Similarly, girls and adolescents who show higher levels of participation in activities viewed as more spatial also score relatively better on spatial tasks (e.g., Newcombe et al., 1983). These data are consistent with the idea that participation in certain kinds of activities—those that are traditionally associated with boys and men in our culture—promotes better spatial skills. Of course, these correlational data are also consistent with the inverse causal possibility, that is, children who have higher spatial skills to begin with are more likely to gravitate toward spatially challenging activities.

One means of exploring the hypothesis that experience *causes* better spatial skills has been to conduct experiments in which experiences hypothesized to promote spatial skills are provided to some, but not other, children and to observe later differences in performance on spatial tasks. In a classic example of this approach, Connor et al. (1978) tested first-grade children's performance on the Children's Embedded Figures Test (Witkin et al., 1971) and found the traditional sex-related difference. They then provided related experience. Both boys' and girls' performance improved significantly, with improvement among girls being large enough that the sex difference was no longer significant after training.

Although other investigations using interventions have also shown significant improvements from training, many have failed to overcome the initial sex difference. A meta-analysis by Baenninger and Newcombe (1989) concluded that training has positive effects on both males' and females' performance, but does not overcome initial differences. We do not know, however, whether group differences remain after interventions because of some inherent sex-related difference or whether the experiences provided by some constrained educational intervention are simply not powerful enough to overcome the accumulated effects of prior years of differential experiences.

The argument for nature effects has also generated a vast amount of research. A number of potential biological mechanisms have been considered as possible factors in the observed sex-related differences in spatial performance.

One possibility is that some spatial abilities are controlled by an X-linked recessive gene. This account holds that—as is true for any X-linked recessive inheritance pattern such as hemophilia—a male's recessive gene cannot be obscured by a dominant gene on the other chromosome because there is no counterpart genetic material on the Y chromosome. This means that if a male and a female each had inherited a recessive gene that is favorable to the development of spatial skills on an X chromosome, for males, that gene would be seen in the phenotype, whereas for females the gene would be seen if and only if that female had also inherited the recessive on her other X chromosome. Had she inherited the gene that is not favorable to the development of spatial skills at that locus, the gene that is favorable (as a recessive) would be obscured in the phenotype. Investigators have reported data on family patterns of spatial abilities that are consistent with this notion (e.g., Bock and Kolakowski, 1973; Thomas, 1983; Thomas and Kail, 1991; Vandenberg and Kuse, 1979), although these data have not gone unchallenged (see Wittig et al., 1981).

A second biological mechanism proposed as playing a causal role in sex-related differences in spatial performance is exposure to different sex hormones in males and females during early and late portions of the life span. The effects of sex hormones are typically discussed under two major headings. One, organizational effects, concern long-lasting, structural influences of hormones on the individual. These occur primarily during the prenatal and perinatal periods. The second, activation effects, concern more transient effects of sex steroids, for example, effects that occur as hormonal levels change with the menstrual cycle or in relation to environmental stress. The term "activation" is used because it is presumed that circulating hormones have their effects on an already prepared organism. Although there is a tendency to equate early effects with immediate structural changes in the brain, there is increasing evidence that effects of sex steroids early in life may affect neural changes at later portions of the life span as well (see Arnold and Breedlove, 1985; Collaer and Hines, 1995; Liben et al., 2002).

Irrespective of the degree to which the two kinds of effects are cleanly separable, hormones may have both long-lasting effects that are traceable to much earlier portions of development and as short-lived effects susceptible to variations that may occur with the seasons, within a month, within a day (see reviews in Alexander and Peterson, 2001; Kimura, 1999; Liben et al., 2002), or even within minutes, with changing environmental contexts (e.g., competitive experiences such as sports events; see Mazur and Booth, 1998).

There is considerable evidence that prenatal exposure to testosterone affects later spatial behavior, although there is controversy about what *levels* of prenatal exposure lead to the highest levels of spatial performance and whether these follow different patterns in boys and girls. Because ethical concerns prohibit manipulation of prenatal hormones experimentally, most human research on early hormonal effects on spatial skills has been conducted with samples that have some atypical hormonal history. Illustrative is research on girls with congenital adrenal hyperplasia (CAH), a condition in which girls are exposed prenatally to excessive levels of androgen. These girls have greater spatial skills than do non-CAH girls, including blood relatives (Hampson et al., 1998; Resnick et al., 1986). Investigators have also examined the effects of levels of circulating sex steroids on behavior, with some evidence that changes in spatial performance may depend on cyclical hormonal changes. To illustrate, Hampson (1990) reported that women who were in the low-estrogen phase of the menstrual cycle performed better on spatial tasks than when they were at their estrogen peak. However, no evidence of an effect of hormones on spatial behavior was found in a clinical investigation in which estrogen and placebo were administered in an alternating schedule to a group of adolescents being treated for pubertal delay (Liben et al., 2002). Taken together with other studies (see reviews in Collaer and Hines, 1995; Fitch and Bimonte, 2002; Hines, 2000; Kimura, 1999; Liben et al., 2002), it is probably most conservative to conclude that sex hormones do have an influence on spatial behaviors, but that the details of this influence are far from certain.

In addition to saying that experiential and biological factors have effects on spatial outcomes individually, there is good evidence that they also have effects interactively. It appears likely that initial differences—even small ones—among individuals may affect the experiences that they seek out or are encouraged to pursue, which in turn have further effects on ultimate outcomes. It is not only that nature and nurture interact in the statistical sense that both components *contribute* in some additive sense to the ultimate outcome (what has been referred to as "statistical interaction;" see Sameroff, 1975). It is also that each can affect the *way* in which the other operates (interaction referred to as "transaction;" Sameroff, 1975). For example, consider a very young child who begins with some inherent predisposition to explore, observe, or represent spatial qualities of the environment. This child may be expected to behave in ways that elicit different kinds of behaviors from adults than those that would be elicited by a child without this predisposition. Furthermore, even when an identical physical and interpersonal environment is encountered by these hypothetical children, they may be expected to take something quite different from their experiences with that environment.

Given the likelihood of statistical and transaction interactions, it is difficult to tease apart the effects of nature and nurture. Two illustrations of an interactive approach follow. In the first, Casey (1996) hypothesized that girls with different brain organization patterns might be expected to respond differently to similar kinds of spatial experiences. She operationalized brain organization on the basis of handedness, which has been linked to different patterns of hemispheric dominance (Annett, 1985). She operationalized spatial experience as exposure to a math-science college curriculum, a curriculum that provides significant exposure to spatial thinking. Although Casey acknowledged that college major is not purely an environmental variable (students self-select into majors; hence those who self-select into math and science may be expected to have relatively strong spatial skills), the self-selection component was held constant because all participants had self-selected into the major. Hence, the critical question was whether there would be differential effects of exposure to that college curriculum as a function of brain organization (measured by handedness). Consistent with the interactive hypothesis, her data show that the same curriculum enhanced spatial performance (measured by a mental rotation task) differentially in relation to students' handedness.

A second illustration comes from work by Berenbaum and colleagues (e.g., Berenbaum et al., 1995; Resnick et al., 1986). Although this work is often taken as a demonstration of direct effects of biology (hormones) on spatial outcomes, it simultaneously speaks to the manner in which biology and experience may interact. For example, CAH girls, subjected to unusually high androgen levels prenatally, show greater spatial skills than do their non-CAH relatives (Resnick et al., 1986). One possible interpretation is a direct effect of prenatal androgens (and hence brain organization) on spatial skills. However, another possibility is that there is only an indirect effect. Berenbaum has shown that CAH girls prefer toys and activities more typical of boys than of girls (Berenbaum and Hines, 1992; Berenbaum and Snyder, 1995). Perhaps these preferences are driven by atypically high activity levels that lead CAH girls to prefer objects and activities that allow active, rather than passive, play. Under this scenario, CAH girls' gravitation toward "boys'" toys stems from the fact that these toys support more action or manipulation, rather than from the fact that they support *spatial* play in particular; however, playing with these toys provides experience conducive to developing higher-level spatial skills.

Appendix D

The Role of Spatial Representations in Learning, Problem Solving, and Transfer

Spatial representations are powerful cognitive tools that can enhance learning and thinking. This position is based on three claims, each of which has significant implications for teaching and learning about spatial thinking. First, creating spatial representations is a powerful way to encode new information that one wishes to recall at a later time. Second, generating images of "old" information that has already been learned and of the situations in which it was learned can powerfully aid in recalling the information at later times. Third, some problems are more readily solved using spatial representations, whereas in other cases, trying to use spatial representations can interfere with problem solving.

LEARNING AND ENCODING NEW INFORMATION

The oldest, best known and most effective mnemonic techniques are based on the power of interactive imagery (Bower, 1973). Possibly the oldest encoding technique using interactive images is the method of loci, which can be traced back to Greek oratory. Like any memory strategy, the method of loci involves two phases: encoding and recall. The key element of the encoding phase begins with imaging a well-known area, generating a perceptually rich spatial representation of a path connecting memorable places through the area, and then encoding each to-be-remembered item by imagining it linked with an easily recalled place along the path. The key element of the recall phase involves generating an image of the familiar path, and then recalling ("stopping at") each place along the way in order to recall the to-be-remembered object associated with that location.

From the standpoint of encoding, retaining, and retrieving information, imagery-based mnemonic systems take advantage of the unique characteristics of interactive images. Consider, for example, the peg word system, where a series of items to be remembered are associated with a series of target objects (denoted by "peg" words), which are embedded in and ordered by a rhyming scheme.

For the method of loci, instead of reciting a rhyme to prompt recall, one calls to mind the details of a route of travel and recalls items that were associated with different places along the route. The peg word system, the method of loci, and other imagery-based systems produce dramatically better memory performance than do the techniques people tend to use in everyday contexts such as verbal rehearsal. Interactive images are remarkably long-lived in terms of their resistance to being forgotten over time, as illustrated in Luria's (1968) book about a famous memory performer who used the method of loci on stage. Imagery-based systems entail a structure—a rhyme in the case of the peg word system, a route in the case of the method of loci—that provides a systematic way to interrogate one's memory and to retain the ordering of items. The spatial version of the system has been used and taught for thousands of years. It exemplifies the power of a spatial representation to encode *any* type of information for later recall.

IMPROVING RECALL THROUGH SPATIAL REPRESENTATIONS

Bower (1973) not only has demonstrated the power of imagery and representation in the construction of memories, but also has shown that the perspective we adopt in constructing such visualizations can influence heavily what we are later able to recall and the properties of the imaginable representations we construct.

Physically reinstating the environmental context in which information was learned (that is, revisiting the physical context) can improve even an infant's ability to recognize information weeks or months later (Rovee-Collier et al., 1999). For older children and adults, however, a physical visit is not necessary: simply imagining the environmental context in which things were learned can improve recall (Bruck and Ceci, 1999; Smith and Vela, 2001). Significantly, mental reinstatement of the original context has about the same benefits as physically reinstating the context itself (Bjork and Richardson-Klavehn, 1989; Smith et al., 1978). Such findings may explain reports from test takers that recalling where, exactly, a needed fact was on a page of text helps them recall the fact.

The fact that mental reinstatement can aid in retrieval of episodic information has been incorporated in the design of cognitive interviews used by police officers (Fisher et al., 1989). The interview procedure depends in part on generating images of the environmental context as a method of prompting memory by eyewitnesses and has been used successfully with children as well as adults (McCauley and Fisher, 1995). Witnesses are asked to replay the event in their minds, first from one perspective, such as the event unfolding as they witnessed it, and then from another perspective, such as a bird's eye view of the event. Details that witnesses are unable to recall from one perspective can sometimes be recalled from another perspective.

Recall is an active process. When people are asked to remember a set of words, recall is better if they are given a task that leads them to generate the list on their own than if they are asked simply to study the list (Slamecka and Graf, 1978). The benefits of generating one's own knowledge are general and include the memory benefits of elaborating the to-be-learned information with one's own experiences (Hirshman and Bjork, 1988; Stein and Bransford, 1979). Indeed, learners are often better off when they think partially through a topic before being told about it than when they are told about the topic before thinking (Schwartz and Bransford, 1998).

The benefits of generating one's own knowledge apply to pictures, graphics, and many other types of spatial representations. For example Wills et al. (2000) asked undergraduate students to study complex sentences and either to use a picture that was provided to help them understand the sentences or to generate their own picture. Students showed better comprehension and later recall when they generated their own pictures. The production of spatial representations—diagrams, flow charts, and concept maps—can create spatial schemas that link related items of information and can provide a way to interrogate one's memory.

Reinstatement and generation techniques can be used in teaching spatial thinking. Reinstatement techniques can facilitate classroom learning, especially in the recall of science experiments, laboratory demonstrations, and other classroom or field experiences in perceptually rich contexts.

Effective teachers understand, at least implicitly, the importance of repetition and creating exercises that lead learners to reinstate the context of what they have learned. Given the effectiveness of regenerating spatial representations of situations in aiding memory, it makes sense for science students to call to mind the perceptual details of laboratory demonstrations and experiences as one method of remembering them when they are needed. Generation techniques show that learners are better at remembering and understanding when they have generated the knowledge or elaborated it on their own, without being "told" to do so. Spatial representations, especially pictures and diagrams, are particularly helpful in remembering and understanding information.

SPATIAL REPRESENTATIONS AND PROBLEM SOLVING

Generating an image of a physical system can help adults reason about the properties of the system. Clement (2000) showed this when he asked adults to reason about why the force exerted by a spring increases as a function of its length. Hegarty and Just (1993) showed the power of images when they asked adults to reason about and explain mechanical advantage in pulley systems. They demonstrated that people generate spatial representations in order to reason about word problems that describe pulley systems. Schwartz and Black (1996) showed that spatial representations aid people in reasoning about systems of interconnected gears. Schwartz (1999) went on to show that physical actions can be integrated with spatial representations, such that physical actions can facilitate how readily people can imagine dynamic changes in imagined physical systems.

How a problem is represented can affect how easy that problem is to solve or whether it can be solved at all. The history of science is rife with examples of where scientists believe they solved difficult problems at least in part because they thought about them in spatial terms (see Chapters 1, 2, and 3). However, using a spatial representation is not a panacea. Spatial representations can interfere when trying to solve problems—the particular representation must fit the problem's structure.

The classic "Buddhist monk" problem, originated by Duncker (1945), is a good example of where a spatial representation can lead to a simple solution:

> One morning a Buddhist monk sets out at sunrise to climb a path up the mountain to reach the temple at the summit. He arrives at the temple just before sunset. A few days later, he leaves the temple at sunrise to descend the mountain, traveling somewhat faster since it is downhill. Show that there is a spot along the path that the monk will occupy at precisely the same time of day on both trips.

The problem is difficult when people try to solve it mathematically by focusing on issues such as relative speeds of travel. A spatial representation can make the answer transparent. If one imagines two monks, one ascending the mountain starting at sunrise, the other descending the mountain starting at sunrise, it is obvious that they must meet on the path, and when they do they will be at the same point at the same time of day. One can do this imagining in different ways, ranging from generating perceptually rich images of monks and mountains to creating a simple schematic diagram to represent the problem's key spatial and temporal features.

The fit of the problem representation to the problem structure is crucial. Ill-chosen spatial representations can lead one down the "garden path" to problem-solving methods that are doomed. Consider a "knock-out" tournament:

> Suppose that 130 children enter a single elimination tennis tournament, where all of the children are originally paired, the winners of the first round are paired, the winners of the second round are paired, and so forth, until the tournament champion wins the final round. How many matches will be played altogether in the tournament. Now consider the general case—how many matches will it take to determine the winner when n children enter the tournament?

To solve this problem, people often represent it by a simple tree structure, reasoning that the first round will include 65 matches, the second round 32 matches plus one "bye," and so forth. However, people using this tree structure approach stumble badly and fail when trying to figure out the general case of n entrants. The problem is that a spatial diagram like a tree structure does not lead to a simple solution; simple solutions arise from considering the verbal fact that in order for there to be a single winner, every other entrant must lose. Given that one match determines one and only one loser, there must be a total of $n - 1$ matches to determine a champion.

In general, problem solving by college students shows that translating a problem into terms that fit it, often spatial terms, aids greatly in solving the problem. The type of representation that leads to the fastest and best solutions depends on what the learner already knows and on the structure of the problem—that is, on what type of solution can, in principle, be used to solve the problem. Novick and Morse (2000) demonstrated that spatially diagrammed representations can help to solve problems, and Novick and Hurley (2001) showed that some problems are most efficiently solved with tree hierarchy schematics, whereas others are best approached via matrices or networks.

Many problems are more readily solved using spatial representations, but in some cases, trying to use spatial representations can interfere with problem solving. Perceptually rich images can enhance reasoning. Barsalou (1999) showed, however, that perceptually rich images do not necessarily help us to think about things in order to recall and reason about their features. For example, in one experiment, participants were asked to think about a situation and then to list all of the characteristics of the main concept. In one condition, people were asked to think about a grassy field and then to generate a list of all of the features of their concept of "grass." In the other condition, people were asked to think about sod being rolled and transported on a truck, and then to generate the same type of list. The results were revealing—in the former condition, people generated relatively few features, and very few listed "roots"; in the latter condition, people generated many more features and everyone listed roots, many listed root hairs, and so forth. The difference between the images is the degree of perceptual richness. Indeed, rich perceptual images involve some of the same neural activation patterns as those apparent when someone is actually looking at such a situation instead of just remembering it.

Appendix E

Software Descriptions and Resources

GIS and Remote Sensing Systems
ESRI: http://www.esri.com/software/index.html
MapInfo: http://www.mapinfo.com/products/products_index.cfm?productcategoryid=1
ER Mapper: http://www.ermapper.com/
Erdas: http://www.gis.leica-geosystems.com/Products/
Idrisi: http://www.clarklabs.org/IdrisiSoftware.asp?cat=2

Geoscience Analytical Systems
Maptek: http://www.maptek.com.au/products/index.html
Surpac Minex: http://www.surpac.com.au/products/index.html
Micromine: http://www.micromine.com.au/products/index.asp
Fractal Technologies: http://www.fractaltechnologies.com/

Computer-Assisted Design Systems
AutoCAD: http://usa.autodesk.com/adsk/servlet/index?id=2704278&siteID=123112
Microstation: http://www.bentley.com/products/
TurboCAD: http://www.imsisoft.com/index.cfm

Mathematical and Statistical Analysis Systems
Mathematica: http://www.wolfram.com/products/mathematica/index.html
Maple: http://www.maplesoft.com/products/index.shtml
Matlab: http://www.mathworks.com/

Production Graphics Environments
Corel Draw: http://www.corel.com/servlet/Satellite?pagename=Corel/Home
Adobe Photoshop: http://www.adobe.com/products/photoshop/main.html
Macromedia FreeHand: http://www.macromedia.com/software/freehand/

Animation Environments
Macromedia Flash: http://www.macromedia.com/software/flash/
Batik SVG Toolkit: http://xml.apache.org/batik/
Macromedia Director: http://www.macromedia.com/software/director/

Information Visualization
Data Explorer: http://www.opendx.org/index2.php
AVS: http://www.avs.com/software/index.html
IRIS Explorer: http://www.nag.co.uk/Welcome_IEC.html

Concept Graphing Tools
Inspiration: http://www.inspiration.com/productinfo/index.cfm
IHMC Concept Map: http://cmap.coginst.uwf.edu/
Personal Brain: http://www.thebrain.com/LPS/PBMM/

Appendix F

What is GIScience?

The University Consortium for Geographic Information Science (UCGIS), a collaboration among approximately 70 academic institutions, private companies, and government agencies, and one of the more prominent manifestations of the rise of GIScience in the United States, is "dedicated to advancing our understanding of geographic processes and spatial relationships through improved theory, methods, technology, and data" (http://www.ucgis.org). This idea of tools in the service of science is echoed by Clarke (1997), who defines GIScience as "the discipline that uses geographic information systems as tools to understand the world."

Yet this is only one of two competing definitions of GIScience. Goodchild (1992) defined GIScience as "the science behind the systems," concerned with the set of fundamental questions raised by GIS and allied technologies, and Mark (2003) has provided a lengthy commentary on definitions. Thus, GIScience is the storehouse of knowledge that is implemented in GIS and makes the tools of GIS possible. GIScience may search for general principles, such as the enumeration of possible topological relationships between pairs of features by Egenhofer and Franzosa (1991), one of the most cited papers in GIScience (Fisher, 2001). It may discover faster algorithms, more efficient indexing schemes, or new ways of visualizing geographic information.

UCGIS has identified 10 "research challenges" representing a consensus on the most important long-term components of the GIScience research agenda: (1) spatial data acquisition and integration; (2) interoperability of geographic information; (3) distributed and mobile computing; (4) future and development of the spatial information infrastructure; (5) extensions to geographic representations (beyond two-dimensional, single-resolution maps); (6) cognition of geographic information and ease-of-use issues (the need to overcome the gap between human cognition and GIS if it is to be regarded by the general public as easy to use or introduced to young children); (7) scale; (8) uncertainty in geographic data and GIS-based analyses; (9) spatial analysis in a GIS environment; and (10) GIS and society (ethics, privacy).

As the science behind the systems, GIScience builds on the accumulated results of many centuries of investigation into how to describe, measure, and represent Earth's surface. The shift to digital technology has revolutionized the older GISciences of surveying, photogrammetry, and cartography, giving new motivation to older research questions, and raising new questions related to the greater flexibility and power of digital technologies. Moreover, the older GISciences evolved in an era of distinct, analog technologies—as long as the paper and pen of cartography had little in common with the analytical stereoplotter of photogrammetry or the theodolite of surveying, there was every reason for them to evolve separately, with separate research agendas. Today, however, all three fields have embraced digital technology wholeheartedly. They serve overlapping applications and face similar issues of representation, database design, accuracy, and visualization.

The world of geographic information has also grown more complex, as new questions have arisen that require the skills and principles of other sciences. Remote sensing, the science of Earth observation, is now an important source of geographic information with its own issues and principles. The unique problems of spatial information have begun to intrigue computer scientists, and spatial databases, computational geometry, and spatial indexing are now recognized subfields of computer science with special significance for GIScience (Liu et al., 2003; Worboys, 1995). Spatial statistics and geostatistics, recognized subfields of statistics, provide important frameworks for the study of accuracy and uncertainty in GIScience (Zhang and Goodchild, 2002), and for the development of advanced methods of spatial analysis, modeling, and visualization (Haining, 2003; Longley and Batty, 2003; O'Sullivan and Unwin, 2003). GIScience is a legitimate subfield of information science, and it is particularly attractive to information scientists because of the well-defined nature of geographic information and the comparatively advanced state of knowledge about this information type. Finally, an important section of the GIScience research agenda asks questions of interest to cognitive scientists: How are geographic knowledge and skills acquired by the human brain, and how can GIS be made more readily understood and usable by humans?

REFERENCES

Clarke, K. C. 1997. Getting Started with Geographic Information Systems. Upper Saddle River, N.J: Prentice Hall.

Egenhofer, M. J., and R. D. Franzosa. 1991. Point-set topological spatial relations. International Journal of Geographical Information Systems 5:161–174.

Fisher, P. F. 2001. Editorial: Citations to the International Journal of Geographical Information Science: The first ten years. International Journal of Geographical Information Science 15(1):1–6.

Goodchild, M. F. 1992. Geographical information science. International Journal of Geographical Information Systems 6(1):31–45.

Haining, R. P. 2003. Spatial Data Analysis: Theory and Practice. Cambridge, U.K.: Cambridge University Press. 432 pp.

Liu, X., S. Shekhar, and S. Chawla. 2003. Object-based directional query processing in spatial databases. IEEE Trans. Knowl. Data Eng. 15(2):295-304.

Longley, P. A., and M. Batty, editors. 2003. Advanced Spatial Analysis: The CASA Book of GIS. Redlands, Calif.: ESRI Press.

Mark, D. M. 2003. Geographic information science: Defining the field. In M. Duckham, M. F. Goodchild, and M. F. Worboys, editors, Foundations of Geographic Information Science, pp. 3–18. New York: Taylor and Francis.

O'Sullivan, D., and D. J. Unwin, 2003. Geographic Information Analysis. New York: John Wiley & Sons.

University Consortium for Geographic Information Sciences (UCGIS). Available at http://www.ucgis.org. Accessed on January 23, 2004.

Worboys, M. F. 1995. Geographic Information Systems: A Computing Perspective. London: Taylor and Francis.

Zhang, J. X., and M. F. Goodchild, 2002. Uncertainty in Geographical Information. New York: Taylor and Francis.

Appendix G

The Introduction of GIS into K–12 Education

A time line for the introduction of GIS in K–12 education between 1986 and 2003 contains many events, activities, and organizations. The contents of the time line, when taken together, reflect a typical pattern of development in that it is haphazard, uncoordinated, and therefore, disorganized. Equally well, the time line shows the impact of enthusiastic pioneers, struggling to influence a massive, fragmented, and inflexible education system. Thomas R. Baker of the University of Kansas prepared the basis for this time line.

1986 National Geographic Society Alliance network (http://www.nationalgeographic.com) started with 8 states and incorporated all 50 states and the District of Columbia in 1993. From the inception of the network, the state alliances, in varying degrees, provided some support for the infusion of GIS in schools and GIS training for teachers.

1989 National Center for Geographic Information and Analysis (NCGIA) (http://www.ncgia.ucsb.edu) was founded. It is a consortium of three universities (University of California, Santa Barbara; University of Maine; and State University of New York-Buffalo) and is funded primarily by the National Science Foundation. Its mission is to advance geographic information research. This mission includes cognition (examining how people conceptualize geographic concepts and how software systems can be made congruent with these concepts), education, and public outreach activities to help meet the demand for GIS professionals and geographically informed citizens.

1989 The JASON Project (http://www.jason.org) uses the Internet, printed curricula, video, and teleconferencing technologies to bring explorations in science, mathematics, technology, and social studies to K–12 students.

1990 NCGIA released the *Core Curriculum,* which was intended to provide a scope and sequence for GIS education at the undergraduate level. Thought was given to adapting this curriculum to the high school level. However, K–12 teachers considered the *Core Curriculum* to be unrelated to the curriculum teachers are tasked to teach.

1991 Association for Geographic Information (AGI) conference organized discussion on GIS in the K–12 environment.

1992   A few schools in North Carolina, Michigan, Kansas, Oregon, and Virginia adopted GIS.

1992   NCGIA launched the Secondary Education Project (SEP) (http://www.ncgia.ucsb.edu/education/projects/SEP/sep.html) with the purpose of identifying existing GIS activities for secondary schools and creating new ones.

1992   Center for Image Processing in Education (CIPE) (http://www.cipe.com) was founded. It trains teachers and students in the use of data visualization tools and produces training manuals and curricula. Since its founding, CIPE has trained more than 3,500 teachers in image processing or GIS.

1992   Environmental Systems Research Institute (ESRI) (http://www.esri.com) established a K–12 Schools and Libraries Division. The mission of the division is to help develop a spatially literate society using GIS.

1994   With the National Geographic Society (NGS), the National Science Foundation (NSF) sponsored the first Educational Applications of GIS conference, called EdGIS, on K–12 applications of GIS.

1994   Collaborative Visualization Project (CoVis) (http://www.covis.nwu.edu) was started by researchers in the Learning Sciences Center, School of Education, Northwestern University, to explore ways in which scientific understanding can be enhanced through visualization tools. Students and teachers met to use specialized software created by the project.

1994   World Watcher program (http://www.worldwatcher.northwestern.edu) was established. It grew out of CoVis and was directed by a senior researcher at CoVis. The program was designed to support student use of GIS in the science classroom. In 2003, it released a vector-based GIS software package for classroom use.

1994   NSF awarded a grant to the Technology in Education Research Consortium (TERC) (http://www.terc.edu) in Cambridge, Massachusetts, for a two-year project to assess the value of GIS in science classrooms. Project researchers concluded that GIS helps students discover relationships among variables, simpler GIS technology encourages open-ended explorations of data, and maps help students focus on the spatial nature of data.

1995   Environmental and Spatial Technology (EAST) (http://www2.eastproject.org/east), a collaborative of hundreds of U.S. high schools, was started. It uses problem-based learning strategies and technologies to stimulate student intellectual development. Using GIS, CAD, image analysis, programming, web development, and data visualization tools, EAST students focus on community issues and service learning. Annual student conferences in Arkansas and California highlight student products and provide teachers with time for training and collaboration.

1995   Visualizing Earth (VisEarth) (http://www.psu.edu) project, a collaboration between Pennsylvania State University's Psychology and Geography Departments and TERC, involved middle school students in the analysis of remotely sensed and aerial photography data.

1996   NGS held the second EdGIS conference.

1996   The Berkeley Geo-Research Group (BGRG) (http://www.bgrg.com) created an *ArcView* GIS extension called *Geodesy*. The objective of *Geodesy* is to help students learn to interpret and analyze geographic information so they can answer questions about where they are, why they are there, and how they can enhance the quality of life in their community and the world. Designed for K–12 education, *Geodesy* is used in nearly 100 schools.

1997   Kansas Collaborative Research Network (KanCRN) (http://www.kancrn.org) was established. It is an Internet-based network of schools aimed to facilitate student research in the natural sciences through high-tech tools.

1997 NGS held the third EdGIS conference.

1998 University of Arizona began a three-year project SAGUARO (http://saguaro.geo. arizona.edu), which developed inquiry-based Earth sciences curricula for use in secondary schools.

1998 ESRI created its Virtual Campus (http://campus.esri.com) for learning about GIScience, GIS technology, and industry-specific applications of GIS. The campus now has more than 200,000 e-mail addresses of people from 185 countries signed into a course. K–12 teachers have found these courses less to their liking than other professional users partly because of course content and partly because of a lack of familiarity with the process of taking courses on-line. By contrast, K–12 students have demonstrated a facility for this style of learning.

1998 Education Division of the Missouri Botanical Garden (http://www.mobot.org/education/ mapping/index.html), in partnership with the University of Missouri-St. Louis and St. Louis public schools, began efforts to incorporate GIS and related technologies in K–12 science and geography classrooms. The Missouri Botanical Garden offers summer classes on themes that use GIS for middle school students.

1999 World Resources Institute (WRI) (http://www.wri.org/enved/datascap.html) and ESRI published an *ArcView* GIS extension called *DataScape,* which enables secondary school students to explore WRI's database of 450 variables for more than 160 countries. Its software allows inexperienced users to take advantage of the capabilities of GIS.

1999 ESRI, NGS, and the Association for Geographic Information initiated an annual GIS day (http://www.gisday.com/news.html). The purpose of GIS day is to educate students and the general public about GIS.

1999 ESRI K–12 Schools and Libraries Division established a core of K–12 educators skilled in GIS (http://www.esri.com/industries/k-12/index.html), and this group of teacher trainers in GIS for schools led to the establishment of the ESRI K–12 Authorized Teaching Program (ATP) (http://www.esri.com/industries/k-12/atp/index.html). ATP training is based on an inventory of what understanding is necessary for teachers to be able to help other teachers use *ArcView* and *ArcVoyager* in particular.

1999 Visualizations in Science and Mathematics (VISM) (http://www.isat.jmu.edu/common/ projects/vism), a three-year NSF program started at the Integrated Science and Technology Center at James Madison University, holds summer workshops in the techniques and application of data visualization for math and science teachers. VISM is a summer program for middle and high school teachers interested in using data visualization technologies in the classroom.

1999 ESRI started the Community Atlas project (http://www.esri.com/industries/k-12/atlas/ index.html). Using GIS, students work on community-related projects during the school year, culminating in a nationwide competition.

1999 Orton Family Foundation established the Community Mapping Program (http:// www.communitymap.org), a place-based, project-based educational program bringing students, teachers, and community mentors together to address local needs and issues. The program works with GIS to enhance the discovery process.

2000 NSF's three-year project, Virtual Immersion in Science Inquiry for Teachers (VISIT) (http://www.piedmontresearch.org/visit/index.html) started at Eastern Michigan University and the Piedmont Research Institute. VISIT was designed primarily to extend GIS teacher training into an on-line setting. By completing activities, teachers earned graduate credit.

2000 EdGIS conference, which was hosted by the California State University, San Bernardino, was held to address the growth in GIS industry, education, and on-line digital libraries.

2000 ESRI established GIS state site licenses for schools. In the United States, Montana obtained the first ESRI GIS state license. Subsequently, Georgia, Utah, South Dakota, and Texas obtained state licenses and Washington, D.C., obtained a district site license. Negotiations between ESRI and other states are under way. The agreements allow schools to acquire GIS software for instructional use at much reduced prices.

2001 California State University, San Bernardino, held the second Education Applications of GIS conference.

2001 ESRI held the first annual Education Conference, a preconference to the ESRI User Conference, in San Diego, California. The Education Conference was attended by nearly 500 educators interested in sharing ideas, attending workshops and paper sessions, and exploring ways to integrate GIS in K–12 curricula.

2001 NSF's program, Extending Scientific Inquiry through Collaborative GIS (ESIC) (http://gis.kuscied.org), was launched at the University of Kansas. A key goal of this three-year program is to develop instructional materials for training K–12 science educators in GIS technologies within the context of problem-based learning. Using both on-line and face-to-face instruction, the program facilitates a cohort of teachers through training, implementation, and evaluation of geotechnologies in the classroom.

2002 ESRI held the second annual Education Conference in San Diego, California.

2002 U.S. State Department and the Association of American Geographers sponsored an international competition called My Community, Our Earth (MyCOE) (http://www.geography.org/ sustainable). One aim of MyCOE is to focus student attention on GIS and sustainable development.

2003 ESRI held the third annual Education Conference in San Diego, California.

Appendix H

Seasonal Differences:
A Customized Eighth-Grade GIS Module

This lesson explores the patterns of monsoon rainfall in South Asia and the relationships between precipitation, landforms, agriculture, and population density in that region.

In the first part of the lesson, students explore patterns of monthly and yearly rainfall in South Asia to identify seasonal changes and differences across the subcontinent. This exploration is accomplished by manipulation of a customized GIS view. The project opens to a view displaying a map of the region and a number of its major cities (see Figure H.1). When a city is selected, its monthly rainfall and yearly rainfall are displayed on two graphs that are also visible in the view. Two or more cities can be compared by holding down the shift key and making the appropriate selection as shown below. This customized project was created by arranging the project in such a way that multiple windows are displayed simultaneously: the view (South Asia) and two graphs (monthly rainfall and annual rainfall). By saving the project in this format, it will always open in the same display mode. The customized project design facilitates the accomplishment of the lesson's objectives by highlighting key patterns and relationships within the data.

As students explore, they are asked to consider inquiry-based questions such as the following:

- As you move northward along the subcontinent's west coast, how does the pattern of rainfall change?
- Although the monthly rainfall amounts differ, what similarities do you see among the overall rainfall patterns in these three cities?
- What happens to the pattern of annual rainfall as you move from west to east across South Asia?

This customized project allows students to *discover* the patterns of rainfall in South Asia's monsoon climate through their own investigation. As they explore they are encouraged to speculate on the causes and consequences of the patterns they observe through questions such as the following:

- How do you think Afghanistan's rainfall pattern will affect the way of life in that country?
- How does the physical features theme help you explain the differences in patterns of rainfall between inland Bangalore and coastal Mangalore?
- Which regions or countries of South Asia are suitable for agriculture and which are not? Explain.

In the second part of the lesson, students compare South Asia's yearly precipitation patterns with those of agricultural activities and population density by adding and observing shapefiles representing those data (see Figures H.2, H.3, and H.4). One customization evident in these maps is that the added themes, derived from global data, have been clipped to the political borders of the South Asia region. Each theme's legend is also customized to facilitate easy analysis and comparison with other themes. Again, these customizations enable the student to focus easily on the content and objectives of the lesson.

In the final part of the lesson, students are guided through a synthesis of their discoveries about the monsoon's impact on agriculture and population patterns with questions such as the following:

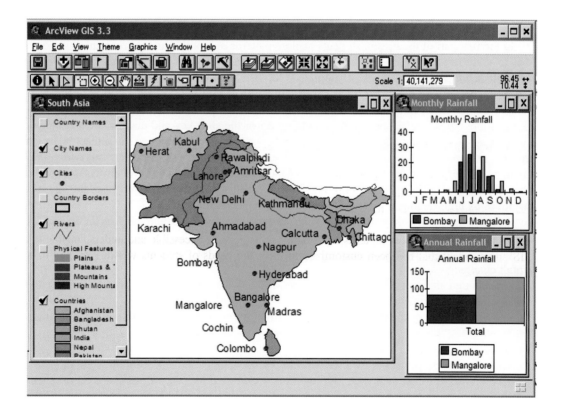

FIGURE H.1 Map of South Asia with countries, rivers, and major cities named with graphs contrasting total and annual rainfall for Bombay and Mangalore. SOURCE: Personal communication from Lyn Malone, 2003.

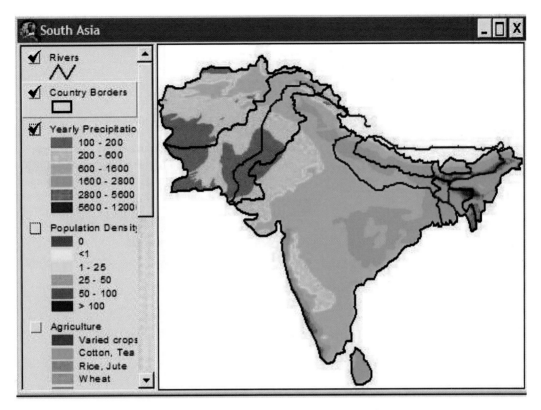

FIGURE H.2 Map of South Asia with countries, rivers, and annual precipitation. SOURCE: Personal communication from Lyn Malone, 2003.

- What is the relationship between agricultural activities and patterns of precipitation in South Asia?
- Why is Afghanistan's population density so low?
- Since most of Pakistan gets little or no rainfall, how do you explain the areas of agriculture and high population density in that country?

In this lesson, complex patterns and relationships become accessible and understandable in a GIS environment that has been customized to meet the needs of students working on particular tasks in a specific context.

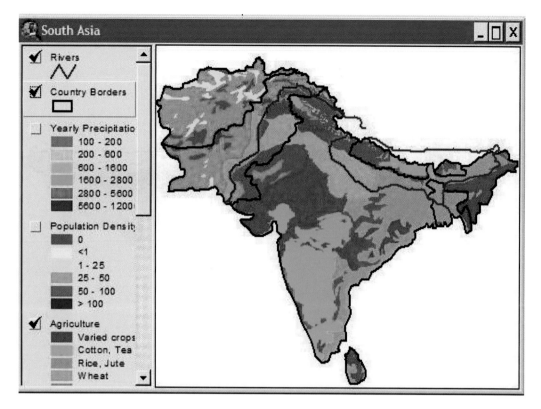

FIGURE H.3 Map of South Asia with countries, rivers, and types of agriculture. SOURCE: Personal communication from Lyn Malone, 2003.

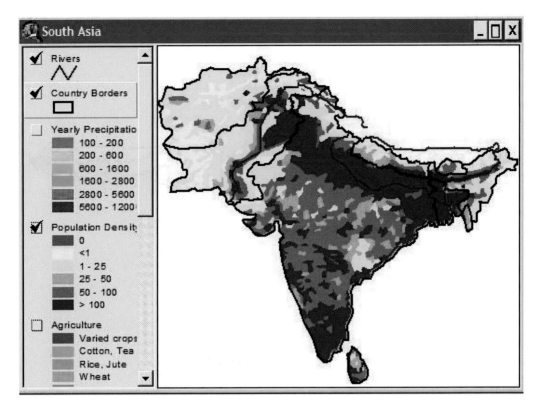

FIGURE H.4 Map of South Asia with countries, rivers, and population density. SOURCE: Personal communication from Lyn Malone, June 6, 2003.

Appendix I

List of Acronyms

ADL	Alexandria Digital Library
AEJEE	*Arc Explorer Java Edition for Education*
API	application program interface
ATP	Authorizing Teaching Program
AVS	*Advanced Visualization System*
BGRG	Berkeley Geo-Research Group
CAD	computer-assisted design
CAH	congenital adrenal hyperplasia
CIPE	Center for Image Processing in Education
CoVIS	Collaborative Visualization Project
CSS	car safety seat
DEM	digital elevation model
DLESE	Digital Library for Earth System Education
DRG	digital raster graphic
DX	*Data Explorer*
EAST	Environmental and Spatial Technology
EdGIS	Educational Applications of GIS
EEG	Electroencephalogram
ESIC	Earth Science Information Center; Extending Scientific Inquiry through Collaborative
ESIP	Earth Science Information Partner
ESRI	Environmental Systems Research Institute
ESSIP	Earth System Science Internet Project

fMRI	functional magnetic resource imaging
GIS	geographic information system, geographic information science
GPS	global positioning system
GRASS	*Geographic Resources Analysis Support System*
GUI	Graphical User Interface
H-R	Hertzsprung-Russell
IMR	infant mortality rates
IP	Internet protocol
IT	information technology
IVNS	in-vehicle navigation system
Kan CRN	Kansas Collaborative Research Network
LAN	local area network
LCD	liquid crystal display
MRI	magnetic resource imaging
MyCOE	My Community, Our Earth
NASA	National Aeronautics and Space Administration
NCAR	National Center for Atmosphere Research
NCES	National Center for Education Statistics
NCGIA	National Center for Geographic Information and Analysis
NGS	National Geographic Society
NRC	National Research Council
NSF	National Science Foundation
PDA	Personal Digital Assistant
PGS	Personal Guidance System
RRRC	Red River Regional Council
SCANS	Secretary of Labor's Commission on Achieving Necessary Skills
SEP	Secondary Education Project
SL	Spatial Language
SMOG	Simple Measure of Gobbledygook
SPC	State Plane Coordinate
SPCS	State Plane Coordinate System
SSST	Support Systems for Spatial Thinking
TERC	Technology in Education Research Consortium
TIMSS	Trends in International Mathematics and Science Study
TOC	Table of Contents
T-S Diagrams	Temperature-Salinity Diagrams

UCGIS	University Consortium for Geographic Information Science
USGS	U.S. Geological Survey
UTM	Universal Transverse Mercator
VAR	value added reseller
VisEarth	Visualizing Earth
VISIT	Visual Immersion in Science Inquiry for Teachers
VISM	Visualizations in Science and Mathematics
WAN	wide area network
WHO	World Health Organization
WIMP	windows, icons, menus, and pointers
WRI	World Resources Institute

Index

A

Abstract concepts, 41, 45-47, 91
  etak, 139-140
Access Excellence, 209
Advanced Visualization System (*AVS*), 157, 170, 171, 286
Age
  and perceptual imaging, 97
  and spatial skills, 101, 108, 270, 274-275
Air traffic control and controllers, 54-55, 93, 95
Alexandria Digital Library, 34-35
Algebra, 19, 91, 92, 117, 126, 130
Alpha Centauri, 62
American Forests, 180, 190
AML, 166
Andromeda Nebula, 64, 67
Animation environments, 46, 80, 105, 108, 149, 156, 157, 158, 159, 171, 182, 219, 224, 286
Anthropogeography, 88
Application program interface (API), 156, 157, 173-174
ArcCatalog, 224
ArcEditor, 222
ArcExplorer, 161, 167, 223
ArcGlobe, 224-226
Architects and architectural design, 12, 28, 40, 43, 54, 55, 95, 97, 100, 104, 141, 155, 156
ArcIMS, 222
ArcInfo, 222
ArcLessons, 209
ArcReader, 222
ArcSDE, 222
ArcView, 156, 166-167, 173, 174, 177, 180, 185-187, 190-192, 194, 196-198, 200, 201, 202, 204, 209, 222-226, 290, 291
ArcView GIS, 166, 184, 188, 222, 226

ArcVoyager, 167, 184, 185-187, 190, 191, 223, 291
Assembly instructions, 50, 51
Association for Geographic Information (AGI), 289, 291
Association of American Geographers (AAG), 292
Association of Research Libraries, 215
Astronomy. *See* Astrophysical spatialization
  parsec unit, 62
Astrophysical spatialization
  absolute magnitude, 62-63, 64, 66
  beyond solar system, 60-67, 68
  Copernican model, 59, 60
  distance scales, 57, 60, 64, 65, 67-68
  Earth shape and size, 57-58, 65, 67
  epicycles, 59, 61
  expertise in, 55, 57-58
  frames of reference, 57-58, 59
  geocentric theory, 60
  heliocentric theory, 60, 61
  Hertzsprung-Russell diagram, 62-64
  Hubble constant and, 64-65, 68
  main sequence, 63, 64
  measurements, 56, 58, 60-67
  parallax concept, 60, 62, 64
  pattern recognition, 56
  period-luminosity diagram, 64, 66
  primitives, 56, 57
  Ptolemaic universe, 59, 60, 61
  role of, 67-68, 94
  solar system, 59, 67
  spectroscopic parallaxes, 64
  standard candle, 64
  time dimension, 56, 57, 59
  universe structure and evolution, 56-57, 64, 68
Atlas GIS, 167
Atmospheric physics/physicists, 80, 81

AutoCAD, 156, 285
Autodesk Map, 167
Avenue, 166, 191, 192

B

Barrington Middle School (Rhode Island), 180
Batik SVG Toolkit (BGRG), 286
Berkeley Geo-Research Group, 290
Bessel, Friedrich, 62
Big Bang theory, 64
Bishop Dunne Catholic School (Texas), 212
Botany/botanists, 53, 69, 209, 291
Brahe, Tycho, 60, 62, 67
Bruner, Jerome, 11-12, 16, 20, 150, 176, 237, 270-271
Bunge, William, 93

C

California State University, San Bernardino, 291, 292
Car safety seat (CSS) installation, 49-50
Cartesian coordinate system, 3, 12, 27, 149, 272
Cartographic modeling, 27, 169-171, 173
Cartography, 83, 113, 156, 222, 287, 288
Center for Image Processing in Education (CIPE), 290
Central place theory, 56, 88-93
Cepheid variables, 64, 66, 67
Charlottesville Education Summit, 111
Chemistry, 27, 43, 181
Chess players, 96, 97
Chorology, 88
Christaller, Walter, 48, 49, 56, 88-93, 95
CITYgreen, 180-181, 190
Cognition/cognitive
    development, 270, 271
    environmental, 26, 29
    geographic, 287, 289
    maps/mapping, 26, 27, 29, 142
    skills, 12, 81. *See also* Spatial skills and abilities
    about space, 30
    in space, 30
    with space, 30
    spatial tool kit, 27
Collaborative Visualization Project (CoVIS), 290
Color
    identifying and classifying objects by, 70
    recognition and evaluation, 41, 42, 43, 53, 56, 138
    representations, 16, 52, 80, 104, 105, 141, 143, 149, 169, 170, 171, 180-181
Columbia University, 83
Communication, in mathematics, 116, 117
Community Atlas project, 210, 291
Community Geography: GIS in Action, 179, 209
Community Mapping Program, 291
Community projects with GIS
    crime reduction, 179, 212
    pollution hazard mapping, 181, 213

vegetation mapping and analysis, 180-181, 190
    water quality monitoring, 179, 180, 212-213
Computer-assisted design (CAD) systems, 12, 19, 20, 141, 155, 156, 158, 185, 290
Concept graphing tools, 32, 157, 286
Concept maps/mapping, 19, 30, 156, 157, 159, 282
Concepts for spatial thinking, 18-19, 26, 29-31, 32, 33
Coordinate systems
    3D, 151
    ability to use, 276
    abstract, 139-140
    Cartesian, 3, 12, 27, 149, 272
    Earth-anchored conceptual, 69, 77-79, 160
    geometry standard, 118, 120, 121, 122, 123
    latitude-longitude, 37, 38, 148, 149, 162, 168
    local, 38
    polar, 3, 12, 123
    raster data, 160, 223
    rotating, 123
    specific, 149
    spheres, 123
    State Plane Coordinate System, 148, 149, 183
    temporal, 171
    transformations, 149, 173
    Universal Transverse Mercator (UTM), 149, 183
    vector models, 70, 160, 223
Copernicus, 59
Corel Draw, 285
Coriolis effect, 123
Crescent School (Ontario), 213
Crick, Francis, 1-3, 55
Crime monitoring, 179, 212
Crystallography/crystallographers, 69, 70, 72, 103
Curriculum. *See* K-12 curriculum
Curriculum and Evaluation Standards for School Mathematics, 165

D

Data
    analysis and probability, 116, 117, 156
    attribute, 162, 163
    collection, 14, 156
    combining spatial and nonspatial data, 88
    correction procedures, 55, 171
    extrapolation and interpolation, 55, 86-87
    generalization, 55
    geometric, 162
    GIS characteristics, 159-162, 171, 173, 175, 217
    management, 13, 16, 30, 32, 34-35, 55, 76-77, 111, 156, 177, 223, 224
    mining, 34, 111
    models, 160-161, 173, 175, 183, 223
    nonspatial, 88, 168-169
    pixel, 32, 175
    quality and quantity, 102, 171
    raster, 32, 156, 160, 161, 173, 183, 223
    retrieval, 34

space for interpreting, 28
spatialization of, 6, 31-33, 34, 35, 111, 148-149, 156, 157, 168-169, 182
vector, 160, 161, 173, 175, 223
visualization, 13, 16, 30, 32, 34, 76-77, 111
Data Explorer (DX), 155, 157, 170, 171, 286
DataScape, 291
Demographics
economic processes integrated with, 180
geographic metaphors, 30, 33
GIS applications, 180, 237-240
workforce needs, 112
Developmental theories, 270-271
Developmentally appropriate education, 270
Diagrams, 19
animated vs. still, 46
central place, 89, 91, 93
devices that focus attention, 46, 47, 102, 177
DNA structure, 2
equal-area projection, 70, 71
flow, 45, 46
GIS output, 169, 189
Hertzsprung-Russell, 62-64
hierarchical, 27, 30, 40
as instructional device, 47-48, 50, 102, 116, 138, 139, 283
mattang stick chart, 138
period-luminosity, 64-66
phase, 27, 36, 133
physiographic, 84, 86, 88
purpose of, 47
reasoning from, 41, 47, 102, 104, 284
and recall, 47, 96, 282, 283
schematic, 27, 50, 282, 283
of spatial operations, 30, 45, 47, 56, 70, 102
T-S, 82
types of, 27-28
Diatoms, 72
Digital Library for Earth System Education (DLESE), 209, 210
Digital Quest, 209
Dimensionality, 12, 47, 102. *See also* Coordinate systems
domain considerations, 37
frames of reference, 53-54
GIS capacity, 169
motion and, 54-55, 56, 59, 80-81
three-space, 37, 53, 54-55, 70, 80, 102, 151
transformation, 40, 149
two-space representation, 13, 16, 32, 37, 53, 70, 76-77, 102, 121, 169
Directionality, 37, 43, 45, 58
Director, 157, 171, 182, 286
Distance, 46, 47, 82
astronomical scales, 57, 60, 64, 65, 67-68
as measure of time, 81-82
Distortions, 40, 41, 45, 52, 72-73
DNA structure, 1-3, 55, 103

Drawing inferences. *See also* Problem solving; Reasoning
expertise in, 47, 53, 72, 86, 88, 102, 104
from shapes, 72-76, 77
from size, 57-58, 74, 90, 91, 92

E

Earth science
competency of students, 114
curriculum, 123, 291
education standards, 119-120, 123, 129
GIS software, 215
Earth Science Information Partners (ESIP), 215
Earth System Science Internet Project (ESSIP), 207
Earthviewer, 171, 172
Eastern Michigan University, 291
Echo sounders and echograms, 84, 86-87
Education Applications of GIS (EdGIS) conference, 290, 291, 292
Education reform, 12, 111-112
recommendations, 131, 133-134
Educational challenges
committee position statement, 7-8, 233-234
concepts for spatial thinking, 18-19
curriculum design, 134
resource-related, 103, 110, 190
support tools, 7-10, 19-20, 144-145, 233-235
Educational software
collaborative model, 215
commercial model, 214-215
customization, 174, 182, 183, 184, 185, 190-192, 218-219, 293-297
Earth Science, 215
geometry, 168, 169, 173, 183
GIS, 164-165, 166, 167-168, 173, 178-179, 184-185, 214-216, 220, 285; *see also individual products*
market, 204-205, 232
open vs. closed architecture, 188-189, 215
redesign challenges, 214-216, 220
resources, 285-286
Seasonal Differences module, 293-297
Einstein, Albert, 45, 95
Electronic circuit design, 95
Embedded figures test, 26
Emergent phenomena, 104
Encarta, 184
Environmental and Spatial Technology (EAST) initiative, 179, 290
Environmental cognition, 26, 29
Environmental Systems Research Institute (ESRI), 19, 166, 167, 177, 184, 185, 186, 188, 190-191, 200, 201, 206, 208, 209, 210-211, 215, 220, 223, 224, 285, 290, 291-292
Epicycles, 59, 61
Epidemiology, 12, 55
arsenic in drinking water, 13
Snow's cholera maps, 13, 14-15

ER Mapper, 285
Eratosthenes of Cyrene, 57-58, 67
Erdas, 156, 285
Etak, 139-140
Everyday life
    GIS in, 158-159
    IT applications, 111
    spatial thinking in, 12, 30, 42, 43, 49-52
Ewing, Maurice, 86
Expertise in spatial thinking
    acquisition of knowledge, 95, 100-101, 103-104,
       107
    age and, 108
    challenges in developing, 103-104
    chess example, 96, 97
    cognitive processes, 98-100, 107
    combining spatial and nonspatial data, 88
    differences in, 95-103
    domain-specific, 40, 53-54, 55, 67-68, 94, 95, 96, 101,
       104, 108
    expertise in creating and understanding, 47, 87-88, 95-
       96, 101, 104
    fostering, 107-108
    inference and intuition, 47, 53, 72, 86, 88
    intelligence and, 95, 96
    memory and recall, 88, 95, 96-98
    nature of, 95-96
    novices compared, 46-47, 54, 55, 56, 70, 71, 75, 77,
       79, 80, 93, 101
    pattern recognition, 42, 54, 87
    projects for, 104-105
    role of, 46-47, 93, 101-102
    in science, 55, 56, 57-58, 68, 69-70, 71, 72, 75, 76, 77,
       78-80, 83-88, 93
    transformations, 44
    visualization, 76-77, 80-81, 84, 88, 103
    at work, 52-53
Explore Your World, 209
Extending Scientific Inquiry Through Collaborative
      Geographic Information Systems, 208, 292

F

Federation of GIS Education Partners, 215, 220
Flash, 157, 171, 182, 286
Foraminifera, 72, 74, 75
Fractal Technologies, 156, 285
Frames of reference, 37, 41, 42, 44, 45. *See also*
      Coordinate systems
    abstract, 139-140
    astrophysical, 57-58, 59
    dimensionality, 53-54
    replotting, 149
    rotating, 123, 129
FreeHand, 157, 285
Function concept, 19
Functional magnetic resonance imaging (FMRI), 19

G

GenScope project, 105
Geocentric theory, 60
Geodesy, 57, 290
Geographic information systems (GIS)
    academic model, 214, 215
    accessibility to all learners, 186-190, 192
    administrative and institutional support, 202-203
    analytical capabilities, 171, 173-174, 177, 190, 210
    animation environment, 171, 182, 219, 224
    appeal to students, 182, 219
    applications, 164, 166, 180
    appropriateness to student needs, 173, 179, 183-192,
       205, 218
    assessment as an educational support system, 176, 182-
       183, 191-192, 203, 213-214, 217-225
    buffer analysis, 175
    capabilities, 156-159, 165, 167-176
    community support, 179-182, 190, 212-213, 218, 220
    compatibility issues, 200
    competitions, 210-212, 292
    component-based or open system architecture, 184
    components, 160
    computing environment in schools and, 200-203
    coordinate system, 171
    curriculum support, 208-212, 213, 218, 220, 237-240
    customizability, 174, 182, 183, 184, 185, 190-192,
       218-219, 224, 293-297
    data characteristics, 159-162, 171, 173, 175, 217
    data management, 177, 223, 224
    design criteria, 176-203, 215, 218-219
    difficulties in using, 193-200
    educational context, 192-203
    for English language learners, 189-190
    in everyday life, 158-159
    expert users, 164, 183, 219
    flexibility in contexts and modes of use, 192-193
    and GPS, 39, 156, 212
    graphic variables, 170
    implementation in schools, 193-214, 219-220
    infrastructure demands, 200-203, 219
    inquiry-based learning with, 176-177, 182-183, 210
    instructional support, 204, 206-208, 213, 214, 222
    Internet access, 202, 204
    K-12 software, 164-165, 166, 167-168, 173, 178-179,
       184-185; *see also individual products*
    logistical support, 205-206, 213, 214, 219
    low-tech learning tools, 205
    material support for, 179, 204-205, 213, 219
    media support, 169, 171
    meeting educational goals, 176-183
    modeling capabilities, 169-171, 173, 175, 190
    nature and functions, 158-164
    and navigation, 38-39, 158
    nongeographic spaces, 168
    novice users, 184, 185-187, 193-200, 219
    operational functions, 18, 40, 158, 162-163, 168, 171,
       173, 174, 175, 176, 177, 187, 205, 207, 218

overlay (thematic layers) analysis, 162-163, 175, 180-181, 193-195

personal guidance system, 38-39

problem solving in real-world contexts, 177-179, 218

proximity analysis, 175

queries, 163, 196-197

recommendations, 9-10, 234-235

representations, 118-119, 170-171

resource constraints in schools, 192-199

role in spatial thinking, 15, 18, 19

size transformations, 169, 170, 171-173, 175, 183-184, 198-199, 225

spatialization capacity, 168-169, 176, 182

standards-based education and, 118-119, 200, 212, 214

status as support system, 164-165, 220-221

teacher-related issues, 189-190, 193, 200-201, 204, 206-208, 214, 219-220

technological evolution, 222-226

time line for introduction into K-12 education, 289-292

time modeling, 171

transfer of learning across domains, 179-182, 218

transformation capacity, 158-159, 169, 170, 171-173, 174, 175, 177, 183-184, 198-199, 218, 225

user interfaces, 9, 171, 173, 174, 177, 182, 184, 185, 188-189, 196-197, 219, 224

virtual applications, 171, 188-189, 237, 291

visualization capacity, 9, 169-171, 176, 177, 210, 214, 217-218, 234

for visually impaired learners, 188-189

workplace applications, 168

Geographic Resources Analysis Support System (GRASS), 167, 215

Geography

active learning, 11-12

central place theory, 56, 88-93

defined, 116

education standards, 116

expertise in, 55, 56

information technology and, 110

as rational sets of induction, 11

spatial thinking in, 55, 56, 116

Geography Network, 209, 211

Geolocation systems, 111. *See also* Global positioning system

Geology/geologists, 43

field, 76, 79-80

structural, 69, 70, 72

GeoMedia, 167, 179

Geometry

activities, 118

computational, 288

coordinate, 118, 120, 121, 122, 123, 130, 132

curriculum, 18, 118, 131

education standards, 114, 115, 116-118, 120-122, 123, 124-125, 130

Euclidean, 123

everyday applications, 142

geography integrated with, 58

GIS software, 168, 169, 173, 183

international student rankings, 114

projective, 274

science content linked to, 123, 124, 125, 129, 130

spatial thinking applied in, 19, 36, 37, 81, 92, 94, 115, 123, 126, 131

transformational, 114, 117, 118, 125, 130

Geomorphology/geomorphologists, 61, 74, 77, 86, 87

Geophysicists, 80

Georeferencing, 37, 143, 159, 180

Geoscience

analytical systems, 156, 158, 285

ascribing meaning to shapes, 72-76, 77

crystal planes of symmetry, 69, 70

describing position and orientation, 77-79

describing shapes, 69-70

equal-area projection diagrams, 70, 71

expert spatial thinking in, 55, 56, 57-58, 68, 69-70, 71, 72, 75, 76, 77, 78-80, 83-88, 101

identifying/classifying objects, 70-72

Miller indices, 70

motion in 3D space, 80-81

novice learning, 56, 70, 71, 75, 77, 79, 80, 93, 101

pattern recognition, 76, 78

processes of spatial thinking, 82-83

recall of object location and appearance, 79-80

representations for nonspatial parameters, 82

sedimentary folding, 69, 70

spatial operations, 68-83

time progression, 81-82

topographic maps, 79

visualization of structures, 76-77, 78, 80-81, 95

Geospatial technology

defined, 112-113

high-tech systems, 156, 158, 179

market characteristics, 112

support for, 179

Geospatial Technology Competency Model, 112-113

GeoVISTA Studio, 188

Geovisualization, 169

Girasek, Deborah, 49-50

GIS Day, 206, 291

GIScience, 159, 287-288, 291

Gladwin, Thomas, 137

Global positioning system (GPS), 55

data collection, 156

GIS and, 39, 156, 212

hand-held receiver, 16

Location Based Services (LBS), 111

mobile devices linked to, 110, 111

ocean navigation, 77, 78, 84, 136, 137, 141

personal guidance system, 38-39

tracking, 111, 143

water quality monitoring, 15, 16, 212-213

GLOBE, 193

Gradmann, Robert, 90

Graphics generators, 157, 159, 179

Graphing calculators, 19

Gravitational theory, 59

Greenbriar High School (Arkansas), 179

H

Haptic mice, 188
Haptic Soundscapes Project, 189
Heezen, Bruce, 83-86, 87-88
Heliocentric theory, 60, 61
Hertzsprung, Edward, 62
Hertzsprung-Russell (H-R) diagram, 62-64
Hettner, Alfred, 88
High-stakes testing, 200, 212
Hubble constant, 64-65, 68
Hubble, Edwin, 64, 67, 68
Human Genome Project, 19
Humboldt, Alexander von, 88
Hutton, James, 72

I

Idrisi, 19, 156, 167, 200, 201, 204, 208, 214, 285
IHMC Concept Map, 286
IKONOS satellite, 16
Imagine, 156
Inferences. *See* Drawing inference
Information
    geographic metaphor, 30, 33
    nonvisual processing, 38-39
    visualization systems, 156, 157, 159, 170, 171, 286
Information technology (IT). *See also* Geospatial
        technology; Support systems and tools; Virtual
        world
    intersection with space, 111
    need for skilled thinkers, 110-111
    skill building with GIS, 182
Inspiration, 286
Instruction. *See* Learning; Teaching spatial thinking
Intellectual space, 28, 30, 31, 32, 48
Intelligence measurement and testing, 26
Interfaces. *See* User interfaces
Intergraph, 19, 179, 207-208, 215
IRIS Explorer, 286
Isotropic plane, 92

J

James Madison University, 291
JASON project, 289

K

K-12 curriculum, 13. *See also* Teaching
    competitions, 210-212, 292
    design challenges, 134
    GIS resources, 105, 121, 124-125, 126, 151, 209-210,
        293-297
    infusion of spatial thinking across, 5, 6, 101, 105-107,
        109, 120, 131, 133-134, 147, 176, 179-181, 182,
        183, 218, 231

interpreting representations, 47-48, 102
    supports, 104-105, 151
    transfer of spatial thinking across subjects, 101, 105-107
Kansas Collaborative Research Network (KanCRN), 193,
        209, 290
Kekulé, Friedrich, 95
Kepler, Johannes, 59, 60, 67
Keyhole Inc. Images, 171
Knowledge. *See* Spatial knowledge

L

Lake Ontario Keeper, 213
Lamont-Doherty Earth Observatory, 84
Learning. *See also* Expertise in spatial thinking; K-12
        curriculum; Transfer of learning
    assimilation and accommodation, 270
    cognitive development and, 270
    collaborative projects, 192-193, 202
    developmental theories and, 270-271
    disabilities, 190
    general principles, 106
    inquiry-based, 133-134, 140, 145, 176-177, 182-183,
        207, 210, 237-240
    interdisciplinary and multidisciplinary, 181-182, 210
    to learn, 101
    multiple examples and, 106, 107
    pattern, 99, 100
    perceptual processes, 97-98, 100
    performance-based environments, 179
    practice and, 98-100, 103, 106, 107
    problem-based, 207, 212
    productivity, 106
    representations, 281-282
    rote, 144-145
    spiral curriculum, 270-271
Leavitt, Henrietta, 64, 66
Life spaces, 12, 28, 30, 31, 48
Literacy. *See also* Spatial literacy
    defined, 4, 17, 49
    verbal, 50
Location Based Services (LBS), 111
Location theory, 88-93
Logo software, 126
Looking at the Environment (LATE) program, 209, 210

M

Mac GIS, 167
Macaulay, David, 28, 29
Magic, 174
Magnetic resonance imaging (MRI), 19, 27
Malone, Lyn, 237-240
MapExtreme, 200
MapInfo, 156, 167, 173, 174, 200, 204, 285
Maple, 156, 285
Mapping Our City project, 191, 208

Mapping Our World: GIS Lessons for Educators, 189-191, 209, 222
Mapping System, 200
MapQuest, 111, 155, 183-184
Maps/mapping
    Albers Equal Area, 173
    cartographic, 27, 28, 33, 36, 57, 83, 85, 142, 145, 149, 156, 162, 169, 170, 171, 173, 288
    chloropleth or isopleth, 188-189
    cognitive, 26, 27, 29, 142
    concept, 19, 30, 32, 156, 157, 159, 282, 286
    contour, 84, 85, 88
    digital elevation models, 86
    environmental, 179, 180-181, 190, 212-213
    geological, 79, 80
    Internet structure, 168-169
    mental, 52
    modified Mercator projections, 27, 141, 145, 146, 173
    paper-and-pencil activities, 133
    reading and interpreting, 33, 36, 79, 104, 142
    satellite-based systems, 84
    seafloor, 56, 76-78, 83-88
    self-organizing, 33
    stellar, 64, 65
    swath-mapping, 84
    topographic, 79
    weather, 104, 105, 223
    web-based interactive, 223
Maptek, 285
Maptitude, 167
Marine geochemists, 80
Mathematica, 156, 285
Mathematical thinking, 25, 144
Mathematics. *See also* Algebra; Geometry
    communication in, 116, 117
    connections among ideas, 118
    education standards, 114, 115-119
    international comparison of student competencies, 113-114
    representations in, 114, 115, 116, 118-119, 120, 121, 122, 123, 125, 130, 132
    spatial concepts, 18
    support tools, 19, 104, 118-119, 136, 141, 142, 144, 156, 159, 285
Matlab, 285
Measurement, mathematics standard, 117
Memory and recall, 11
    chunking information, 97
    classic model of, 97-98
    diagrams as aid to, 47, 96, 282, 283
    domain specificity, 100
    and expertise, 88, 95, 96-98
    learning and encoding new information, 281-282
    long-term, 97, 142
    method of loci, 281
    mnemonic techniques, 281
    overlearning and, 97
    pattern recognition, 27, 40, 41, 42, 44, 53-54, 68, 76, 78, 82, 86, 96, 100, 276

peg word system, 281-282
reinstatement and generation techniques, 282-283
representations and, 45, 46, 47, 97, 98, 102, 107, 281-283
sensory storage, 97
sex differences, 277
structural differentiation, 98
support systems, 144
verbal materials, 97, 98, 282
working (short-term), 46, 97, 98, 100, 101, 107, 140-141
Mental imagery/practice, 43, 44, 55
Mental rotation, 18, 26, 27, 31, 40, 43, 44, 47, 52, 83, 98, 99-102, 107, 123, 130, 133, 150, 266, 267, 268, 274, 275, 276-277, 280
Meta-cognitive knowledge, 100, 106
Metaphors in spatial thinking, 12, 25, 34, 41, 93, 94
    in everyday life, 45
    geographic, 30, 33
    graphics, 36
    overlay integration, 180
    root, 36, 56, 110
    in science, 82, 83
    "space" used for nonspatial parameters, 82
    for virtual-world access, 110-111, 184
Meteorology, 27, 98, 103
Mfworks, 167
Micromine, 156, 285
MicroStation, 156, 285
Mineralogy/mineralogists, 69, 70-71, 76
Missouri Botanical Garden, 209, 291
Modified Mercator projection, 27
Motion/movement, 149, 170, 225, 271, 272
    and angular estimation, 78
    astrophysical, 56, 59, 61, 62, 68
    describing, 129
    directionality, 43, 45, 50
    through geospaces, 82
    parallactic, 62
    representations, 43, 45
    rotating frames of reference, 123, 129
    through 3-D space, 80-81
    in 3-D space-time, 54-55, 56, 59, 80-81
    tracking, 38-39
    and transformations, 102
    visualization, 47, 69, 80-81
Multidimensional scaling (MDS), 12, 27, 111
Multiscalar analysis, 56
My Community, Our Earth: Geographic Learning for Sustainable Development, 210, 212, 292
My World, 167

N

National Aeronautics and Space Administration (NASA), 112, 215
National Assessment of Educational Progress (NAEP), 113
National Center for Atmospheric Research (NCAR), 215

National Center for Education Statistics (NCES), 113-114, 207
National Center for Geographic Information and Analysis (NCGIA), 208, 289, 290
National Education Goals, 111
National Education Standards
    coupling between mathematics and science, 120-131
    geography, 116
    goals, 114-115
    mathematics, 114-119
    organization, 115
    role of spatial thinking in, 6-7, 114-115, 208-209, 232
    science, 114-115, 119-120
National Geographic Alliance, 208, 289
National Geographic Society (NGS), 290
National Geography Standards, 116, 165
National Science Education Standards, 165
    categories, 115
    content standards, 115, 119-120
    mathematics standards linked to, 120-131
National Science Foundation (NSF), 208, 289, 290, 291
Navigation, 30, 94
    angular estimations, 78-79
    buffers, 39
    celestial, 84, 87, 138, 140
    computer programs, 38-39, 122
    dead reckoning, 78-79, 84, 87, 138, 139
    GIS technology, 158
    GPS, 78, 84, 136
    homing vector/path integration procedure, 142
    knowledge of physical environment and, 138
    landmarks, 38, 52, 53, 94, 142, 143, 213, 272, 277
    map reading, 79
    Mattang stick chart, 138
    neurophysiology and, 52
    oceanographic techniques, 77-79, 84, 87, 135-140, 141
    personal guidance systems, 38-39
    "piloting" system, 142
    Puluwatan islanders, 135-140
    sex differences in, 142
    size evaluation and, 42
    vehicle navigation systems, 111, 135-136, 142-143
    virtual, 110, 193, 206, 207, 224
    workplace networks, 53
Networks, 123
Neural networks, 33
Newton, Isaac, 59
No Child Left Behind Act, 114, 134, 186-188
Northwestern University, 290
Numbers and operations, 116, 117, 119

O

Objects
    ascribing meaning to shapes, 72-76
    concrete vs. abstract, 27
    defined, 36-37
    describing shapes, 69-70
    distinguishing figures from ground, 41-42
    embedded, 26, 44
    identifying and classifying, 70-71
    motion visualization, 80-81
    position and orientation, 77-79
    properties, 37-38
    recall of, 40, 41-42, 44, 79-80
    recognizing shapes or patterns, 76
    remembering location and appearance, 79-80
    shape change processes, 81
    visualizing from 1D or 2D data, 76-77
Oceanography. *See* Physical oceanography/oceanographers
Onstar System, 142
Operations. *See* Spatial operations
Orientation. *See* Mental rotation; Spatial orientation
Orton Family Foundation, 291

P

Paleontology/paleontologists, 70-71, 72, 76
Paper folding test, 26, 81
Parallax concept, 60, 62, 64
Patterns, 5, 19, 32, 33
    description and analysis, 47, 91, 92, 150
    in epidemiology, 13, 14-15, 16
    with GIS, 18
    noisy background, 76, 78, 86, 92
    operations, 40, 41, 76
    perceptual learning of, 100
    process modeling, 150
    random vs. systematic, 40
    recognition, 27, 40, 41, 42, 44, 53-54, 68, 76, 78, 82, 86, 96, 100, 276
    transformation of, 100
Pennsylvania State University, 290
Period-luminosity diagram, 64, 66
Personal Brain, 286
Personal Digital Assistants (PDAs), 111
Personal guidance systems (PGSs), 38-39
Perspective, 3, 12, 26, 27, 28, 31, 44, 47, 98, 100, 102, 118, 123-124, 131, 141, 143, 149, 225, 282. *See also* Frames of reference
Petrology/petrologists, 69, 70-71, 82
Philosophy, 101
Photogrammetry, 287, 288
Photoshop, 19, 157, 285
Physical oceanography/oceanographers
    conductivity-temperature-depth profiles, 76
    seafloor mapping, 56, 76-77
    visualization of structures, 76-77, 80
Physical science/physics
    achievement of U.S. students, 114
    curriculum, 18, 27, 47, 133
    education standards, 114, 115, 119, 123, 124, 127-128
    spatial concepts, 12, 18
    spatial representations, 47, 57, 102
    and spatial visualization, 76

Physical space/environment, 28, 29-30, 31-32, 48, 118,
    138, 177, 268, 271-272
Physiographic diagrams, 84, 86, 88
Piedmont Research Institute, 291
Pixel data, 32, 175
Plate tectonics, 86, 100
Point concept, 19
Pollution hazard mapping, 181, 213
Position of objects. *See* Spatial orientation
Precision data recorders (PDRs), 84
Pressure-temperature space, 82
Primitives, 25, 36-37, 40, 56, 57, 86
Principles and Standards for School Mathematics
    content standards, 115
    expectations for students, 115, 117-118
    and GIS support, 118-119
    process standards, 115
    science standards linked to, 120-131
    spatial thinking and, 115-119
Problem solving, 12, 13, 27-28, 48, 53
    age and sex differences, 52
    Buddhist monk problem, 283
    car safety seat installation, 49-50
    in everyday life, 49-52
    knock-out tournament problem, 283-284
    mathematics standard, 117, 120
    representations and, 27, 107, 108, 283-284
    in science, 83-88
Production graphics environments, 156, 157, 159, 285
Psychometric testing, 273
Ptolemaic universe, 59, 60, 61
Ptolemy, Claudius, 59

R

Radiologists and radiology, 53, 54, 95, 97, 98
Raster data models, 32, 156, 160, 161, 173, 183, 223
Ratzel, Friedrich, 88
Reading, 50
Reasoning. *See also* Drawing inferences; Problem solving
    ascribing meaning from shapes, 72-76
    from diagrams, 41, 47, 102, 104, 284
    examples, 3, 12-13
    from first principles, 75
    mathematics standard, 117, 120, 121
    problem solving, 121
    processes, 28, 29, 40, 44, 45-46
    scientific, 44
    technology and, 126
Recall. *See* Memory and recall
Recommendations
    GIS, 9-10, 234-235
    spatial literacy goals, 7, 232-233
    timetable for implementing, 236
Red River High School (North Dakota), 212-213
Relativity theory, 45, 95
Remote-sensing applications and imagery, 32, 42, 113,
    149, 156, 158, 162, 183, 200, 285, 288, 290

Representations. *See* Spatial representations
Ritter, Carl, 88
Rodgers, John, 79
Russell, Henry Norris, 62
Russell Sage Foundation, 112

S

SAGUARO Project, 209
Satellite imaging, 16
Scale and scalar relations, 92. *See also* Size
    multidimensional, 12, 27, 111
    progression, 31
    properties, 37
    terminal values (bounds), 37
    transformation, 27, 149
Schematization, 45, 46
Science. *See also* Astrophysical spatialization; Geoscience
    concepts of spatial thinking, 19
    forms of thinking in, 12
    international comparison of student competencies, 113-
        114
    IT applications, 111
    spatial thinking in, 27, 42, 43, 55-56
Seafloor
    mapping, 56, 76-78, 83-88
    sediment deposition patterns, 81, 84
    spreading, 84, 86, 103
Secondary Education Project (SEP), 290
Secretary of Labor Commission on Achieving Necessary
        Skills (SCANS), 111-112
Sedimentology/sedimentologists, 69, 72-73, 74, 76, 81, 82
Sex differences
    developmental emergence, 277
    memory for spatial locations, 277
    in navigation, 142
    origins of, 277-280
    problem solving, 52
    in spatial performance, 269, 273, 276-277
Shapes. *See also* Size; Spatial orientation
    ascribing meaning to, 72-76, 77
    change processes, 81
    describing, 69-70
    identifying and classifying, 70-72
    recognizing, 76
Simple Measure of Gobbledygook (SMOG) statistic, 50
Sims Superstars, 169
69 Cygni, 62
Size
    comparison, 42
    evaluation, 41, 42, 43, 45, 52, 53, 189
    GIS modeling, 169, 170, 171, 172, 175, 225
    inferences from, 57-58, 74, 90, 91, 92
    scaling, 47, 56, 92
    transformation, 44, 149, 169, 170, 171-173, 175, 183-
        184, 198-199, 225
    zooming, 198-199
Small Magellanic Cloud, 64, 66

Smallworld, 174
Smith, William, 79-80
Snow, John, 13, 14-15, 16
Software. *See* Educational software; *individual packages*
Space
  as basis for spatial thinking, 36-40
  economic model of, 91-92
  examples, 12
  forms of thinking about, 25-27
  as framework for understanding, 28-33
  GIS context, 168
  Internet intersection with, 111
  for interpreting data, 28
  languages of, 37, 40
  objective vs. subjective, 27
  properties, 12
SPACESTARS program, 209-210
Spatial ability. *See* Expertise in spatial thinking; Spatial
    skills and abilities
Spatial agnosia, 94
Spatial amnesia, 94
Spatial analysis, 88-93, 158-159
Spatial attitude, 27
Spatial cognition, 26, 30, 272
Spatial development
  age-linked, 271-272
  theoretical approached, 272-273
Spatial knowledge, 18-19, 27
  domains, 12
Spatial location, 40, 45
Spatial literacy
  components, 16-20
  fostering, 3-4, 12, 15-20, 89-90, 105
  and problem solving, 49
  student characteristics, 4, 20
Spatial operations, 25
  ability to perform, 26
  analytical, 160
  ascribing meaning to shapes, 72-76, 77
  cognitive, 5, 12, 230
  describing shapes, 69-70
  diagrams of, 30, 45, 47, 56, 70, 102
  distortions in patterns, 40, 41, 45, 52, 72-73
  encoding, 41-48, 281-282
  in everyday life, 52
  externalization, 28
  in geoscience, 68-83
  GIS, 18, 40, 158, 162-163, 168, 171, 173, 174, 177,
      187, 205, 207, 218
  identifying/classifying shapes, 69-72
  learning, 49
  mental, 43, 46, 101
  metaphors, 36
  motion of objects through space, 80-81
  on nonspatial parameters, 79
  opacity-transparency issue, 144
  ordering, 52
  pattern recognition, 40, 76, 78
  position/orientation of objects, 37, 77-79

problem solving, 12
remembering location and appearance, 79-80
research needs, 7, 15, 232
scaling, 37, 40
sensory modality and, 26
shape-changing processes, 79
spatial location and, 40
support systems, 8, 134, 140, 141, 148, 150, 158, 233
time factor, 79-80
transformations, 36, 37-38, 41
visualization, 76-77, 80-81
Spatial orientation, 26, 52. *See also* Coordinate systems
  changing, 44
  describing, 77-79
  determining, 42-43
  inferring meaning from, 74
  of natural objects, 74, 77-79
  real-world relative to conceptual coordinate system,
      77-79
Spatial perception, 26, 29, 276, 277
Spatial representations, 4, 5, 7, 14, 15, 17, 20, 26, 40, 57.
      See also Diagrams in spatial thinking; Maps/
      mapping; Metaphors
  animated, 46, 80, 105, 149
  classes and forms, 149
  color, 16, 52, 80, 104, 105, 141, 143, 149, 169, 170,
      171, 180-181
  of concepts in space, 30
  curriculum, 47-48, 102
  decomposition of, 41
  digital, 34, 86
  dimensionality, 13, 16, 32, 37, 53, 70, 76-77, 102
  effectiveness, 46, 80, 103
  encoding processes, 41-48
  in everyday life, 32, 52
  examples, 3, 12, 19, 150
  external, 25, 27-28, 46, 102
  GIS support, 118-119
  imaging technologies, 19
  interference with problem solving, 283
  internal (mental) forms, 25, 27-28, 41, 102
  interpreting, 47-48, 102
  and learning and encoding new information, 107, 108,
      282-282
  limitations of, 104
  maps and mapping, 33-34, 36
  mathematics, 114, 115, 116, 118-119, 120, 121, 122,
      123, 125, 130, 132
  and memory performance, 45, 46, 47, 97, 98, 102, 107,
      281-283
  of movement/motion, 43, 45
  for nonspatial parameters, 82
  and orientation, 42-43
  physiographic diagrams, 84, 86
  practice in creating and transforming, 98-100, 101, 108
  in problem solving, 27, 107, 108, 283-284
  properties of, 41-42
  reasoning with, 47, 87-88, 95-96, 104
  relations between dynamic entities, 43

relations between static entities, 42-43
role of, 46
science, 47, 57, 102
sensory modalities, 36, 149
structure of classifications, 40
support system capabilities, 149
systems of, 12
and transfer of learning, 101, 281-284
transformations of, 41, 43-45, 98, 274-275
on 2-D space, 30, 33-34, 37, 70, 121, 169
virtual auditory system, 39
Spatial skills and abilities, 19-20. *See also* Spatial
  development
  angular estimations, 78-79
  categories, 26
  chronological age and, 101, 270, 274-275
  defined, 26
  differences among learners, 266-268, 269
  Euclidean, 70, 77
  gender differences, 268, 269
  group differences in performance, 267, 268-269
  intuition, 75, 77, 84
  measurement, 274-275
  memory, 80
  observational skills, 91
  organizational ability, 80, 91, 92
  sex differences in performance, 269, 273, 276-280
Spatial structures, 25, 36, 37, 95
  analysis, 149, 150
  extracting, 47, 102
  relationships between, 106-107
Spatial thinking and acting
  approaches to, 25-28
  catalog of elements, 41
  committee position statement, 5-7, 230-232
  concepts, 18-19, 26, 40, 29-31, 32, 33, 40
  contexts for, 29-31, 32, 33
  defined, 33
  developmentally appropriate education, 270-273
  DNA structure as example of, 1-3
  educational challenges, 18-19
  in everyday life, 12, 49-52, 93, 94
  functions of, 3, 5-7, 33, 36
  primitives, 36-37, 40
  as problem solving, 27-28
  processes, 3, 16, 26, 28, 40-48, 82-83, 93; *see also*
    Spatialization
  in science, 14-15, 16-17, 55-93, 94
  space as basis for, 3, 36-40
  value of studying differences in, 209
  at work, 12, 52-55, 93, 94
Spatial visualization. *See also* Concept maps/mapping
  age and, 97
  classroom activities, 121, 124-125, 126
  content standards, 123, 125
  courses, 210
  data management, 13, 16, 30, 32, 34, 76-77, 111
  defined, 118

design issues, 46
DNA molecule, 3
effectiveness of, 55
expertise, 76-77, 80-81, 84, 88, 96-97, 103
GIS capacity, 9, 169-171, 176, 214, 217-218, 234
information exploration, 156, 157, 158-159, 169, 171,
  185, 286
in mathematics, 114, 117, 118, 120, 123, 156
measurement, 26, 81, 276-277
motion of objects through 3D space, 80-81
multidimensional scaling, 12, 27, 111
negative spaces, 81
nonspatial input, 82, 97
problem solving with, 117, 120-126, 131, 133, 276-
  277
process, 60-61
and recall skills, 282
Science magazine wards, 103
scientific, 3, 36, 46, 55, 56, 73-77, 80
sex differences, 277
of shape changes, 81
skill development in learners, 79, 122-123
spatialization and, 111
in statistical analysis, 155, 156
support systems, 8, 135, 143, 155, 156, 158-159, 169,
  217-218, 233, 286
of 3-D objects from 1-D or 2-D data, 13, 16, 32, 37,
  53, 76-77, 78, 79, 131
virtual reality systems, 36
for visually impaired people, 36, 188-189
Spatialization, 25, 41. *See also* Astrophysical spatialization
  ability, 26, 31
  in communications, 116
  concept graphing tools, 157
  of data, 6, 31-33, 34, 35, 111, 148-149, 156, 157, 168-
    169, 182
  defined, 30, 168
  GIS capacity for, 168-169, 176, 182
  high-tech support systems, 148, 156-159
  and information retrieval, 34
  of mapping domains, 111
  multidimensional scaling, 111
  of nonspatial data, 168-169
  in numbers and operations, 116
  process, 31-32
  software tools, 156, 157
  support systems for, 8, 148, 156-159, 168-169, 182,
    233
  visualization and, 111
Spatialized query user interface, 35
Speech recognition software, 188
Standard candle, 64
Standards. *See* National Education Standards
State Plane Coordinate System (SPCS), 148, 149, 183
State University of New York–Buffalo, 289
Statistical analyses, 12, 19, 82, 89-90, 91, 92, 117, 141,
  149, 155, 156, 159, 175, 183, 190, 205, 273, 285,
  288

Statistical interaction, 279, 280

Struve, Friedrich von, 62

Support systems and tools, 13. *See also* Geographic
information systems; *other specific systems and
software packages*
    analytical capabilities, 150
    appropriateness to student needs, 141, 146, 147, 151
    barriers to classroom use, 179
    committee position statement, 7-8, 233-234
    context considerations, 147
    costs of learning, 20
    design criteria, 145-147, 218-219
    discipline-specific, 19
    educational challenges, 7-10, 19-20, 144-145, 233-
        235
    end-means issue, 144
    expert users, 141-142
    functions of, 140-141, 143
    high-tech, 19, 135, 136, 141, 142, 155-165, 179
    implementation, 144, 151-152
    instruction process, 144
    in K-12 context, 150-152
    limitations of, 141-145, 146, 157
    low-tech, 19, 84-86, 87, 135, 136, 137-140, 141, 142,
        150-151, 155
    meeting education goals, 145, 147
    nature of, 135-140
    need for, 147-148
    novice users, 144
    opacity-transparency issue, 144
    operations capabilities, 150
    power-limitations issue, 145
    representations, 149
    requirements of, 148-150, 217-218
    rote learning-comprehension issue, 144-145
    spatialization of data, 148-149
    and transfer of learning, 142, 143, 147, 176, 179-181,
        182, 183
    transformation capability, 149
    visual, 55
    visualization of results, 149

Surpac Minex, 156, 285

Surveying, 287, 288

T

T-S diagrams, 82

Teachers
    demands on, 200-201, 212
    GIS skills, 208, 219
    professional development opportunities, 207-208, 222
    training issues, 13, 45-46, 189-190, 202, 206-208,
        219-220, 291

Teaching spatial thinking, 3-4, 26, 45-46. *See also*
Educational challenges; K-12 curriculum
    diagrams as aids to, 47-48, 50, 102, 116, 138, 139, 283
    examples of using GIS, 11-12, 179-181, 212-213,
        237-240

    facilitating GIS, 179
    formal instruction in spatial ideas, 131
    inquiry approach, 133-134, 140, 145
    reasoning, 3, 47
    reinstatement and generation techniques, 282-283

Technology, 13, 55
    barriers to classroom use, 179
    collaborative, 192-193
    coordinators, 202
    mathematics education standard, 119

Technology in Education Research Consortium (ERC),
    191, 208, 290

Temperature, 82

Tetris, 100, 105

Texture, 36, 41, 42, 43, 70-71, 72, 84, 169

Tharp, Marie, 48, 56, 76-77, 79, 83-88

ThemeRiver, 157

Thinking. *See also* Spatial thinking and acting
    forms of, 12

Thought experiments, 95

Time, 40, 55
    coordinate, 171
    dimension, 56, 57, 59
    distance in space as measure of, 81-82
    geological, 81-82
    leap year, 57
    GIS modeling capability, 171

Topology, 36, 113, 171, 173, 272, 287

TouchGraph, 157

Transfer of learning, 52
    curriculum infusion and, 5, 6, 101, 105-107, 109, 120,
        134, 147, 176, 179-181, 182, 183, 231
    direct application theory, 106
    domain specificity, 5, 45-46, 99, 100, 105-107, 108,
        109, 145, 231
    education standards and, 120
    far, 100, 105, 106
    instruction and, 106-107, 134
    mental rotation skills, 101
    near, 100, 105
    negative, 143
    pattern recognition skills, 53, 100
    practice and, 95, 99, 101, 105, 107
    preparation for future learning, 106
    representations and, 101, 281-284
    support systems and, 142, 143, 144-145, 147, 176,
        179-181, 182, 183
    testing for, 106
    visualization skills, 100
    ways to facilitate, 46, 95, 105-107, 143, 147, 176, 179-
        181, 182, 183

Transformations, 3, 5, 12, 27, 230
    age and skill in, 274-275
    in coordinate systems, 149, 173
    defined, 149
    detecting embedded figures, 44
    dimensionality, 40
    domain specificity, 100
    enacting, 43, 44-45, 47

geometry standard, 114, 117, 118, 125, 130
GIS, 158-159, 169, 171-173, 174, 177, 218
learning, 102
mathematical and statistical analysis systems, 130, 156
memory and, 46, 100
mental rotation, 18, 26, 27, 31, 40, 43, 44, 47, 52, 83, 98, 99-102, 107, 123, 130, 133, 150, 266, 267, 268, 274, 275, 276-277, 280
novices vs. experts, 47, 108, 274-275
operations, 30, 37-38, 44, 59, 173
ordering, 45
orientation changes, 44, 102
of patterns, 100
perspective changes, 44
practice in, 98, 100, 101, 102, 108, 274-275
processes, 45, 98
properties of, 41
and reasoning, 45
reconfiguring parts, 44
of representations, 41, 43-45, 98, 274-275
in scale, 28, 36, 47, 56, 102
shadow projection task, 274-275
support systems for, 8, 148, 149, 150, 156, 158-159, 169, 171, 173, 174, 177, 218, 233
Trends in International Mathematics and Science Study (TIMSS), 113-114
TurboCAD, 285

U

Universal Transverse Mercator (UTM), 149, 183
University Consortium for Geographic Information Science (UCGIS), 215, 287
University of Arizona, 291
University of California Santa Barbara, 38, 289
University of Kansas, 289, 292
University of Maine, 289
University of Minnesota, 207
University of Wyoming, 207
U.S. Army Corps of Engineers, 215
U.S. Department of Education, 113, 201, 220
U.S. Environmental Protection Agency, 16
U.S. Navstar, 38
U.S. Navy, 84
U.S. State Department, 292
User interfaces, 222, 224, 234
application program interface, 156, 157, 173-174, 177, 184, 188
command-line style, 177
customized, 224
for English language learners, 189-190
GIS, 9, 171, 173, 177, 178, 182, 183-184, 185, 188-189, 191-192, 193, 196-197, 214, 215, 218, 219, 222, 224
nonvisual, 188-189
pictorial, 177, 178
query, 34-35, 173, 175, 196-197
standards, 215

vehicle navigation systems, 143
virtual auditory display, 39
WIMP, 173, 174, 177
wizards, 9, 177, 184, 219

V

Vector data model, 70, 160, 161, 173, 175, 223
Vega, 62
Vegetation mapping and analysis, 180-181, 190
Verbal thinking, 25-26
Video games, 100, 105, 169, 182, 188
Virtual auditory display, 39
Virtual Campus, 291
Virtual Immersion in Science Inquiry for Teachers, 291
Virtual reality systems, 27, 36, 141
Virtual world
access to, 110-111; *see also* User interfaces
displays, 39, 111, 141
GIS applications, 171, 188-189, 237, 291
teacher training, 291
for visually impaired learners, 188-189
Visual Basic, 166, 174
Visual browsing query process, 34
Visual exploration systems, 157, 159, 169, 177, 179
Visualization. *See also* Spatial visualization
Visualizations in Science and Mathematics (VISM), 291
Visualizing Earth (VisEarth), 290
Visually impaired people, 36, 38-39, 188-189, 218
von Thunen, Johann Heinrich, 88
Vulcan, 156

W

Water quality monitoring, 179, 180, 212-213
Watson, James, 1-3, 55
Wayfinding, 38-39, 94, 142. *See also* Navigation
Weber, Alfred, 88
Wegener, Alfred, 72
Wegner, Mark, 49-50
Work force
adequacy of education, 112
cognitive skills, 110-113
GIS applications, 168
international competition, 111-113
IT applications, 111
Workplace
demand for knowledge workers, 110-111
spatial thinking, 12, 52-55
Workplace Investment Act of 1998, 17
World Health Organization (WHO), 16
World Resources Institute (WRI), 291
World Watcher program, 290

Z

Zoologists/zoology, 69